**BLACK
MONTMARTRE
IN THE
JAZZ AGE**

BLACK MONTMARTRE IN THE JAZZ AGE

ROBERT TOMLINSON

The University of Georgia Press
Athens

© 2026 by the University of Georgia Press
Athens, Georgia 30602
www.ugapress.org
All rights reserved
Designed by Melissa Buchanan
Set in Garamond Premier Pro

Use of any part of this book in training for any artificial intelligence (AI), large language model (LLM), machine learning technologies, or similar generative language system without license is expressly prohibited.

Printed digitally

EU Authorized Representative
Easy Access System Europe—Mustamäe tee 50, 10621 Tallinn, Estonia,
gpsr.requests@easproject.com

Library of Congress Control Number: 2025030363
ISBN: 9780820375014 (hardback)
ISBN: 9780820375021 (paperback)
ISBN: 9780820375038 (epub)
ISBN: 9780820375045 (PDF)

CONTENTS

Acknowledgments   vii

Introduction: "A Joyous Tower of Babel"   1

Part I. In the Rue Caumartin: From Clandestine Dance Halls to "Society *Dancings*"

Chapter 1. Shimmy Parlors and Deluxe Dives:
The Era of Dubious *Dancings*   13

Chapter 2. The Dancer and the Drummer:
"Weird and Wonderful Sounds" in the Rue de Clichy   29

Chapter 3. "America's Sweetheart," the "Jazz Baby,"
and the Sister of the "Colored Gentleman"   46

Chapter 4. A Gala in My Sister's Garden:
Grandeur and Decadence of a "Society *Dancing*"   62

Part II. On the Rue Fontaine: Conflict and Collaboration

Chapter 5. "Smoke upon the Waters":
An Elegy for the Tempo Club   81

Chapter 6. Zelli's Royal Box: A Bordello in the
Country of the Abencerrages   94

Chapter 7. "M'soo Kee-lay and His Snow-White Russian
Wolfhound": Conflicted Dreams of a Dance Hall King   111

Part III. Around the Rue Pigalle: Triumph and Failure on the "Great Black Way"

Chapter 8. "An Ostrich Feddah Suit o' Cat's Pajamas":
Louis, Flo, and the Prancing Princes   129

Chapter 9. Bricktop and Buddie at the Grand Duc:
"Black and Laughing, Heart-Breaking Blues in the Paris Dawn"   146

Chapter 10. "Still Longing for de Old Plantation": Miscegenation, Violence, and the Collapse of a Utopian Dream   162

Epilogue: "No Doubt One Must Bid Them Adieu"   183

Appendix: Bars, Cabarets, *Dancings*, Restaurants, and Theaters Cited in the Text   187

Notes   191

Bibliography   229

Index   237

ACKNOWLEDGMENTS

My thanks go out to the many anonymous staff members of the Bibliothèque publique d'information du Centre Pompidou and the Bibliothèque Nationale, in particular the Département des Arts et des Spectacles; to the Research Division of the New York Public Library, especially the attentive librarians of the Schomburg Center who introduced me to the treasures of the Black newspapers, and last but not least, the African American Collections of the Stuart A. Rose Manuscripts, Archives, and Rare Book Library at Emory University, with a special salute to its guardian spirit, Randall Burkett.

I am also deeply indebted to Dr. Monique Wells of Entrée to Black Paris for her encouragements, editorial eye, and communicative passion for the history of the Black expatriate community of Montmartre. My sincere thanks to my editor at the University of Georgia Press, Nathaniel Holly, for his fruitful suggestions and continual encouragement. Lastly, I wish to extend special thanks to Makoto Ishiwa.

RUE CAUMARTIN
9e arrondissement

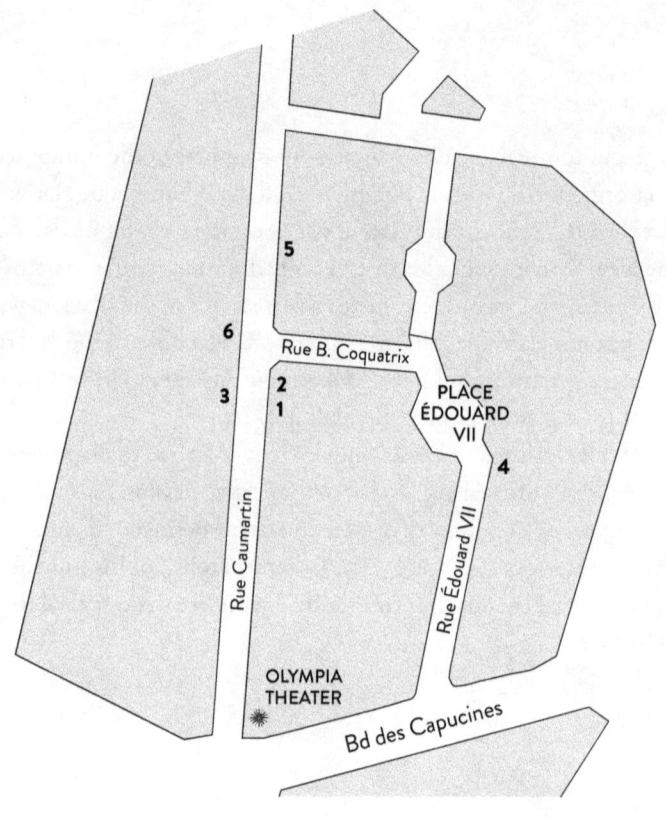

1. Maurice's Club 1 (Hotel Grande Bretagne)
2. Club des Lapins
3. Cadet Rousselle
   Zelli's Club
   Chez Harry Pilcer
   Le Sans Souci
   Le Jardin de ma Soeur
   The Blue Room
4. Louigi's Elmano
5. Le Grand Teddy
   The So-Different
6. Le Théâtre Caumartin
   The Savoy Dancing Club
   The Clover
   Maurice's Club 2

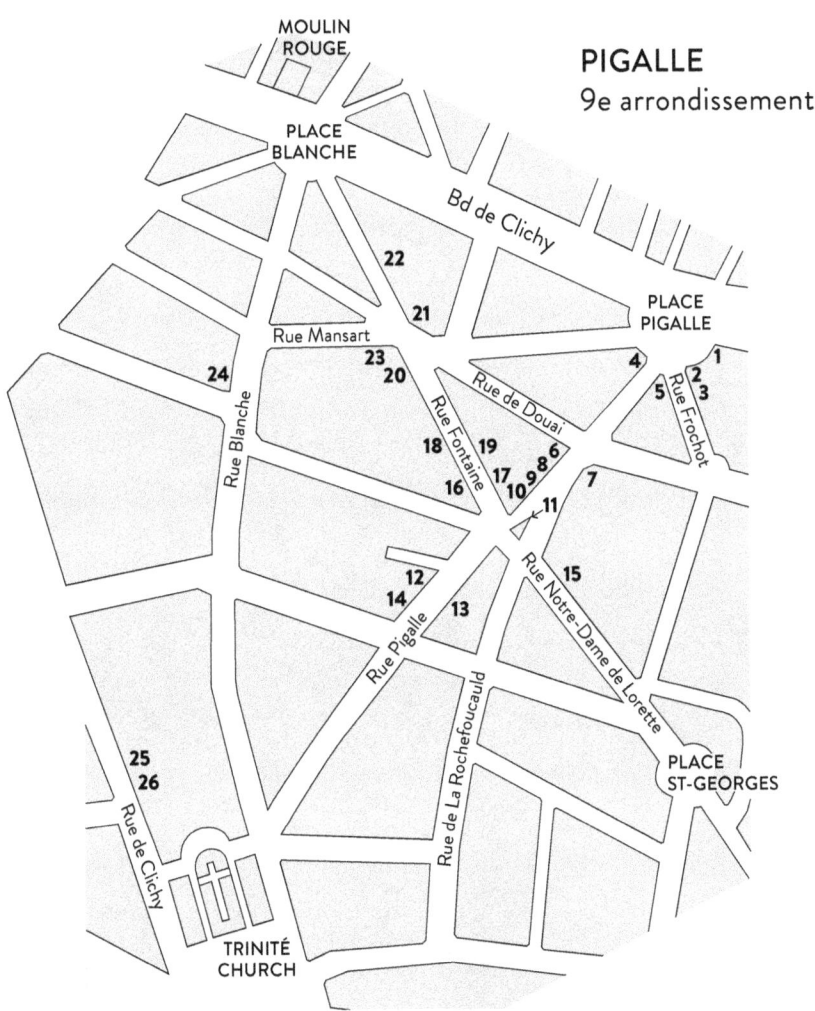

1. L'Abbaye de Thélème
2. Le Rat mort
3. L'Esperanto
4. Pigall's
5. Le New Monico
   Bricktop's Monico
6. Le Yar
7. Château et Caveau caucasiens
8. La Perle
   Le Floresco
   Bricktop's
9. L'Impérial
   Joséphine Baker's Impérial
   Bricktop's Impérial
   Pile ou Face
10. Le Harem
    Harlem
    Bricktop's Harem
    Music Box 2
11. Le Grand Duc
12. Music Box 1
13. Mitchell's 1
    Chez Florence 1
14. Mitchell's Quick Lunch
15. Le Capitole
    La Plantation
16. Costa Bar
17. El Garrón
    Kiley's
    Shanley's
    Le Palermo
18. L'Escadrille
19. La Féria
    Zelli's Royal Box
    The Tempo Club
    Omar Khayyam
20. Kiley's Gaiety
    Merrick's Gaity
    The Comedy Club
21. La Troïka
    Le Normandy
22. Chez Joséphine
23. Arsène's
    La Cloche d'Or
24. Le Ver Luisant
    Mitchell's 2
    Chez Florence 2
25. Harry Pilcer's Dancing (Apollo Theater)
26. Le Perroquet (Le Casino de Paris)

**BLACK
MONTMARTRE
IN THE
JAZZ AGE**

INTRODUCTION
"A JOYOUS TOWER OF BABEL"

Foreigners from all nations of the world gather there. They bear witness to the fact that pleasure is perhaps the most practical form of internationalism. Voluptuous Argentines stand cheek by jowl with the mysterious Japanese and the athletic American cowboy. The gigantic blond Swede is not astonished to find himself rubbing elbows with the romantic Italian or the fatalistic native of Madrid. The strong-jawed German is beginning to reappear without shocking those around him, whether it be a supple golfer from Oxford, an inscrutable and unpredictable Chinese, a wide-eyed Canadian or some nouveau riche Brazilian covered with jewels.
—Jean Gravigny

In current guidebooks "Montmartre" refers to the one-time suburban village, with its cobbled streets and steep stairways clinging to the side of the "Mountain of Martyrs" and crowned by the instantly recognizable onion domes of Sacré Coeur, the neo-Byzantine wedding cake celebrated in the paintings of Utrillo and many lesser talents. With the Boulevard de Clichy as its northern border, the half circle of the Place Pigalle lies to the south, harboring a venerable quartet of prewar pleasure haunts: the fantasy Gothic of the Abbaye de Thélème (1886), flanked by Le Rat Mort (ca. 1867), reputedly an importunate rodent condemned for disturbing the endearments of an amorous couple, and lastly, on the southernmost point of the Place, at the head of the rue Pigalle, Pigall's (1907) and Le Monico (1905).[1]

In the 1920s a new Montmartre emerged (known as Lower Montmartre or Pigalle), relegating the old artistic cabarets, like the Chat Noir, to the status of nostalgic memories. Before the First World War, Black American entertainers had made punctual appearances in Paris, performing the cakewalk and early ragtime. However, the postwar period represented something new. A more permanent Black population invested the artists' studios and cafés so well known from the Impressionist era. Responding to a clientele eager to dance to American rhythms, even the hallowed entertainment venues acquired jazz orchestras, and a plethora of jazz clubs sprang up in the network of narrow streets south of the Place Pigalle, principally around the rue Pigalle and the rue Fontaine. On this self-contained urban island, far from the shores of the racist homeland, a tight-knit group of Black American performers established a community that represented an imperfect Utopia, a metropolitan version of the island society imagined by sixteenth-century English humanist Thomas More (1516). Situated in the New World discovered by contemporary explorers, his ideal Utopia was protected from the ills of the mainland by a wide channel dug by its founder, King Utopos. The irony is that jazz-age voyagers in search of a more egalitarian society left the New World to return to the Old. In one way or another, all had fled the burden of discrimination—if France was not wholly color blind, it was at least free of the stifling constraints of segregation. Certainly, few of the Black expatriates of Montmartre had read More's famous work, but they would have recognized the striving of Utopia's citizens toward a just and equitable economic and social order.

Their audience consisted of foreign aristocrats, American tourists, and wealthy expatriates in search of a good time. These pleasure seekers visited the *dancings* (a French neologism) of the tiny enclave as they might an alcohol-soaked amusement park. They were principally from the other side of the ocean for, despite its ethnic diversity and the shadowy French partners required by law, Montmartre was very much a Yankee tale and reflected American disquiets. Anglo American journalist Basil Woon's oft-cited tome, *The Paris That's Not in the Guide Books* (1926), announces that "five Americans have left their mark in Montmartre. Oscar Mouvet is one, Joe Zelli is another, the third is Gerald Kiley, the other two are American negroes: Mitchell . . . and his former partner Florence."[2] Woon's list is divided between white and Black Americans, but beyond that it betrays an ideological bias. Despite the grudging acknowledgment, this is the only mention of legendary drummer and leader of the Jazz Kings, Louis Mitchell. Singer Florence Jones, "the colored queen of Montmartre," does not fare much better, receiving only two glancing references, and for Woon, her pianist husband, Palmer, does not even exist.[3] By contrast, the three white Americans are treated in depth: the much-decorated Belgian American war hero Oscar Mouvet, who began his career as a professional dancer but whose managerial exploits in the joy palaces of Montmartre brought him fame; Joe Zelli, the jovial "Chief Mogul of Montmartre"; and Gerald "Jed" Kiley, not the least of whose honors was the title of "Dance Hall King."[4]

At the same time, Woon disregards individuals of both races who deserve to figure on his hit parade: Oscar's celebrated sibling, Maurice, the "aristocratic dancer" who often performed in his brother's clubs, as well as two other notable white Americans, namely, Elsa Maxwell, the stout frump from Keokuk, Iowa, who became the doyenne of Parisian society, and the handsome Austrian American dancer Harry Pilcer. Among the Black Americans, one would have hoped to see mention of the brilliant percussionist Buddie Gilmore, "King of Jazz," although it is perhaps too soon to see in Woon's text the name of the inimitable Josephine Baker, who at the time of publication had just recently arrived. But one would expect to find Montmartre personality Eugene Bullard. Born poor in Jim Crow–era Georgia, he became the first Black American fighter pilot and later an indispensable impresario of the quarter's nightlife. Last, but not least, one cannot overlook the "Queen of Montmartre," singer and dance coach Ada Smith, better known as Bricktop, hostess of the fabled Grand Duc.

Many major actors of Montmartre have been erased from their own stories, hardly or inaccurately mentioned, as though they deserved no more than approximate references. Admittedly, despite the autobiographies of a few participants (Bricktop, Josephine Baker, Elsa Maxwell), the record is ephemeral, filled with people and establishments that have left only a faint imprint. The lives of Montmartre's denizens are not those of veritable kings, queens, and emperors. Unlike the reigns of a Louis XIV or a Napoleon, detailed in historical chronicles and contemporary biographies, the stories of the leading figures of Montmartre are, with a few exceptions, largely forgotten, blurred images of ersatz monarchs in papier-mâché crowns. We are obliged to reconstruct the details of their existence out of fragments, seek connections, propose interpretations, somewhat like reassembling the oddly shaped pieces of a jigsaw puzzle. Providing a more detailed and documented history of the social structures and racial dynamics of the Montmartre *dancings* may help fit the pieces together and cast fresh light on certain familiar episodes of Montmartre life in the 1920s.

During my preliminary research I was struck by the fact that despite extensive scholarship on Montmartre, much that was taken to be well documented was in fact characterized by verifiable errors, omissions, and misconceptions.[5] For example, William Shack's influential *Harlem in Montmartre: A Paris Jazz Story Between the Great Wars*, source of a major PBS series, seeks to lay out the postwar rise of jazz and some of the racist obstacles faced by its protagonists. His pioneering study was necessary, but research resources of the time did not allow him to dig deeply enough into the historical record. Egregious inaccuracies and reliance on a synchronic approach render his account confusing and falsify its conclusions.⁶ It seemed to me then that the first task was to establish a sounder factual framework, but if we seek to resuscitate the particulars of this period, what evidence can we draw on? Many secondary sources such as Shack seemed inadequate. Despite its voluminous detail, a study such as Louis Chevalier's monumental and poetic opus is of limited use, as it allocates relatively few pages to the 1920s (75 out of 452), and aside from some discussion of the "Americanization" of Montmartre, he focuses on the French.⁷ Others, like Nicholas Hewitt's more recent *Montmartre: A Cultural History*, are broad historical surveys that cast a wide net and in so doing are often victims of some of the same faults as Shack: expansive overviews, inexactitudes, and factual contradictions.⁸ Lastly, studies like those of Colin Nettlebeck or Bernard Gendron are outside of the time frame I had set for myself (1918–1930) or deal with theoretical issues irrelevant to my interests.⁹

Confronted with a paucity of detailed information on the life of the quarter in favor of vague generalities or half-truths, I returned to primary sources. One would expect firsthand reporting in the Parisian press, particularly the popular European edition of *The New York Herald*, but more surprising is the wealth of material to be found in the syndicated articles that Basil Woon and others wrote for the provincial American press. It might seem odd to seek news of Montmartre in such an unlikely place, but correspondents on the Paris beat devoted a great deal of space to doings in Montmartre, unlike contemporary observers such as Wambly Bald and Sisley Huddleston, whose chief focus was the Montparnasse literary set or the wider cultural scene.¹⁰ On the contrary, Woon was deeply implicated in the nascent café society of Montmartre and, though subject to caution, his book and neglected journalism track the mores of a moneyed elite who passed the essential of their evenings dining and dancing in its cabarets. Thanks to him and his confrères, Black and white, a stereotypical American housewife idling over her late morning coffee in some forsaken hamlet of the Republic probably knew more about Montmartre nights than the average Parisian.¹¹

Woon's work is therefore indispensable, but it presents three problems. Firstly, if properly understood, he is often correct, but interpreting his comments is at times like reading the entrails of a goat. Secondly, his chief concern was not to provide historical testimony but to entertain his small-town readers. As a result, he is often careless and not above distorting facts in the interest of an attention-grabbing story. Finally, like all authors, he writes out of a set of ideological biases: He was dazzled by wealth and celebrity; he was a snob; and he was a racist.

Most studies cite him but seldom assess the veracity of his statements. An example is Jackson's *Making Jazz French*. Although it deals chiefly with the relation of jazz to French cultural identity, the first three chapters tackle my subject directly. He and others adopt Woon's breezy narrative of Jed Kiley's debuts in the clandestine clubs of 1919 without question, although much of it is mythologizing.[12] As laid out in the first chapter of the present book, the real story is quite different. Nevertheless, despite Woon's fabulations and narrative nonchalance, he functions not only as a valuable if reluctant witness to the successes of Black performers, but as an emblem of the sniping racist strategies to which they were subjected by bigoted American journalists. These denigrations were the localized workings of a virulent American racism that attempted to impose its biases on a more permissive French social and legal environment that did not enable their excesses. Thus, the protective isolation inherent to the utopian model was constantly menaced by the insidious pressure of American racial prejudices.

For other sources, I drew upon the many important French primary texts that have not been translated, or only sporadically, such as the literary sketches of the caricaturist Sem, author Jean Gravigny's accounts of Paris after dark, surrealist Philippe Soupault's evocations of the Tempo Club, or the writings of poet Louis Aragon, both actor and observer of the tumultuous decade of the twenties. His novel *Aurélien*, and above all his 1925 memoir, *Le Mauvais Plaisant*, are virtually unknown in the English literature on nighttime Montmartre. Yet they furnish essential information on this vibrant world of bars and cabarets, reconstituting not only the concrete reality but its metaphysical dimensions.

The elaboration of a more accurate factual context reveals a previously undeveloped narrative: the decline of the clannish white "society *dancings*" of the rue Caumartin and the parallel rise of the more diverse Black-owned and -managed clubs of Pigalle. Beginning at the Olympia Theater, on the corner of the Boulevard des Capucines, and extending a few blocks north/northwest toward the Trinité church, the rue Caumartin might be regarded as a southern suburb of Montmartre. Yet, even though there are random references to its society *dancings* (particularly the fancifully named Jardin de ma Soeur), the street's key role in the creation of Montmartre's dance culture has never been recognized, nor has it been identified as a discrete social and geographical subset with an evolutionary history that positions it in opposition to the Black clubs of Pigalle.

While the story of this shift is not a history of jazz, it is of necessity bound up with the constantly changing narrative of the *dancings* that featured the new music.¹³ Unfortunately, this story is often obscured by a tendency to view Black Montmartre in the twenties synchronically as a moment frozen in time, a stagnant muddle of clubs and eras, rather than diachronically as a mutable narrative. The static synchronic model masks this development and blurs the relations between causes and effects. For example, in the summary list of dance clubs operating between 1917 and 1926 proposed by Olivier Roueff, he amalgamates Cadet Rousselle, an early pioneer of the rue Caumartin, with a decadent latecomer, l'Hermitage Muscovite; the Tempo Club, a precursor of the Black-owned cabarets, with a late flowering of the phenomenon such as Chez Florence.¹⁴ All are placed on the same temporal plane, introducing errors and obscuring the significance of their historical progression. The ideal approach would be a balanced combination of overlapping synchronic and temporal narratives; a chronological account of Black Montmartre that, at the same time, recognizes the horizontal relations between people and events.

My book is divided into three parts. The first chapter of part 1 details the origins of the clandestine *dancings* in the wartime ban on dancing, a restriction that lasted until early 1919 and beyond, due to continuing limitations on closing hours. It focuses on the untold stories of two flamboyant impresarios, Jed Kiley and Joe Zelli, the most prominent personalities of this outlaw period. Paradoxically, the ensuing society *dancings* described in chapters 2, 3, and 4, with their codes of white privilege, grew out of the socially and racially permissive atmosphere of the illicit dance halls. Though the former did not hesitate to make use of Black talents, they remained socially hermetic and, in the eyes of many of their leading figures, contemptuous of the entertainers whom they employed.

Part 2 highlights the recurring theme of the interactions between those talents and Zelli and Kiley, whose successes were predicated on an exploitation of their gifts. The activities of these relatively benevolent white club owners expose a series of racial conflicts and interracial complicities. In this respect, Zelli's ill-defined connection with the Tempo Club is of particular significance (chapter 5). Even as the society *dancings* of anti-jazz dancer Maurice Mouvet were triumphing in the rue Caumartin in 1921 and 1922, the emergence of Black-owned clubs in the Pigalle area was gestating on the rue Fontaine in the transient and little-studied Tempo Club (1921–1922), the first of the Black-owned clubs of Pigalle. Aside from mistaking its location, Shack tells us virtually nothing about this seminal establishment, and other references are equally fragmentary, yet it was an essential seedbed of the Black musical virtuosi who would eventually dominate Montmartre.

Part 3 deals with the transfer of hegemony from the society *dancings* of the rue Caumartin to what was caustically known as "the Great Black Way," consisting of the successful cabarets of Louis Mitchell, Florence Jones, Ada Smith (aka Bricktop), and others.[15] This influx of Black performers, characterized by some observers as "the Black invasion," has led modern critics to speak of "Harlem in Montmartre," a phrase inspired by Harlem Renaissance writer Gwendolyn Bennett's label "the Harlem of Paris."[16] Such a depiction is based on a misunderstanding. Socially and demographically, Montmartre was the opposite of Harlem. The latter's residents were predominately people of color, interacting with a relatively small but dominant white culture, represented by people attracted for commercial and cultural reasons or banal thrill seekers who dared the journey uptown to visit segregated night clubs. In Paris the situation was the inverse. A small number of Black Americans, perhaps several hundred (estimates varied, and the numbers were constantly changing), mingled with an overwhelmingly white population, in the framework of a relatively benign and racially tolerant French legal system. Even though they faced resistance from a number of their white compatriots, this sympathetic climate allowed them to attain a level of social and economic achievement that would have eluded them in America—a narrative of troubled race relations marked by advances and retreats, what Stovall fittingly called the "nation's conflicted journey into the modern age."[17]

The story of this postwar social phenomenon has understandably been presented as a tale of Black Montmartre, but in reality the account is multifaceted. Blacks were not the only marginalized group to find refuge in Montmartre—there were the Argentines and the Russians, to name only the most prominent. If Black Americans occupied a unique position, it was because the ascendance of jazz accorded them a preponderant place. Studies like that of Boittin deal largely with the integration or non-integration of populations linked to France by its colonial history, but apart from a few exceptions like the Franco-Senegalese boxer Battlin' Siki (Louis Phal), the Dahomeyan Prince Tovalou Houénou, or a small number of Black gigolos, Black French were not a major presence in the huis clos of Black Montmartre, which was characterized by the typically insular quality of utopian communities.[18]

The two cultural soirées organized by the prince in late May and early June of 1924 were among the rare exceptions to this isolation. For an evening, at least, the inward-looking Montmartre community connected with other peoples of color. The first was a "Grande Soirée de Noirs Américains." Tovalou gave a talk on Black Americans and Africans, and the program featured Florence Jones and the leading lights of Montmartre: Buddie Gilmore, Palmer Jones' International Five, Sonny Jones, all entertainers whom the prince had met at the Grand Duc. The second, on June 7, consisted of Dahomeyan music and dances, sponsored by Tovalou's Franco-Dahomeyan Friendship Association.[19] We do not know if Florence and the others attended.

Despite this deviation from the rule, most of these performers seldom left Montmartre except to tour or follow their affluent audiences to summer extensions of the quarter like Deauville, Biarritz, and Venice. The cosmopolitanism suggested by their international travel does not necessarily suppose a geopolitical worldview, and Paris remained, as Miller puts it, "the *gare centrale* of jazz on the Continent during the 1920's."[20] Even in the French capital Black expatriates had relatively little interaction with the broader society and lacked a citywide as well as a global perspective—when the narrator of Robert McAlmon's roman-à-clef invites banjo player Joe Caulk to Montparnasse, the latter replies, "Sure, Kit. I been hearing about the place so long I got a curiosity," and that after years of residence in the city.[21]

Centered on an emblematic night café, La Plantation, the final chapter of part 3 offers three case histories illustrative of the evils and failures of jazz age Montmartre: a paranoid white fear of miscegenation, a characteristically American surfeit of violence, and the pernicious stereotypes conveyed by the myth of happy days on "the old plantation." Apparently liberated from the shackles of racism, Montmartre presented, in the words of Andy Fry, "an idealized vision for the future of America."[22] The chief obstacle to realizing this dream of a society free of the constraints of American bigotry was the fact that, unlike classical utopias, Montmartre was not an island enclave, and thus vulnerable to the negative influence of American prejudices, perpetuated by resident expatriates, narrow-minded tourists, and biased journalists.

Ironic echoes of heroic historical figures—moguls, kings, queens, countesses—for these insubstantial Black royals, grandiloquent titles served as emblems of the utopian dreams that flourished in the twisting streets of Montmartre. Like the spectators in Northrop Frye's comment on the dénouement of Shakespeare's *Tempest*, they sought "the island that the world has been searching for since the dawn of history, the island that is both nature and human society restored to their original form, where there is no sovereignty and yet where all of us are kings."[23] If their lives seem at times to be the trivial chatter of old-school gossip columns, the battles they fought were nevertheless essential and not without significance for our own time. In the drafts of F. Scott Fitzgerald's great expatriate novel *Tender Is the Night*, two characters are seen at the conclusion of a night of dissipation in Pigalle "drifting like America itself towards some ignoble destiny," a fate whose conflicts were vividly mirrored by Black Montmartre, as was the hope of a possible redemption.[24]

To write history means to write a certain history. One can never seize the totality of things. The detailed narrative of Montmartre that I wish to write begins on the rue Caumartin. This street witnessed some of the earliest manifestations of jazz and, with the exclusion of Bricktop and Josephine, who did not arrive until 1924–1925, and Kiley, whose early clubs were itinerant, all the personalities I have mentioned were initially associated with this modest thoroughfare. To begin the history of Montmartre outside its traditionally recognized borders may appear arbitrary, but it is justified by both history and geography.

PART I

IN THE RUE CAUMARTIN
From Clandestine Dance Halls to "Society *Dancings*"

CHAPTER ONE

SHIMMY PARLORS AND DELUXE DIVES

The Era of Dubious *Dancings*

That was the heroic epoch, the time of persecutions and catacombs.
—Sem

It is a commonplace to state that European jazz began with the entry of the United States into the Great War. On January 1, 1918, the 369th Infantry Regiment, a segregated Black unit known as the "Harlem Hellfighters," disembarked at Brest with a regimental band led by famed conductor James Reese Europe. But one should not forget that along with jazz and ragtime, Europe's band played Sousa marches and assorted French and American selections, even if the "jazz" pieces aroused the greatest interest from the locals, who had never heard anything like them.[1] And while Europe's impact is undeniable, in November 1916 drummer extraordinaire Louis Mitchell and a ragtime band had already accompanied the popular dance team of La Belle Leonora and Signor Valentino at the Alhambra Theater in Paris.

A month before the landing of the Hellfighters, Mitchell was back at the Alhambra with his Seven Spades. The name may offend modern ears, but others were equally incorrect, such as the regrettable Ciro's Club Coon Orchestra in London. Though the French probably missed the racial connotation of "spade," advertising as a Black band was not necessarily a handicap vis-à-vis the American and English soldiers who flocked to their performances. The Spades were a sensation. Their two-week contract was extended till January 1918, followed by equal success at the Olympia Theater.

The war was ending, and Paris was ready to explode. Some of the first detonations were heard on the unpretentious rue Caumartin. According to music hall star Maurice Chevalier, "Night life in Paris recruited more and more votaries. English, American, and French officers on leave embraced it enthusiastically. Hundreds of apartments were transformed into places of amusement;

champagne flowed like water. American jazz bands and dance halls mixed heroes, society women, industrialists, artists, and demimondaines—a nocturnal world to which the police closed its eyes, an exacerbated gaiety, as if there were an imperative to enjoy oneself."[2] Out of "compassion for the suffering at the front" dancing had been banned during the war, but after the November 1918 Armistice soldiers emerged from the horrors of the trenches executing a panoply of North American dances to the revitalizing rhythms of jazz.[3] The feeling among many was that their sacrifices had earned them the right to an animated "warrior's rest."

The new passion was born in clandestine dance clubs and nurtured in the novel "surprise parties"—characterized by impromptu merrymakers who arrived at the door of unsuspecting hosts prepared to one-step or tango, the latter a prewar craze imported by the sons of Argentinean cattle barons, come to Paris to complete their "sentimental educations."[4] Though the tango maintained its popularity, the imperious need to gambol was satisfied primarily by North American dances. Devotees of these transatlantic novelties came to be known as "*fox-trotteurs, shymmistes, bleuseurs, charlestoniers,* or *black bottomiers*"—terms designating the dances that overlapped and replaced each other with dizzying speed. All were executed to the sound of jazz, a word that surfaced in French lexicons in 1918. Close on its heels, a neologism was created to designate the new clubs. Derived from English, its use as a common noun is uniquely Gallic. Granting this novel institution a metaphysical dimension, terpsichorean critic André Warnod proclaimed, "Modern dance, the new goddess, had its high priests and its faithful followers . . . It was necessary for her to have her temples, that need was met, they were designated by an Anglo-Saxon name: *dancing*."[5]

The ban on dancing persisted for several months after the Armistice, but even when it was lifted on April 3, 1919, dance enthusiasts were unable to indulge their passion without constraint. Closing hours were restricted due to persistent shortages of coal, a product that the *dancings* relied on to produce the electricity that illuminated their gleaming parquets. On November 26 of that year, dance halls—from the elegant *dancing* in the Apollo Theater to the humblest back alley *bal*—were closed by order of Prefect of Police Fernand Raux, generating desperate appeals from proprietors and ardent supporters of the dance. A comic sketch even showed a young girl on her knees, beseeching a haloed "Saint Raux": "Please don't close the *dancings* at 10 p.m.!" His laconic response to these pleas was that "he did not dance."[6]

The rationale for the curfews—the shortage of coal—was greeted with disbelief. Dance hall proprietors pointed out that "theaters, large hotel lobbies, restaurants and countless tea rooms consumed more coal than they did and that closing dancing places was only a drop in the bucket." The director of Harry Pilcer's *Dancing* underlined the human element: "They are throwing out of work thousands of musicians, waiters and professional dancing instructors as well as shops employing countless girls manufacturing cotillon favors. Closing dance halls is an act of oppression and is engineered by the theatrical and moving picture men, who are jealous because the dance halls are getting all their business."[7]

This distrust was echoed by sceptics like Warnod for whom coal shortages were only a pretext for the "fierce defenders of public virtue" to attack what they deemed to be dens of vice and iniquity.[8] In November 1919 the archbishop of Paris, Cardinal Léon-Adolphe Amette, a prudent Norman opposed to modernity, "issued a pastoral letter protesting against immodest toilettes and indecent dances."[9] Nonetheless, Amette's condemnation of "modern dances" is distinct from transatlantic critiques. For the prelate it was a question of public morals, while for many Yankees protests took on racial overtones. Noting the popularity of the Charleston and the Black Bottom in Parisian nightspots, a condescending American later commented that "these two dances are danced exclusively on music hall stages or in night clubs. No one in *polite society* has any familiarity with them!" [my italics].[10]

An unexpected consequence of police regulations was the persistence and spread of the clandestine balls. In Montmartre's heyday, the clubs hardly woke before midnight. Thus one can imagine that the limited hours of 1919 and 1920 were a serious constraint on aspirant nighthawks. Caricaturist Sem graphically describes the 11 p.m. closing of a legitimate club. Groups of bereft dancers wandered about like abandoned children. "Languishing, disoriented, some bubbly ladies whom the abruptly suspended *dancing* has left unsatisfied continue to move to the rhythm, to find relief in tracing on the rain-glazed sidewalk the final tremors of an embryonic tango."[11] Finally, one member of the party suggests a solution: a covert *dancing*!

The best known of what Warnod terms "these fugitive *dancings*" were the fruit of the bold efforts of John Gerald "Jed" Kiley, youthful scion of a Chicago Irish American family.[12] He had arrived in France during the summer of 1917 as an ambulance driver with the American Field Service before becoming a civilian chauffeur for the American Expeditionary Forces (AEF).[13] Following the termination of hostilities he settled in Paris where, as travel author Ralph Nevill writes, he "did his best to keep jazz and One-step going."[14] For most critics, the chief biographical source on Kiley has been the mythmaking of Basil Woon. The latter declares that his old friend Kiley began his career shortly after the Armistice with invitation dances for American officers, which continued until May when music and dancing were legalized, causing him to abandon jazz and go into the ice cream business—with dire results in October due to French reluctance to consume frozen products in winter.[15] This account is generally accepted without blinking, despite Woon's fondness for false causalities (dancing was authorized in April, not May, while Kiley did not "abandon" jazz until the following August, and then only provisionally).

A closer look at contemporary sources rectifies the legend drafted in embryonic form by Woon in 1924 and elaborated two years later in his book.[16] After the war, Jed commenced a stint at the Paris office of the *New York Herald*, a job he promptly lost due to overindulgence in the fine Beaujolais served at a luncheon talk given by the American ambassador.[17] Armed with a week's severance pay, he and another ex-ambulance driver, Harold Fitch, began to organize after-hours dances. Defying the ban on all night one-stepping, in January 1919 they planned a "Wilson Welcome Ball" to honor American President Woodrow Wilson's arrival at the Versailles Peace Conference. Although the latter snubbed the invitation, they netted over ten thousand francs, allowing them to expand their activities.

Woon's picaresque version has Kiley moving from one impromptu dance hall to another, always one step ahead of the police. There may be some truth to this as Kiley himself states that the Wilson Ball's success was duplicated at "The Dixie Club" dances—plausibly the parties with jazz band held at the Dixie Club, in the vicinity of the faubourg Saint-Martin, which then as now harbored a colorful nightlife.[18] What is undeniable is that several months later he was running a similar operation on the affluent Avenue Montaigne: the American Foxtrot Club.[19]

This "shimmy parlor" was not hidden away in some back alley but niched in the rehearsal rooms of the historic Théâtre des Champs Elysées, a venue that would witness the celebrated 1925 debut of Josephine Baker in *La Revue nègre*. We know little about the music except that it was performed by a jazz band of American doughboys led by Bill Henley.[20] That spring, Henley and other former AEF members had formed the White Lyres, an allusion to the insignias worn by Army musicians as well as to the conspicuous fact that they were a white band. Nevertheless, on the evidence of his later ventures, it seems likely that Kiley also featured Black musicians, a stance consistent with his ambiguities about race.

In August the American Foxtrot Club was closed by police, not due to jealous rivals but at the request of U.S. Army authorities. The latter had denounced it as the resort of intoxicated soldiers absent without leave and declared the parties off-limits to officers and rank and file. However, the military police had no authority over sailors, and when they attempted to block their entry, "a pitched battle roared out over the avenue Montaigne to the accompaniment of jazz music tinkling from the open windows six floors up." Kiley demanded to know why his club was off limits to the Army yet "respectable" for the Navy, and in reprisal threatened to "name brigadier-generals and major-generals who have spent quiet evenings at my dances and I may include numerous attachés of the peace conference who tried to forget their troubles regulating the world by a little relaxation."[21]

One may wonder why the police had tolerated this prohibited activity. There are two credible reasons. Initially, Kiley catered only to military personnel; it is also likely that money changed hands, which Kiley could afford—he was credited with making half a million francs before the shutdown. For a time, the flamboyant Foxtrot King amused himself with his earnings, buying "a string of cars and the entire output of a fashionable tailor," but in late October he reunited with ex-partner Fitch to set his sights on the less nerve-wracking title of "Ice Cream King."[22] They bought the machinery of the American YMCA, a defunct wartime enterprise, and formed the Dixie Ice Cream Company.

The new enterprise was a huge success, and Kiley swore he was through with dance palaces forever. With a measure of hypocrisy, he even allied himself with anti-saloon groups proselytizing for prohibition.[23] Nonetheless, perhaps bored with his frosty crown, in early 1920 he returned to the shimmy and champagne trade with the "Author's Club," located on the western outskirts of Paris. Though some clandestine *dancings* lay within the precincts of the city, most were positioned in the close-lying suburbs of Passy, Neuilly, and Auteuil, boasting names like the Flirting Club or Aladdin's Lamp. The gain in discretion is evident, but why to the west? In addition to an abundance of deserted mansions large enough to house itinerant dance halls, I believe the choice was dictated by proximity to the fashionable districts of the 16^e and 17^e arrondissements, which furnished a significant part of their clientele.

It is perhaps unexpected to find such clubs still functioning at this late date, but ongoing coal shortages obliged the government to continue restrictive hours. Thus, there was a continuing demand for surreptitious dance halls. In a vain attempt to evade police scrutiny, a *dancing* like the Gold Club claimed that its members practiced golf strokes while sipping champagne and one-stepping. Kiley's ploy was to present his Author's Club "as an association for the studiously inclined to read late at night," an ironic preface to his literary ambitions. The police were not taken in by these pretentions. In February they began a campaign to put a lid on late-night *dancings*. Kiley's learned circle was shut down, along with the less scholarly Flirting Club and the popular Aladdin's Lamp. Conserving electricity was not the only concern. Waiters at the Flirting Club were alleged to be selling cocaine, morphine, and opium![24] Not in the least daunted, Kiley launched the appositely named Mr. Will Stay-Up-Late Club, housed in a château in Auteuil. This time he offered no justification other than his clients' insatiable craving to remain vertical until the wee hours. It was intermittently closed by police.

In contrast, Dixie Ice Cream continued to prosper ... until August. Woon's explanation for its failure (French aversion to the "crazy" Yankee habit of ingesting ice cream in winter) is ingenious, but he manipulates the facts to support his false narrative. The Ice Cream Kings did not launch their business in May 1919, as he maintains, but in October (when he has them closing) and, in fact, the company thrived through the winter, only foundering the following summer.[25] Moreover, the reason for its collapse was not French mores but a violent dispute between the partners over profit sheets that left Kiley sitting in the doorway of the Dixie factory, with a battered head but triumphant, the Stars and Stripes floating bravely from the handle of an ice pick.[26]

Fortuitously, in a text dated April 1920, Sem offers a detailed depiction of an unidentified *dancing* similar to Kiley's Mr. Will Stay-Up-Late Club.[27] Plausibly, it chronicles the final days of the Aladdin's Lamp Club in Neuilly, run by aspirant dance king Clarence M. Glover and fellow ex-AEF members familiar with sub-rosa activities, for example, White Lyre Bill Henley. The club was frequented by well-known personalities, such as Kiley's future wife dancer Joan Sawyer and a cohort of peace conference attachés exhausted by a year of negotiations.[28] A French journalist reminisced that astride the upright piano of this "deluxe dive," Johnson, King of the Banjo, instilled "with generous laughter the poison with which we were going to intoxicate ourselves."[29]

I am tempted to cite Sem's text in its entirety, but I will limit myself to a few vivid passages. The brief extract cited showed frustrated dancers stranded by the closing of a legitimate *dancing*. Sem and his party then pile into two cars. Inundated by incessant rain and the ether-soaked breath of one of the women, they file past the Arch of Triumph in the direction of Neuilly. Eventually, they arrive at a suburban villa set in a "funereal garden that exudes the vague impression of a deconsecrated cemetery." From hermetically closed windows leaks a "ghostly clamor."[30]

In the spider-webbed vestibule, a tuxedo-clad gentleman at a rusty garden table collects "dues," a ruse to maintain the fiction of a private club. Having remunerated the elegant Cerberus, they are propelled into a "whirling crowd of men and women in evening clothes who, swept along by an unbridled Negro orchestra, dance furiously in a half-light blurred by smoke."[31] As Maurice Chevalier intimated, the chaos of war had upended societal codes. "The *dancing* was a social incubator in which different social arrangements were tried, tested, and destroyed," facilitating a mixture of "hookers, demimondaines, and even authentic society women. Thus far the latter had held themselves apart. But now these ladies and demoiselles lean on the same tables, exchange cigarettes, swap dance partners"—a cohabitation that anticipates the future promiscuity of the more diverse boîtes of the rue Pigalle and the rue Fontaine.[32] Age, social status, racial origins—all are dissolved in the heady rhythms of jazz. "The cadence of the *Shimmy Shake* creeps into their limbs, sends an electric current through their bodies, causes them to writhe against their will like Volta's dead frogs."[33]

In effect, these were the years of the Shimmy, a Yankee craze involving vigorous agitation of hips and shoulders—one critic described it as "a dog exiting the water, which shakes itself to dispose of the liquid clinging to its coat."[34] French dance professors deemed these "violent" American dances an upshot of the recent conflict, to be rejected along with other wartime lapses in propriety.[35] The concomitant of such attitudes was that one-steps, shimmies, and jazz were the province of Black Americans. In effect, French performers were rare in the first years of the decade (a native jazz culture would not develop until the thirties), and outside a few successful groups like the White Lyres or the Billy Arnolds, jazz was largely synonymous with Black musicians.[36]

Therefore, noblesse oblige, the band animating Sem's furtive revels is a Black ensemble. One of his witty sketches shows a banjoist (Johnson, "King of the Banjo"?) enthroned on an upright piano, surrounded by frenzied colleagues and a raft of empty champagne bottles (see gallery 1).[37] "In a sadistic fury, the pianist completes his destruction ... of the keyboard. The one-man band intensifies the rapid beating of his drum set, alternates the base and the tom-tom, activates the cymbals, unleashes ear-splitting devices with his hands and feet; while, with a megaphone contrived from sheet music, ... his comrade shrieks out a Negro song, vainly shouting above the fracas of instruments that mask his high-pitched howling. This uproar is contagious, for all the dancers sing or whistle in time."[38] The overheated prose reflects the impact of the band on its enraptured listeners. The relation is symbiotic, as the two sides spur each other on in a mutual frenzy. Nevertheless, eventually the band falters. A lunatic American insists they continue. Several ladies intervene, one kissing the pianist—a gesture that elicits a violent reaction typical of a culture haunted by the fear of miscegenation. The American leaps forward "to lynch" the pianist. Later he will silence the orchestra with a shot from his Browning, but for the moment, stylish Florence Nightingales prevail.[39] "Sympathetic nurses, they strive to invigorate the faltering musicians, rousing them with infusions of champagne cut with whisky, as one might revive half-dead battling cocks. 'Hello! drink, my darling. You, good Negro, never sick, never die!' [they croon in a pidgin French that betrays a naive, well-meaning racism]. They succeed. The stalled motor revs up anew. The musicians step on the gas and the hullabaloo begins again."[40]

Sem's stance is that of amused observer, but his final image contains an implicit moral judgement on the shimmying classes. It is 5 a.m. As the weary night owls depart, "the livid dawn of an execution vaguely lights the long suburban boulevard veiled by the mists of the Seine. Some truck farmers and laundrymen pass in their wagons and gape."[41]

With the legalization of public prancing, dance clubs had sprung up all over Paris like spring flowers, but nowhere more vigorously than in the hothouse atmosphere of the rue Caumartin, a choreographic blossoming accompanied for the most part by banal French bands and sagely conducted during mandated operating hours. Devotees of Terpsichore fox-trotted, shimmied, and tangoed in the early evening, leaving the clandestine clubs to continue till dawn, though at times the legitimate *dancings* pushed the envelope on closing hours.

The seeds sown by the authorization to dance burgeoned in two emblematic night cafés. Warnod explains that "the small theatres of the rue Caumartin, all more or less in a state of collapse, sought a new fortune."[42] Such was the case of Cadet Rousselle at number 17 and the Savoy Dancing Club at number 25 (former Théâtre Caumartin), among the first *dancings* to emerge after the lifting of wartime proscriptions. As the war was winding down in March 1918, Louis Mitchell and the Seven Spades followed their triumphs at the Alhambra and Olympia with appearances at the Théâtre Caumartin.[43] Since prewar days this tiny theater had functioned alternately as playhouse and cabaret, but in 1918 singer/actress Clara Faurens assumed the direction, presenting a revue titled *Ramasse-les donc!* (Pick them up, then!). Her aim was to create a spectacle of international quality, and the Seven Spades were essential to her project. As the *Figaro* declared, Mitchell's band added "a definite [American] spice to this ultra-Parisian program."[44]

Mitchell asserts that Mme Faurens promoted the revue's lead act at his group's expense and finally enticed the band away from him.[45] If this is true, apparently there were no hard feelings, for in July he united the Casino de Paris band with former Spades (listed as the band of "the Théâtre Caumartin") for a performance at the American Soldiers and Sailors' Club.[46] Subsequently, several American groups would appear at Faurens' theater to meet the demand Mitchell had helped to create. These Yankee interventions were still in the context of traditional music hall presentations, but seizing on the new vogue, Clara Faurens was the first to convert her theater into an up-to-date dance hall: the Savoy Dancing Club. American-style revues, a ubiquitous "American bar," and the Seven Spades had been insufficient. Patrons wanted to dance. Newspapers announced a transformed "ex-Théâtre Caumartin," with a new parquet and a Franco-American orchestra. In this mood of worship of all things American, the theater quickly engaged the White Lyres.[47]

However, the notoriety of the Savoy Dancing Club was short-lived. An ultimate ad appeared on May 15, 1920, and the *dancing* quietly metamorphosed into the Clover Club, managed by Clarence Glover and other former owners of the recently padlocked Aladdin's Lamp. The transformation inscribed itself in a cycle in which the venue ricocheted between theater and cabaret—the Comédie Royale in 1901; then a satirical cabaret; followed by Faurens' Théâtre Caumartin, which became the Savoy Dancing Club before mutating into the Clover; then reverting to the Théâtre Caumartin; succeeded by Maurice Mouvet's brief dance season; only to be reborn as the second Clover, and ultimately returning to its theatrical vocation—as though ceaselessly reiterating the genesis of the rue Caumartin *dancings*.[48] Nevertheless, if the fame of the Savoy Dancing Club was quickly forgotten, Mme Faurens' Théâtre Caumartin is still remembered for having hosted one of the groundbreaking Parisian engagements of Louis Mitchell.

Less chic than the Clover, which numbered among its adherents "a select, but not too snobbish, group of princesses who are American by birth and Parisian by inclination," the raffish Cadet Rousselle was more important in the history of Montmartre.[49] It was managed and owned by two fascinating personalities: Serge Alexandre Stavisky, a Russian émigré known as *le beau Sacha*, and his mistress Fanny Bloch, née Dreyfus, aka Jeanne Darcy—"Lulu" to her intimates. The former is best known as the protagonist of the infamous

"Stavisky Affair," the politico-financial scandal that precipitated the fall of two prime ministers, triggered fascist riots in 1934, and rocked the foundations of the Third Republic. However, at the time of his meeting with Jeanne in the spring of 1917 he was only a charming petty swindler with large, languorous eyes, a glance full of Slavic charm, and a penchant for exploiting vulnerable women.[50] Jeanne was an actress and demimondaine whose prewar reputation on the café-concert stage was fast fading.[51] Eight years older than Sacha, she fell madly in love. He was more attracted by her cash and assets, inherited from a lover and fellow drug user killed during the war. The couple promptly launched a series of covert gambling dens and began to dabble in cocaine cut with bicarbonate of soda and talcum powder.

By June of that year le beau Sacha had persuaded his mistress to invest in Cadet Rousselle, a cabaret founded by the beloved chansonnier Maxime Guitton on the site of the Sans Souci, a prewar tango palace. Stavisky became codirector, she a silent partner. During the waning days of the war, its revues veered from traditional French song, featuring American orchestras and English titles such as "Mind Your Pips." Following the Savoy's lead, in April 1919 Stavisky began to present thés dansants and evening galas animated by a jazz ensemble; by September he had fully embraced the new mode with the booking of a white group, Kelly's Jazz Band.[52] Throughout the fall they regaled delighted dancers, but the real revolution in Cadet Rousselle's fortunes occurred in December when Stavisky hired soon-to-be cabaret legend Joe Zelli as manager.[53]

The new dispensation had the further distinction of initiating the career of another Montmartre icon, fighter pilot and war hero Eugene Bullard. Most descriptions of Zelli's tenure in the rue Caumartin rely on Woon's brief remarks and Bullard's unpublished memoir, *All Blood Runs Red*, as cited in the biographies of Craig Lloyd, P. J. Carisella, and James W. Ryan. I refer chiefly to Lloyd's paraphrase of Bullard's at best ambiguous story of a shady chapter in his past:

> After becoming proficient enough as a drummer (he admits several times that he was never more than that), Bullard found work with a band employed in a nightclub owned by Joe Zelli on the rue Caumartin.... Zelli realized that if he could secure a license permitting him to remain open past midnight, something then forbidden by Parisian law, he could steal a march on his competitors in the cabaret business.... Bullard contacted Robert Henri [a lawyer friend] "and told him that I would have an interest as artistic director for Zelli if he got a [all night] club license.... Fifteen days later Joe Zelli and I were instructed to meet the lawyer at the License Bureau. There we received the club license."[54]

The reality is more complex. Giuseppe (Joe) Salvatore Zelli was an Italian American who began his career in 1904, at the age of fifteen, running a bar in New York, followed by the direction of a London club in 1911. When Italy joined the Allies in the summer of 1915, he enlisted in the Italian Artillery and two years later was wounded at the battle of Caporetto. 1919 found him in Tours running a restaurant/café patronized by officers of the American SOS (Service of Supply), headquartered in the city. Apprehensive about returning to an America threatened by the Volstead Act that established prohibition, he tried his luck in Paris, where the vacuum created by the departure of AEF officers had been filled by a horde of parched American tourists and temporary residents, lured by a favorable exchange rate, plentiful liquor, and an eagerness to dance.

As for Bullard, in the spring of 1919 he returned to Paris armed with French citizenship he had earned by his wartime service, numerous medals, and an honorable record that did not protect him from racist compatriots. One evening, he accidentally brushed against a white officer in the street. Infuriated by the offender's color, the American beat him to the ground, necessitating evacuation to a hospital. Thankfully, his wounds were slight.[55] This was not the last time he would be obliged to defend himself against American bigots, but such incidents did not weaken his determination to profit from the relatively bias-free conditions offered by Paris.

Like his mentor, Zelli, he saw an opportunity in the flood of visitors who had joined Parisians in their passion for dancing. Conscious that jazz was considered the specialty of Black Americans, he set out to become a drummer. The expatriate community was small and, if we are to believe Lloyd, he became acquainted with Louis Mitchell's Seven Spades and was soon learning to play drums from the master himself.[56] By June, the romantically alluring aviator was frequenting the boulevards and playing in a number of jazz bands.[57] "I think I was rotten," Bullard avowed, "but it seemed every dancing place wanted a colored drummer, and they had auditioned me before hiring me, so what could I lose."[58] This seemingly hasty conversion to show business is not as startling as it seems. As an eighteen-year-old boxer in London, he had supplemented his income by appearing with New Orleans entertainer Belle Davis' cringe-inducing "Freedman's Pickaninnies." It was while traveling with her troupe that he first visited and fell in love with Paris.

Indicative of his readiness to exploit Black talent, Zelli recruited Bullard to play drums in Cadet Rousselle's "frenzied jazz band" and before long engaged him as artistic director.[59] The club was a hit with dance fanatics, but its vogue was not solely a consequence of the Black drummer's professional relations; Cadet Rousselle had begun staying open after the legal closing hour of 10 p.m. and the result was a continuous game of cat and mouse with the police. Again, one wonders why the authorities did not simply close the offending cabaret; however, as in the case of Kiley, the situation was sensitive. "Police captains who raided these establishments were on occasion extremely discomfited. What could they do? Finding themselves face to face with some highly placed personage, or the sovereign of an allied country, the captains were sometimes obliged to be accommodating."[60]

Weary of this constant jousting, in mid-April 1920 Zelli acquired a French associate, Pierre Monzat (editor of an ephemeral revue, *Paris-Danse*) and, to circumvent police regulations, transformed Cadet Rousselle into a bogus administrative entity known as "Zelli's Club," with Monzat as "president" and himself as "manager."[61] Bullard may have been helpful in obtaining a so-called [all night] club license, but it was only a standard "license" (the interpolation is Lloyd's), one that recognized the debatable incorporation of Zelli's as a private association with artistic and sporting ambitions.[62] There is no evidence that sports or the arts played any role at Zelli's, but the advantage of this stratagem, vainly employed at Kiley's Author's Club, was that unlike ordinary *dancings*, private clubs were granted later opening hours on condition that they admit only authorized members. "One paid thirty francs for a 'card of membership' [the more upscale Clover demanded 60] which, needless to say, was obtainable by anyone at the entrance."[63]

In the early hours of June 11, 1920 (the day that *Paris-Danse* published a dithyrambic review refuting the presence of "questionable elements" and launched a hypocritical tirade against clandestine *dancings*), the carousing was disturbed by the inopportune visit of a certain "Captain Metten."[64] The dismayed officer discovered "*illicit dancing*.... After the legal hour for authorized frolicking—one o'clock in the morning—the patrons gave themselves up to the pleasures of the dance. At Cadet Rousselle, 17 rue Caumartin, some engaged in the foxtrot, and at the Savoy Club, number 25 of the same street, others passionately swayed back and forth."[65] In effect, the foxtrot, the shimmy, and the tango were the reigning favorites, above all the gay, supple foxtrot, punctuated by lively syncopated steps: "Fox trot music—*Where the Black-Eyed Susans Grow*. The razzle is on." Observing the eager dancers, the affable Zelli is quoted as saying, "Oh, fox trots for this tea crowd. They're for the nifty tunes. That's *Peaches Down in Georgia*. Now we'll give them *Just a Baby's Prayer at Twilight*."[66]

The Herald's account of the raid cites inflated champagne prices as the cause, but the *Journal* makes it clear that while liquor tariffs were a contributing factor in the raid, Captain Metten and his joyless men were motivated chiefly by the infringement of the rigorous curfew, admission of nonmembers, and the legitimacy of the club status.[67] Monzat tacitly acknowledged the final point when, writing as "Le Noctambule," he "certified" vociferously that Zelli's was "really a club, founded and directed according to the law."[68]

The Clover's claims to "member-only" status were perhaps more convincing, but the police were not fooled for long by the patent ruses of the jovial Italian. Notwithstanding the high-flown rhetoric of *Paris-Danse* (probably the work of Monzat), announcing "a sort of great family, pleased to see each other, discuss their common interests, and pursue friendships," on raiding Zelli's in November the police observed that it was "'the same *dancing*' [Cadet Rousselle]. Same management [Zelli], same orchestra [Jack, the incomparable Negro jazz band], same faces [and, particularly troubling to defenders of public virtue], same young people accompanied by the same foreigners"—presumably of a mature age. All this joyous company "was passing the night drinking and dancing."[69] Therefore, the court issued a writ against MM. Monzat and Zelli on the grounds that the "pseudo club" was an illegal operation and ordered its dissolution.[70]

Zelli's aborted adventure (it lasted little more than five months) suggests the intricacy of the profitable finances of the *dancings*. The name was "Zelli's," but Jeanne Darcy (under Stavisky's influence) and Guitton were the actual proprietors.[71] As for le beau Sacha, in October court papers still referred to him as "codirector" of Cadet Rousselle.[72] Clearly, he was the éminence grise behind Zelli and Monzat's questionable operation. He was no stranger to ghost firms of dubious legality; Charlier and Montarron affirm that "his field of action, his real hunting ground was that of offices with fraudulent façades, of falsified documents, of devoted straw men."[73] Undoubtedly Zelli and his partner figured among the latter. Though he was noted for his bonhomie and good nature, less favorable critics described Zelli as a sleazy racketeer. This was certainly true of his later years when he served as front man for the infamous gangster and bootlegger Owney "Killer" Madden in an upscale New York speakeasy, but his equivocal activities had begun with the sulfurous Stavisky.

In the light of this evident state of illegality, the myth of the "all night" license does not stand up to scrutiny. The disastrous series of events recounted above shows that Zelli's only escaped the rigors of draconian closing hours by masquerading as a members-only club, a status that continued police raids exposed as false. It is not surprising that in his memoir Bullard makes no allusion to his involvement in the duplicitous affairs of Zelli, Monzat, and the disreputable Stavisky. He prefers to dwell on more exemplary episodes, like his presence at a homage to French Foreign Legion war dead, held less than two months after the June raid.[74]

All current histories overlook Cadet Rousselle's problematic transformation into an ersatz private "cercle," and its bouts with the law, as if "Zelli's Club" had tranquilly followed its course until, "not long after receiving the ["magical"] license, the club moved to an even more lucrative location on the rue Fontaine" in Pigalle.[75] If, for a time, the future "King of Cabaret Keepers" had been able to avoid the most unpleasant consequences of police incursions, it was likely due to Stavisky's good offices. Police files suggest that the latter was an informant and may have benefited from official protection.[76] Where Zelli's illegal operation was concerned, "the police was not a faithful friend and never hesitated to denounce an informer when the wind changed."[77] Not a problem. Despite the "dissolution" of his club, in January 1921 Zelli was back at the old stand until, several months later, he opened his new moneymaker, the Royal Box.[78]

Behind Zelli's problematic public maneuverings lay the sordid private affairs of "Lulu" and "le beau Sacha," marked by turbulent financial disputes, messy court cases, and Stavisky's repeated thievery. Bemused by passion, Jeanne Darcy had forgiven earlier larcenies, but shortly before the November closure of "Zelli's Club" she took him to court over the theft of personal effects and the receipts of Cadet Rousselle. The reported sum varies but it was substantial; the *Journal* estimated her romantic relations had cost her more than a million francs.[79] After a firestorm of recriminations and reconciliations, Stavisky was found guilty in February 1921.

With the irrepressible Zelli having decamped to Pigalle, in March Jeanne installed popular American dancer Harry Pilcer as artistic director and *vedette maison* (house star). The club was rechristened "Chez Harry Pilcer" but the new incarnation was transitory. Stavisky had appealed! Stricken again with remorse, "Lulu" withdrew her complaint. Result: on May 6, 1921, he was acquitted.[80] Four days later she abruptly fired the new director, who countered with a successful suit to have his name removed from the marquee.[81] The next day Chez Harry Pilcer became the Sans-Gêne, only to be advertised six days later as a Tango-Tea: "Chez Jane Darcy, ex-Cadet Rousselle."[82] However, Jeanne's fraught efforts were to no avail. After a few weeks the Tango-Tea discontinued operations, and its owner found herself assailed on all sides. Since his triumphant acquittal, Stavisky had conducted a subversive campaign to force her to cede the club. Fearful of accusations of drug dealing and intimidated by Sacha's underworld relations from the boisterous faubourg Saint-Martin district, Jeanne capitulated.[83] She and Guitton were ruined.

Theoretically, Stavisky now possessed a profitable night club where Harry Pilcer had prospered (half the net profits, a financial arrangement no doubt enjoyed by Zelli). In reality, he was confronted with a series of disasters: Zelli's departure, Pilcer's dismissal, the short-lived Sans-Gêne, and the ephemeral Tango-Tea. August passed (a time when most nightspots closed), but in September 1921 the club acquired a new identity. The ex–Cadet Rousselle reopened as the Sans Souci, with a "Zazz Américain" [sic].[84] The new Argentinean manager was probably more sensitive to the music of Manuel Pizarro (whose orchestra alternated afternoons at the club with evenings at tango rendezvous El Garrón), but as the latter confirmed in his memoirs, the American leaning "Stavinsky" [sic] was still in charge.[85]

The last recorded encounter between Zelli and his erstwhile patron took place in August 1923 apropos of "the incident of the falsified check." One evening a Romanian medical student called Popovici entered the Royal Box posing as a well-to-do patron. Having run up a large champagne bill with the ubiquitous hostesses, he paid with a fifty-dollar bill and then, pleading an inebriated state, asked for the change in the form of a bank check from the proprietor. The latter, for 600 francs, was altered to read 48,200 and promptly cashed. Given Stavisky's past dealings with the restaurateur, he was careful not to be seen during the swindle, but he was clearly its author. Zelli was justifiably wary of "le beau Sacha" for, despite Charlier and Montarron's postulation of their "excellent relations," he filed charges.[86] When Popovici returned to Paris (having made himself scarce for a time in Bucharest), he was arrested and immediately riposted by accusing his partner in crime.[87] At that point, as so often in Stavisky's affairs, a "miracle" occurred; Popovici retracted his charges, asserting that he had only denounced his accomplice to gain revenge, and the incriminating check "vanished" from police headquarters. The consequence of a benign police connection? The truth was never known, and in the absence of the unique piece of evidence, Stavisky was released.[88]

The unsavory intrigues surrounding Cadet Rousselle and "Zelli's Club" represented both the swan song of a raucous, freewheeling era and an improbable prelude to the fashionable society *dancings* of the rue Caumartin. In an ironic tribute to the clandestine dance halls, Sem likened the votaries of the goddess Terpsichore to Christian martyrs: "That was the heroic epoch, the time of persecutions and catacombs. Since then, time has trotted by, even fox-trotted. The fever has fallen; dance has become an endemic condition.... We are no longer scandalized, no longer astonished, no longer even stare. We have gotten as used to watching the shimmy as to seeing women smoke, show their backs, or their legs. It seems that this worn-out subject has lost its spice."[89]

Notwithstanding Sem's mock elegy for proscribed pleasures, for Zelli the scandalous era never wholly ended. A lingering impression of impropriety clung to his persona like a persistent odor. Woon asserts that the Royal Box resembled a place on the Barbary Coast—the thriving red-light district of early twentieth century San Francisco—a rough and ready Western ambiance that Woon knew well, having debuted as journalist in an Alaskan gold camp at the age of seventeen.[90] The parallel with the criminality and social transgressions of the underground *dancings* is evident. Zelli had the reputation of an amiable and generous soul, but as the old adage has it, "if you lie down with dogs, you get up with fleas." Beginning with Stavisky, Zelli would frequent an inordinate number of canines. It was the price of his success but inevitably it exposed him to what Nevill termed the "dark side" of the night life of Montmartre.[91]

CHAPTER TWO

THE DANCER AND THE DRUMMER

"Weird and Wonderful Sounds" in the Rue de Clichy

One of the first jazz bands heard in Paris was, I believe,
the band of the Casino de Paris.
—André Warnod

It would be misleading to suggest that Parisian jazz originated in the rue Caumartin. As 1917 morphed into 1918, it flared up at several flashpoints like a raging wildfire. In December 1917, while Louis Mitchell's group was triumphing at the Alhambra Theater, "weird and wonderful sounds from a variety of unknown instruments" were heard for the first time at the Casino de Paris in the rue de Clichy.[1] The owner of the Casino and the neighboring Apollo Theater was a Frenchman, Léon Volterra. Along with his four uncles, he held sway over much of the entertainment life of the quarter. The eldest, Jules, "Father of Montmartre," ran the Capitole restaurant and *dancing* in the rue Notre-Dame de Lorette, aided by his half-brother, Joseph; the second, Albert, officiated at the Abbaye de Thélème; a third, Elie, presided over the tango club El Garrón. Given the family's central role in the leisure economy of Montmartre, Woon appropriately grants them a page, but it is symptomatic that he downplays the importance of Black Americans in Montmartre's musical culture, while paying homage to white bands like the Lyres.[2]

However, one may risk focusing on Black Americans as if they existed in a racial vacuum. The true story is less clear cut, a complex narrative of cultural and racial interactions, and of a potential social Utopia—notably as played out at the Casino—an intricate web woven by Louis Mitchell and the Austrian American dancer Harry Pilcer, both adepts of ragtime. The young hoofer was the first to appear. Served by lush good looks and an unmistakable talent, he would pursue a lengthy career, always under the sign of the new music. On December 12, 1917, he and his French partner, Gaby Deslys, debuted in an epochal revue created to inaugurate a renovated Casino, *Laisse-les tomber!* (Let 'em fall!)—comic Louis Boucot's defiant challenge to the German bombs raining down on Paris: "Is your hair falling?" he sang, "Let it fall! Are they launching bombs? Let 'em fall!"[3]

The couple had worked together since Gaby's 1911 arrival in New York, trailing reports of a liaison with King Manuel II of Portugal reputed to have cost him his throne. They wowed Broadway in a string of musicals, rivaling popular dance teams such as Maurice Mouvet and Florence Walton. They had long manifested an interest in ragtime; their signature dance, the "Gaby Glide," already exploited ragtime rhythms and blues harmonies. By proposing an American-style revue in Paris, they were mounting a spectacle that was novel for local audiences. Above all, it contained a jazz band, an innovation of historical significance!

The Casino possessed the artistic and financial resources to produce the type of show of which Stavisky and Faurens could only dream. Entering in an extravagant gown smothered in rhinestones and plumes, head weighted down by a mop of dyed blonde curls and a towering headdress of pink ostrich feathers, Gaby introduced a trailblazing model for subsequent music hall revues based on spectacular staging and the orchestral format of the jazz band.[4] As her biographer asserts, on "that evening in 1917, the old Parisian *café-concert* was laid to rest. Gaby introduced Paris to the Black American music that was to overwhelm the world."[5] A grandiose finale, "The Human Flags," paid tribute to the Allied Forces. Dozens of beaming showgirls descended a dizzying thirty-foot staircase clothed in red, white, and blue, representing the Union Jack; on turning, the dancers displayed the Star-Spangled Banner. "United by a noble but ill-placed sentiment, the audience rose to render homage to the American flag created by an assemblage of the charming posteriors of delicious young women."[6]

Like Warnod, cultural man of all trades Jean Cocteau received his first exposure to jazz at the Casino. In *Le Coq et l'Arlequin*, a compilation of notes on art and music, he ignores the indelicate incarnation of the American flag and concentrates on the syncopated rhythms that energized the choreography:

> This is what the dance was like. The band accompanied it on banjos and large nickel pipes. To the right of this little troupe in white tie and tails stood a barman of noise under a gilt pergola laden with bells, triangles, boards, and motorbike horns. With these he fabricated cocktails, occasionally adding a dash of cymbals, rocking back and forth with a beatific smile. Mr. Pilcer, in evening dress, thin and rouged, and Mademoiselle Gaby Deslys, a great ventriloquist's doll with a

porcelain face, flaxen hair, and a gown of ostrich feathers, danced to this hurricane of rhythms and drums, a sort of controlled catastrophe that left them utterly stunned and intoxicated under a shower of six anti-aircraft searchlights.[7]

Curiously, though the couple's choreography is at the heart of Cocteau's text, he has little to say about it. Léo Vauchant explicitly dismisses Harry's performance, stressing that he "liked jazz" but that "he wasn't a tap dancer. So he'd just glide around the floor, put his arms over his head and fall on his knees on the floor. Then he'd straighten himself up again as he put his arms down. That was his big trick."[8] Vauchant's assessment is perhaps excessively harsh; most critics were more laudatory: "Singer, dancer and mime . . . behind the free execution, one senses the determination and taste of a true artist . . . from the pirouettes of Russian popular dance with its crouching steps to the hesitant syncopations of modern American dances."[9]

Unlike Vauchant's negative judgement, Cocteau's inattention to the dancing is better explained by the fact that he is not really interested in the couple's terpsichorean skills, portraying them as painted puppets in thrall to the irresistible energy of the music. The same shock was experienced by French pianist Jean Wiener: "I was amazed the first time I heard syncopated music. It was before the First World War at the Casino de Paris. There was an English dancer called Harry Pilcer who was with a very pretty girl called Gabby Deslys. And they did a number—it was something by Handy, I think. This was absolutely the first kind of ragtime. It was incredible. I can't remember now if it was a French orchestra or not, the details escape me, but it was certainly not Black musicians."[10] If the musical jolt was still fresh in Wiener's mind, time had blurred his memory of the particulars. It was not before the war, ragtime was in its final phase, W. C. Handy did not compose the music, and Harry Pilcer wasn't English. But on one point Weiner was right: The orchestra was not composed primarily of Black instrumentalists.

The group that produced Cocteau's "controlled catastrophe" was the "Sherbo American Band," led by Harry's younger brother, Murray, even though for decades the phrase "barman of noise" was thought to refer to Louis Mitchell.[11] A photo reproduced in the program shows that the "gilt pergola" poetically described by Cocteau was a rack hung with an odd array of objects designed to create a percussive din: cymbals, wood blocks, sirens, cowbells, toy pistols, and what resembles a frying pan.[12] This panoply was not exceptional. A photo from 1917 shows Louis Mitchell, impeccable in white tie, surrounded by a similar display, including a garden shovel (see gallery 1). Having said that, the ethnic makeup of Murray's purportedly "white American band" presents certain paradoxes. If we are to judge by the program photo, several members—the pianist, one of the banjoists, and possibly the violinist—were men of color, presumably British, the band having just arrived from London. Both Louis Mitchell and Murray Pilcer played crucial roles in the implantation of jazz at the Casino. The difference lies in the quality of their music. Judging by surviving recordings, the performances of Pilcer's group were abysmal. A doughboy from Santa Cruz wrote, "The hit of the evening was a jazz orchestra from the States—they played real 'jazz' music in the lobby during the acts"; but, out of tune, key, and time, their rendition of "K-K-K-Katy," with its excruciating vocal, suggests that the war-weary soldiers were not demanding.[13] Equally cacophonous is a one-step from the revue: "The Wild, Wild Women Are Making a Wild Man Out of Me." Harry Pilcer's choice of the Sherbo Band may perhaps be ascribed to brotherly indulgence; as shown by his involvement with Mitchell or the Red Devils, his taste in ragtime was excellent.

Evidently, the impact of Murray Pilcer's band must be attributed to extramusical criteria. European civilization had engendered a bloody, destructive war. For some, the shattering of the old order initiated a quest to revitalize an exhausted civilization, and for many jazz embodied that renewal. At worst, this enthusiasm resembled a patronizing negrophilia. At best, it represented a sincere appreciation of the qualities and virtues of other cultures. Surrealist writer and poet Michel Leiris detailed the connotations of jazz for the postwar generation: freedom, modernity, and the rejection of outdated antebellum values. "During the period of great license that followed the hostilities, jazz was a rallying cry, an orgiastic banner colored by the spirit of the time. It operated like magic and its mode of action may be compared to a possession. That was the element that gave these fêtes their true meaning: a *religious* sense expressed by a communion through dance, a latent or overt eroticism, . . . an underlying desire for a new life in which a greater role would be accorded to the savage candor we so ardently desired."[14]

Even with the Sherbo Band's manifest deficiencies, *Laisse-les tomber!* triumphed. Nevertheless, Pilcer and Deslys left the show in early March of 1918, to be replaced by Maurice Chevalier and Gaby's rival, Mistinguett. The star was fatigued, plagued by a dry cough, desirous of the physical and emotional comforts of Marseille, the childhood home she had fled twenty years earlier.[15] Given their fascination with ragtime, one imagines that were it not for this retreat to the Mediterranean metropolis, the couple would have welcomed the collaboration of Louis Mitchell. For, after concluding his engagement with

Mme Faurens at the end of May, he was increasingly present at the Casino. Pernet and Rye assume that from April to June Mitchell led a band in the second edition of *Laisse-les tomber!* but advertisements specify that the "American orchestra" in question was led by a certain Bobby Berschad, of uncertain origins.[16] Moreover, Mitchell's ongoing performances with Faurens' troop preclude his participation. A more likely date is after May 28 but before June 23, when an American correspondent attested to his growing celebrity: "The big attraction at the Casino theatre here and the big attraction for every Parisian theatre that can bid high enough for his services, is Louis A. Mitchell, a coloured American drummer, who has literally 'drummed' his way to Paris and into the hearts of Parisians."[17] The *Figaro* endorses this homage, assuring visiting soldiers that they would "be amused by the drummer who, displaying extraordinary deftness, tickles with his sticks all the pots, tambourines and other more or less resonant instruments."[18] It is difficult to imagine this referring to anyone but Mitchell.

However, it is not simply a question of dating; rather, it is the story of a complex cross-fertilization between two racial groups that were polarized in America, and two cultures, French and American. After the baffling success of the Sherbo Band it was almost obligatory to advertise an American ensemble. Appellations varied. In the 1918 revue *Pa-ri-ki-ri*, different names were given to the house band: the "Great American Jazz Band" or the "Jazz Band of the Casino de Paris."[19] The word "American" served as "open sesame" and assured that, whatever its origins, the music would be something calling itself jazz. This blind rhetorical allegiance masks the fact that the Casino's pit orchestra was made up almost wholly of white musicians and led by a white Frenchman.[20] (The drama editor of *The New York Age* specified, "The only Negro in it is Louis Mitchell.")[21] At times it may have contained a few Black transatlantic elements (an ad for *Pa-ri-ki-ri* vaunted the presence of a "Jim Poker of Kansas City"), but these "American" ensembles were Yankee only in name.[22] Audiences were beginning to appreciate the qualities of Black musicians like Mitchell but confronted with an essentially white "jazz orchestra" the charmed patrons did not seem unduly troubled.

Mitchell did not display the same indulgence. A letter to composer Eubie Blake, dated August 21, 1918, is instructive on this point: "I have just formed another band of Frenchmen," he writes, "and I am teaching them to play rags and they are getting along fine, better than I thought they would." But, he adds, "it is hard to teach these Frenchmen to play ragtime."[23] At that moment Mitchell was appearing in *Boum!*, a revue that claimed the mantle of *Laisse-*

les tomber! and boasted the much publicized "National Dresses" (another showgirl tribute to the Allies) and the evening's highlight, "The Arrival of the Americans." Among these Yankee artifacts was an "American orchestra."[24] Although Mitchell is uncredited, these were evidently the "Frenchmen" he had been training and probably the core of the ensemble that he took into the Folies Marigny in September as Mitchell's Midnight Frolic Jazz Band.[25] Ideally, he had envisioned "a band of coulard [*sic*] boys"; realistically, he worked with what he had. Léo Vauchant, who at fourteen was playing in the Marigny's orchestra, suggests that Mitchell's critical attitude was not unwarranted: "When the French would play, there was no sense of beat. They were playing things with rubato—there was no dance beat. It didn't swing. It didn't move. . . . I would fix all the trumpets and the glissandos on the trombones. But it had to be written out before the French guys could play the syncopations."[26]

A significant point in Mitchell's letter is not that he was working with white musicians (Blake had collaborated with white vaudevillians), it is that the cultural context of Paris supported the interaction. He assured his friend, "This is the finest Country in the world and if you once get over here you will never want to go back to N.Y. again. I intend to stay here the rest of my life, as you can go where you want . . . and have the time of your life. . . . The work that we do over here now is different than the work in the States and not half so hard, we never work over two hours a day . . . [and] we only work fifteen minutes a day and thirty minutes on the days that we have Matenees [*sic*], so you can see it is like stealing money, and you are treated white wherever you go as they like spades here and these Yanks can't teach these French people any different."

Mitchell was not exaggerating when he vaunted the short hours and excellent pay, but coming on the eve of the Armistice, his attitude betrays concerns other than congenial working conditions. During the Great War, many Black citizens had closed ranks with white compatriots, not only out of patriotism but from an implicit belief that their sacrifices would elicit more equitable treatment. Instead, their return was often greeted with hostility and lynch mobs. Thus, when Mitchell states that he was "treated white," he is not expressing a rejection of his skin color but rather reacting to bitter American experiences that had taught him that being born white was the criterion for simple justice.

Until July 1919 Mitchell and Pilcer had been ships passing in a not entirely somber night. They may have met the previous year, at a gala organized by Volterra that included Gaby and Harry; however, when the couple returned permanently in 1919, Mitchell was in New York.[27] Their real collaboration began after the founding moment of postwar Montmartre: the revocation of the dancing ban. If Mitchell's ex-patron Mme Faurens was the first to take advantage of the new privilege, Volterra was quick to follow with the opening of "Harry Pilcer's *Dancing*" at the Apollo Theater. Relying on the business sense that had brought him from peddling programs before the Olympia to a position as czar of Montmartre's nocturnal amusements, he envisaged the potential of a fashionable *dancing* located in a popular music hall. His chief problem was unfair competition from club owners tempted to brave the restrictions on opening hours.

Volterra's efforts to obtain special privileges were fruitless, but he *was* able to use his influence to bring the other clubs into line. Around this time he learned of a gentleman who had become a thorn in the side of the legitimate *dancings*: Jed Kiley, whose joy parlor in the Avenue Montaigne was happily jazzing until the early hours. One Saturday at midnight Volterra climbed the six flights of steps to the American Foxtrot Club and confronted Kiley with threats "to have him closed."[28] Though he was unsuccessful, other misfortunes would drive the foxtrot king out to the suburbs.

Volterra's second problem was staffing. Despite ill feelings due to Deslys and Pilcer's infidelity with a "Franco-American" revue at the Théâtre Fémina, differences had been resolved, and with this show's failure Harry was amenable to hosting the new *dancing*. There remained the question of music. The impresario's interest was commercial. For Pilcer there were also artistic concerns. The answer to both their prayers was Louis Mitchell. Recognizing that patrons increasingly demanded jazz performed by Black artists, Volterra had sent him to New York the previous January to recruit a large orchestra.[29] The ambitious project fell through; nevertheless, Mitchell returned with five veterans whom he dubbed the "Jazz Kings." On July 6, fresh off the boat, the band was featured at the launch of Harry Pilcer's *Dancing*, making them a double threat since they were also appearing in the Casino's summer revue, *Ouf!*

The first allusion to the fledgling band speaks nebulously of "six Black musicians"; after one week their Apollo salaries were doubled and they were touted as the "sensational highlight of *Ouf!*"[30] Their performance inspired Cocteau to write, "Art is regaining its virility through these savage contacts ... the Jazz Band can be considered the essence of those forces. It is there that they reach their peak, chanting a cruel and melancholic song.... These good Negroes [dangling] in the air in a sort of cage, sway, thrash about, toss pieces of raw meat to the crowd, accompanied by blasts of trumpets and 'cog' rattles. Played in counterpoint, a jagged, fragmentary dance tune rises to the surface from time to time. The overheated theatre . . . resembles a typical saloon in some Western movie."[31]

As in his comments on *Laisse-les tomber!*, Cocteau's critique is not musical in a technical sense, and despite his much-trumpeted passion for the "weird" new sounds, the tone is condescending. Pilcer's jazz-fueled performance had elicited the remark that "these spectacles are not art. They excite us in the same way as machines, animals, landscapes."[32] The text on the Jazz Kings expresses a worn-out civilization's reappropriation of a lost virility through an imagery of caged creatures and instinctual abandon, except that the meat destined for savage beasts is now thrown back at the audience to arouse their primal appetites, an act of cruelty, rather than joy, that betrays an implicit sadness. All this was encoded in the image of the "Far West," that phantasmagoric country revealed in the new motion picture palaces, where the law of the jungle reigned, and primitive passions found easy expression. However, the animalistic fury invoked by Cocteau is better exemplified by the caterwauling of Murray Pilcer's Sherbo American Band than the music of the Jazz Kings, which Goddard lyrically describes as "the sad sweetness of ragtime, whose lovely but slightly ailing quality reminds one of a consumptive child who, though beautiful today, will die tomorrow."[33]

Which raises a question: What did the Jazz Kings actually sound like?[34] On hearing them in Brussels, Belgian poet and jazz critic Robert Goffin stated that "Mitchell's band didn't exactly play jazz, rather fox-trots played in unison without improvisation."[35] In sum, comments Goddard, it was something resembling jazz but that contemporary "purists may not consider to be jazz at all." He also affirms that the French did not understand jazz but thought they did.[36] What is significant for my purposes is not whether French audiences understood jazz but that they invested it with the ideological values enumerated by Leiris: exoticism, primitivism, and a syncopated beat perceived as the pulse of modernity.

The collaboration between Pilcer and Mitchell lasted a scant six months. There were two major reasons for their parting. The first was Mitchell's departure in January 1920 for Volterra's Alhambra Theater in Brussels with a new edition of *Laisse-les tomber!* His band was replaced at the Apollo in February by the impressive sounding "Jazz Band du Majestic Hotel de New York," whose most illustrious members were banjoist Opal Cooper and saxophonist Sammy Richardson. Their manager was banjoist Seth Weeks, president of the Clef Club (a combination trade union, booking agency, and fraternal society for Black artists excluded from the American Federation of Musicians). Straightaway they made their mark on the musical scene, performing for tea at the Apollo from 5 to 7 p.m. and headlining from 9:30 to 11:30 at Morgan's *Dancing* near the Champs-Elysées, the first Black-owned club.[37]

There has been some doubt about Weeks's involvement, as he is not mentioned in pianist Elliot Carpenter's interview with Goddard, but the evidence is unequivocal.[38] In the *Chicago Defender*, Weeks enthused that the Clef Club men were making a great record in the French city, and he confirmed their engagement at the Apollo and Morgan's.[39] His touting of the band's success was justified. In a comment conceivably aimed at strident bands like Murray Pilcer's, a French critic heaped praise on the Majestic Hotel musicians: "In this creole music there is something much superior to the epileptic agitation to which we have become accustomed with most American bands in London and Paris. It is, in a word, very artistic . . . without being cacophonic, gay without being grotesque."[40]

If we are to believe Opal Cooper, having broken with Weeks in June, the band became the Red Devils and moved to London for more than a year and a half.[41] On their transitory return in 1921, and even more strongly in 1922, they began a brief but distinguished career, which ensured that after their dissolution in 1923 former members, notably Cooper and Richardson, were able to integrate into the best bands in Montmartre.

"The sad sweetness of ragtime"—this was appropriate music for the end of these fleeting moments of congruence between the dancer and the drummer, the more so in that the second reason for their separation was Gaby's abrupt demise. Exiting Volterra's Théâtre de Paris on December 1, 1919, she caught cold waiting for her limousine. The cold turned into what may have been a late case of the Spanish flu that destroyed millions of ordinary lives. Operations failed to stem the progress of the disease, causing Harry to abandon the direction of the Apollo *Dancing*. According to a January 13th article by popular columnist O. O. McIntyre, "Pilcer, who is appearing in a French revue next door, runs in between acts to dance with American sightseers. . . . Once a week Gaby shows up at the Apollo and dances with Pilcer and this proves a great drawing card."[42] Based in New York, McIntyre's information was not always current; here it was tragically out of date. In October Harry had made a few appearances in the Casino revue, *Tout feu . . . tout flemme*, and Gaby may have been seen a few times during the summer, but she spent the greater part of the fall in New York, and after December she was in no condition to dance.[43]

She died on February 11. Harry was prostrated. He retreated to their ornate apartment and fashioned a shrine adorned with candles, flowers, and portraits framed in black velvet.⁴⁴ After visiting Pilcer's memorial, Woon asserted that "for months he was not seen in public"; according to Prasteau, it was years.⁴⁵ In this case, Woon is closer to the truth: two and a half months. Harry's ostentatious mourning was doubtless sincere, even if by April he was managing Chez Harry Pilcer, housed in the Oasis (a *dancing* installed by fashion designer Paul Poiret in his eighteenth-century gardens). Confirming the end of his bereavement, in the fall he returned to the Casino in *Paris qui Jazz* (Swinging Paris), with the droll Mistinguett as costar. Recent critics make short shrift of this interesting revue, which deserves closer examination.

Firstly, we should be careful not to overstate its jazz content. Despite the stars' sincere interest in ragtime, the show leaves the impression of a superficial gloss intended to surf on the vogueish connotations of the new rhythms, a music hall cabaret flavored with a hint of early jazz. Its biggest hit, "Mon Homme" (My man), featuring Mistinguett and Pilcer, was a quintessential story of Parisian low life in which she played a working-class prostitute. Written as a Schottisch espagnole, a slow polka that could include syncopated steps, "Mon Homme" was hardly jazz. Yankee influence lay less in the revue's musical modes than in a subtle mirroring of the increased visibility of racial and cultural diversity that was becoming part of the DNA of Montmartre.

Poet Louis Aragon depicts these varied performers as the latest in a wave of historical invaders. "The modern *dancing* is set apart by its music, its unique atmosphere, and the floating population that it implies," he writes, characterizing its musicians as contemporary nomads who are to the modern life of cities what itinerant bards from "the troubled frontiers of Arabia" were to the medieval period. "One year, the Argentine enveloped Paris with its rogues, another year the Pacific lifted up the ash-grey Hawaiians with a great wave to depose them on the shores of Montmartre with their concerts of sighs. Then the Russians, with daggers and furs, arrived to weep in Paris; then the Negroes of America, who have spread like an ink blot in the environs of the Place Saint-Georges."⁴⁶

The tableaux that best exemplify Aragon's parallel are *The Harem* and *The Gri-Gri of Love*. Drawn from the *One Thousand and One Nights*, the former exploited a traditional exoticism originating on the "frontiers of Arabia." Aragon relegates this migration to the distant past, but the music halls sought to infuse it with elements of modernity. For *The Harem* Maurice Yvain, author of most of the show's music, wrote "La Lune indiscrète ou le Sultan jaloux" ("The Inquisitive Moon or the Jealous Sultan"), a foxtrot danced by Pilcer and la belle Dherlys (Simone Dherlys). Like the other songs, it was written to a dance tempo, but it was far from anything that could be termed jazz. At best, Yvain was sensitive to the rejuvenation of a stale musical tradition by rhythm and syncopation, coupled with an ambition to naturalize the new musical force by suffusing it with a Parisian fragrance. For the real thing Pilcer was obliged to look to the legendary Southern Syncopated Orchestra's *Jazzing the Harem*, seen four months earlier, and he may have infused some of its feeling into his dancing.

"La Lune indiscrete" was subtitled "Tale of the Thousand and Second Night," a reference to the memorable 1911 soirée hosted by Paul Poiret, creator of the *Harem* costumes.[47] His collection of that year featured turbans and pantaloons in which a decorative orientalism (inspired by Léon Bakst's designs for the Ballets Russes' *Scheherazade*) was merged with the simplicity of the modernist aesthetic.[48] After 1913 this style fell out of favor, but the influence on the *Harem* costumes is patent. Harry Pilcer's green-eyed Sultan wore a magnificent outfit, striped with gold and topped with an ostrich plumed turban. As for his dance partner, one newspaper quipped, "You could never say that Mlle Dherlys ever wears enough to be dignified by the name costume."[49] The couturier had imagined a bare-breasted "dancer" attired in gilded "hot pants" with latticed side panels. To judge by the Sabourin photos, the statuesque beauty hardly danced, remaining immobile as Harry spun around her in a ballet of submission and domination—at her feet in an excess of adoration or hovering like a glittering bat as she knelt, bound in chains of pearls.[50] Disappointingly, the implicit ideology of Mlle Dherlys' poses ("the slightly servile, softly brutal look [of Bakst's women] . . . was not unpleasing to men: they had the illusion of being masters, Sultans") was at odds with the emergence in the first quarter of the century of a dynamic, new feminine type known as the "New Woman": self-confident, independent, and often politically engaged.[51]

Thus, despite his contributions to art deco modernity, Poiret found himself caught between avant-garde innovation and a penchant for ancien régime values, a tension already evident at his Oasis. During the dogdays of August and early September 1919, when the social elite usually deserted Paris, the designer had devised a dazzling series of costume parties in his garden, notably the blue and silver gala "Clair de Lune." We might be tempted to imagine a host of shimmying flappers such as those that had been seen at Jed Kiley's jazz-house. Not at all! Dainty Columbines offered male invitees the cap and ruff of Pierrot, and lulled by summer breezes, guests swayed to the cadences of the waltz. As *Vogue* put it, "Those who danced at the Oasis left all thoughts of 'jazz' behind them."[52]

If the resurrection of the Viennese dance seemed novel, it was because prevailing taste had already embraced American rhythms. At the final "Hunt Ball" gala, tangos were tolerated but only when punctuated by the thematically appropriate hunting horns of the Duchesse d'Uzès—retainers in scarlet coats "blowing a fanfare between each dance, each tango! Sublime mixture. . . ."[53] Were the guests aware that the tango's roots were to be found among the former slaves of the Rio de la Plata quarter of Buenos Aires? Apparently not. At the fourth fête, "The Equator," Black people were present, but only as decorative elements of a colonialist fantasy ("negresses," heads bound in brightly colored bandanas, presided at the entrance, and Black waiters serving succulent sweetmeats circulated under South Seas palms).[54]

A year later, under Pilcer's direction, syncopation infected the Oasis. Perhaps influenced by the hoofer, Poiret's attitude evolved. Following the final curtain of *Paris qui Jazz* in March 1921, he acquired the Clover Club, hailed as "the temple of jazz," a progression in musical taste confirmed by his engagement of Buddie Gilmore, "King of Jazz."[55] The décor reflected this evolution. Betraying a vision hesitating between the old and the new, it was decisively branded with the stamp of the new music, which critic Jed Rasula terms "a generic signifier of modernism."[56] In the carriageway leading to the former Théâtre Caumartin hung "exotic fabrics," while on the walls of the club starlit landscapes evoked the eighteenth-century rose gardens of the Oasis. At the same time Poiret "caused to be painted in behind the musicians' stand a score or more of Black faces so scarlet of lip and white of rolling eye that they must rather disconcert the orchestra if it turns to inspect its mural background. And the smiling spectator doesn't know which is which, Black flesh or Black fresco."[57]

The band members might well have been taken aback, for the painted Black musicians sound disturbingly like ethnic stereotypes. For the reporter, the identity between the real musicians and their caricatures seems unproblematic. The same readiness to confuse travesty and reality is evident in another verbal portrayal: "The Clover Club is equipped with a jazz band of East Side boys, whose foreheads slope back from their eyebrows like a shingle roof."[58] Poiret's thinking is impossible to evaluate with certitude, but the actual murals should perhaps be seen in the light of art deco stylizations, such as Paul Colin's Josephine Baker poster for *La Revue nègre*.[59] It is unreasonable to expect that people of an earlier time totally transcend their cultural horizons, but deftly positioned between celebration and exploitation, Poiret's intention appears to have been benevolent.

As a modern counterpart to Arabian Nights exoticism, Aragon evokes a new wave of nomadic troubadours, "the ash-grey Hawaiians." The latter were a significant strand of the ethnic tapestry of Montmartre, though their presence is more complicated than appears at first glance. Transmitted by the sounds of ukulele and steel guitar, the "languorous charm" of Hawaiian music experienced a vogue in wartime America.[60] With the arrival of jazz in Paris, island music followed. As Leiris reminisced, "We bathed in the melancholy of certain records that were said to be of Hawaiian origin."[61] One of the most prominent examples of this phenomenon was the integration of ukulele players Kelvin and Alvin Keech into the White Lyres, even if the Honolulu-born brothers were not native Hawaiians.

This pervasive presence found expression in a composition by Yvain showcasing Mistinguett and Louis Boucot: *Le Gri-Gri d'Amour, a Hawaiian Legend for Children*.[62] Subtitle notwithstanding, the lyrics were not suitable for toddlers, being a tasteless collection of double entendres about a phallic gri-gri and a castration executed by the tale's audacious heroine. The word "gri-gri" designates an African charm or amulet designed to bring good fortune, in this case not so fortunate as the male Hawaiian loses his "pretty little amulets" to the avidity of a "large" Hawaiian lady. At best, this scabrous tale can be seen as an extreme validation of the "New Woman," at worst, a pandering to the lowest music hall tastes. The first interpretation might suggest considering the tableau as an overt parody of the team of Kanui and Lula, then enjoying success at the Olympia. The couple incarnated the exotic myth of the beautiful, voluptuous wahine, the perfect sexual object, undulating to the melodious ukulele of a half-savage partner.[63] *Le Gri-Gri d'Amour* subverts the fable as the young lady was played by the bold and witty Mistinguett, and the unlucky gentleman who loses his virility to a voracious wahine by the diminutive Boucot.

Perhaps the most interesting aspect of this "frivolous divertissement" lies in its implicit classification of Hawaiians as a subgroup of Black Americans, an assimilation already hinted at in Aragon's "ash-grey" musicians and the ethnic incoherencies of Poiret's ostensibly South Sea fête, "The Equator." On the musical plane, a ukulele ad from 1917 vaunted the "equal facility" with which the instrument "lends itself to the syncopation of ragtime."[64] Although some critics created a false opposition ("if the Hawaiian orchestra that the Casino reveals to us . . . could depose, through its popularity, the barbarian, the horrid jazz band . . . what progress for Paris!"), others tacitly recognized an affinity.[65] In a racist remark, one journalist commented that Harry Pilcer's solo of "Swanee," George Gershwin's half-parodic/half-sincere evocation of the Stephen Foster classic, was later "jazzed ad nauseam in the *promenoir* by a Hawaiian jazz band that... had evidently been recruited from the tropics of 135th Street."[66] Regrettably, we have no information on the band's veritable ethnicity, nor is it clear if it was the "Strange Hawaiian Orchestra" featured in *Le Gri-Gri d'Amour.*[67]

An implicit racial element already underlay the *Harem* sketch; after all the Sultan was not a Nordic European, a fact accentuated by the casting of a darkly handsome Jew in the role.[68] Nor is it accidental that Roger de Valerio's cover for the sheet music of "La Lune indiscrète" shows a fair-skinned young woman conversing with a conspicuously Black sultan, outlined against a looming moon.[69] More directly, Mistinguett and Boucot's duo reflected the increased sensitivity to race that had accompanied the invasion of Black Americans into the Montmartre microcosm. A first indication is the fact that the song is a one-step, a ragtime dance characterized by James Reese Europe as the "national dance of the Negro."[70] Even more conclusively, one of two sheet music covers by de Valerio for *Le Gri-Gri d'Amour* shows a frenetic jazz band and an inset photo of Mistinguett and Boucot. She wears a grass skirt and sleeveless bodice, strings of beads, and an odd hat; Boucot is dressed in loose pants, a striped top, a short grass skirt, and a conical straw hat, both costumes reminiscent of photos of Kanui and Lula. The second, a cover for the piano score, hints at the miscegenation that so preoccupied white American visitors to Montmartre. Boucot retains his droll hat and shapeless pants, but he has been transformed into a strapping Black man, naked to the waist, while Mistinguett holds an amulet in one hand and with the other seductively strokes his neck, an image that echoes the sexual dynamic of de Valerio's design for the sheet music of "La Lune indiscrète."[71] Supported by the perceived ethnic and musical parallels between Hawaiians and Black Americans, a shifting racial framework facilitates this substitution; and the lyrics of *Le Gri-Gri d'Amour* explicit the subtext: "One night when the *Negro* was sleeping... [my italics]." Gillett reminds us that "the socio-cultural impact of the *tumulte noir* coincided with increased migration into the French *métropole*" and that "anxieties associated with racial difference became a very present feature of French life."[72] Notwithstanding the seeming absence of Black Americans and any meaningful jazz content, the racial dynamic foregrounded by the presence of modern-day troubadours from the Pacific left its mark on the lighthearted revue.

In March Mistinguett abandoned *Paris qui Jazz* for the staging of *Madame Sans-Gêne* that probably inspired the desperate Jeanne Darcy.[73] Her costar also struck out on his own, opening Chez Harry Pilcer in the former Cadet Rousselle. Lacking Mitchell's Jazz Kings, he engaged the Red Devils, remnants of the Seven Spades, and Joe Puni's island ensemble, a group similar to the Casino's Strange Hawaiian Orchestra. He also envisioned a Gaby Deslys Theater as a tribute to the late star, but Mlle Darcy put a stop to that![74] His hopes of a public shrine dashed, he remained faithful to their shared passion for ragtime. His presence was noted at two events central to the development of Parisian jazz. On the eve of the shuttering of Chez Harry Pilcer, he was blithely attending the premiere of the celebrated Southern Syncopated Orchestra, and that summer he was seen at Léon Volterra's new *dancing*, Le Perroquet.[75] The featured band was that of his old colleague Louis Mitchell, recently returned from Brussels. The new venue provided a more authentic musical vision than the superficial pastiches of *Paris qui Jazz*, and thanks to Mitchell, it became a seminal venue for the innovative new music.

Volterra's experiment at the Apollo had convinced him of the viability of a *dancing* housed in a music hall. This was the Perroquet (which opened on March 26, 1921), known as the "Half-Way House" because of its position midway between the *dancings* of the rue Caumartin and the burgeoning cabarets to the north.[76] But this opening must also be placed in the context of relaxed controls on dancing establishments. To the north, even the traditional pleasure palaces of the Place Pigalle were adopting the codes of the modern *dancing* and Joe Zelli had just opened the Royal Box. To the south, this conversion had taken place immediately after the war with the Savoy Dancing Club, Cadet Rousselle, and more recently Pilcer's champagne palace, which set the standard for the society *dancings* to follow. Aware of this geopolitical context, Volterra inaugurated his new club.

Although the feeble jazz coloration of *Paris qui Jazz* had little to offer Volterra's *dancing*, where décor was concerned, he called again on Paul Poiret. The designer was not responsible for musical programming; nevertheless, this involvement confirms his evolving attitude toward jazz. His design contained a unique feature commented on by Nevill, who noted "the curious decoration of the walls on which brightly coloured parrots abound."[77] This was a nod to the name of the new night resort, but parrots were also frequent in art deco iconography.[78] Materialized in the neon parrot perched above the marquee, it was more than an ornamental motif; in style, medium, and content it was a sign of modernity.[79] Passing beneath, men in tails and women in sumptuous furs mounted the staircase to a high-ceilinged entresol above the Casino lobby, hung with tasseled lamps of vaguely "oriental" design that resembled those of Bakst's set for *Scheherazade*. Above tables and modernist armchairs, an arched, art deco mural echoed the ample curve of the facing stained glass window.

The living birds of Poiret's "Equator" fête were mimed by painted parrots, peacocks, and flamingos, flying and strutting about in a stylized jungle.[80] The decorations confirmed the marriage of tradition and avant-gardism that had characterized his work in *Paris qui jazz*, a blend of Bakst-inspired orientalism and a rococo-tinged art deco (see gallery 1).

In this setting, delicately balanced between present and past, Mitchell and his band planted the supreme symbol of modernism, what Leiris called the "orgiastic banner" of jazz. The Perroquet espoused the trappings of the nascent society *dancings* (champagne, evening dress, chic clientele); yet at its heart, it acknowledged the central role of Black jazz. As usual there was a tango orchestra, but Mitchell's group was the main attraction. Their debut is commemorated in a series of familiar but often misidentified photos. One, cited by Pernet and Rye, shows the band members in white tie, standing before a stained-glass window, with a white man seated in front. Basing their claim on the testimony of Robert Goffin and music promoter and publisher Félix-Robert Faecq, the authors maintain that the picture was taken at the Brussels Alhambra and that the window was a painted canvas.[81] However, the stained glass is very real and the tufted banquettes the same seen in Séeberger frères photos of the Perroquet.

Regarding the white man, Goffin asserts that he is Albert Glazer (Blazer), maître d'hôtel of the Brussels theater; according to Faecq he was Oscar the bartender. Pernet and Rye opt for the latter, and critic Jody Blake, who reproduces the photo, identifies him as Léon Volterra in 1918–1919.[82] At that time the Perroquet did not exist, and the slight, fair-haired figure bears no resemblance to the stout Volterra. In fact, Goffin was correct about Blazer's identity, but the photo dates from his tenure as the Perroquet's urbane maître d', not his previous stint in Brussels.[83] Predictably, Woon credits Blazer with the cabaret's triumph.[84] In effect, his cordiality, discreet hospitality (he knew the favorite drinks and sexual tastes of his patrons), and marketing strategies (fashion dolls, perfume, and chocolates for the ladies) were effective tools, but the overwhelming reason for the club's success was unquestionably the music of the Jazz Kings.

Inopportunely, on May 8, 1922, disaster struck. The Casino was consumed by flames. After a seven-month restoration it reopened with a new revue, *En Douce* (Softly). In tandem with their nightly sessions at the Perroquet, the band had been appearing regularly on the Casino stage.[85] But for Mitchell, *En Douce* would be his last hurrah. These final performances were typical of the easy duty he had vaunted in his letter to Eubie Blake: a fifteen-minute stint during the intermission, eight minutes in the second act to accompany American dancer Marion Forde, and an intervention in the tableau *Les Ponts japonais* (The Bridges of Japan), one more example of the facile exoticism of the Casino revues. When *En Douce* closed on May 24, 1923, Mitchell passed the figurative baton to trumpeter Crickett Smith, who renamed the group "The Real Jazz Kings."

The band had been an unqualified success, but hardly had Mitchell begun his residency at Le Perroquet than he began to question his path. As early as November 1921 rumors circulated that, like Pilcer, he was "soon to open and operate what is known as a night café."[86] The gossip was premature (it would be more than a year before Mitchell assumed the management of the Grand Duc), but in a landscape dominated by Oscar and Maurice Mouvet to the south and Zelli and the Volterra family to the north, Mitchell's eventual move to the rue Pigalle would be an effort to establish an autonomous jazz kingdom. Jazz had become an intrinsic element of the Casino revues, but the white dancer who started it all had already moved on and soon it would be the turn of the influential Black drummer. Mitchell appeared at the Casino again only on a few special occasions; Pilcer briefly in the late twenties. But thanks to a fruitful series of encounters, near encounters, and even missed meetings, the "weird and wonderful sounds" heard in the rue de Clichy were on their way to becoming the heartbeat of Montmartre.

CHAPTER THREE

"AMERICA'S SWEETHEART," THE "JAZZ BABY," AND THE SISTER OF THE "COLORED GENTLEMAN"

[*Within the Quota*] is nothing but a translation on to the stage of the way America looks to me from over here. I put into the play all the things that come out of America to me, you see, as I get things into perspective and distance. Paris is bound to make a man either more or less American.
   —Gerald Murphy

With the unrestricted operating hours of 1921, new clubs opened, and old ones transformed into all-night venues. The possibility of dancing till dawn without fear of inopportune police raids was greeted with enthusiasm from the Boulevard Montparnasse to the Place Pigalle, but nowhere more eagerly than in the rue Caumartin. Describing the street in 1922, Sem exclaimed, "It is there that the throbbing rhythm of Americano-Parisian life beats with the greatest frenzy."[1] Since the days of Cadet Rousselle, the Savoy, and the Clover the street had been a beehive of American nocturnal activity, but with the departure of Yankee troops a gold-plated swarm descended, justifying Sem's characterization of "Broadway in miniature."[2] Gilded insects such as Fanny Ward, Peggy Hopkins Joyce, and Mabelle Gilman Corey, all veterans of the New York theatrical scene, glittered retrospectively in "the glamour and the light of Broadway, mayhap a little dimmed by torpid liver and stomachs that know their lobster but too well, but glamourous and luminous still."[3] Members of a nascent café society, these affluent patrons sparked the emergence of what became known as the "society *dancings*."

"The first really smart club on the rue Caumartin," asserts Woon, "was Harry Pilcer's Sans Souci, which he opened in Zelli's old place.... At that time there were not enough spenders in Paris to support more than one night club, so when the dancers Maurice and Leonora Hughes, under the direction of Oscar [Mouvet] and [Jules] Ansaldi, opened the Maurice Club just across the street, Pilcer's closed up."[4] Again Shack and others adopt Woon's chronology without reserve, but as usual it is marred by distortions.[5] That Chez Harry Pilcer (not the Sans Souci) failed because Maurice's new club in the Hotel Grande Bretagne attracted the limited clientele postulates a fictitious chain of cause and effect. As Woon well knew, the real reason for Pilcer's closure in May was his abrupt dismissal by Jeanne Darcy.

If Woon's conflation of the Sans Souci and Chez Harry Pilcer were accurate, we would be crediting the dancer with initiating the Parisian career of singer Florence Jones who, accompanied by her pianist husband, Palmer, leader of the International Five, would soon be hailed as one of the glittering decade's leading entertainers, courted by wealthy Americans and titled Europeans alike. Yet the situation was quite the opposite, as we have seen that honor belongs to the nefarious Alexandre Stavisky, owner of the Sans Souci, the man who introduced American-style revues to Cadet Rousselle and obtained the services of the jocular Joe Zelli and his "nifty foxtrots." At the Sans Souci Stavisky employed a formula that became universal, the alternation of a jazz band and a tango ensemble. Teatime was the province of Manuel Pizarro's tango orchestra. The rhythms for late-night dancing were the work of the anonymous "Zazz," which was quickly replaced by Florence and the International Five.

The couple's first appearance was on an exceptionally warm October evening.[6] Unable to display their costly fall mantles, female dance enthusiasts arrived in furs designed "for summer without a calorie of heat in them. A woman has one of broken marten tails that looks as if it could weather the artic and [yet] she almost freezes in it of a Paris evening."[7] Having descended from their vehicles, the fashionable horde pressed through the narrow entry of the old town house, and down the luxuriously carpeted corridor leading to a small pink-and-white room. Lacking a detailed description, Warnod's evocation of a typical "bonbonnière" may serve: "A subdued and expertly colored light bathed the room with a soft clarity; refined, voluptuous tones had been chosen for the rugs, the wall coverings and the fabrics that covered the seating. . . . In these small *dancings* reigned a sweet and troubling atmosphere. The air was impregnated with subtle perfumes; the sighs of the banjo, the lamentations of the clarinet became even more maddening, and for the habitués more enticing."[8]

In this sensual atmosphere, rendered tropical by the unseasonable weather and the heat emanating from the perspiring dancers, Florence was introduced to Parisian audiences. The engagement proved ephemeral. After two months, she and Palmer moved up the street to the didactically named So-Different. "All winter Americans patronized the So-Different in the rue Caumartin.... Then Maurice and Leonora Hughes opened across the street.... The following night the So-Different was a desert and Maurice's packed to the doors."[9] Here, Woon's chronology is exact. He refers to the dance team's brief apparition at the defunct Théâtre Caumartin, with Maurice's brother Oscar once again acting as manager. As usual, the season was only projected to last six or seven weeks. Opened on April 21, 1922, by June the club was shuttered, and the duo was dancing at a fashionable restaurant in the Bois de Boulogne.[10]

Yet, for a fleeting moment Maurice's was all the fashion. "It is there," declared Sem, "that the tide of elegance flows at present. It is there, and nowhere else, that one must be seen."[11] Entertainment in an intimate second floor cabaret was assured by two white musicians recruited in New York: pianist Roy Barton and singer Tommy Lyman, the man whose whispery voice had earned him the nickname "the Tubercular Tenor." Sometimes described as practicing "vocal jazz," he was not strictly speaking a jazz singer, even if his performances were appreciated by Bricktop.[12] However, the principal draw was the nightly exhibition of Maurice and Leonora.

Here is Sem's description of the scene: On the evening of his visit four hundred people have been crammed into a space meant to hold a bare hundred. The decoration is summary. A few flowers and hangings (vestiges of Poiret's "exotic fabrics?") suffice to transform the former theater into a dance hall. An "ah!" of ecstatic pleasure rises as Maurice and "Miss Leonora" make their entrance. His olive skin, slicked-back hair, and smoldering eyes exercise an unquestionable fascination, but for many they serve only to set off Leonora's vaporous, Nordic charms (see gallery 1). Ignoring Maurice, Sem concentrates on his partner. He acknowledges her choreographic talent but proposes another source of her appeal: a modest grace and a "pure, wholesome charm lacking in perversity, and even in sensuality." Notwithstanding her very "modern fox-trot," Sem sees no hint of seduction in Leonora's movements. Surprisingly, the jaded chronicler of the clandestine *dancings* waxes rapturous over her fresh-faced appeal: "She appears to be the Anglo-Saxon angel of the fox trot. There is no coquetry in her smile, only an innocent playfulness ... and perhaps a hint of insipidity. She is the ideal *America's Sweetheart*."[13]

"America's Sweetheart!" The phrase evokes a creation of Cole Porter and his Yale classmate, wealthy expatriate Gerald Murphy, principal inspiration for the character of Dick Diver in F. Scott Fitzgerald's *Tender Is the Night*. This "jazz ballet," *Within the Quota*, premiered at the Théâtre des Champs Élysées on

October 25, 1923. It was commissioned by wealthy dance patron Rolf de Maré's Ballets Suédois as a curtain-raiser for Darius Milhaud's avant-garde "ballet nègre," *La Création du Monde*—a work based on African folk legends and the jazz rhythms the composer had discovered on his visit to Harlem in 1922. The cryptic title refers to the Emergency Quota Act (1921), which severely limited immigration into the United States. In a series of lively meetings, a naive "Nordic" immigrant is confronted with a cavalcade of types drawn from Hollywood categories: the "American Heiress," the "Jazz Baby," the "Colored Gentleman" (a Danish dancer in blackface), the "Cowboy," and a silent film star: "Sweetheart-of-the-World (La Reine-de-tous-les-Cœurs)!"

The ballet's roots lay in the culture of the *dancings*. This was reflected in the audience, where high society, Hollywood, and Montmartre intermingled: among them wealthy Mrs. Freddie Havemeyer, screen idol Rudolph Valentino, and cabaret queen Elsa Maxwell.[14] Three years later, Porter would receive Charleston lessons from Bricktop, but he was already sensitive to the fascination of Black dance rhythms. His score exhibited a blend of ragtime, jazz, and popular melodies, each of the immigrant's encounters giving rise to a different tempo: a foxtrot for the bejeweled Heiress, a shimmy for the alluring Jazz Baby, a ragtime tap dance for the Colored Gentleman, and a rhapsodic parody of popular tunes and silent film music for the Sweetheart. Repeatedly, the immigrant's anticipated pleasures are frustrated by a sinister, black-clad figure incarnating diverse forms of interdiction: Social Reformer for the Heiress, Prohibition Agent for the Colored Gentleman, Puritan Preacher for the Jazz Baby, etc. All of this was played out before Murphy's Dadaist collage of newspaper headlines that echoed the ballet's satire of American hypocrisy, repressive puritan values, and worship of money.[15] As Murphy explained, the argument was "a translation on to the stage of the way America looks to me from over here. I put into the play all the things that come out of America to me, you see, as I get things into perspective and distance."

Murphy's scenario was built on the Hollywood clichés that nourished both American and French imaginations. As Michel Leiris recalled, "We particularly liked the American comedies with their simplistic sentimentality, or those violent films where one saw either good people gone wrong or stray lambs who reform themselves and fall into the arms of an ideal woman."[16] The conduct of Murphy's Nordic immigrant conforms to these schemas. The prototypes are easily identifiable—the Jazz Baby was an avatar of sultry movie vamps like Pola Negri—but, as Murphy acknowledged, the Hollywoodian source is particularly evident in the case of the heroine.[17] She is a carbon copy of silent screen star Mary Pickford, known as "America's Sweetheart" (justifying my assimilation of Leonora Hughes to the Sweetheart-of-the-World), as seen in photos from her greatest success, *Pollyanna* (1920). Here, we find the same lacy, tiered skirt, straw bonnet, and blond sausage curls, her smiling, Cupid's bow mouth displaying an "innocent playfulness."[18]

Obviously, Leonora's persona is a more sophisticated version; her curling blonde hair is bobbed, and the filmy layers of her gown an art deco translation of Pickford's elaborate layered skirt. Musical chronicler of this extravagant decade, Porter was not fooled by the Sweetheart's flirtatious chastity, bucolic basket of roses, and overstated flaxen curls. He recognized that the fantasy of American innocence encoded in her smile was an illusion of happiness founded on a spurious purity, that her artless traits masked American guilt and moral irresponsibility. Thus, for critic Gilbert Seldes the rhapsodic theme that Porter wrote for her is a perfect example of "his marvelous talents for parody and exaggeration."[19]

If Leonora assumes the role of the Sweetheart in my makeshift allegory, who represents the seductive Jazz Baby? The leading candidate was the most notorious habitué of Maurice's club: the infamous Peggy Hopkins Joyce, central figure of one of the major scandals of expatriate Paris. She succeeded in marrying three extremely wealthy magnates, a Swedish Count and two lesser trophies, earning the sobriquet of "million-dollar doll" by dilapidating a fortune in a one-week shopping spree. With her plunging neckline, provocative fringed skirt, and syncopated shimmy, the "Jazz Baby" echoes the sensation created by Peggy's "daring gowns, usually of the super-décolleté type," and the fact that she did not disdain "Negro dances" (in consonance with her alter ego, Peggy was credited with being the best shimmy dancer in Paris).[20] Both traits illustrate the sins enumerated by that nemesis of modernity, Monsignor Amette: immodest toilettes and indecent dances. Linking Leonora to a musical mode, Sem hails her as the "angel of the fox-trot," but the phrase inevitably suggests a Manichean opposition with the Jazz Baby's shimmy. Murphy's evocation of cinema stereotypes points to a schizophrenia in the American psyche; the tabloid readers who rhapsodized over Leonora's guileless charms were equally entranced by Peggy's scandals.

Here, another emblematic figure of postwar Paris enters the story. Peggy's misadventures were immortalized in one of the six "experimental sentences" composed by Ernest Hemingway in the spring of 1922, a distillation of scenes from his first five months in Paris: "I have seen Peggy Joyce at 2 a.m. in a *dancing* in the rue Caumartin quarreling with the shellaced [sic] haired young Chilean who had long pointed fingernails, danced like Rudolph Valentino, and shot himself at 3.30 that same morning."[21] Some of these remarks were based on observed events, but Peggy and the novelist had never met, and in April he was in Genoa covering the Economic Conference. Returning at the end of the month with an inflamed throat, he discovered the scandal in the Paris edition of the *Chicago Tribune* while ensconced in his bed.

Owing to its gripping denouement, the story was widely covered. Hemingway reduced it to a terse evocation, but the tabloids expanded on the juicy details ad infinitum. The young victim was a married diplomat from a monied Chilean family, Guillermo (Billy) Errázuriz. When he first made Peggy's acquaintance in New York in 1917, he fell madly in love with the twice-married siren. When they met again in Paris in 1922, Peggy was fresh from divorcing her third husband, Stanley—the Joyce in Peggy Hopkins Joyce. Freed of her lightly worn marital chains, Peggy returned to her old stamping grounds.

The fatal night of April 29, 1922, began at the epicenter of fashionable Paris, Ciro's restaurant, an obligatory halt on any Saturday round of gaiety. Peggy had recklessly invited the besotted Errázuriz to dine with his rival, multimillionaire Henri Letellier. Afterwards, the trio went dancing at Maurice's club. Exacerbating the awkward situation, Peggy's divorce from Joyce had been announced a year earlier at the inauguration of Maurice's first *dancing*, provoking unrestrained hilarity among gossip-hungry patrons when it was revealed that the dancer had been cited as corespondent along with Letellier.[22] Her reputed lovers both disrespected her. The newspaper magnate dismissed Peggy as "a gilded butterfly, . . . she was never more to me than an exquisite creature with whom I delighted to dance."[23] Maurice was even less chivalrous. He flatly denied the allegations and added, "When I pick a girl, I'll pick a prettier one than Peggy."[24] The Jazz Baby responded in kind. Evoking a turn with the dancer at the fashionable Deauville Casino on the Brittany coast (he sheepishly confessed that he had danced the shimmy with her "a few times," but always with "proper decorum"), she confided to tabloid readers that one "requires no formal introduction to a dancer of this type—he is like a crossing policeman, doorman or head waiter."[25]

It is not recorded that Peggy danced with the "crossing policeman" the night of April 29, but she granted a foxtrot to Letellier and, in a bow to his Latin origins, a tango to Errázuriz. To fuel these terpsichorean exertions, the fraught triangle consumed twelve bottles of champagne. Further intoxicated by her powers of seduction, on leaving Peggy was heard to exclaim, "Here are my two lovers." Prior to this tactless declaration, the inconsolable Billy had requested the most melancholic tunes in Tommy Lyman's repertoire: "I'm Sorry I Made You Cry" and "Some of These Days You'll Miss Me Honey."[26] The apologies were to no avail, and the prediction would be hollow. The imprudent revels ended before dawn with a nightcap in Peggy's suite at the tony Claridge Hotel, where Billy again professed his passion. Letellier took his leave and Errázuriz retired to his room. A few minutes later a shot rang out. Forcing the door, employees discovered the expiring Chilean, casualty of a suicide.[27]

Midnight the following day Peggy held court for reporters, reclining in her bed at the Claridge in a dark blue lace negligée—a sort of half-mourning. True to her self-dramatizing nature, she compared herself to history's most celebrated vamp: "The secret of my charm? I cannot tell. Probably Cleopatra, or those other women before me could not have told."[28] It was obvious that Peggy would have to leave town. On May 7 she embarked for New York, but before long she was back defending her title of Queen of the Shimmy, despite having declared to reporters, "I never want to see a dance place, hear a jazz band, or taste champagne again."[29]

Ms. Joyce was a symbol of the opulence, frivolity, and self-indulgence of the dawning jazz age flaring up in the society *dancings*. Avatar of a postwar generation obsessed with money and sex, and instilled with contempt for prewar values, the Jazz Baby indulged her every whim. But if Peggy is a symbol, it is a complex one. Though she had no education to speak of and showed no interest in progressive causes, her sexually liberated behavior could be seen as emblematic of the New Woman, freed of confining stays, cumbrous skirts, and subjection to a hypocritical double standard. Seen negatively, she appears as an exemplar of the mindless dissipations of her time. In a rare foray into social criticism, Woon cautions that "one of the saddest possible experiences Paris offers is a night with a party of those incorrigible *noctambules* who make night-trotting their profession . . . surfeited with sexual pleasure, their stomachs ruined by bad champagne, their brains feverish from insomnia, their principal occupation in life a knowledge of 'the' people, 'the' places and the way to wear the 'right' clothes."[30]

But where is the "Colored Gentleman" to be found in all this (Louis Mitchell for the purposes of my allegory)? Or rather the "Colored Gentleman's sister?" Not far. Sem's account of Leonora's triumph includes the following. Faced with a stampede of fans, Maurice is obliged to intervene. With a faint Belgian accent, he informs a desperate woman, "'Excuse me, for once, you understand, dear friend! Not the smallest free table!'" And Sem concludes that the rejects resign themselves to taking "refuge in another *dancing* across the street. Since then, it is known as the *Salon des Refusés*."[31] Sem's allusion is to the 1863 exhibition of Impressionist paintings rejected by the official Salon. He does not name the subaltern *dancing*, but the only suitable candidate is the So-Different (almost directly opposite), where Florence Jones had been singing since December.

Notwithstanding his usual nonjudgmental attitude, Sem was too astute an observer to ignore the differences between the social codes of clandestine shimmy parlors like Aladdin's Lamp and the cliquish society *dancings*. His humorous anecdote may thus be read at another level. Florence, the "Colored Gentleman's sister," is implicitly consigned to a secondary zone, an act of ideological import. For with his straw boater, cane, and modish spats, the Black vaudevillian in Porter's ballet represents the pungent image of a diverse, multiethnic society. His strutting tap dance to a music of "witty and jaunty syncopation, ... followed by wild drums and chaotic strings and woodwinds" fascinates the immigrant until a "Revenue agent enters to confiscate the scofflaw's liquor" and, having chased the nimble dancer, hypocritically guzzles a drink.[32] Incarnating difference, the Black character taps out an alternative tune, and in so doing opposes a subtle resistance to the norms of a disingenuous and oppressive white America.

Maurice's tacit relegation of Florence and Palmer to the "Salon des Refusés" was not only a question of professional rivalry. The dancer obviously did not care for jazz and, unlike Poiret, gave no evidence of an evolution in his attitude; any concessions he made were purely commercial. Contemptuously, he confided that "as long as the public continues to demand the Argentine-African dances, being the servant of the public, I shall supply them."[33] However, unlike the feckless tango aficionados of Poiret's fêtes, Maurice was well aware of the dance's origins in the Black working-class districts of Buenos Aires; his Parisian version was inevitably "sanitized." As Sem observed, it was "a little toned down ... with an easy, decent grace."[34]

In a curious outburst, Maurice railed against "artistic bolshevism" (shorthand for an assault on the traditional order), which he claimed was invading modern ballrooms. He deplored "the grotesqueness, ugliness and freakiness" introduced by Bolshevik "rebels" and blamed this decadence on syncopated music. His rejection was not purely aesthetic. The denunciation veered toward racism. "Jazz music," he maintained, was "almost wholly confined to third and fourth rate places," and since these "dubious steps ... originated in low Negro haunts," of necessity they "had an unhealthy and unpleasant significance."[35]

Despite this choreographic conservatism, Maurice and Leonora were one of the many popular dance teams of the period who performed to syncopated rhythms, using steps derived from Black American dances. The explanation of this seeming contradiction is that, as with his tango, the boisterous, erotic edges were ironed out. A perfect example of this decontamination may be found in his remarks on his signature dance, the "Maurice Glide," a combination of the waltz, two-step, foxtrot, and shuffle. While praising the cakewalk as "a product of the fantastic musical imagination of the Negro," he added with an insidious, racist tone, "There are a great many different ways of shuffling, as you know if you have ever seen a real cakewalk . . . the modern adaptation is not the heavy shuffle of the flat-footed [read "Black"] laborer but a light, brisk shuffle that imitates the heaviness without having it."[36]

Bending to fashion, during the intervals, he accepted "the spasmodic cadence of jazz," but his performances were free of such impurities, and at the time of his death he was perceived as "the last of the guild of aristocratic dancers to withstand the eccentric Charleston and Black Bottom craze"—damning praise that consigned him to the junk heap of history.[37] At the height of his success at the Hotel Grande Bretagne, it must have galled him to perform at a charity affair organized by the Marquise de Polignac, christened the "Black and White Ball," along with "a choir of 40 Negroes" drawn from the fabled Southern Syncopated Orchestra.[38] Nor, in 1921, could Maurice claim ignorance of the "Colored Gentleman." Two dancers, epitomizing the antipodes of attitudes toward jazz, visited the Perroquet on a summer evening of 1921. The first, as I have noted, was Harry Pilcer, the second Maurice! The newspapers inform us that "notwithstanding the heat, few of [those present] missed a single dance."[39] One may suppose that Maurice and his partner restricted themselves to the conservative foxtrots and polite tangos that were part of their stock in trade.

There is no explicit evidence of Leonora's thoughts on the matter, but about this time the couple was invited to London by Foreign Secretary Lord Curzon and Lady Curzon to dance at a reception for the British sovereigns. On that occasion Queen Mary was quoted as confiding to America's Sweetheart, "I think the English owe you our best gratitude for the courageous stand you have taken for the old-fashioned waltz and against the new dances, which are ungraceful and inharmonious . . . I have always believed that, despite the modern craze for the syncopated movement, the old waltz, combining true poetry with the genuine grace, would ultimately triumph."[40] As a consequence of the queen's disapproval, the foxtrot and the shimmy were banned in noble houses frequented by royalty. Although Leonora may have found Queen Mary's prohibition a trifle extreme (at a slow tempo, the foxtrot could resemble a waltz), she would surely not have ventured to contradict her, and in large measure she probably shared her views. Therefore, it is understandable that she and Maurice may have been reluctant to collaborate with groups such as the International Five, lending a perhaps unintended resonance to Sem's pleasantry on the "Salon des Refusés."

At this point a certain confusion arises. I have identified the "Salon des Refusés" as the So-Different, at 24 rue Caumartin, but this edifice also housed the Grand Teddy. Could the latter not lay equal claim to being the humiliated *dancing*? The building still stands—an imposing edifice with two commercial spaces flanking the central portico: a pharmacy to the left and a pizza parlor on the right. A contemporary photograph shows the Grand Teddy on the left, so I initially imagined that the So-Different occupied the site of the pizzeria.[41] However, further research revealed that in 1922 this space harbored a sweetshop.[42] Where then was the elusive dance salon? The answer is that Le Grand Teddy and the So-Different were one and the same!

How this could be requires a bit of history. A hotel was built on the site in 1898 and later renamed in honor of President Theodore Roosevelt. The magnifying adjective attests to French veneration for the champion of the 1917 American intervention in the war. The Grand Teddy was inaugurated on January 3, 1919. Initially only a restaurant and tearoom, two months after the abolition of the ban on dancing it yielded to the postwar passion. Because of early closing hours, evening dancing was confined to a few steps between courses, rhythmed by a prosaic French ensemble. That changed in December 1921 when the management announced a new formula. In the afternoon the café was the Grand Teddy; in the evening it metamorphosed into the So-Different.[43] Between 5 and 7 p.m. clients danced the tango, but from 11 p.m. to 3 a.m. the International Five offered the syncopated sounds of jazz and the blues of Florence Jones.

The setting of Florence and Palmer Jones' first prolonged exposure to a Parisian audience is well documented. Designed by Francis Jourdain, a forerunner of the modern school, the fittings were sufficiently unusual to be remarked upon by the press: "salons luxuriously furnished and decorated by François [sic] Jourdain. Paintings by [Edouard] Vuillard."[44] If the Grand Teddy is remembered by the public today, it is for Vuillard's avant-garde pictures, referred to as the "Grand Teddy tearooms paintings." It has been suggested that the Japanese-flavored interior of the largest painting represents a mise en abyme of the restaurant and its patrons; however, this is at odds with Jourdain's resolutely modern design, and a publicity fan rectifies the error.

The image on the fan affords a view of the Grand Teddy around 1920—a series of salons whose unadorned geometry announces the nascent art deco style.[45] It is teatime, the hour of the tango. Pastries and teacups are laid out on tables peopled by gentlemen in formal dress and women in designer gowns, their coiffures crowned with aigrettes. The tables ring the floor where an exhibition dance is taking place. That was 1920. A year or so later, in the evening, Florence and Palmer Jones would appear on the small bandstand shown on the fan. The petite chanteuse was not yet the elegant, aloof Black woman who ruled nighttime Montmartre, but even at this early stage, she displayed three qualities that accounted for her success: beauty, style, and a distinctive voice. One critic described her in terms that suggest their interdependency: "beautiful; majestic in manner and speech; with class; elegance; finesse; to match her talents."[46]

The relative importance of these traits varied with the observer. Poet Langston Hughes, who worked with her in 1924, opined that "she was no Raquel Meller"—the Spanish vocalist who in the fall of 1922 was appearing with the White Lyres at a revived Clover. However, he suggests that beauty compensated for any deficiency in her performance.[47] French critics were more responsive to what *Time* referred to as her "sultry blues voice."[48] Espousing a perhaps feminine point of view, Bricktop deemed that she was not pretty, but "striking in her beautiful clothes."[49] Notwithstanding the redhead's negative assessment, many felt that beauty was part and parcel of the impact of Florence's unique voice.

One of the few images documenting her appearance allow us to judge for ourselves. A 1922 passport photo shows a perfect, sepia oval marked by large, somewhat plaintive, almond-shaped eyes. Short hair is brushed away to the right and left but three delicate ringlets curl across a smooth forehead and her sensuous, rouged lips are lifted in the faintest of smiles (see gallery 1). On Bricktop's second comment, however, everyone agrees. At the time of her death in 1932, all obituaries mentioned her jewels and furs; yet even in her debuts she was recognized for an acute sense of fashion. Bathed in colored spots, standing erect before the spare elegance of Jourdain's décor, she might have been wearing something like the ensemble that she wore some two years later at the Grand Duc: "an evening gown of gold and a spray of orchids in her hair."[50]

Both Woon and Nevill associate Elsa Maxwell of Keokuk, Iowa, with the transubstantiation of the Grand Teddy into the So-Different; if only in nebulous terms.[51] Elisabeth de Gramont, whose memoirs span the belle époque and the jazz age, portrays Maxwell as "short and round, with a plump profile, always dancing; born between two blues, she has rhythm in her blood and leads the farandole; the busiest of bees fulfills her mission, which is *to organize pleasure*; she knows where the honey is located and how to spread it around."[52] With the initiation of the new formula, on December 15, 1921, Elsa began to disseminate that nectar at the So-Different.[53]

Elsa did not own the club. The proprietors included an anonymous Frenchwoman, "and others."[54] As she boasts in her autobiography, she functioned as a social director and "pioneer press agent," a task for which she was eminently suited thanks to her extensive social relations.[55] One can sense her hand in the naming of the fledgling cabaret, a marketing tool to distinguish it from the plethora of *dancings*, all more or less the same. Advertising for the late-night rendezvous also appears to bear her fingerprints: "This luxurious establishment is not a *dancing* such as one imagines it today but a haven of pleasure that was lacking, where one can socialize with the right crowd."[56] Elsa strove to exploit the rampant snobbishness of her target audience, a strategy she would pursue at all her society *dancings*.

Undoubtedly, Elsa was also responsible for Florence and Palmer's precipitous move. Always on the lookout for the latest trend, she had shrewdly noted their arrival in Paris. Having declined the Maharajah of Kapurthala's invitation to visit India during a tour by the Prince of Wales, Elsa organized a "Children's Ball" to commemorate the Armistice. Guests cavorted in juvenile costumes designed by Chanel while Florence, the Sans Souci's new sensation, sang "all of the latest New York ragtime songs."[57] Thanks to Elsa the couple quickly met the Grand Dukes Dimitri and Boris, the Princess di San Faustino, the Marquis and Marquise de Polignac, and other members of the Parisian gratin who were to become crucial elements of their fan base. But Elsa was far from disinterested. The society maven recognized that for the venerable Grand Teddy to become smart again, the aura of modernity attendant on a jazz-driven *dancing* was essential. Similarly, the following year she would engage the Red Devils for a new venture, the Acacias, insisting, with some exaggeration, that "then, to get an American jazz band seemed like finding the Kohinoor."[58]

Elsa's personal history may help to explain her openness to Black entertainment. Among her many gifts, she was an accomplished pianist, and before becoming the most popular society hostess in Paris, she had honed her skills on the American vaudeville circuit, a fact Bricktop highlighted by an amusing anecdote recounting a party given by Elsa at the Ritz Hotel, where she performed along with a team of comic dancers. "Like many entertainers of the time, Negro and white, they blackened their faces with burnt cork." Bricktop thought they had been a hit, but Elsa told her not to use them again. Believing that it was the continental thing to do, they had kissed the ladies' hands, leaving half a dozen society women smeared with burnt cork. "And, Brick," Elsa scolded, "if you don't know how hard that is to clean off, I do. I used to wear cork in vaudeville."[59] Laying aside the negative connotations of blackface, it is probable that her theatrical past had rendered her more receptive to Black culture than Maurice or many of her American social connections.

After a successful winter at the So-Different, the restless hostess departed, at which point, according to Woon, "the French owner thought she could run it by herself, when of course it ended by being No Different, and flopped gracefully."[60] As usual, he is willing to sacrifice truth for the sake of a witty sally. Even though obliged to beat a provisional retreat before the onslaught of Maurice's popularity, Florence and the cabaret nevertheless continued until January 1923.[61] As for Elsa, she had left to inaugurate Les Acacias, situated on an eponymous street near the Etoile, a club previously exploited by Maurice Chevalier and others. Her partners were Oscar Mouvet, the club's former dance director, and Capt. Edward Molyneux, a British war hero and rising dress designer. Molyneux and Oscar provided the financing, with Elsa again as social counselor. While she easily convinced the couturier to promote his fashions among the clientele of a chic night club, rallying Oscar to the new project was a more noteworthy achievement, one that his brother Maurice experienced as a betrayal, causing a temporary rift.[62]

The opening on May 24, 1922, was touted as the major event of the season. Equipped with parasol-covered tables and a platform for dancing under the moonlit trees of the garden, it featured Jenny Dolly (of Jenny and Rosie, the celebrated Hungarian American dancing twins), partnered with Clifton Webb, renowned as a hoofer long before his Hollywood fame. The guests included not only members of the social elite but leading artistic figures such as Serge Diaghilev, impresario of the Ballets Russes, and Elsa's long-time friend Cole Porter.[63]

Considering that the inauguration made such a large splash in the small pond of nocturnal Paris, it seems strange that it produced so few echoes in the French press. *Comœdia* picked it up, noting the Molyneux gowns of the "bewitching Miss Dolly" but making no mention of the changed management.[64] *Vogue* suggested a reason for this odd silence: "Les Acacias has reopened its exquisite gardens under a new direction whose names, well-known to true Parisians, are whispered in low voices, since they must remain anonymous."[65]

Actually, they were an open secret, one that American newspapers did not hesitate to share; this feigned discretion was simply an extension of the policy of exclusivity elaborated by Elsa at the So-Different. As she explained, "Molyneux and I sat at separate tables flanking the entrance and personally passed on everyone admitted to the Acacia [*sic*]. If one of us didn't like the appearance of the people in a party or we wanted to snub them, we gave a high sign to the maître d'hôtel."[66] Exploiting the glamour of snob appeal, Elsa perfected the prototype of the society *dancing* drafted by Harry Pilcer and Maurice. Well acquainted with "society," the much-married Jean Nash wrote of the dynamo from Keokuk:

> She knows what snobs people are, and takes advantage of this common human weakness. Thus she has at her service, so to speak, a great deal of royalty, hard-up Italian princes, fleeing and hungry Russians and many discarded monarchs of unsettled Central Europe. On an opening night she will draw up her battle plans like a general.... "In this corner," she says, looking at a list, "oh yes in this corner it's all right. The left side is a little empty. I think I will transfer Lord Neverpays from the right. Yes, there is enough nobility there, we can spare him. Then Prince Lastdimesky—where shall I put him? Oh, but I suppose he won't have dined, knowing he can get something here. I will put him nearer the kitchen so as not to have waiters crossing the floor with Russian food. I will thus have nobility at the main posts."[67]

Jean acknowledges that this monologue, which was reported to her, is a bit exaggerated, but it is true to the spirit if not the letter. How much of Maurice's success at the former Théâtre Caumartin was due to Elsa's prior departure from the So-Different is difficult to assess; he was playing the same game. The Grand Teddy/So-Different was larger and better appointed than his cabaret, but that was irrelevant. The second-best status of the So-Different was not the fruit of objective evaluation but the result of fashion and an intangible snob appeal. The vogue in *dancings* changed as rapidly as the gowns of their female patrons, without any concrete reasons to explain the sudden shift. Even the accumulated efforts of Elsa's publicity machine, which hailed Florence and Palmer as "incomparable...unique" and "celebrated," were unable to alter the inexorable judgement.

Ironically, as the artistic virtues of Florence's voice were beginning to be recognized by the "refugees" of the "Salon des Refusés," the shimmy-shaking Peggy Joyce, famous for being famous, was acting badly at Maurice's Club and being rewarded for it with the headlines of two continents. Not that Peggy harbored any prejudice against the So-Different. Unconcerned with club rivalries, she simply loved to dance. Indeed, it was a spin at the So-Different with visiting champion Jack Dempsey that first aroused Errázuriz's fatal jealousy.[68] As Florence watched Peggy carelessly juggling the young Chilean diplomat and the brawny "Manassa Mauler," she must have felt a justifiable sense of her own worth—something like the sentiments expressed by Zora Neale Hurston: "At certain times I have no race, I am *me*. When I set my hat at a certain angle and saunter down Seventh Avenue, Harlem City, feeling as snooty as the lions in front of the Forty-Second Street Library, for instance. So far as my feelings are concerned, Peggy Hopkins Joyce on the Boule Mich with her gorgeous raiment, stately carriage, knees knocking together in a most aristocratic manner, has nothing on me."[69]

But what of the "Colored Gentleman" himself? Identifying Mitchell with this allegorical figure is not gratuitous; handsome, nattily dressed, with a slim waist and broad shoulders, he was the embodiment of the dapper entertainer seen in a costume drawing by Sara Murphy.[70] During the period I have been discussing, he was still producing "weird and wonderful sounds" in the rue de Clichy, but within months he would transfer his "vaudeville dance" to the rue Pigalle and the "colored nightingale" of Montmartre would take wing to join him.

As in the case of their move to the So-Different, Elsa's multifarious activities impacted the careers of Florence and Palmer, this time indirectly. She attributes the demise of the Acacias to the fiction that she and Molyneux "were too busy having a good time to check incoming revenue against outgoing expenses. Half the bistros in Paris must have been stocked with liquor stolen from us."[71] In fact, the club was never intended to be more than a distraction to lighten the dog days of summer, something on the order of Poiret's legendary fêtes of 1919 or Maurice Chevalier's seasonal operation the previous year. In mid-August Oscar Mouvet and a new associate relocated the *dancing*, and the Dolly Sisters, to Biarritz for the late summer season.[72] Thus Elsa was at liberty. As we know, the devil finds work for idle hands. She was soon announcing the creation of a new dance palace, again with Oscar as her partner.[73] The declaration was premature but would eventually result in a lavish new club at 17 rue Caumartin: Le Jardin de ma Soeur.

At the conclusion of the "dance hall wars" of 1922, a victorious Oscar Mouvet rapidly claimed the musical spoils personified by the International Five.[74] It is true that he had never shared his brother's virulent aversion to jazz, but the underlying issues were more complex. Mitchell's move to the rue Pigalle, with Florence at his side, would prepare the dance hall wars of 1924 and 1925, opposing not just two cabarets but two streets and two cultures. The imminent ascension of the northern thoroughfare and decline of the rue Caumartin were in progress. However, the story of that transfer of hegemony is an integral part of the rise and fall of the most celebrated of the society *dancings*, the whimsically named My Sister's Garden.

CHAPTER FOUR

A GALA IN MY SISTER'S GARDEN

Grandeur and Decadence of a "Society *Dancing*"

> In the old days we should now go to the Jardin de ma Soeur, but this has just been closed and transformed into a billiard hall.
> —Basil Woon

The So-Different, Maurice's Club, Elsa's Acacias, the revived Clover, Harry Pilcer's Acacias, Le Jardin de ma Soeur . . . For an entire winter the So-Different held the high ground, until Maurice's ultrafashionable *dancing* flared up like a round of artillery fire. Over the space of a summer, Elsa's Acacias filled the void left by his withdrawal with the jazz of the Red Devils, but by fall the *Tout-Paris* was eager for a new combatant, one more exciting than a resurrected Clover or Pilcer's recycled Acacias. Elsa's retreat was strategic. With Molyneux as silent partner, on December 5, 1922, she and Oscar Mouvet opened Le Jardin de ma Soeur "in a blaze of glory."[1] The final entrant in the dance hall wars of 1922 would appear to have triumphed.

Elsa's memoirs make no mention of Oscar, which is not surprising. Despite a deceptive candor about money matters, her account of the affair is less than forthcoming. If we are to trust her word, Molyneux supplied the funds for Les Acacias; all she had to offer was "an old tablecloth and some new ideas."[2] In reality, Oscar is likely to have provided half the capital. She then explains Le Jardin's eventual end in terms similar to those proposed for the Acacias—"It took the employees two years to steal us blind"—implying that she left in 1924.[3] In truth, she and Mouvet quarreled less than three weeks after the opening. He claimed they had agreed to put the lease in his name; Elsa alleged it was to have been shared. "Mouvet is what he would call a pretty smart businessman," she added tartly and slammed the door.[4] She would later return, remaining till the Jardin's closure on New Year's Eve 1925, but this precipitous exit explains why, though her name is regularly associated with the club, Oscar is cited as owner and credited with making the Jardin an establishment "much frequented by fashionable Society."[5]

Elsa's friend, writer Anita Loos, remembered it as "the most elegant place to greet the Paris dawn." My Sister's Garden was not just an intriguing name. "It occupied an ancient town house," Loos explained, "with a lush, well-kept garden where we dined and danced out of doors."[6] The interior echoed the garden ambiance, giving the impression of an alfresco picnic. In a space ringed by concrete columns, Elsa and her decorators had elaborated a pastoral fantasia, with art deco murals of antique ruins, banks of cypresses, and an aqueduct reflected in a lake. May Birkhead took it to be an Italian garden.[7] In fact, it was merely the Southern plantation of Les Acacias restaged in a generic Arcadian vein.

Two images bring the setting to life: a postcard in the author's collection and a sketch in *Vogue*.[8] Maurice and Leonora had missed the inauguration, but after their return in April 1923 they started to attract huge crowds.[9] The drawing captures the excitement of those spring evenings. From an ironwork balcony, elegant clubbers gaze down at the dance floor where among tables littered with champagne glasses a spotlight picks out the silhouette of Leonora Hughes, "so fragile that one would really imagine watching a petal about to land [see gallery 1]."[10] Surrounding this enchanting vision the guests sit on bentwood chairs with calico backs, but the imitation grass that cushioned their feet at the club's opening has disappeared, and servers have resumed the evening dress that—to appease society men weary of being mistaken for waiters—Oscar had replaced with corduroy knee breeches, buckled shoes, and William Tell hats.[11]

Even in the last year of its existence, the *dancing* remained the theater of extravagant gestures. Gay millionaire Howard Sturges hosted an "amazing evening" at which he and Elsa sang the leads in Gounod's *Faust*, while their friend Cole Porter accompanied them on the piano. In an excess of solicitude for his guests—or perhaps from egomania—he had caused the words "Sturges Gala" to be emblazoned over the entrance in electric lights.[12] At a moment when many Parisians struggled to survive in a crippled postwar economy, such antics were galling; a few years earlier the Communist tabloid *L'Humanité* had urged the unemployed to march on "the gilded dance palaces of Montmartre as a demonstration against the reckless expenditure of money."[13]

On April 14, 1924, a remarkable event signaled both the dazzling apogee of Le Jardin and the onset of its decline: a "Gala Night" to celebrate Maurice and Leonora's triumphant return from New York. In their absence, Le Jardin had been renamed the Embassy Club (a promotional stunt—ads still included "Jardin de ma Soeur" in parentheses). Yet, though the gala betrayed a smug air of self-satisfaction, the situation more closely resembled the engagement of a fresh young star to invigorate a failing box office. All the usual suspects were on board, but the unchallenged headliner was Edward, playboy Prince of Wales, later Duke of Windsor. He had already patronized the Embassy during a brief visit in January. Throngs of visitors gathered to gawk, and Oscar labeled him "the greatest drawing card in the world"; nevertheless the Prince's actions on April 14 heralded a changing of the guard that would prove fatal to the Jardin's supremacy.[14]

The prince arrived on Monday of Holy Week, transparently disguised as the Earl of Chester (in fact one of his lesser titles). He had been resting in Biarritz after a series of equestrian accidents. Planning a short visit, he remained for five days, precipitating a whirl of activity that would prove anything but restful. Woon begins the story with the discovery of two young men dining at Ciro's with a pair of anonymous American beauties. The columnist's party, including the ubiquitous Erskine Gwynne, ogles the prince: "'Why—he's no bigger than I am!' a young woman in the group remarks. (She is five feet one-and-a-half.) . . . 'Look at that flower in his buttonhole—I wonder which of them gave it to him?' . . . 'So this is the way he takes a rest cure!' says a lady with an Illinois accent"—doubtless meant to encourage identification for a provincial readership.

The prince and his guests quickly finish and leave. "Within two minutes everyone in the room knows that they have gone on to the Casino de Paris," then featuring Crickett Smith's Real Jazz Kings.[15] "What is that noise?"[16] a woman in the audience is heard to ask. "It must be a jazz band," her husband tentatively replies.[17] A longtime aficionado, the prince surely has no difficultly recognizing the "noise"; what he does not know is that in the course of the evening he would also discover the other two entities of the Holy Trinity of Black jazz bands, the Crackerjacks and the International Five.

"And after that?" someone inquires. Woon replies, "The Embassy, of course! But not the Embassy of Great Britain! . . . This Embassy is a Champagne Palace."[18] With this preface, "the Boswell of the boat train crowd" offers a complacent enumeration that contrasts the social freedom of the clandestine dance halls and the exclusionary character of the society *dancings*.[19] By granting habitués of Le Jardin Homeric epithets ("much-married Mrs. Jean Nash" is the rhetorical equivalent of "swift-footed Achilles"), Woon haloes them with a spurious prestige.

From the Riviera arrive "Mr. and Mrs. Berry Wall, whose return . . . presages the real beginning of the Paris season." From London come "two American ladies—Lady Curzon of Kedleston and Lady Cunard. Just beyond, Grand Duchess Marie of Russia, entertaining five friends. Next to her, Infante Don Luis of Spain, rumored to be engaged to Mrs. Maybelle [sic] Corey. Across the room, Grand Duke Dimitri," the Grand Duchess' handsome brother, who was involved in the death of Rasputin, and "Mr. and Mrs. Axel Wichfeld, with a big party, Lord Pembroke, Marquis and Marquise de Polignac, Princess Cystria." Among the theatrical folk is "Mrs. Jack Dean—better known as Fanny Ward, receiving congratulations on her recovery from a bad attack of influenza and looking the youngest person in the room. Not far away from Fanny another big party from Baltimore, the hosts being Prince and Princess Jerome Bonaparte and the guests including Mr. and Mrs. Griswold Thompson," etc., etc. "The Prince [of Wales] comes in accompanied by Mr. and Mrs. Freddy Bate—Freddy is his highness' inseparable companion in Paris—. . . and an Argentine young millionaire named Alda, who once was reported engaged to the much-married Mrs. Jean Nash. A very gay crowd." In addition, from the East have come the Shah Ahmad Shah Qajar, (styled Prince of Persia), the Maharajah of Kapurthala, and others whose names have been long forgotten. All these charming people have congregated on the first night of Holy Week for a gala celebrating Maurice and Leonora's return to the newly christened Embassy Club, "sometimes known by the more appropriate name of *Le Jardin de ma Soeur*."[20]

Drawn by rumors of the prince's presence, "Society with a big S" (Woon's fetishistic phrase) has gathered. Elsewhere, he expounds on the demographics of Montmartre: "The crowd of spenders which Paris facetiously calls 'Tout-Paris' and which more justly might be named 'Tout-Etranger' is limited in number . . . Americans and English form a majority of the spendthrifts during the season, with South Americans and Spaniards next in numbers. The French only succeed in keeping a short jump ahead of the Italians, the Swiss and the Germans."[21] The motley assembly included the famous and the infamous, veteran socialites and dewy-eyed debutantes, the up-to-the-minute and the out-of-date, royalty and aristocracy—legitimate and dubious—together with refugees from Broadway and Saint Petersburg.

There was no lack of run-of-the-mill Yankees such as the Thompsons, but many of the "European" aristocrats were, in fact, American, for instance Lady Grace Curzon, née Hinds, wife of the British foreign secretary, the Marquise

Nina de Polignac, née Crosby, or Lady Maud Cunard, née Burke, wed to the grandson of the Cunard Line's founder. Mixed with the titled and garden-variety Americans were bright lights of Broadway. Though stars like Mabelle Gilman Corey and Peggy Joyce were not present that night, one did encounter the eternally young Fanny Ward, who, fifty-two years old, was credited with sixty-one and looked like thirty.

Finally, in keeping with Elsa's formula, a full battery of royals had answered the call: Sir Jagatjit Singh, potentate of the princely Indian state of Kapurthala, and the chubby, not too bright-looking Shah Ahmad, whose titles ranged from "Zil Allah," Shadow of God, to "the King Whose Standard Is the Sun." (When the hero of Fitzgerald's *Tender Is the Night* commandeers the silver-wheeled auto of the Shah of Persia, whose interior "was inlaid with innumerable brilliants," one senses a novelistic extravagance, but the author is only documenting the routine life of Montmartre.[22] Lastly, there was Don Luis-Ferdinand of Bourbon-Orleans, black sheep of the Spanish royal family. Of the rumor that he was engaged to Mabelle Corey, Woon coyly opines, "I never believed that report because Don Luis is not the marrying sort," a veiled allusion to his homosexuality.[23]

The presence of the two Asian princes was unexceptional: They were only the most prominent of the Eastern royalty who frequented the quarter. The Indians were particularly conspicuous—the Maharajah of Indore, to name only one. Though the population of the subcontinent was rural and highly traditional, a small elite embraced the frivolous Montmartre lifestyle. As future king of Great Britain and Ireland, defender of the faith, emperor of India and of the dominions over the seas, the Prince of Wales outranked them all, including his vassal, the ruler of Kapurthala. When the P.O.W., as he was familiarly known, toured India in 1921 and '22, "princes spared no effort ... in honouring the heir to half the world with fabulous, if disquieting, hospitality."[24] Reveling in the humbler salons of the Embassy Club, the Maharajah may have fondly remembered the elaborate banquet he had offered the imperial visitor in his pink-and-green marble palace. He might also have recalled that during the trip Edward often danced the shimmy, attended by what was jokingly referred to as "a princely jazz band."[25]

Even if Maurice disapproved of shimmying, a passion for dancing and money was the de facto glue that bound together the patrons of the society *dancings*. The cash-poor Russian aristocracy was an exception (Grand Duke Dimitri worked as a champagne agent, and the Grand Duchess Marie furnished embroidery for Chanel). For them, sonorous titles and exquisite manners were sufficient. But if the Prince of Wales was arguably the wealthiest person in the room, the Maharajah of Kapurthala, nicknamed the "Modern Solomon" because of his vast fortune, ran a close second, and one of his younger sons, Prince Karam, was "considered the finest male dancer in Paris."[26] Even a lesser figure like Berry Wall, "King of the Dandies," had run through two fortunes and, despite his sixty-odd years, was known to shake a mean leg.[27] As for Erskine Gwynne, grandson of Mrs. Cornelius Vanderbilt, it was said that "any time he dares to show his face in any of the dancing houses . . . the professionals take a back seat."[28] Also legendary was the P.O.W.'s appetite for dance. Years later, in New York, he would ask Bricktop to teach him the Twist, reminiscing, "I used to know all the new dances, and Brick can tell you how many different girls I danced them with."[29]

The third salient trait of this insular world was its almost total pallor. Black performers such as Florence and Palmer Jones or Buddie Gilmore occasionally featured, but in the early period entertainment tended to be white. This bias reflects the partiality of a portion of the American clientele. A prime example is Lady Cunard who, despite her "purified-of-that-horrible-American-twang voice," remained profoundly Yankee.[30] She was not yet famous as the mother of Nancy Cunard, female half of the most scandalous interracial romance of 1920s Montmartre, nor the object of her daughter's scathing condemnation in the 1931 essay "Black Man and White Ladyship," but like Woon, she combined the prejudices of upper-class English snobbery with the blunter forms of American racism. Asked about Nancy's liaison with jazz pianist Henry Crowder, she replied, "You mean to say my daughter *does* know a Negro and that you know him too? Well don't speak of it to anyone—nobody knows anything about it."[31]

One guest who could bear eloquent witness to Lady Cunard's hypocrisy is curiously omitted from Woon's list, Elsa Maxwell. However, she *was* there, entertaining a large party that certainly excluded Lady Maud.[32] Elsa detested her social pretensions and contempt for Americans, contending that she only received those whose names might decorate the society columns.[33] They had clashed again at the opening of the Jardin. As Elsa noted, the décor contained "more birds in cages than the Paris Zoo. . . . Lady Cunard, my old sparring partner, decided to create a scene when she condescended to visit our establishment. Expressing more solicitude for our feathered friends, the birds, than she ever had shown for her human friends, Lady Cunard opened the cage of a 'poor, tortured' pigeon. The pigeon proceeded to show its appreciation by making an indiscretion on her ladyship's head. Her shrieks echoed in Paris and

London newspapers, which reported the incident on a tip from a certain press agent who had cleared it with the management."[34]

Lady Maud's daughter, Nancy, was no more dupe of her mother's posturing than Elsa. "I am told," she wrote, "that Her Ladyship was invited to a night club, saw some coloured singers, turned faint and left."[35] Fortunately for Lady Cunard's health and sense of propriety, Palmer Jones' group was absent the night of the gala, as were the insolent pigeons! In her groundbreaking anthology *Negro*, Nancy raised the issue of her mother's double standard in a context pertinent to the demographics of the Embassy Club. Apropos of a photo of Lady Maud posing with a bejeweled Maharajah, Nancy angrily questioned, "How is it that Indian Rajahs are not discriminated against?"[36] Of the Asians attending that night, the Prince of Persia was relatively fair skinned, but the Maharajah of Kapurthala was "very dark in complexion, being rather darker than the average person of half-black and half-white ancestry. In his sack suit he could very easily be taken, if in a Negro gathering, for a colored preacher, doctor or other professional."[37] Intimidated by the aura of royalty, Lady Maud may have succeeded in convincing herself that the maharajah was not a "person of color," even though his skin was as dark as that of Nancy's lover. For Lady Maud, titles, jewels, and wealth excused any defect of pigmentation. This indulgence was shared by the clients of the society *dancings*, resulting in a rash of interracial marriages involving dusky princes.

Again, Fitzgerald's *Tender Is the Night* seems more like social documentation than literary invention. Mary North's second husband is the staggeringly rich Indian, Hosein, Count Minghetti. Though his exalted rank is only a papal honor, dark-skinned bearers of European titles were not unknown, often the result of unions that the American psyche sought to ignore. In the cosmopolitan atmosphere of the old continent, Count Minghetti's wealth, like that of Kapurthala's ruler, allows him a freedom inconceivable in America—Fitzgerald's narrator wryly notes that Hosein "was not quite light enough to travel in a Pullman south of Mason-Dixon."[38] In effect, notwithstanding Lady Cunard's elastic tolerance, according to cultural historian Andrew Rose, "'Black' at that time was used indiscriminately to embrace virtually anyone with a skin darker than pink. Thus, Egyptians, such as Ali Fahmy, were 'coloured' or 'Black,' as were all Asians in the Indian Empire."[39]

Rose's "Egyptian" is Ali Kamel Fahmy Bey, the ill-starred husband of a conspicuous absentee, one who by all rights should have attended the gala: Princess Marguerite Marie Laurent Fahmy Bey, née Alibert, aka Maggie Meller.[40] This scarlet lady owed her title to marriage with the young royal. Their idyll ended on July 10, 1923, in a suite of the exclusive London Hotel, the Savoy, thanks to her homicide of Ali with a Browning automatic. Her defense exploited the stereotype of the sadistic Oriental preying on innocent white women, a "ferocious brute with vilest tempers and habits."[41] Marguerite was acquitted, some said thanks to agents of the Prince of Wales. For behind the public scandal lay a private one: the potential exposure of compromising letters written to Marguerite by the prince during their wartime liaison.

Many of the guests at the gala were likely to have been familiar with these facts, particularly Lady Curzon. Before the princess' trial, Lord George Curzon had written his wife about a rumor that might "amuse" her: "The French girl who shot her so-called Egyptian prince in London, and is going to be tried for murder, is the fancy woman who was the Prince's 'keep' in Paris during the war . . . and they were terribly afraid that he might be dragged in."[42] A few days prior to the gala Marguerite had become the laughing stock of Paris over a failed plot involving medical certificates attesting the birth of a dead baby, a fiction designed to bolster claims to her late husband's estate.[43] These mortifying circumstances may explain her absence. Or did she hear reports of the prince's attendance and consider discretion the better part of valor?

For many reasons then—echoes of his peccadillo, restiveness, ennui—the prince may have felt that the ostensibly festive occasion was more like one of the tiresome duties to which his rank constrained him. If the Bates and the Polignacs were personal friends, Lady Cunard and Princess Cystria were merely card-carrying members of his restricted social circle.[44] During his January visit the same monotonous faces had haunted a banquet given by the British ambassador, Lord Crewe, and a dinner by the Princesse de Polignac. The princess at least had the originality to prolong the evening with a soirée wherein Elsa Maxwell and Cole Porter interpreted pieces written by the latter for two pianos. His jazz-inflected works are likely to have delighted the prince.

In contrast, although the Embassy Club band did its utmost to please, Edward was unsatisfied. (One wonders what Lady Curzon thought of their efforts. Queen Mary's 1921 ban on "modern dances" in the houses of the nobility had specified Lord and Lady Curzon.)[45] The uninspiring Embassy band would perhaps have contented the exigencies of his mother, but it was insufficient for the jazz-mad prince. Having essayed two turns on the floor, he and his party left—their destination Jed Kiley's establishment in the rue Fontaine. Fifteen minutes later, Woon learned the astonishing news in a message from Kiley:

"Dear Basil... the Prince is up here at my place, tell the gang and come!" Evidently reluctant to offend the star dancers, the sycophantic author delayed for an hour before wending his way "up the hill" to Pigalle.[46]

At this point we dispose of a second eyewitness, journalist C. F. Bertelli. Though informality was the rule at Kiley's, the prince "nearly bowled [him] over by addressing him as 'old man,' and asking whether he couldn't have a whisky and soda instead of the proverbial champagne."[47] One can imagine the P.O.W. speaking with his trademark boyish simplicity, a democratic air he could assume so easily, the question of equality being unimaginable. Having flabbergasted his host, the P.O.W. executed, as he would two nights later, "fancy steps for 25 minutes without rest while a band of American Negro jazz artists [the Crackerjacks] plays their heads off," causing Kiley to comment in awe, "He may have broken a shoulder-blade, but I'll tell the world his legs are sound enough."[48]

The prince was what Woon categorizes as "a royal die-hard," one of those "who simply don't know when to go home."[49] In this he resembled his grandfather Edward VII. However, at that earlier time dancing was confined to professionals. His forebear occasionally danced a jig step or two at the Abbaye de Thélème, but the P.O.W. was more radical. As signs of a disdain for ceremony, he danced the new choreographies and sat in on the drums with Montmartre bands. Trumpeter Arthur Briggs tactfully observed, "He was OK. He didn't worry us. His tempo was reasonable. We didn't pay much attention to his left hand as long as he kept what you might call the 'oom-cha' going."[50]

Spying him at Shanley's, author Jean Gravigny offered a tongue-in-cheek tribute to this "timid young man, his face flushed with happiness... who honors our champagne with one of the youngest and prettiest actresses of a Parisian *bonbonnière*. Allow him to enjoy himself, everything is not rosy in the metier of king. Ask nothing more of the heirs to the last crowns than to serve for the launching of a casino or a great bar. They will come to know the human heart more deeply in this way than by listening to diplomats."[51]

Bertelli argues that despite their differences, the P.O.W. was following his elder's example: "He does not go where society says he should go, but where he wants to go and as a result some amazing transformations have taken place in the night life of Paris."[52] In fact, he did more than follow, he traced a new path. Oddly, Woon takes no notice of any further visits; he concludes his observations with the prince's exclamation at Kiley's, "Cripes! After three, and I've got to go hunting tomorrow."[53] Was he unaware of the P.O.W.'s further peregrinations, or is the omission deliberate? In any event, after leaving Kiley's, Edward went on to consecrate Louis Mitchell's club at 36 rue Pigalle. According to Bertelli, "The prince had evinced a wish for something to eat and he had been told by Kiley that buckwheat cakes and sausages, washed down with coffee and milk, would probably reach the spot. 'I'll try anything once,' said the prince or words to that effect and went to Mitchell's. There he downed five buckwheat cakes and four sausages and was enthralled by Florence, the colored queen of Montmartre, who sings jazz as they used to sing it down in Alabama before the war. It was the first time anything like that had ever happened to a prince of Wales. He liked the sausages, he liked the cakes, and he liked Florence. And every morning thereafter during his stay in Paris, about five a.m., he would be seen at Mitchell's."[54]

Bertelli's comment that this was "the first time that anything like that had happened" is not elucidated. Does "that" refer to making Mitchell's acquaintance, the wheat cakes and sausages, or the "surprising" circumstances? And he adds in amazement, "Mitchell's with an American colored proprietor, waiters and entertainer and orchestra, is now the very swagger breakfast place of Paris."[55] It is not certain that the staff was entirely Black, but the assertion betrays Bertelli's view of the establishment as a uniquely Black phenomenon and his astonishment at such an aberrant state of affairs. His article concludes with barbed criticism disguised as humor: "All fashionable Paris that can get in may be seen there in the wee hours and what those buckwheat cakes have done to carefully pampered digestions is a thing to be imagined, not described."[56] In reality, the situation was not unusual. Mitchell's and Kiley's affected an unceremonious style, offered greater social diversity than the segregated society *dancings*, and both were to the prince's taste. Even Bertelli was dimly aware of the import of his choice. The Prince of Wales' adoption of Mitchell's was certainly the most revolutionary of the "amazing transformations" that he fostered in Montmartre nightlife.

That the prince's desertion marked the beginning of the Embassy's collapse is seen most clearly in a rapid resumé of the adversarial relation between Maurice and jazz, as embodied by Florence and Palmer Jones. Mark Miller states laconically that "after a year at the So-Different, they returned to the Sans Souci, which in the interim had become the Jardin de ma Soeur, . . . their base until 1925."[57] This is essentially true (for the band, if not Florence), but it does a disservice to the obscure nature of a period lacking a detailed narrative.

A jazz band presided at the Jardin's opening, but it was not the International Five.[58] Maurice was also missing. In July 1922 he had suffered a lung hemorrhage at Deauville, where he, Leonora, Jenny Dolly, Clifton Webb, and other soldiers of the dance wars had gathered to compete. He was not expected to live. The prognostic was premature, but it prompted Oscar to declare, "The doctors have ordered my brother to the mountains . . . after that all depends on his constitution."[59] In Maurice's absence Oscar had engaged the International Five, but the fundamental opposition between musical styles and social modes was not resolved. When Maurice and Leonora returned in April, they found that the barbarians were not just at the gates, they had entered the city! From that moment on, a game of hide-and-seek began between the bandleader and the dancer. Similar to Maurice's 1921 stint at the Hotel Grande Bretagne (where an American jazz band played for dancing, while the couple were accompanied by an imported Rumanian ensemble), Palmer's group only performed in the intervals and at thés dansants.

As the season drew to a close in June, Maurice and Oscar imagined a humiliating exercise, framed as a benefit for the widow and baby of deceased International Five banjoist Usher Watts. Perhaps inspired by a Dolly Sisters sketch, the evening's theme reenacted a persistent Montmartre folklore: a "Plantation Night," presented by Maurice and Leonora, two figures as distinct as possible from the image of "happy days" on the old plantation—unless they saw themselves as benevolent slave owners! The benefit, which involved the embarrassing sale of a "doll baby," netted 6,817 francs, including 1,000 from the Mouvets, but the price was submission to a demeaning charade.[60] On this racist note, Maurice and Leonora initiated their farewell appearances.

With the couple gone, in November the International Five returned for the much-touted conversion to the Embassy Club. The key moment of the festivities was a reconciliation between Elsa and Oscar, the latter gallantly "presenting Miss Elsa Maxwell with a bouquet of roses to bury the hatchet."[61] This "touching" reunion explains her presence at the Embassy gala, an event from which Palmer's band was conspicuously absent. However, the Prince of Wales' Holy Week escapades were a game changer. When the band reappeared at the Jardin in May 1924, it was haloed by royal patronage. Hard on the heels of Edward's visit, the king of Rumania had also stopped in at Mitchell's for griddle cakes and bacon, and a month later the band was convoked by the king and queen of Spain.[62] Oscar characterized this trip as a "Command Performance of Oscar Mouvet and the International Five."[63] But the band had already played before the sovereigns during the summer of 1922, so it is an open question as to whose coattails were being ridden.

A seismic shift in the Montmartre landscape occurred in the fall of 1924. All secondary sources assert that Mitchell renamed his club Chez Florence in her honor. This narrative is exploded by an ad dated November 18 announcing that "from now on the house of 36 rue Pigalle formerly known as Mitchell's will be known as Chez Florence."[64] In fact, the Joneses had taken over the club, and Mitchell moved on to 61 rue Blanche. We can only speculate as to the reasons for the rupture. The genial drummer may be credited with the pancakes, but what had really captivated the P.O.W. was Florence's singing and Palmer's jazz. He was so taken that on Holy Wednesday the couple was invited to entertain at an intimate dinner in his honor given by his friends the Munns.[65] Did this excess of royal sponsorship create tension between Mitchell and the couple? If so, it only prompted a temporary divorce.

More significantly, it showed that the balance of power had shifted from the rue Caumartin to the rue Pigalle. Though Palmer returned to the Jardin in November with a revamped band, he continued to perform at Chez Florence, as he had at Mitchell's. One reporter wrote of the earlier period, "2: 40—Mitchell's. . . . Small, but intimate and most amusing crowd. . . . Griddle cakes, sausage, corned beef hash with poached egg, champagne. Negro jazz players from Jardin de ma Soeur."[66] The hours of the Jardin and Chez Florence were compatible, allowing Palmer to manage this frenetic dual activity. But the fluidity tends to conceal the essential fact that his continuing presence in the rue Caumartin was only a vain attempt by Oscar to recuperate the excitement of the new Black clubs.

An unrelated episode would contribute to the Jardin's decline: Leonora's passion for a young Argentinean, Carlos Ortiz Basualdo, scion of one of those "beautiful and rich families so linked to the society life of Paris that their disappearance would greatly diminish its brilliance."[67] They met at the Embassy Club, probably the night of the gala—as a leading light of "the Spanish-American element," his attendance was de rigueur.[68] Whatever the case, by July the romance was in full flower at Deauville. After that the relation skittered between rumors and denials. On October 1, Maurice and Leonora set sail for America to honor a contract. Owing to family pressure and probably proverbial cold feet, Carlos denied their engagement but he was soon on a ship to New York, and the ensuing February he and Leonora were married at Saint Patrick's Cathedral.[69] A weeping Maurice swore that he loved her "as a sister, she meant everything to him, and he would never dance again."[70] Yet in May he was back at the Jardin partnering with actress Barbara Bennett.

The collaboration was doomed. They quarreled over money and, supreme indignity, it was rumored she was being courted by Carlos' polo-playing younger brother, Luis.[71] Eventually she decamped, but a few banal words in the final ads for their engagement are an indication of Maurice's more profound defeat: "*accompanied by the International Five*" [my italics]![72] Scornfully, he had asserted that "as long as the public continues to demand the Argentine-African dances" he would supply them, yet he had contrived to avoid any direct association with jazz. February 1925 had seen the band respond to a "royal command" to appear before the king of Italy, emanating from the eccentric American Princess Jane di San Faustino.[73] Did the accrued weight of royal favor cause Maurice to yield? Whatever the explanation, he was obliged to "eat crow" and accept the collaboration of the International Five!

His aborted partnership with Miss Bennett marked his final appearance at Le Jardin. After Oscar's June wedding to an English dancer, Maurice regained New York and recruited a new partner, Eleanora Ambrose, whom he soon married. It was also Palmer's final season in the rue Caumartin. He and Florence used the summer hiatus to launch an outpost in Biarritz. Oscar had not waited for the advent of Le Jardin to engage the International Five. In August 1922 they had played for the Dollys at the Biarritz Acacias.[74] Now, in 1925, Palmer and his wife were performing at their own club, in an area of the Basque resort ironically known as La Négresse, so-called by Napoleonic soldiers after the Black servant of a local inn. In a "rustic" cabin, men in tuxedos and ladies in Chanel gathered to hear Florence "evoke in her songs the distant native land or decant a nostalgic blues."[75] Proudly casting off the yoke of the declining Jardin, she paid a delicate tribute to her anonymous nineteenth-century sister.

The couple returned to Paris with a bang, relocating to the rue Blanche.[76] Ten days later, the Embassy's fall season began. The two clubs were manifestly in competition. In a deprecating diatribe aimed at Chez Florence, Woon declared that "former American social haunts in Montmartre bitterly complain of the so-called 'color fraternizing,' saying society's new fad is ruining their business."[77] While racist, his observation was correct. Le Jardin had become increasingly irrelevant, "a family resort compared with some of the other places. The real rounders . . . pass on to other places in search of keener thrills."[78] Even Oscar seems to have admitted defeat. After the Prince of Wales' defection, his attention shifted to the north. In September 1924 he took the reins of the Abbaye de Thélème.[79] "Smart, yet not too formal" was his motto for the new Abbaye, a "lively place [where] persons that have been quiet and well behaved at the fashionable Jardin arrive humming and shimmying... with the expression 'Now for fun' written on their faces."[80]

Some trivial celebrity gossip is revelatory of the Embassy's dimmed allure during its final crepuscular nights. Bertelli relates that silent film star Bessie

Love and Deering Davis, "the most popular Charleston dancer in Paris," were glimpsed at My Sister's Garden, where "he declined the offer of Elsa Maxwell, who runs the club, to become her star Charleston performer. Bessie, accompanied by Deering, is the first amateur able to show visitors at the Florida Club, Mitchell's Dance Hall, etc., the really graceful Charleston."[81] This anodyne text reveals two noteworthy facts. Firstly, it confirms Elsa's ongoing commitment to the Jardin. Secondly, it suggests that lacking the talents of the International Five, the club sought an infusion of Black choreography to preserve its former luster.

One ploy was to bring in the latest rage for its winter opening: the *Revue nègre*'s Charleston Jazz Band (even Josephine Baker made a brief appearance), completed by pianist Leon Crutcher and the Palm Beach Six, who functioned as a substitute for the International Five.[82] Profiting from their notoriety, the Charleston troupe was seen everywhere, including the Abbaye de Thélème, where Oscar was investing most of the energy of Crutcher's band.[83] Notwithstanding the presence of Coco Chanel, the Polignacs, and the Cole Porters, the inaugural evening heralded the final agony.[84] The roots of the dynamic dance lay outside the pale confines of the rue Caumartin, with Josephine, Bricktop, and the ebullient Frisco.[85]

On New Year's Eve the wannabe *charlestoniers* were still desperately dancing—to a callow student band from the University of Michigan—but the small type in an ad for the evening conveyed a less festive message: "Closing following provisionally during change of policy [*sic*]."[86] The club never reopened. A comic eulogy was pronounced by the humorist Chéron. Responding to the announcement of a *fête de nuit* at which guests were to dress as flowers or vegetables, Chéron offered a play on words: "The *fête* that you've publicized . . . will never take place for the good reason that the Jardin de ma Soeur is presently out of the running ('dans les choux')."[87] The most celebrated of the society *dancings* had come to an end, not with a bang but a droll whimper.

Rapidly the fabled cabaret passed into nostalgic memory. "The glories of the Jardin de ma Soeur have ended," Woon opined, "and the place is closed. And Oscar dreams of retiring."[88] In February of 1926 Oscar *did* abandon the management of the Abbaye for health reasons.[89] But before their closing bows the brothers attempted to recapture the old magic. Taking a lease on the Acacias, they opened "Maurice and Eleanora's Club."[90] Sadly, the tubercular Maurice was racing against the clock. Since his lung hemorrhage in 1922, Maurice had been performing "a sort of dance micawbre [*sic*]. Frequently during that period, he would slump into his ringside chair after an exhibition dance to be caught by a paroxysm of coughing that would stain his handkerchief pink. His raven black hair accentuated waxen pale features. But he continued to dance and smoke innumerable cigarettes."[91] Within a year of launching his last club he would lie dead in a clinic in Lausanne.

Seen in hindsight, the folding of My Sister's Garden and Maurice's demise foreshadowed the waning of the rue Caumartin. As Woon noted, the celebrated Jardin had been "transformed into a billiard hall," even if, following Nevill's prediction, the walls of number 17 would "re-echo to the sound of jazz."[92] Rejecting its prosaic fate as a pool parlor, the pretentiously labeled Palais du Billard was resuscitated as "The Blue Room."[93] Trading on the faded glamour of the name, the owners billed it as "ex–Jardin de ma Soeur."[94] Maurice had been dead a little over five months when, like a ghost haunting the scene of its earlier triumphs, Leonora returned from her gilded exile for the opening—a radiant apparition but a specter all the same.[95] The rue Caumartin had become a simulacrum of its former splendor; the junction of the rue Pigalle and the rue Fontaine was now the nerve center of Montmartre.

Not content with his relentless week of gaiety, prior to an early morning pilgrimage on Good Friday to reaffirm his allegiance to "the colored queen of Montmartre," the P.O.W. attended a supper hosted by the Polignacs at the chic Chez Henri. Mythic designer Coco Chanel was a member of the party. If we are to believe *Vogue* editor Diana Vreeland, that night the indefatigable prince was smitten by the alluring couturier and managed to fit in what Vreeland described as "a great romantic moment together."[96] The fact that she was just beginning a long relationship with Edward's close friend the Duke of Westminster did not appear to trouble the free-spirited Coco. Nor did it seem to bother the prince.

Misbehaving royals were no novelty in Montmartre. A capable ruler, the Maharajah of Kapurthala was perhaps the sagest of the regal revelers. Yet even he was not immune to certain follies—his chief flaw a reputation as "an Eastern Don Juan" fond of dancing with European women at Le Perroquet to the syncopations of Mitchell's Jazz Kings.[97] More seriously compromised were the Shah of Persia and Don Luis-Ferdinand. A headline neatly summed up the latter's situation: "Too Outrageous to Be Allowed to Live Even in Gay Paris." Five months after the gala, the wayward prince was stripped of his titles by King Alfonso XIII and expelled from France for scandalous behavior. "Where did Alfonso get so much virtue?" riposted Don Luis apropos of his royal cousin—the latter being no stranger to the dance floors of Montmartre, Deauville, and Biarritz, where he had created the "Barcelona Glide" and instituted the diamond-studded "Order of Girls Who Have Danced with Me."⁹⁸ Like the king, the hypocritical clientele of the society *dancings* was willing to overlook Don Luis' cocaine habit—he was not alone—as well as his homosexuality, as long as it remained discreet, but his highly publicized excursions to the sleaziest haunts of Paris strained even their tolerance and led to exile in Lisbon.⁹⁹

If Don Luis had no throne to lose, the same was not true of the Prince of Persia. After an accession at age nine, and a fragile regency, the young potentate had been evicted from power by Reza Khan, founder of the Pahlavi dynasty. The remainder of his spectral reign was passed in the *dancings* of Montmartre and the watering holes of the rich, where he was known as the author of the "Harem Hug," a fast shimmy that he originated with Jenny Dolly at the Biarritz Acacias to the rhythms of the International Five and made into the craze of the 1922 season.¹⁰⁰ One paper quoted Jenny to the effect that the corpulent ruler was "plump but makes up in energy what he lacks in grace" or (in sister Rosie's embryonic but more candid critique), "He danced not so—how shall I say it, not so—never mind!"¹⁰¹

Five days before the Embassy gala, the press announced that if the news of Reza Khan's flight were confirmed, the Shah would be returning post haste to his kingdom.¹⁰² The bulletin was precipitous; yet the *Houston Post* was already asking, "While this young Eastern potentate enjoys the pleasurable life of the Riviera and Paris and invents new dance steps with pretty Americans, is revolution indeed seething in his kingdom and will the actual overthrow of his reign result if he does not soon pack his dancing pumps and go back home?" Along with noting their shared admiration for the Dolly Sisters, the *Post* drew other parallels between the Shah and the P.O.W.: "Both of them love dancing, both are extremely democratic, and both have shown a tendency to fight shy of the job of ruling."¹⁰³ If so, their wishes were granted. The Shah definitively lost his throne in 1925, and in 1937 Edward VIII was obliged to abdicate in order to marry the sulfurous American divorcée Wallis Simpson.

During his Holy Week marathon, the Prince *did* honor two semiofficial engagements, one of them Lady Cunard's Friday luncheon at the Ritz.¹⁰⁴ Despite the presence of Vera Bate and a few friends, it more closely resembled one of the tedious obligations he was always fleeing, such as his Wednesday lunch with British ambassador, Lord Crewe. The latter found him looking "well and apparently quite recovered from his fall."¹⁰⁵ The prince was putting a good face on things, but looks were deceptive. On the eve of his departure, he sat down in a remorseful mood and penned a self-pitying letter to his married mistress—an epistle that reads like a judgement on the circumscribed little world of the society *dancings*. Headed "Good Friday," it began, "I'm off to Le Touquet tonight." Then, reverting to the third person, Edward wrote, "He's got pretty rotten on this trip . . . God, what a bloody life this is & it's a great pity I was not killed in the Army." He signed it, "Your very sad little David."[106]

Shallow, neurotic, and self-indulgent, Edward filled the emptiness of his life with frivolous interests and a dissolute lifestyle. No fool, on occasion Woon was capable of insightful analysis. Two and a half years after the legendary Embassy gala he met the prince again at Louigi's, a popular American hangout off the rue Caumartin. Obviously flattered that the prince remembered him, Woon's habitual passive-aggressive stance elicited a viperish commentary: "The English don't like his private life and they don't like his passion for American jazz and American cocktails, and they don't like paying his losses at baccarat. Their attitude is that they're paying him a huge salary to learn to be a king, and they think he should be a little more serious about it."[107] Ironically, the democratic openness denounced by Woon was the very trait that assured the prince's popularity.

The prince's defection to Pigalle was less likely to have been motivated by ideological considerations than by an insatiable thirst for novelty. Exhausted, but thrilled by his gala's "success," Maurice whispers hoarsely to Woon, "This is the best bunch we've ever gotten together."[108] "Society with a big S" had turned out; however it is a hollow victory. In 1923 prominent members of "the bunch" (Fanny Ward, the Marquise de Polignac, and Elsa herself) had already prefigured the prince's infidelity (albeit with less éclat), unable to resist the lure of Mitchell's Grand Duc and its charismatic star, Florence Jones.[109] The P.O.W. did not initiate the shift of hegemony from the rue Caumartin to the rue Pigalle, but his actions during Holy Week acted as a catalyst and contained an implicit political statement—an endorsement of the multicultural joys of Mitchell's over the pallid social rituals of the Embassy Club. Henceforth the "Colored Gentleman's" ragtime capers, now decisively a jazz step, would hold sway in the nocturnal kingdoms of Pigalle.

PART II

ON THE RUE FONTAINE
Conflict and Collaboration

CHAPTER FIVE

"SMOKE UPON THE WATERS"

An Elegy for the Tempo Club

The Tempo Club was a private *cercle*. Not that it was selective about the quality of the members who sought admission, but because the doors at 16 bis rue Fontaine were discreet and well-guarded.
—*Le Figaro*

It is an early morning in the spring of 1925, a year after the Embassy gala. Imagine that we are standing with Louis Aragon at the junction of the rue Fontaine and the rue Pigalle, "one of the principal crossroads of the intrigues and enigmas of night-time roaming."[1] He will come to be recognized as a major figure of twentieth-century literature; at present he is only a young writer of twenty-seven who describes himself as "a pillar of the *dancings*."[2] Ahead of him the rue Fontaine stretches out, a glittering tunnel of neon culminating in the illuminated red windmill sails of the Moulin-Rouge. Before his bemused eyes, taxis and chauffeured Rolls discharge a stream of stylish merrymakers garbed in furs and white tie, a scene as elegant as any at the society *dancings*. Yet, he is aware that behind this festive image lies a sordid marketplace, with its complement of cocaine addicts, procurers, and whores.

Setting off, he purchases cigarettes at the Tabac on the left, then crosses to the opposite side of the street and arrives under the glittering marquee of Zelli's Royal Box, one of his favorite haunts (see gallery 1). A doorman in Persian dress attempts to lure him up a narrow, dim-lit staircase, whose gaudy neon announces "Omar Khayyâm, Persian *Dancing*"—another improbable expression of the polyglot exoticism of Montmartre.[3] Paying no heed to the importunate doorman, he hesitates a moment before entering Zelli's. But before we follow him in, let us turn the clock back to the spring of 1921, a pivotal moment in the history of Montmartre, the birth of what Séité calls a veritable musical and literary myth.[4] At that time there was no illuminated sign, no doorman in a long Persian coat. An anonymous stairway led to the obscurely famous Tempo Club. It would be several years before Black-owned and -managed clubs came to dominate the nightlife of the quarter, but the "ink blot" that Aragon imagined spreading across the quarter had already begun its inexorable diffusion in this low-ceilinged mezzanine, hidden above Zelli's brilliant marquee like a utopian island isolated from a debased reality.

Surprisingly, little has been written about this seminal establishment, initiated by Black banjoist Joe Boyd in collaboration with Mazie Mullins, wife of Jazz King Frank Withers—some diffuse but musically perceptive comments by Séité, and two useful but scant pages by Mark Miller.[5] Unofficial headquarters of the Southern Syncopated Orchestra—the remarkable group of which Mazie and Frank were former members—it served as a haven for Black American musicians. In this sanctum sanctorum, they were able to practice their art, free of the demands of the vulgar and often-indiscriminate public of the *dancings*. A syncopated heart, beating covertly among the frantic cabarets, the new club was the epicenter of a ferment that would nurture the major jazz artists of Montmartre.

One might imagine that the appellation Tempo Club evoked the members' rhythmic skills. In fact, it referred to a defunct New York organization created by James Reese Europe as an alternative to the Clef Club. However, the name was not mere nostalgia. Aspiring to serve as head of a comparable placement service in Paris, Boyd adopted the quaint title "general manager jazz banders."[6] The other face of his activity (and ultimately the cause of his ruin) was only visible in "the back room," where his booking agency housed an "unexpected branch office. While awaiting engagements the idle jazz musicians occupied themselves with poker, craps, blackjack, and other games."[7]

These comments are posterior to the Tempo Club's sudden demise in April 1922; gambling was certainly apparent in 1921, but the character of the club was quite different. Recognized as a Black refuge, it was not restricted to Black patrons. The young Frenchman Léo Vauchant was introduced into its hermetic precincts by Louis Mitchell, according to him the club's creator.[8] It is true that Mitchell had been active in the New York Tempo Club and, given his passion for gambling, would certainly have enjoyed the ancillary activities of its Parisian namesake, but nothing suggests that he founded the Paris edition. Vauchant penned his reminiscences years after abandoning Montmartre for the sound stages of Hollywood, and his memories are at times inaccurate. Nevertheless, Mitchell had pioneered the introduction of jazz and ragtime to Paris and, boosted by his success at the Casino, was on his way to becoming what one of Fitzgerald's fictive mouthpieces carelessly calls "the most important nigger in Montmartre."[9] If not the club's literal progenitor, he might be considered its spiritual father. He was associated with its leading figures—Frank, of course, but also Mazie. As affirmed by Robert Goffin, she had been signed for the Casino orchestra that Mitchell was supposed to have brought back to Paris in 1919.[10]

If Mitchell had chosen Mazie and Frank for his aborted band, it was because they ranked among the leading Black artists of New York. Born in Denver circa 1889, Mazie met Frank in "the Mile-High City" when she was still a young woman and he eight years her senior. Charming, pretty, extremely talented, she received her first trumpet as a gift from Frank. For a year they frequented Chicago's musical scene, before moving to New York in 1912. While he was noted for his tone on the trombone, "curiously like a voice, and more sensitive and full of a hundred subtle shades of color and inflection than anyone could dream the instrument to be capable," she was considered one of the most versatile instrumentalists in the city, easily mastering the saxophone, piano, and trombone.[11] Apparently Mazie possessed a timid nature; surrealist writer and poet Philippe Soupault avers that "before blowing into one of the strangest instruments ever invented [the slide trombone], she felt the need to smile. Doubtless to pluck up her courage."[12] But as one critic enthused, "her tone, ringing and triumphant in heroic phrases, nevertheless is tender and velvety in the purely melodic."[13]

In September 1919 Frank took a leave from the Jazz Kings and left for London, accompanied by Mazie. In December they integrated the Southern Syncopated Orchestra, an organization central to the introduction of jazz to Europe, led by Will Marion Cook and managed by George William Lattimore. Sometime after April 1920, Frank rejoined the Jazz Kings for their Brussels residency, and when the band returned to Paris in March 1921, he and Mazie came with them. Frank began his long tenure at the Perroquet, and she commenced her brief association with the Tempo Club. Conveniently, their apartment at 41 rue Pigalle was around the corner from the rue Fontaine and close to the Casino de Paris. Mitchell and Bricktop would open the first Music Box at this address in 1926, but Mazie did not live to see it. On October 14, 1921, she expired at the American Hospital in Neuilly.[14] She had spent only six months as codirector of the Tempo Club, but it was enough to mark indelibly Philippe Soupault and the memory of Montmartre.

One day a teenaged Léo Vauchant found Mazie seated at the piano, Frank with his trombone at her side, another trombone at her feet. Vauchant reckons it was around 1920. His dating may be faulty, but his memories are vivid. He states that Frank shouted out, "'Hey, we're going to play.' So he gave me the notes and I played. . . . In that club there would be a lot of sitting in. . . . It was the first time I heard jamming going on. We just sat there and played the tunes that we knew. . . . We didn't play the Dixieland tunes—more sort of ballads and the tunes that were in vogue at the time, but we improvised on them"—a practice crucial to the evolution of early jazz. Vauchant was eager and quick to learn. Though young and of a different color, he shared with the couple an authentic passion for the music. Of Frank he wrote, "He was old enough to have been my father and I was like a son to him."[15] Short, slender, and balding, Frank indeed had the look of someone's ancestor. Vauchant dates their relations from 1918 and the showcase of Mitchell's "Midnight Frolic Jazz Band" at the Marigny Theater; however, at that time the Jazz Kings had not yet arrived in France. Nevertheless, the artistic influence is unquestionable—the young Frenchman openly modeled his style on that of Withers.

That is the way it was at the Tempo Club. It was therefore inevitable that the Southern Syncopated Orchestra (which included many of Montmartre's future talents) would gravitate to 16 bis rue Fontaine. Offshoots of the group visited in May 1921 and February 1922. A rift between Cook and Lattimore over ownership had caused the orchestra to fragment, some like Frank and Mazie staying with Cook; Buddie Gilmore and others joining the dissident Synco-Synco Orchestra. Nevertheless, both Parisian engagements were led by composer Harry Wellmon, known as General Wellmon because his colorful regalia resembled that of a Brazilian commander in chief.[16]

However, this quintessentially "Negro" orchestra was not made up exclusively of Black performers. Montboron, a French reviewer, noted that "the ranks of the former Southern Syncopated Orchestra have definitely become a bit lighter, both in number and even in the color of its executants . . . there are all the varieties of black, from a mat ebony to a deep and brilliant mahogany with here and there the lighter shade of a mulatto, a creole or a full-blooded white."[17] The antithesis of the American "one drop rule," this description reflects the French penchant for minute gradations of racial categories, but the only discernible "full-blooded white" was Wellmon's partner, British vocalist and songwriter Dick Carlish. Indeed, the latter claims to have been the lone white person in the company and to have hidden his pallor "under a liberal smear of black cork," even though the blackface is not evident in a photo published by Montboron.[18] He poses in the image with Wellmon, Buddie Gilmore (whose banter with the "General" was a highlight of the show), and the drummer's wife Martha (Mattie), known as "Lady Gilmore."

This was in February of 1922, at the time of the encounters with the bandleader narrated in Soupault's 1927 novel, *Le Nègre*. The first chapter begins with an evocation of those polar nights:

> Darkness and a certain impatience crueler than anger, or perhaps the cold, or simply the rain, drove me often during the winter of 192[2] . . . to the threshold of a house painted cream yellow, situated on the rue Fontaine. . . . When I pressed the little door of the entresol, I had the impression of penetrating with measured step onto another continent. . . . [Having doffed his white gloves and blue jacket trimmed with gold epaulettes], my friend Wellmon . . . was seated at the piano and the moment I arrived, in sign of welcome he greeted me with a smile and began to play *Saint Louis* [*Blues*], that strange yet familiar melody that I liked so much. The Tempo Club was the meeting place of all the Black musicians of Paris. They drank whisky, grenadine, and a thick green liqueur whose name I have forgotten; they played at dice and occasionally, without anyone paying the slightest attention, someone opened the piano and for hours on end one of my Black friends would lose himself in its vertigo.[19]

Just about any musician of color active in Montmartre at that time could be found at the Tempo Club. The presence of some is certain, for others we can only speak of probabilities. Though he is not cited in any text, Gene Bullard could not have ignored the activity taking place on the mezzanine above his head. Also represented were members of the major bands: noblesse oblige, Frank Withers and the Jazz Kings, also Florence and Palmer Jones and the International Five, Bobby Jones of the future Crackerjacks, and finally Opal Cooper and Sammy Richardson of the Red Devils who, in the spring of 1921, had just returned from London to perform at Chez Harry Pilcer.

Nevertheless, as I have noted, the Tempo Club was not limited to Black entertainers. Vauchant, Carlish, and perhaps a few "full-blooded" members of the SSO were the only white musicians to gain entry, but the premises were also frequented by adherents of the circle surrounding Dada and Surrealist theoretician André Breton. Zelli's and its hidden satellite were directly on their path when, after a reunion, they exited Breton's studio at 42 rue Fontaine. In the words of writer Jacques Baron, "At the bottom of the rue Fontaine, paved with good and bad surrealist intentions, in the crude chiaroscuro of the pleasure quarter, Zelli's glittered with all the glamour of a fashionable cabaret."[20]

These Dadaists—later Surrealists—who visited the Tempo Club included artists Marcel Duchamp and Man Ray, probably Aragon, and of course Philippe Soupault.[21] As *Figaro* avers, the doors were discreet and well guarded, so it is unclear how Soupault found his way to the unobtrusive retreat, but his memoirs suggest that it was thanks to the Jamaican musician who inspired the iconoclastic hero of *Le Nègre*.[22] In turn, Soupault may have initiated Aragon. If so, having tasted the genuine pleasures of the Tempo Club, one can understand why they may have found the papier-mâché exoticism of Omar Khayyâm Persian *Dancing* prodigiously inauthentic. Others, like Marcel Duchamp, may not have needed Soupault's intercession, and the painter undoubtedly sponsored Man Ray. They had been close friends during the former's 1915 New York sojourn, and upon the photographer's relocation to Paris in July 1921, Duchamp took him under his wing and introduced him to the Dadaists. Soupault promptly offered him a show at his bookstore/gallery near the Invalides. Most of the pieces were brought from New York, but Man Ray added three new works, one a painting titled after the mythical club.[23]

That fall, Duchamp steered another American to the cloistered rendezvous, modernist painter Charles Demuth. In fact, all three artists knew each other well. In New York they had frequented the salon of steel heir and art patron Walter Arensberg. Demuth's hitherto unnoticed visit is divulged in a letter to Eugene O'Neill dated September 17, 1921, where he recounts a nocturnal rendezvous: "Marcel is here and he sent word to me one night before I had seen him to meet him at an address in Montmartre. So I went, he said one o'clock. I got to the place and knocked on the door expecting to enter his apartment, but the door opened only to allow a rolling eye to be seen,—then it opened wide enough to let me in, and I was back on 53rd street in my favorite café, Marshall's. It has moved over complete,—Florence, all. The only thing that is missing is the 6th Ave. El., and the only thing added is a room in which they play 'craps.' . . . It looks just like a nigger parlor. I have never on any stage—not even on David's—seen such complete realism. . . ."[24] I think Florence has her eye on Marcel or whatever,—so things are cheap for us and they don't make us drink champagne."[25]

Demuth does not identify the club and misunderstands its character, taking it to be a trendy *dancing* like Poiret's Oasis, which is perhaps why editor Bruce Kellner believed it to be the Grand Duc. However, that is unlikely. In 1921 the newly opened cabaret was not yet a "chic Black nightclub frequented by American celebrities and tourists."[26] Nor is the artist likely to have mistaken it for a private residence: The Grand Duc was a storefront, with the name in bold letters above the windows.[27] However, the crucial detail is the "room in which they play 'craps'"; 52 rue Pigalle did not possess a back room. Everything suggests that Demuth discovered Florence at the Tempo Club, at the time the only cabaret other than Zelli's patronized by Dadaists.

Thus, although a notice for Florence and Palmer's October appearances at the Sans Souci announces their arrival from Britain, they were already in Paris in late September.[28] This was to be expected. Palmer had performed with Mitchell's Southern Symphony Quartet between 1912 and 1914, and Mazie had played at many of the same New York venues as Florence. Fresh off the boat, the couple would naturally have headed for this inescapable rendezvous, seedbed of the "Great Black Way"—Woon's contemptuous name for the nexus of minority-owned or -managed clubs springing up around the rue Pigalle and the rue Fontaine. "Manager of jazz banders" Joe Boyd may even have negotiated the couple's contract at the Sans Souci, or Florence's presence at Elsa's ball. Nor is it odd that Demuth found in the Tempo Club a reminiscence of the café at Marshall's, a renowned New York hostelry on West 53rd Street. It was a center for Black social, intellectual, and artistic life and a focal point of interracial contacts. Doubtless, Demuth recognized the multicultural ambiance that had made Marshall's a target of the anti-vice Committee of Fourteen, which equated race-mixing with immorality.[29]

Lodged in a palm court, the dining room at Marshall's featured string music, but its chief attraction was the basement bar. In the summer of 1915 Demuth allegedly introduced Marcel Duchamp to the racier aspects of New York nightlife, among them the cellar café, an occasion thought to be depicted in a flowing watercolor titled *At Marshall's*, which shows Duchamp seated in the center.[30] Demuth is also credited with three intensely felt watercolors of a jazz band and singer that art scholars identify as Florence performing at the hotel.[31] However, despite this doxa, and Demuth's recollections, Duchamp never visited Marshall's and Florence never sang there! The hotel was closed in September 1913, victim of an administrative order.[32] The source of the error may lie in the fact that the premises were resurrected a year later as the Dunbar Hotel, an enterprise that continued Marshall's musical tradition.[33] It was there that Florence actually appeared, that Duchamp presumably met the singer, and Demuth painted his watercolors.[34] Years had passed and Demuth was perhaps amalgamating the two hotels in his mind. In any case, for him, as for many, the iconic underground bar, under any name, would always incarnate the essence of the animated New York musical scene of the teens.

Demuth was not a Dadaist, but he shared their mistrust of the outmoded values of Western bourgeois culture and their interest in the transgressive new music. At war with European cultural norms, the Dadaists perceived jazz as a liberation: "I developed the taste for jazz," Michel Leiris proclaimed, "as if it were something that came from elsewhere and appeared like a slap in the face to European art and music."³⁵ The appeal was also technical. Although it is hazardous to make parallels between materially different arts, for these writers the free flow of improvised jazz rhythms was apparently analogous to their experiments in "automatic writing." Unfortunately, their admiration was often based on stereotypical evaluations, as Leiris later recognized: "I reproduced, in a positive sense, the naïve stereotypes of blacks that were common currency ('sensual,' 'illogical,' etc.)."³⁶

But Soupault's empathy went beyond formal considerations and erroneous labels. He perceived an artistic ideal, incarnated by the vision of Mazie Mullins dancing. In his narration of this experience, the setting is late one night in a deserted Tempo Club. Tired of restless roaming, the author arrived before his friends had finished their gigs in the Montmartre *dancings*. A single light bulb provided feeble illumination. Lighting a cigarette, he seated himself in a shadowy recess. "Mily" (the name Soupault gives to Mazie) entered and launched into a dance: "She began to turn, then fling her legs into the air and wave her arms about. Her dance was not at all savage; it was natural and spontaneous." Despite her sophistication, Mazie retained some of the artlessness of the vivacious young woman Frank had met in Colorado. "She danced as some sing or others whistle," a synthesis of body and soul in which, freed of the obligation to please, she expressed the truth of her inner self, "drawing upon mysterious inner powers of creativity."³⁷ "I realized," Soupault writes, "that Mily was in the habit of dancing for her own pleasure." Later, she danced again, but "she was not the same." Before her peers, she no longer danced for herself but for the admiration and approval of an audience.³⁸

For the white male viewer, the apparition of the exotic other inevitably contains an element of eroticism, but for Soupault this dimension is secondary. Foremost is the candor of Mily's dance, a metaphor for a utopian purity and integrity, be it in the domain of music, choreography, painting, or literature. Writing in 1927, he evoked the ideal of which he had been the awed eyewitness: "I remembered the strange woman who danced with all her strength, not before a mirror or in search of praise, but before the mystery of her joy."³⁹

At the time of her malaise, Mazie was jamming with drummer Arthur (Dooley) Wilson and two ex-colleagues from the Southern Syncopated Orchestra, trumpeter Bobby Jones and pianist Joseph Hall. Shortly after, she died at the American Hospital.⁴⁰ Soupault states his belief that her demise was "due to alcoholism"; however, based on Frank's letters, African American newspapers wrote of the cause as being complications from an appendectomy.⁴¹ One might hypothesize that Withers was seeking to protect her reputation; still, appendicitis is consistent with a sudden malaise, even if intoxication is more in accord with Soupault's tragic view of the "Negro." If Mazie's Parisian career was as fleeting as the Tempo Club's existence, it was nevertheless a brief effusion of gaiety and joy. Yet Soupault sounds a more somber note: "I cannot recall without a certain sadness a Black woman whom I knew in Paris long ago."[42]

After Mazie's death Boyd continued with a new associate, a Mr. Reed of Kentucky, but their partnership abruptly ended with a police raid in the early hours of April 30, 1922, a peripety far from the idealistic aura of Mazie's dance.[43] Dick Carlish describes a flamboyant confrontation that culminated with the arrival of the law. His autobiography presents a series of racy, somewhat novelized anecdotes, although there is much credible detail. Whether it be embroidered truth or fiction, Carlish's story vividly details the gritty atmosphere of the club in its last days. The text appears to conflate two narratives, the April 30th raid and a gunfight between French and Americans that supposedly occurred two weeks earlier:

> Above Joe Zelli's place was another club run by a character called Joe Boyd, who ran a gambling room as well. Blackjack was the favourite game at the time and it was during a blackjack session that I saw the Apaches in action for the first time.[44]
> ... I knew that the Apaches were feuding with Joe Boyd, though I had no idea what the trouble was, as it was not wise to ask too many questions in the area about anything or anyone. Joe certainly was not very anxious to see them because the night they came into his gambling joint, he dived down the chute and landed up still in one piece in the kitchen. This upset the Apaches no end.... They lined us all up against the wall and began to rob us systematically.... I must say that they were very polite about it all, until they came to one reluctant customer who refused to part with her rings. One of the Apaches gave an exasperated grunt and gestured with his knife to hurry her up. Still she refused and suddenly the gangster realized that she was serious, that she had no intention of parting with her diamonds. Without another word, he dragged her to the gambling table; held her hand flat on its surface and hacked off the finger that held most of her rings.[45]

The *Herald* offered conflicting justifications for the raid. In May it claimed that the invasion resulted from an earlier French/American shootout—a scenario similar to Carlish's. In October the paper announced that the real cause was an incident involving stolen gems and an assault on Boyd's wife, a white Englishwoman purportedly beaten and stripped of her jewels by masked robbers, causing her demise and leaving Boyd alone with a small son, an episode reiterated by the *Journal* and *Comœdia*.[46] Understandably outraged by the vicious attack on his spouse, Boyd is alleged to have filed a complaint. In accordance with this storyline, an inquiry into the robbery was initiated and a sweep of the premises ordered. In his agitation Boyd had neglected to conceal all signs of gambling activity, thus triggering another raid.

Despite these dissonances, news reports concur on the second police incursion. Again we meet the fearless Captain Metten, last seen raiding Zelli's Club in the rue Caumartin, still saving the world, one night resort at a time. In this instance, the jovial Italian American was not the target, but the captain *was* very interested in Joe Boyd's extracurricular pursuits. The *Petit Parisien* recounts that "to surprise the gamblers in flagrante delicto Monsieur Metten, captain of the special gambling squad, and the thirty policemen who accompanied him on this expedition were required to mount a stairway where even a slightly overweight gentleman would have been unable to pass." Having gained entry, Metten focused on the dapper owner, but Boyd was no more eager to meet him than he had been to confront Carlish's Apaches. Few news articles neglect to mention his farcical attempt to escape by maneuvering his plump figure through a narrow window, only to find himself embraced by the heroic Captain Metten who, after an animated struggle, confiscated his gun (a Browning of course).[47] The club was padlocked, and Boyd was ultimately fined 500 francs.

What is striking in all these reports is the exclusive focus on gambling. The *Herald*'s condescension is particularly egregious in this respect. The article sarcastically proclaimed that the Tempo Club enjoyed "a wide reputation among devotees of African Golf, as the Paris temple of that exalted pastime, where the tuneful saxophone and traps, so conspicuously active in the front room, were only an accompaniment to the more subtle melodies of rattling 'bones' in the inner shrine."[48] Gambling had always been part of the club's DNA; however, the final months of its existence saw a marked change from the period when Soupault had spied on Mazie's dance, or even early 1922 when Wellmon greeted him with a poignant rendition of "Saint Louis Blues." The Synco-Synco Orchestra was gone, and the Tempo Club had acquired a French doorman (even if he did not sport showy Persian regalia as would the chasseur of Omar Khayyâm's) and a white clientele quite different from the likes of Vauchant, Soupault, and Demuth—the *Petit Parisien* evokes touts cajoling thrill-hungry tourists into enjoying the club's covert pleasures.[49]

Perhaps Boyd had been seduced by the lure of easy money. At his trial, he explained that playing the banjo earned him 175 francs per performance, while his percentage on gambling at the Tempo Club brought in a minimum of 300 francs a night.⁵⁰ All the French papers comment on this drift toward illegal but highly remunerative activities. However, a few, like the ill-informed Clément Vautel, seem more concerned with deploring the mores of the patrons than informing their readers. For Vautel, assuming the moralizing tone of the "defenders of public virtue," the brave Captain Metten's endeavors were insufficient. He accuses the police of laxity toward "known criminals." Adopting the opera *Manon* as a metaphor, he states that "the des Grieux of the *Tango-bar* [*sic*] need have no fear for their girlfriends or themselves, and to the sound of banjos playing tunes other than the airs of Massenet, they go their merry way with compete freedom."⁵¹

Yet, for all his virulence, Vautel's stance differs from that of the Americans. The *Herald* was particularly derogatory, portraying "a notorious dive . . . a motley gathering [of] professional gamblers, jail-birds, cocottes, jazz artistes and some innocent sightseers."⁵² The *Los Angeles Times* further darkened the picture, adding cocaine, morphine, and hypodermic needles in the stockings of French cocottes.⁵³ An evocation of the club's degenerate atmosphere in its latter days is not unwarranted, but American journals go beyond an image of Montmartre's free and easy mores. Their tone reveals an implicit racist bias. *The New York Times* details the alleged race of the club members, who included "colored musicians, dancers and demi-mondaines," as well as "several men and women badly wanted by the police."⁵⁴ In 1922 there were few American women of color in Montmartre, thus it is difficult to imagine who these "demimondaines" might be. Even Vautel evokes a local French variety: "the des Grieux of the *Tango-bar*" and "these Gabys of the place Blanche."⁵⁵

The New York Times adds that the police were "attracted by revolver shots during a dispute in which half the members held up the other half and took furs and jewels off the women." The article then evokes a Harlem stereotype, declaring that "the police also found a number of guns and razors which were thrown away by the habitués" (in a hyperbolic comparison, the *Herald* declared that the police "seized enough razors, revolvers and knives to stock a crime museum").⁵⁶ The entire thrust of the American reports is to suggest an equivalency between delinquency, "Negroes," and jazz such as that found in English news stories cited by Rose, which conflated "Negro haunts of crime . . . hot beds of evil" and "a member of a jazz band."⁵⁷

This bias becomes explicit in Hemingway's comment on "Zelli's, Kelly's [*sic*], now Shanley's, and several nigger joints."⁵⁸ The author of *The Sun Also Rises* had a regrettable fondness for the word "nigger." He is unlikely to have known the Tempo Club, but his reference to "nigger joints" seems to echo Demuth's "nigger parlor." Both are representative of the vocabulary of the era, but are they equivalent? Demuth's editor attributes his usage to "ignorance" rather than "crudity or malice," and one might note that "joint" is a low or shabby bar whereas "parlor," although sometimes used to describe night haunts, is a sitting room in a private house.[59] If Demuth's phrase "parlor" is intended in the same sense as "joint," it is nonetheless redeemed by a grain of irony. More eloquently, his sympathetic portraits of jazz performers, the denizens of gay bathhouses, and the habitués of Black cabarets demonstrate a deep empathy with marginalized groups.

Although there are ideological differences between French and American accounts, in both cases the emphasis on gambling is at the expense of the club's function as a retreat where Black performers were allowed to cultivate the utopian ideal incarnated in Mazie's dance. The *Petit Parisien* brushed off Boyd's claims at promoting the arts as a "fallacious pretext," even though two years earlier Jules Volterra, the respected owner of the Capitole, had appreciated Boyd's vocal talents and consented to testify as a character witness at his trial.[60] More broadly, these critiques ignore the Tempo Club's role as a source of inspiration not only for Black performers but for white musicians, writers, and visual artists.

This burlesque tragicomedy sounded the death knell of the club, if not of its owner. Given the gravity of his alleged crimes, and the extent of his nightly earnings, the fine was relatively light, and Boyd resumed his career, eventually performing with Tempo Club habitués Bobby Jones and Harry Wellmon and even appearing in 1927 as the "King of Negro Singers" at Louigi's, a club that in 1922 was still a bigoted enclave.[61] However, where the entresol at 16 bis rue Fontaine is concerned, sometime before June 1924 the site of so much creative energy became a Russian cabaret, the Samovar, replaced later in that year by a Russian restaurant, then, in April 1925, by the preposterous Omar Khayyâm's, and finally by another Russian club, which was gutted by fire in early 1927.[62] That the Tempo Club should come to an end was probably inevitable. It was an ephemeral Utopia, and like all Utopias doomed by its divorce from the real world but also by its inherent vices: gambling and violence, failings that scarred the lives of many Montmartre musicians.

In the concluding weeks of April 1922, two events marked the nightlife of Montmartre, one an ostensible victory, the other a seeming defeat: the opening of Maurice's in the former Théâtre Caumartin and the raid on the Tempo Club. Despite the spectacular suicide of Peggy Joyce's Chilean lover, Maurice's *dancing* triumphed. Yet, in a deeper sense his success and the Tempo Club's failure were only apparent. It is no coincidence that Florence Jones and Louis Mitchell were frequenting the modest hideaway on the rue Fontaine at precisely the moment that the drummer was imagining a launch of his own club. The decline of the rue Caumartin loomed on the horizon, while the Tempo Club would symbolically rise from its ashes in the guise of new Black-owned or -managed clubs such as the Grand Duc, Mitchell's, or Chez Florence.

Nevertheless, the elegiac tone of the Tempo Club's Proustian chronicler, Philippe Soupault, is appropriate for its material dissolution: He evokes "ephemeral smoke upon the waters," drifting above the sodden embers of the recent conflagration. In notes related to Wellmon's rendition of "Saint Louis Blues" he lamented:

> This music, which gallops and agitates us incessantly before becoming a tedious refrain, perhaps possesses a charm that allows us to savor it even more since it has the air of ephemeral smoke upon the waters.... I know that all these melodies, these blues are today in fashion for a few months, like Negro sculpture and the Charleston.... Of this music flowing past, I wish only to regard the reflections. I put aside that intolerable mania and those songs that are, purportedly, perfect. I am witnessing an agony, and it pleases me to see it surrounded by melancholy songs or ones too gay. The random notes that rose from Wellmon's piano are, to my mind, the debut of a funeral march or that of a murderous hymn. Those Negroes knew much better than I, than we, that they were singing in the shadows. As for me, I heard only the noise of their galloping.[63]

vif, d'où jaillit, comme un flot de sang, un torrent de notes bouillonnantes. Pendant que ce sauvage lui administre cette raclée à tout casser, un autre nègre, gratteur de banjo, installé dessus à califourchon, les jambes ballantes, de ses larges souliers carrés l'éperonne sans pitié, précipite son galop trébuchant de pauvre bique exténuée, à bout de souffle. A côté, le joueur de saxophone, les joues gonflées à craquer comme une outre de cornemuse, meugle lugubrement à perdre haleine, tandis qu'un démon noir, agitant des bras innombrables, armés de baguettes tourbillonnantes, se démène furieusement au milieu de son établi à tintamarre. Je reçois en pleine figure ce fracas cadencé, comme une volée de claques. Ça me secoue à me déplomber les dents. D'ailleurs tout danse, tout rebondit dans ces trois chambres étroites, gorgées de bruit à éclater : les verres, les bouteilles qui encombrent le dessus du piano, jusqu'aux musiciens qui, eux-mêmes, se dandinent en mesure sur leur chaise,

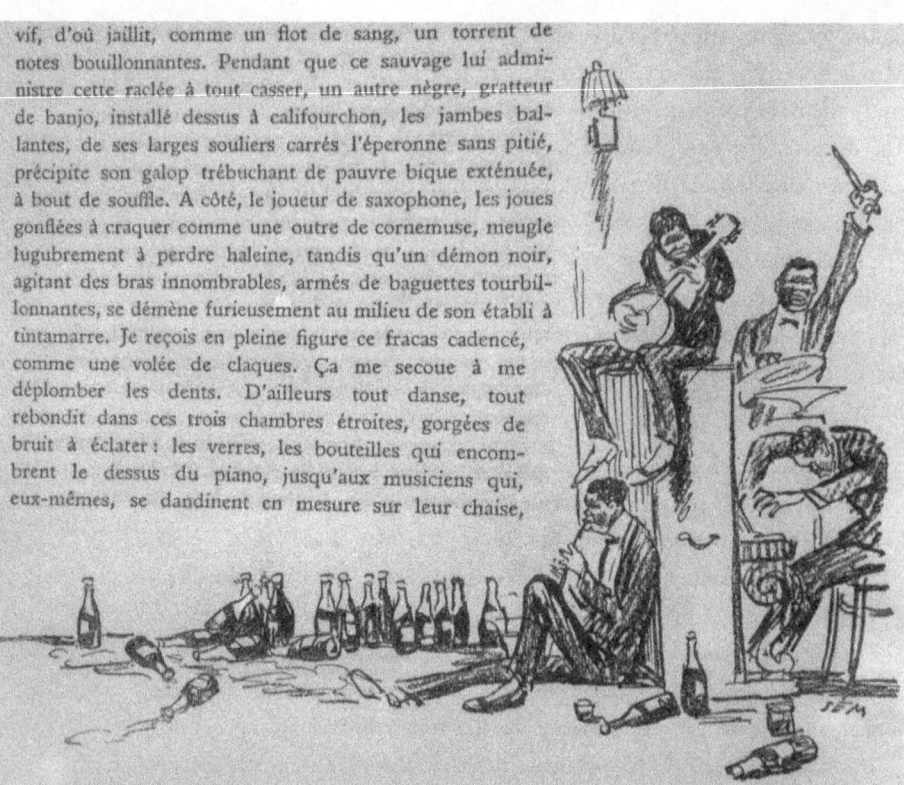

Jazz band in a clandestine dancing [Aladdin's Lamp Club], Sem (Georges Goursat), 1920. From *La Ronde de Nuit*.

Eugene Bullard, 1918.
Science History Images /
Alamy Stock Photo

Harry Pilcer and Gaby Deslys, ca. 1912.
Cineclassico / Alamy Stock Photo

Louis Mitchell with the Seven Spades, London, 1917.
Courtesy of Mark Berresford Rare Records.

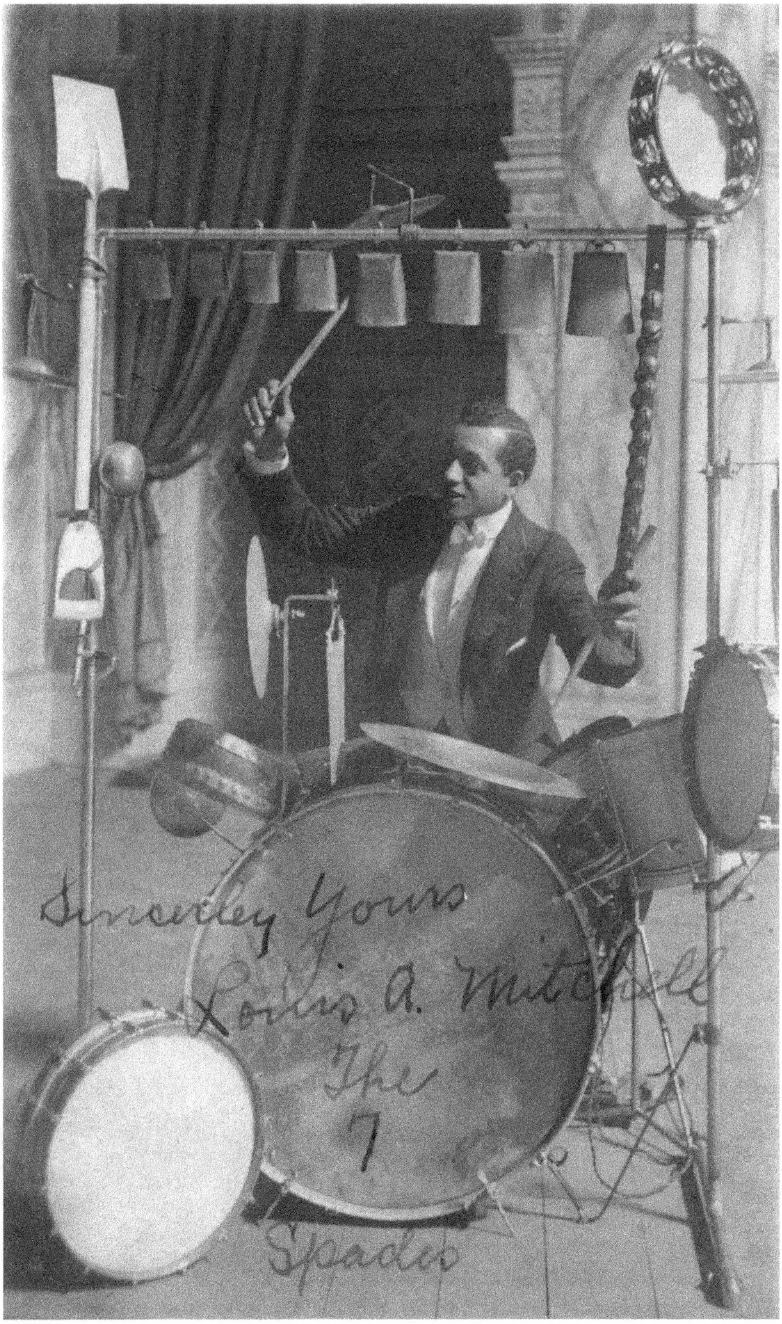
Sincerley Yours
Louis A. Mitchell
The
7
Spades

"Le Perroquet," Séeberger frères, 1928.
© Ministère de la Culture / Médiathèque du patrimoine,
Dist. RMN-Grand Palais / Art Resource, N.Y.

Maurice Mouvet and Leonora Hughes,
Sem (Georges Goursat), 1922.
From *La Ronde de Nuit*.

Leonora Hughes dancing at the Jardin de ma Soeur. Leslie Saalberg. *Vogue* (French ed.), June 1, 1923.

Edward, Prince of Wales, later King Edward VIII. Akpool / Arkivi / Alamy Stock Photo

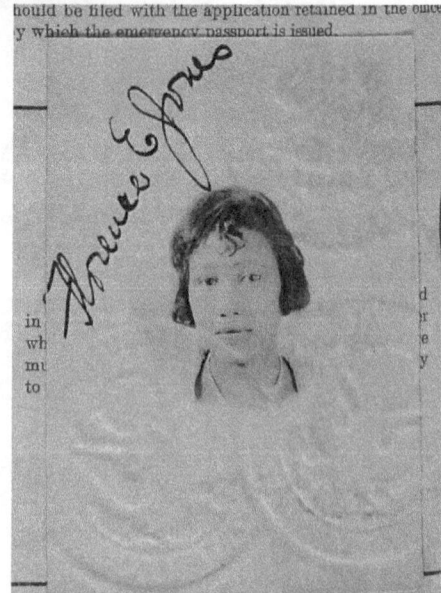

Florence E. Jones passport photo. Courtesy of Dr. Rainer E. Lotz.

"Joe Zelli's Royal Box, façade," Séeberger frères (1925). © Ministère de la Culture / Médiathèque du patrimoine, Dist. RMN-Grand Palais / Art Resource, N.Y.

"Joe Zelli with the 'Royal Box Smile.'"
Pittsburgh Press, September 6, 1925.

CHAPTER SIX

ZELLI'S ROYAL BOX

A Bordello in the Country of the Abencerrages

The artificial moonlight suited the music in the same way that this Abencerrage décor suited the girls of Montmartre.
—Louis Aragon

We have been examining the shift of supremacy from the rue Caumartin to the rue Pigalle. The pioneer in this domain was Joe Zelli who, with prophetic insight, had recognized that the wave of the future was breaking to the north. The inaugural date of Zelli's Royal Box (usually said to be 1922) is unknown—either late March or early April 1921, which coincides with the return of Mazie Mullins, Frank Withers, and the Jazz Kings from Brussels.[1] Zelli's Royal Box opened about the same time as the Tempo Club, and Zelli was likely implicated in the activities of his upstairs neighbors Joe Boyd and Mazie Mullins, but his exact role remains unclear—leaseholder, silent partner, or more? Dick Carlish describes sitting on the balcony of the Royal Box one evening when "police poured in and made straight for Joe Boyd's gambling saloon where the blackjack game was being run."[2] I cannot confirm an access route from the balcony to the Tempo Club's back room, but if one existed, this would suggest Zelli's complicity in Boyd's illegal undertakings.[3] The problem is that Carlish situates the anecdote in 1925! Nevertheless, vivid details again lend veracity, even if the date is incorrect.

Whatever his function, the good-humored Zelli was a benevolent neighbor. "He plays a stellar role in all the little dramas of life and death which breed in fertile Montmartre," writes old friend Basil Woon.[4] What the journalist fails to mention is that his mediations extended to members of both racial communities. A complicity with Black artists, combined with an unimpeachable status among white expatriates, designated him as the conciliator of volatile affairs. In November 1923 Palmer Jones and the International Five sued the management of the Club Daunou, near the Opéra. They had been signed for the cabaret and to accompany showgirl Edith Kelly Gould, ex-wife of multimillionaire Frank Jay Gould, at the Alhambra Theater. But the contract was cancelled when Miss Gould objected to performing with colored men! Zelli was called in and arbitrated a 10,000-franc settlement of the three-month contract—which, despite his efforts, their manager haughtily refused.[5]

Despite this high standing in the Black musical community, journalist Robert Abbott avers that the Royal Box had "the reputation of being a bit of Mississippi planted in the very heart of Paris." Notwithstanding, he absolves the cabaret keeper of any bias, declaring that he was "a very courteous gentleman. It is the southerners who flock to his place that has given it that reputation. When they get drunk they are likely to shy a champagne bottle at a Colored guest who should come in."[6] The profits at stake were enormous—Zelli was rumored to have made half a million dollars in his first five years as owner of one of the most emblematic dance halls of Pigalle. However, even if his efforts to placate his white American patrons can be seen as motivated more by cupidity than racism, he does appear to have pandered to their worst prejudices.

Thanks to Aragon's *Le Mauvais Plaisant* and his novel *Aurélien*, we possess a vivid portrait of the theater of these contradictory postures.[7] Like the author in 1925, the titular hero of the novel enters through a mirrored corridor leading to the foyer and bar, filled with patrons in conversation, dancers taking a break, and "'*poules*' gossiping among themselves."[8] The walls of the bar are plastered with club insignias, college pennants, and the tasteless paintings of a penniless Uruguayan artist left as guarantee.[9] From June to September it becomes a de facto Yale-Harvard-Princeton annex, and when a football team arrives in uniform, the band strikes up *Yankee Doodle* or *Swanee River*.[10]

Near the entrance to the *dancing* a thin-lipped blonde, Mme Zelli, sits behind a cash desk, plump fingers covered with diamond rings, a string of pearls around her neck as she totes up the profits, a responsibility she had assumed since the dodgy days of the rue Caumartin.[11] Zelli calls her "baby doll." (She is barely taller than his shoulder and he is not very tall.) Every evening a limousine ferries her to Montmartre from the château where her husband enjoys the bourgeois pleasures of a country gentleman: riding, tennis, and raising chickens and dogs, "the necessary counterbalance to the deadly Montmartre atmosphere in which he is obliged at night to live."[12]

Heavy drapes separate the vestibule from a cavernous hall circled by a balcony. All smiles, Zelli greets wide-eyed tourists from the provinces of the Republic: "A *Royal Box* for the Prince and Princess of Venice' [at which the maître d' seats the flattered rustics at any available table]. Farcical, man, farcical."¹³ From these august heights the princes of Paducah and princesses of Punxsutawney lean over the delicately scalloped railing, gazing down at the crowd cavorting on the dance floor, a square of polished wood impinged upon by tables among which white-coated waiters navigate, balancing shining buckets of champagne.

Aragon conveys the desperate gaiety that reigns under the streamers and shimmering garlands of lights:

> the music that comes from the Moorish *dancing*, and the clamor of voices, the laughter, the hysteria of solemn, drunken men, of Americans and ladies of the evening, of women with plunging necklines escorted by dusky cavaliers, the habitués, Suzy, Georgette, Yvonne . . . this décor of insomnia and alcohol, and the weightiness of the long night, of all the thoughts one wishes to avoid, all the missed occasions, the dance of those who are afraid to sleep, afraid of not sleeping . . . and the great hall bathed in a blue glow for a waltz, the light glancing off the skin of the women, off their sequined gowns, the men in black with their white dickeys, the projector's colored waves . . . the flurry of light, the pale flakes that seem to rain down from the vaulted ceiling onto the simulated patio, petals that vanish on the ground, poetry of two minutes to midnight rue Pigalle.¹⁴

A photo from 1925 (the year chronicled in *Le Mauvais plaisant*) shows a beaming patron weaving among a throng of relentlessly gay dancers, dispensing the famous "Royal Box Smile" (see gallery 1). Zelli is Italian, and the club favored by Americans, yet he cries out periodically: "'Ole! Ole!' with appropriate gesticulations."¹⁵ His lapse into the Iberian tongue is perhaps a wink at the club's décor, vaguely reminiscent of the Hispano-Arabic "Mudejar" style of the Alcazar of Seville or the purely Arabic Alhambra, residence of the Moorish rulers of Granada. Dating from prewar days, the interior is a legacy of La Féria, created for a renowned flamenco guitarist, with furnishings imported from Spain.¹⁶ This counterfeit décor stages a bizarre fantasy world, peopled with suave, predatory gigolos and grasping harem beauties, an exotic kingdom ruled over by Zelli, "Chief Mogul of Montmartre."¹⁷

As the gullible vacationers gaze down in wonder, dances follow one another, rhythmed by alternating orchestras, one for the tango, waltz, and an occasional java, the other, a jazz band, for the one-step, foxtrot, and shimmy. In the early years of Zelli's Royal Box the jazz band was Anglo-American: Tom Waltham and his Ad-Libs.¹⁸ Waltham had arrived during the war at the head of a British military orchestra and seized on the opportunity to fraternize with American colleagues like James Reese Europe, who introduced him to ragtime piano. It is difficult to know how the Ad-Libs sounded in 1921, but later recordings provide an indication. Goddard finds that on "C'est Bouche à bouche" (1925) "the trumpet player makes a feeble attempt to play a hot 'wah-wah' chorus and the bass saxophone solo, which follows it, gives an appalling rendering of the tune. ... The piece completely fails to swing as none of the musicians can play even four beats to a bar. Instead this two-beat rendering gives a stiff, corny feel."[19] However, Vauchant thought Waltham a fine musician: "He played good dance piano. He would have made you dance just playing the piano alone. He'd pull the time around and anticipate the beat. . . . Waltham was the first pianist I heard who really played different—American."[20]

This hints at a problem that became increasingly acute in the twenties: the opposition between "soft jazz," a symphonic tendency chiefly represented by white orchestras, and "hot jazz," played principally by Black bands, an approach incorporating a strong rhythmic pulse, a more flexible structure, and a greater role for improvisation. Cocteau wrote, "There are two schools, two sects of jazz. The real jazz, known as hot—which involves playing hot, adding spice to the music—and symphonic jazz, the bastard, Europeanized jazz, which is the province of Witman [Paul Whiteman], Hilton [Jack Hylton], etc."[21] Known as the "King of Jazz," Whiteman downplayed improvisation in favor of formal written arrangements, as did Hylton, styled the "British King of Jazz." On this point, Cocteau concurred with the most advanced French thought on the subject. A few years later, influential French jazz critic Hughes Panassié would expostulate, "There isn't any swing. Consequently, no one can properly say that Hylton's music is jazz." As regards Whiteman, he decried the "empty, pompous performances nicknamed symphonic jazz."[22]

After 1928 the Ad-Libs' arrangements became less "hot," due perhaps to Whiteman's influence (some members are reputed to have played with him in the summer of 1926).[23] Most noticeably, the designation "Ad-Libs," revelatory of an aesthetic, was jettisoned in 1930. Individuals and groups evolve; nevertheless comments by Vauchant suggest that in its early years the Royal Box was home to a tolerably "hot jazz." And he points to a sociability and a musical ambiance somewhat like that of the Tempo Club: "It was a jazz place, you know. Except it was limited to just that one band. But anybody could sit in. It was Tommy Waltham. It was a white band, but Black guys would come in and sit in. . . . The music was basically fox trot. It was pretty formal stuff but it was already very jumpy."[24]

Admittedly, it is tempting to imagine a dichotomy between the low-ceilinged Tempo Club and the vast reaches of the ornate Royal Box—one club

Black, the other white, Mazie and members of the Southern Syncopated Orchestra versus the Ad-Libs. But Vauchant's observation demonstrates that this would be an oversimplification. As I have pointed out, white visitors penetrated the cloistered Tempo Club; at the same time Waltham consorted with Black musicians, and people of color were not unknown at the Royal Box.[25] Illustrative of this racial diversity, in the spring of 1922 Dick Carlish and "General" Harry Wellmon were hired by Zelli for a spot in the cabaret, which allowed them easy access to the Tempo Club.[26]

However, the most prominent of the "Black guys" to sit in was Buddie Gilmore. Intended "to give patrons an excuse for lingering over their aperitifs," the cabaret consisted of acrobatic dancing, singing, and comic routines by assorted nationalities, what *Variety's* London correspondent called the "International Parisian style, viz: An American fox trot, the everlasting tango and then a turn."[27] According to *Variety*, "One of the most cheery of these is the nightly appearance of Buddy, the trick drummer."[28] Gilmore was the recognizable model for the infantile virtuoso of *Aurélien*, "Tommy," even if his presence corresponds to a later reality—in 1921 it would be an anachronism.

In addition to seating credulous guests, animating the dancing, and ejecting troublemakers, the omnipresent Zelli also presented the cabaret. Jacques Baron and Louis Aragon were both struck by his florid introductions, amalgams of Italian volubility and American good humor—a contrived buffoonery that seduced even those who were not deceived: "Tararabadaboum boum boum! Spotlight. King of the fête, memory of the world, Joe Zelli positions himself in the blinding circle of light."[29] Corseted in a close-fitting tuxedo, arms outstretched, hands waving, he pretended to bring the drumroll to a climax, and then "with an accent mixing Florence and Chicago, he announced Tommy, the one and only Tommy, the best drummer in the world":[30]

> A small Negro, pale and plump, with short greying hair and astonished eyes... Tommy made himself comfortable in a crossfire of spotlights... Tommy, who with all sorts of juggling of his drumsticks and small metal brushes, played without accompaniment the tom-toms, the cymbals, the little bells... and the arms and feet of Tommy flew around the large drum, caressed the drum kit with the gestures of a chicken shocked at having made so much noise, his neck folding back on itself in rolls of dark flesh martyrized by an immaculate false collar.... Glued to his chair he leapt up and fell back in a delirium that infected the audience... bowing, perspiring, breathing heavily like a seal seated in a toy automobile.[31]

By 1927 Tom Waltham and the Ad-Libs were gone, playing for tea dances, and Buddie had left Paris to tour in the Netherlands and South America. A new group provided music for the assembled masses, the Royal Box Orchestra. Despite a sabbatical from December 1923 to oversee the Grand Duc, Gene Bullard had remained faithful to his mentor. After ceding the management to Bricktop in August 1924, he was again available to oversee the band at Zelli's dispensary of froth and frivolity. In a photo taken at a benefit concert for graduating student nurses of the American Hospital, he appears seated behind a drum set inscribed with the name of the band.[32] Among the figures ranged around him are his colleagues Crickett Smith, Glover Compton, Frank "Big Boy" Goudie, and Ferdie Allen. On either side are gathered a Who's Who of leading jazzmen: Frisco, Frank Withers, Bobby Jones, Joe Caulk, Palmer Jones, Sidney Bechet, Sammy Richardson, and a score of others (the only absentee is Buddie Gilmore, who also performed), a tribute to the prestige of Zelli's band in Montmartre's musical community.

An earlier photo from 1927 captures the Orchestra in its native setting. The mirrors of the octagonal half-rotunda that houses the bandstand transform the reflected balconies into an Expressionist Alhambra of jutting angles and clashing diagonals. Seated in the rear to the left, an affable Joe Zelli accepts a sip of champagne from a lovely young lady.[33] Regardless of the uncharacteristic discretion, we should not underestimate his role in promoting this preeminent group of musicians, part of the pool of Black talent on which he had relied since his days at Cadet Rousselle.

In the center, surrounded by revelers and two thuggish-looking waiters, a baton-waving gentleman imitates Zelli and feigns to lead the orchestra. Between the giddy, would-be bandleader and a party-hatted merrymaker stands a composed Gene Bullard, the man whose relations gave Zelli access to the finest Black musicians.[34] Over were the hectic days of "Jack's Negro Band" and turbulent exchanges with Alexandre Stavisky. Bullard was now a settled married man with two young daughters, but those early experiences had forged an indefectible bond with the cabaret king. When, in 1924, he and his French wife, Marcelle Straumann, christened their first child, Zelli and his spouse were among the guests, and each of the restaurateur's suppliers provided a case of bubbly, the accredited nectar of Utopia. Nor was this unusual: the Zellis attended all of Bullard's fêtes, for example, the "sumptuous afternoon wine party" given in 1929 in honor of Marcelle.[35]

If he ultimately abandoned his patron, it was due to circumstances beyond his control. Plagued by waning business, the winter after the wine party Joe Zelli shuttered the Royal Box for three months. Added to the lowered temperatures were the chilling effects of the Wall Street crash of 1929, which sent numbers of cash-strapped clients fleeing back across the ocean. Following on their heels, Zelli and his wife departed for the more clement skies of Palm Beach by way of New York. Left at loose ends, on May 3, 1930, Bullard launched The Comedy Club, located in the depths of the Gaity Theater at 25 rue Fontaine. The club quickly folded. Unfazed, the dynamic Bullard took over the second Music Box and ultimately bought L'Escadrille, a jazz rendezvous that prospered until the advent of the Nazis.[36]

But to return to the 1927 photo of the Orchestra. Deployed behind Bullard and the tipsy "bandleader" is Cricket Smith with his signature melon hat (the Real Jazz Kings had intoned their swan song at the Casino in 1925).[37] At the keyboard sits J. Glover Compton, a veteran of the Chicago jazz scene, "massaging the keys with his cigar at an angle of 45 degrees and that unique expression on his face."[38] On either side of Crickett figure banjoist Ferdie Allen and saxophonist Big Boy Goudie. Like Crickett, Ferdie could claim ties to Louis Mitchell, being an ex-Spade, but along with Compton and Goudie he was also a survivor of the unforgettable Palm Beach Six.

Sadly, they are often recalled for a tragic reason: the murder in February 1926 of Leon Crutcher, the group's coleader, at the hands of his jealous French wife, Marie-Louise Boyard, a hostess at the Royal Box. Always ready to introduce a literary allusion, one French journalist invoked a classical tragedy of Pierre Corneille, dubbing Crutcher "the Cid of the Charleston" and adding that his wife was not the only lady "to have Chimène's eyes for him (a colloquial expression inspired by the play's heroine)."[39]

In October 1925 the band had done its best to invigorate the final nights of the Jardin de ma Soeur, while doubling up at the more animated Abbaye de Thélème. It was there that the curtain rose on the first act of the modern tragedy. Marie arrived at 5 a.m. to fetch her husband, but he preferred to remain, carousing with assorted ladies at the Grand Duc and returning home the next afternoon humming a Charleston. Provoked by boasts of amorous conquests, Marie menaced him with a revolver. He dared her to shoot. She did—a single shot that laid the "colored Don Juan" out dead on the floor of their hotel room.[40]

So much for "froth and frivolity!" Leon Crutcher's woeful fate highlights a somber facet of Montmartre: Nevill's "dark side." With British phlegm, the nightlife chronicler opines, "Though at first sight life in Montmartre seems to be almost entirely given up to gaiety and dissipation, there is a serious and even tragic side to it which the casual visitor who goes to the *Butte* only for purposes of amusement does not see."[41] Leveled directly at the Royal Box, Aragon's analysis is even more trenchant: "Everything here is presented in a false perspective, a façade so correct that you would hardly imagine what this throng signifies if your heart were not already depraved. All is smiles, dancing, and neither love nor obdurate perversity show on faces flushed with champagne."[42] The very fact that Zelli felt obliged to offer an appearance of propriety condemns him. Referring to two hulking American sailors, Simone, a hostess in Aragon's novel, informs the hero with a sigh, "There're no two ways about it... They're drunk, but good-looking, those guys over there... really good-looking... Too bad they don't know how to behave... If it weren't for that... You see, Zelli, for him, proper behavior... If we picked up one of those birds over there, right away he'd notice... and you know he doesn't fool around, Zelli... Once outside, anything goes... But in the house, no soliciting" (ellipses in original).[43]

Simone belongs to a class of men and women known as "professional dancers." The restaurateur owed a good part of his success to a modus operandi he had experimented with at Zelli's Club, a phalanx of "for hire" hostesses (absent from the society *dancings*) who danced with patrons and received a percentage on their consumption of the obligatory champagne. Estimates of their number varies from 30 to a stunning 150. Inevitably, this relentless gaiety and social promiscuity produced an atmosphere conducive to illicit sexual activity. In French slang *poule* ("chicken") means "whore," thus Aragon's use of the term to describe Zelli's hostesses. But Simone's confidences make it clear that strictly speaking they were not prostitutes (Crutcher's wife insisted loudly on the "respectability" of her occupation).[44] Nevertheless, the frontier between the streets and the *dancings* was permeable, and for all Zelli's ostentatious policing, Simone does not hesitate to arrange a meeting with one of the handsome Americans, a suppleness evident in the biting lyrics of Cole Porter's "Love for Sale" (1929), a song inspired by this sentimental commerce.[45]

Of these questionable ladies Aragon writes, "The artificial moonlight suited the music in the same way that this Abencerrage décor suited the girls of Montmartre." The Abencerrages were a medieval Moorish tribe of the fifteenth-century Kingdom of Granada, and the subject of a legend recounting how the last Arab king, Boabdil, jealous of the romance between an Abencerrage and his Sultana, massacred forty of the clan in the hall of the Alhambra that bears their name. Considering the discernable allusions to the famous fortress in the décor of the Royal Box, the use of this curious appellation is not just a bizarre whimsy.

Zelli's artificial illumination might also have suited the music. On the cutting edge of atmospheric lighting, the Royal Box was a luminous world of enchantment. Lights hung everywhere—along the edges of balconies, the ribs of ceiling vaults, in little Moorish lanterns, reflected in the mirrors circling the room, and spilling out of projectors whose rotating gels diffused waves of color: an orange known as "tango" for the Argentinean numbers, a pale blue reminiscent of moonshine for a slow foxtrot. But one might still ask in what way the factitious Abencerrage décor "suited" the girls of Montmartre?

By invoking the name of an obscure clan, Aragon invests Zelli's semidisreputable ladies with the fatal glamor contained in the image of the Alhambra and its exquisite patios and water displays—such as the courtyard containing the Fountain of the Lions, whose graceful jets spatter before the so-called Hall of the Abencerrages. He then strips away the aura of romance, revealing a darker image: "an Alhambra without fountains, with so many *almahs* that it's rather nauseating. Like whipped cream tartes."[46] The reference to *almahs* (Egyptian dancing girls whose postperformance favors titillated nineteenth-century European travelers) reduces the hostesses to their commercial function in a mercenary harem. Given the number of Middle Eastern and Asian princes who frequented the Montmartre *dancings* in search of boarders, it is not far-fetched to assimilate Zelli's sisterhood to these exotic dancers. (Nevill jested that "Paris has a way of fascinating the Oriental . . . offering as it does some of the main attractions of the Mahometan heaven!")[47] Cued by this extraordinary décor, Michel Leiris conjured up a disquieting vision of rapacious, lethal women, a harem of venal *almahs*: "Dream: I am in a bordello that resembles Zelli's in its décor but where the women, instead of being there to make love, are there to tell our fortune. For the rest they are dressed as prostitutes usually are." In another version of this text a group of fortune tellers arrives with "a smudge of blood in place of a mouth. This last detail proves that they are vampires."[48]

The same moral ambiguity hovers over their male colleagues. With exaggerated contempt, O. O. McIntyre declared that "oiled and herring-hipped gigolos . . . they emit the faint glow of the rotting, phosphorescent fish. They are superbly groomed, manicured and perfumed. And dance divinely."[49] Ostensibly based on observation, this comment resembles Hemingway's assimilation of Peggy Joyce's unfortunate lover, Billy Errázuriz, to a gigolo ("the shellaced haired young Chilean who had long pointed fingernails [and] danced like Rudolph Valentino"), descriptions based purely on their fevered imaginings. Yet, even allowing for these prejudices, the morality of real-life gigolos was clearly open to question.

It was in this shadowy milieu that Josephine Baker met the man who became her manager and lover, the self-styled aristocrat "Count" Giuseppe "Pepito" Abatino. A distinctive feature of the Royal Box was the framed caricatures of celebrated personalities lining the walls, and though Zelli's public was predominantly white, the gallery included "several colored persons."[50] The caricatures were the work of a young Sicilian named Vincenzo Maria Zito, known simply as Zito, whose art and person Aragon detested, excoriating "the satirical sketches of that horrible little Italian ... who goes from table to table bowing and scraping." He added that "the most elegant people here are some Italians, friends of Zito, dressed to the nines, with beautiful light cravats and dark clothes. They dine next door at Arsène's place. Later, they're here. At times at the Palermo."[51] Zito's compatriots may have had the honor of sharing a bowl of onion soup and a glass of dry white wine with the Prince of Wales, reputed to frequent Arsène's in the neighboring rue Mansart, a rendezvous favored by workers of the night. Along with gangsters, gigolos, and royal heirs, one might find "actors, chorus girls, American drunks... and diverse company."[52]

Demographically the "professional dancers" of Montmartre were overwhelmingly Latin: Argentine, Italian, or Spanish. Though a distinct minority, there were also Black gigolos (Aragon's "dusky cavaliers?")—correspondent J. A. Rogers speaks of two Antilleans whose "tall, athletic figures, dark faces, clever dancing and flashy clothes won them a certain popularity" in a Montmartre cabaret.[53] For obvious reasons, the corps at Zelli's favored the Italian persuasion, and Zito's "cousin," the vacationing Pepito Abatino, might have figured among the supper companions of the Prince of Wales. There is some question as to whether they were really related or just from the same hometown, but most people believed it.

The previous April Josephine had debuted at the Folies Bergère, clad only in the mythic banana skirt. Her celebrity was such that in October the owners of the Impérial, across from Bricktop's Grand Duc, invited her to dance.[54] "They didn't pay me," she wrote in her memoirs, "but I was fed. I was introduced to soufflés ... Oh! là là ... how I ate them ... with cheese, mushrooms or sweet with vanilla, chocolate or liqueurs."[55] Later Josephine would move in grander social circles, but in the fall of 1926 she was part of a group that circulated between Bricktop's, Zelli's, and the Impérial.

Bricktop recounts that Josephine "used to come into Le Grand Duc with a fellow named Zito.... Zito wasn't much of a date, but there are always times when a woman in the spotlight doesn't have much choice. Many boys who might have asked her out were too shy, and too frightened by all the publicity she was getting.... One night Zito was sick. He got his cousin Pepito to take Josephine around.... Pepito had just arrived from Rome. His real name was Giuseppe Abatino and he was working as a gigolo at Zelli's."[56] That would have been in late August or early September, not in October, as is generally thought—a passionate missive dated September 24 and written on the letterhead of the Italian Finance Ministry evokes the "pleasant moments" they had spent together.[57]

At the time of their first encounter, Pepito was a minor Roman bureaucrat visiting his "cousin" Zito, who since 1925 had become a familiar figure in the Montmartre night world. Were there previous visits during which Zito introduced him to the joys and profits of foxtrotting with ladies "of the age that our grandmothers had before the invention of the *dancing* . . ., clad in short skirts and revealing distressing treasures?"[58] It is difficult to say; we know very little about Pepito's life before Josephine, but Canadian jazzman Arthur Briggs maintained that "he'd go to tea dances and dance with ladies and they'd tip him between fifty and one hundred francs. We all knew what Pepito was, but Josephine fell in love with him, it was just one of those things."[59]

Bricktop is dismissive of Zito's charms but, in all fairness, he was rather dashing in the genre exemplified by Pepito—heavy-lidded eyes, devilish eyebrows, hair slicked back with Gomina, and a debonair moustache like that of movie actor Adolphe Menjou—a male beauty to which Josephine was clearly susceptible.[60] Much later, she wrote with distinct nostalgia, "He had delicate features, his eyes at once gay and serious behind his monocle, his mouth ironic but tender."[61] But Abatino's questionable moonlighting and shortage of funds caused the mordant Bricktop to dub him "the no-account count," adding derisively that "he and the others preferred to call themselves 'dance instructors.'"[62]

Bricktop is perhaps too harsh in her view of his career choices and the plausibility of his noble pretensions; aristocratic gigolos were not unknown—there had been much talk the previous year of a Polish princess, related by marriage to the soon-to-be deposed Shah of Persia, who had been aided in swindling schemes by her titled brother, "a dancing instructor in the Montmartre cafés."[63] The legitimacy of Pepito's noble lineage was less likely, but he had distinct qualities, and if he exploited Josephine, he also fostered her career. "I am not *richman* [*sic*]," he wrote from Rome; all he could offer was honeyed words ("my sweetheart . . . my love . . . my adorable doll"), sweeter than the Impérial's soufflés, plus a business sense that Josephine clearly lacked. He proposed to leave his dead-end job and rejoin her.[64] Presumably she encouraged him, and after his return in late October or early November he quickly arranged for her to abandon the Impérial's sugary delights for her own club, Chez Joséphine, a block north of Zelli's, where their marriage was announced six months later. The sham nuptials galvanized a pervasive American anxiety: miscegenation, the more so in that French mores not only permitted race-mixing but may even have encouraged it. It was just a publicity stunt (he was not a real count, and she was still married to Pullman porter, Will Baker), but in the land of the free the adventure might have had a crueler denouement, in the vein of Billie Holiday's iconic classic, "strange fruit hanging from a poplar tree."

An amusing anecdote involving two of Pepito's compatriots illustrates the gigolos' modus operandi. Jack Pickford, brother of film pioneer Mary Pickford and widower of screen beauty Olive Thomas, was dining at Zelli's with his second wife. Approached by two Latins, the couple invented a new technique to discourage them—the use of bulldogs as protection had failed, they were too easily bribed by raw pork chops. Jack asked the two gigolos where they were from.

—"I come from Florence," said the first.
—"Florence's?" Jack reflected with false naïveté. "I thought it had shut down."[65]
—"Florence will never sit down—I mean shut down," replied the Italian. "It is the greatest city in Italy...."
—"Oh, I see," said Jack, "I had thought you were referring to the cabaret down the street, operated by American Negroes."

He then introduced the befuddled Latins to his wife and, feigning susceptibility to their charms, she held out her hand. With horror the first Italian "found he had kissed the head of a three-foot snake coiled around the lady's arm." Havoc ensued, with fleeing gigolos, overturned tables, and a runaway snake christened Sydney. The author wryly concludes that even Argentines (the worst offenders) "are beginning to look at both of a lady's wrists before they go close to her table."[66]

The inept Italians were not necessarily sexual predators, but like their sisters they sometimes erred—at times with more serious consequences, as in the case of Rogers' Black cabaret dancers, who were charged with the murder of an elderly woman, a crime, he adds, "committed frequently by white men."[67] For his part, Nevill advances an even-handed evaluation: "The profession of a dancer at a night resort cannot ... be said to be a very dignified one, being at best but a sort of 'blind alley' occupation not unlikely to degenerate into something worse. The sum such a dancer receives per night is not large [however] the less reputable of these young men ... often make far more than this out of skittish old ladies who take a fancy to them." And, he sums up, "On the whole, considering the rather demoralizing atmosphere in which they live, these men, outwardly at least, behave themselves correctly and well."[68]

The link between the nocturnal activities of the *dancings* and the evils of drugs and prostitution is apparent. French artist Edouard Chimot made this theme his stock in trade, producing a series of sensitive etchings of the "daughters of perdition," with titles such as "Little Pale Jeanne No. 2—Waiting for the Drug in the Cabaret." Subjected to harsh working conditions, Zelli's harem lovelies were vulnerable to the appeal of artificial stimulants. An article on Chimot's work commented, "The resorts of Montmartre are filled with the pretty, frail women who make the lure of Paris. . . . It is among these women that the greatest number of addicts occurs for the burden of their lives becomes at times so terrible that they can crave anything that will give them a few moments of forgetfulness."[69]

The report of Commissioner Caron of the Sureté Générale stated that "the majority of the personnel of the night dives, if not all, take an active part in the traffic either as sellers, go-betweens or addicts."[70] It would be remarkable if Zelli's were exempt from this widespread abuse. In effect, Baron discloses that "there was certainly a little drug dealing in the toilets and, naturally, the inevitable prostitution, but of *bon goût*."[71] The functioning of this traffic is outlined by the editor of Francis Carco's *Rue Pigalle* (1928), a novel set in Montmartre's drug culture: "A wink of the eye was sufficient, the doorman or the bartender understood; a 100-franc coin slipped discreetly into their hands and one headed towards the toilets. . . . The packet could be found as usual, affixed with thumbtacks to the washbasins or in the telephone booths."[72]

The problem captured the attention of American tabloid readers in 1920 with the shocking demise of Olive Thomas, Pickford's first wife, who died poisoned at the Ritz after a night of revelry in Montmartre joy palaces. The first major Hollywood scandal, it spawned stories like one that appeared in the *Pittsburgh Press*. Driven by the fevered ruminations of a Reverend Beekman, the article indicts "the modern Babylon," and although it says little about Thomas' death, it details at length the perverse pleasures of Montmartre. With delectation, the Reverend enlightens us about morphine, opium, and hashish, as well as a puff of cocaine mixed in a drink or sprinkled on floral bouquets, trick lead pencils called "respirettes" that held a gram of the drug or poisonous dashes of liquid ether added to a cup of tea.[73] Despite the vogue for this last narcotic, which combined maximum intoxication with minimal damage to the digestive organs, the drug of choice was "the dream powder," cocaine. No need of a needle, as with morphine. According to one informant the flat end of an indispensable nail file sufficed for the girls of Montmartre, known as "snowbirds," to sniff their "coco."[74] And one was spared the unpleasant odor of ether or the elaborate opium ceremonial.

Despite a 1916 classification of opium and cocaine as illegal substances, the plague of coco was widespread. If Parisian consumption was sometimes exaggerated—one newspaper claimed that "more cocaine is sold in a single night than elsewhere in Europe in a whole month"—the phenomenon was of genuine concern.[75] Between 1916 and 1922 the number of addicts was estimated to have increased by 800 percent.[76] Given the huge profits, severe penalties were not enough to stem the traffic.

However, the abuse of narcotics was not confined to what Caron calls "public women." He acknowledges that cocaine was used "by an increasing number of society people, by many writers, actresses and professional men."[77] Bricktop took a more indulgent view of the habits of the society folk who constituted her clientele than she did of the professional activities of Pepito. "They were maybe ten or fifteen among the real crowd who smoked opium," she wrote, "including a very rich marquise in Paris. Others carried cocaine in little jeweled boxes. They always did it in a classy way though."[78]

Notwithstanding these questionable aspects of the Royal Box, Joe Zelli strove to maintain a semblance of decorum. This mask of respectability supposed a complicity between the restaurateur and his "upstanding" clientele in an effort to maintain what Aragon terms a "joyous calm." After all, it was precisely to be titillated by racy amusements that the princes and princesses of Paducah and Punxsutawney flocked to the Royal Box. Their conviction of moral superiority was coupled with a hypocritical enjoyment of forbidden pleasures. For those who violated the implicit pact another fate was reserved. Zelli boasted that he had no need of a bouncer, but only because he occupied the function himself.[79] If the slightest "onset of revolt appears in a violent man," wrote Aragon, "immediately a sort of whirlpool plucks him from his fury and tosses him out into the street, and the dancing couples have not so much as interrupted their fox trot when, adjusting their tuxedos, one can already see Joe Zelli returning with his somewhat less fleshy second . . . single-handedly the two of them are sufficient to preserve this joyous calm."[80]

Zelli and his wife formed a redoubtable tag team. The genteel Mme Zelli, daughter of a well-to-do farmer near Fontainebleau, was equally adept at preserving outward decorum in the middle of this Moorish bordello. "Baby doll" demonstrated that she could "tame the wildest of men." One evening, an obstreperous cowboy threatened to shoot anyone who disagreed with him. With a "sweet smile" she admonished him not to be "a great big silly child" and gently steered him to the door where the chasseur installed him on a comfortable square of asphalt![81]

This sort of anecdote is typical of the blithe tone adopted by journalists when speaking of Zelli's whoopee emporium. They chose to present an image of harmless debauchery, as if the hypocritical mask of decency covered nothing more than a good-natured indulgence in slightly "naughty" pursuits. This stereotypical Montmartre "wickedness" constituted a second mask concealing a deeper depravation, one in which Zelli was complicit: young women addicted to cocaine, ether cocktails, rapacious Italian gigolos, not-so-discreet prostitution, and ultimately death, an aspect to which Aragon was particularly sensitive. Recalling a novel by Dickens in which a knife is inserted so efficiently that hardly a drop of blood appears on the victim's shirt and the body remains upright in the doorway where it was slain, he observed, "More than any other, Paris is the city where cadavers remain standing. One sees few drunks, the cocaine addicts know to behave, there are tranquil havens for every human pleasure. . . . But Paris is a bloody city. At the moment when the idea of violent death is furthest from your mind, in this *Zelli's* filled with music and light . . . always picture in the darkness of your imagination the upright cadaver with merely a speck of purple confetti on its heart."[82]

By the time of his January 1930 trip to New York, Zelli had become a larger-than-life figure. He is said to have visited the much-admired recreation of the Royal Box for Cole Porter's musical *Fifty Million Frenchmen*. While inspecting the set, the curtain rose and Zelli ended up playing himself.[83] An excited young lady assured him she had never seen such marvelous makeup; he "was the exact counterpart of the original!"[84] Backed by gangster Owney Madden, Zelli then attempted to open a New York Royal Box but the venue was shut down on New Year's Eve 1931 by Prohibition agents.[85] A brief five-month triumph in 1931–1932 as codirector of the Apollo Theater was not enough to realize his dreams of becoming a theatrical producer. Predictably, his Broadway production of *Papavert*, an adaption of a British version of a French comedy based on a German play, closed after two performances.[86]

Spring 1932 saw the French Royal Box metamorphosed into a café chantant, then "Zelli's Chez les Nudistes."[87] Zito's famous caricatures were replaced by paintings of noted Parisians in the nude (including, side by side, rivals Mistinguett and Josephine Baker). In late 1933 he made a final stab at reviving his Parisian career, briefly opening the "Club des Lapins"—directly across from Cadet Rousselle where he had earned his first battle stripes.[88] Again his partner was a dodgy character: Jack May, an American restaurateur who had run a string of successful London nightspots reputed to be covers for an extensive drug operation. He was finally deported from Britain in 1930. The Club des Lapins didn't last long. By May 1934 Zelli was back in America. There followed a series of night cafés in New York and Florida. None were able to recreate the exhilaration of the rue Fontaine. The forties saw him as maître d'hôtel at the Hotel Brevoort in New York, cheerfully offering the Royal Box to baffled members of a younger generation unfamiliar with the once-famous champagne palace.

His final gig found him in Hillsdale, New York, bottling gourmet sauces for high-end restaurants. It was there that Zelli was buried in 1971 at age eighty-two. A 1958 news photo shows him comfortably installed in a lawn chair, caressing his collie, Duke. The idyllic Hillsdale slopes stretch out behind him in the late afternoon sun. A self-satisfied smile widens his mouth. He seems content. Comparing his densely wooded sylvan retreat to the celebrated landscapes of Europe, he muses, "Why should I ever want to leave when I have everything in the world right here at my doorstep?"[89] If he thinks for a moment of his opportunistic alliances with unethical imposters like Monzat, his uneasy relations with the scandalous Stavisky, or the homicidal Owney "Killer" Madden, the harem girls, the "discreet" drug commerce in the toilets, he tells himself that perhaps these concessions to a less-than-strict morality had been necessary compromises.

And the Black entertainers on whose talents he had built his fortune? Despite a frequentation of racist circles and an occasional bottle of champagne lobbed by patrons at a colored guest, he was generally supportive of Black artists, both professionally and socially (a 1927 photo shows him posing at the Royal Box with Pepito and Josephine, bending over as if to kiss her hand). Any compromises that he had been compelled to make with his essentially tolerant stance on race relations were contrary to his nature and determined solely by the profit motive. But, along with the neon glitter of Montmartre, he appears to have put all that behind him, perhaps retaining only the image of Buddie Gilmore in the spotlight, juggling his drumsticks to the rhythm of a muted ragtime; the excitement of presiding over the animated presentations of the

Royal Box Band; or the recollected pleasures of champagne parties in Gene Bullard's apartment near the Eiffel Tower.

As for the dance hall that had brought him fame, in 1934 it was reportedly converted into a Turkish bath, prompting a journalist to quip, "which is hardly any change at all!"[90] Clever! But he was wrong on two counts. Chez les Nudistes lasted until early 1939 when it was superseded by another nude cabaret, the Paradise, destined to satisfy the "degenerate" tastes of the future Nazi occupiers. Secondly, the columnist was confusing two equally exotic but quite dissimilar décors, a Turkish steam room and a kitschy Moorish bordello in the country of the Abencerrages.

CHAPTER SEVEN

"M'SOO KEE-LAY AND HIS SNOW-WHITE RUSSIAN WOLFHOUND"

Conflicted Dreams of a Dance Hall King

Kiley's principal profession is that of Fatal Man.
—Basil Woon

At mid-decade Zelli's and Kiley's cabarets were the most prominent white-owned establishments in Pigalle. However, their personalities were quite dissimilar. Zelli was of a generous nature, a cheerful disposition, and partial to genteel pursuits. Kiley was volatile, impulsive, and insensible to rustic pleasures, preferring the gambling rooms of fashionable casinos or boxing matches at the Vélodrome d'Hiver. Even so, they shared certain traits. Endowed with expansive personalities, both had opened their first clubs during the heroic era of the clandestine *dancings* and both owed their success to the talents of Black artists. Given the conflicted nature of his personality, for Kiley, this endorsement sometimes led to tensions. Although he does not appear to have been strongly biased, he sought the approval of a white establishment less enlightened than he. Beyond mundane business failures and the melodramatic epithet "fatal man" lay a complicated reality: Kiley's inability to choose between committed relationships and frivolous liaisons, art, and commerce, the Black performers who made his name and the racist critics who harassed them.

Unlike Zelli, who finished his days peacefully seated in a lawn chair in Hillsdale, Kiley obsessively pursued the twin chimeras of literary glory and love. Yet, for most of his life he remained a bachelor, "the boy whose love affairs were to intrigue all Europe."[1] This notoriety earned him the fatuous sobriquet of "fatal man." Woon did not invent the expression, nor does he necessarily assign it an amorous meaning; with good reason he refers to the financial misadventures caused by a "fatality" in Kiley's nature.[2]

The label was born in the fertile imagination of a feature writer at the *Pittsburgh Press*, where a sensational subhead trumpeted, "Astonishing Fatalities

Destroyed Seven Sweethearts of Mr. Gerald Kiley Before He Could Marry Them."³ As recounted by the tabloid, the series began in 1914 with a young Chicago society woman, Ebba Johnson. The twenty-one-year-old beauty, whom Kiley had purportedly been wooing, died of a suspected suicide. Kiley was twenty-five years old. A year and a half later, as a cub reporter on the *Chicago Examiner* he and future dramatist Charles MacArthur were assigned to cover the departure of the First Illinois Cavalry for a punitive expedition against Mexican rebel Pancho Villa. Having patronized one too many saloons, the two confrères inadvertently enlisted. During his seven months on the Texas border, Kiley cemented his reputation as a Don Juan by pursuing an obliging army wife.⁴ This was unexceptional. As MacArthur's colleague Ben Hecht wrote, "During the heroic campaign, wherever [he] and Kiley trod, rivers flowed uphill, senoritas stormed the tents, rum poured out of the palm trees, and commanding officers were torn between suicide and desertion."⁵

Concerning Miss Johnson, the *Pittsburgh Press* echoes comments circulated by Kiley that he had been her "forbidden suitor." The family denied this, and a coroner's jury ruled her death accidental.⁶ As with the other six fatalities, the story is composed of approximations and vague allegations. Moreover, having reviewed the folklore of the "fatal man" or "woman," the author blithely admits that none of it applies to Kiley unless "he had lived in the superstitious Middle Ages."⁷ Most of Jed's fatal beauties remain obscure. One exception is the ravishing young Princess Francesca Rospigliosi, offspring of an American mother and a Roman prince. Her sudden death in June of 1920 elicited a deluge of press reports that demonstrate how a legend is born and nourished.

Kiley was then at the peak of his success as "Ice Cream King" and, according to the *Pittsburgh Press*, living at the prestigious Ritz Hotel. Enamored of the princess, also in residence, he allegedly obtained her mother's consent to marry. Though secretly engaged to an Italian cavalry officer, Francesca was said to be attracted by the "handsome" Chicagoan who danced so well. Not being choreographically gifted, the desperate Italian committed suicide during a telephone quarrel over Kiley. Dashing across the place Vendome, the princess discovered him lifeless in his room at the Hotel du Rhin. Less than two weeks later she herself was dead of an overdose of the sedative veronal—the *Pittsburgh Press* speaks of an accident while implying suicide.⁸

The general outlines of the story are accurate. Although no other reports on the princess' demise mention Kiley, he may well have met the young woman during a tea dance at the Ritz and been drawn to her beauty; however, despite his fondness for the hotel, he was not living there but in Montmartre.⁹ As for her sentiments, Kiley's buddy Floyd Gibbons claimed that "almost every girl in France, from princesses to *midinettes* were running after Jed."[10] It is difficult to fathom his physical appeal (see gallery 2). Doubtless the secret lay in his personality and social flair. The princess may have been charmed and enjoyed dancing with him—after all, he was the man said to have introduced the foxtrot to Europe—but there is no evidence of anything more. And Princess Mary Rospigliosi's consent to their marriage is a complete fabrication, as is the transcription of the telephone dispute between Francesca and her fiancé.[11] The Italian officer's suicide was due to her mother's opposition to his marriage with the princess and, despite romantic suggestions of death from a broken heart, reliable newspapers attributed the young woman's death to chronic malaria.[12] Manifestly, the story was revised by the *Pittsburgh Press* to fit the narrative of the "fatal man."

After the calamitous and likely fabricated passion for Princess Rospigliosi and the Dixie Ice Cream fiasco in August, Kiley began what the French call "une traversée du désert" ("a time in the wilderness"): a flamboyant period during which he lived through a tragic love affair in Berlin with Dora, a German skater who died on the ice from lung congestion. While in the German capital, he also found the time to operate a dance school in partnership with his ex-rival of the Aladdin's Lamp, Clarence Glover.[13] This failed venture highlights the fact that although not directly linked to the rue Caumartin, he was associated with two of the Clover Club's owners: Glover and Bill Henley, whose White Lyres had played at his American Fox-trot Club, establishing a clear filiation between the clandestine clubs, the semilegal boîtes of the rue Caumartin, and their legitimate successors, the society *dancings*.

During this chaotic time, an incident occurred that is symptomatic of Kiley's ambivalent relations with his compatriots of color. In the early morning of January 1, 1923, as he exited the New York Bar in the rue Daunou (ruminating, perhaps, on his varied misadventures), Jed noticed a scuffle. Seconded by ex-Spade Fernando Jones, the proud and prickly war hero Gene Bullard was slugging it out in front of Ciro's with Harry McClelland, a white lawyer from California. Bullard's patronage of the chic restaurant suggests the ease with which the son of an ex-slave navigated the social strata of Paris. However, that was not always the case. When a Frenchwoman in the lawyer's party spoke to him, the Californian objected that he "didn't want any 'damn nigger' talking to women in his company."[14] Unaware of the reasons for the quarrel, Kiley revealed his divided loyalties. Noted for "a Cyrano de Bergerac flair for taking sides in public," he spontaneously responded to the sight of a white man being pummeled by a Black one.¹⁵ Leaping into the fray, he landed a blow on the startled Bullard, while a white passerby belabored Bullard with an umbrella. Police promptly hauled the main actors and the umbrella warrior off to the station house, while Kiley rapidly disappeared.¹⁶

Three years is a long time to wander in the wilderness. Longing for his abandoned throne of Foxtrot King, in the fall of 1923 Kiley discovered a locale suitable to realize his dream of the "largest cabaret-café on the hill": the expropriated Théâtre des Deux Masques at 6 rue Fontaine, a few doors south of Zelli's.¹⁷ However, he did not, as Woon implies, discover Montmartre in 1923.¹⁸ He had been living close to the rue Fontaine since the war and was certainly aware of both Zelli's success and the changes gestating in Pigalle.

The projected dance palace was to have borne a whimsical name: the "Volstead Café." "To drink under the auspices of the author of the National Prohibition Act," one journalist remarked, "would not have been lacking in imagination. Unfortunately, Mr. Volstead, who apparently lacks the sense of humor that characterizes the compatriots of Mark Twain, has just forbidden Mr. Kiley to use his name."¹⁹ In effect, Kiley had been scolded by the abstemious senator: "Undoubtedly, you consider this very clever and expect to reap huge profits from the sort of Americans, like yourself, who consider it very smart to ridicule the laws of your country."²⁰ Tongue in cheek, Kiley riposted that Volstead was the name of an Austrian composer best known for his "Jolly Fellows Waltz."²¹ The senator did not buy the explanation. On February 5, a few days before the opening, the club was prudently renamed "Kiley's."²²

Unanticipated delays had allowed the installation of an opulent décor.²³ A drawing by Jean Dulac reveals a vaguely ecclesiastical ornamentation (see gallery 2).²⁴ The image dates from the club's reincarnation as the Palermo, but a photo of the original décor suggests no substantial difference.²⁵ Once past the vestibule of this ersatz temple, one entered the Holy of Holies. Over the bandstand loomed an ironic altarpiece, a mural in the modern style representing a lost golden age. Kiley flatly declared, "My place was no church," but with its square, reflecting columns, vaulted ceiling, and arched mirrors that served as narcissistic side chapels, the vast hall resembled nothing so much as a Byzantine art deco cathedral.²⁶ Only the gods venerated were Bacchus, Venus, and Terpsichore, and the one-eyed doorman, boxer "Blink" McCloskey, with his glass eye, cauliflower ears, and no-neck-to-speak-of, served as a most unorthodox sexton.²⁷

For opening night, Kiley relied on the Crackerjacks, one of the finest and most enduring of the Montmartre bands, augmented by the drums of Buddie

Gilmore.[28] At the height of his Parisian celebrity, the champion drummer's participation represented a hallmark of jazz authenticity. Ads announced "dancing**attractions**suppers."[29] Dancing was well provided for, as were the attractions, the sort of cabaret acts popularized at Zelli's, but as for "suppers," in the early hours of April 17, repasts posed a problem. Led by his hostess Mrs. Charlie Munn, and attended by the indispensable Bates, the Prince of Wales learned that the personnel of the café were on strike.[30] Displaying his proverbial common touch, he declared, "Lock the doors and we'll have a good time, I've always wanted to wait on table anyway," and donning an apron, he pitched in to serve drinks and clear dishes.[31] For his efforts, he was rewarded with a platter of ham and eggs and the griddle cakes he had learned to appreciate at Mitchell's, concocted in extremis by the socially prominent Mrs. Freddie Havemeyer. Ensconced in the kitchen in a grease-stained designer gown, she headed an amateur staff, with Dorothy Munn on dishwashing duty.[32]

Despite sniping journalists (Kiley's "native sons orchestra believes musical America is bordered on the north by the Mason and Dixon line"), the prince clearly preferred the Crackerjacks.[33] Between bussing tables and wolfing down griddle cakes, he requested two of his favorite numbers: "Some Sunny Day" and "You Gotta Kiss Mamma Every Night, or You Can't Kiss Mamma at All."[34] The central figures of the band that inspired him were trumpeter Bobbie Jones and his partner Joe Caulk, a bandolinist of Black and Mexican origins (Pancho Villa was rumored to be his father).[35] The prince's riding accident hadn't dimmed his passion for dancing; it even turned to his advantage. Owing to an oscillating right kneecap caused by his fall, he was able to enlarge the royal repertoire of King Alfonso and the Shah of Persia, inadvertently inventing the "Prince de Galles Trott," a wobbly dance step imitated by all the young dandies of Montmartre![36]

In early September, Kiley's became Shanley's, a name calling up memories of an eponymous series of New York restaurant-cabarets that had flourished in the teens. The new owners, however, were not American. Sensational assertions of the *Pittsburgh Press* aside, it is obvious that the fatal man was unlucky with women. Jed was associated with a lady anxious to make her fortune, declares Woon, but they "quarreled, and it is the woman who now owns the place."[37] Despite a paucity of detail, Woon was on target. Six months after the heralded opening, the mercurial entrepreneur ceded his club to French associates. To avoid "long court proceedings" he accepted the modest sum granted by the judges and, with a promise to open a new jazz emporium, embarked on a tour of the casinos of Deauville and Ostend.[38]

His retreat left an eerie afterimage. A 1925 advertisement for Shanley's, illustrated by Josephine's erstwhile boyfriend Zito, exhibits a scantily clad young woman brandishing a bottle of bubbly as she swoons in the arms of a top-hatted Don Juan bearing an uncanny resemblance to Kiley.[39] The central figure cannot refer to him; however, some elements can be identified with certainty. On the left, a Black banjoist strums his instrument. The hugely popular Crackerjacks continued at Shanley's and its successor the Palermo, so the musician may represent Joe Caulk or a generic personage signifying jazz. On the right, a text announces, "Billie [sic] Trittle and his I.B.F. Band." Trittle, a talented white trombonist, had been part of Billy Arnold's "millionaires" band. Goddard's critique of the Arnolds' recording of "Stop It" is devastating: "The rhythm section of piano and drums has all the retarded momentum of a Model-T Ford being driven with the handbrake on . . . only the trombone player makes a reasonable showing, but even he can do nothing to impart some swing to the corny staccato lead and the tuneless twittering of the clarinet."[40]

It was perhaps this difference in quality that prompted Trittle to go out on his own at Shanley's. His motivations do not concern us, but the name of his band is key to a reading of the advertisement. If the connotation of the banjo player is evident, what does the enigmatic appellation I.B.F. Band signify? The mystery is quickly dispelled. I.B.F. stands for "International Bar Flies." The creation of this burlesque organization was intimately bound up with Billy Trittle, Harry's New York Bar, and Kiley, many of whose friends were among its charter members.[41] Kiley's future editor, Arthur Moss, offered a comic rendering of the group's creation: "You've heard so much about the *Birth of a Nation*, the "Birth of the Blues," and the birth of quintuplets to a prominent Slovak society woman in Pottsville P. A., that it's about time to recall the *Birth of the Barflies*."[42] The impetus for the I.B.F.'s founding was an article by Kiley's friend columnist O. O. McIntyre, in which he facetiously bemoaned the sad state of the "barflies" of Paris. With an eye to publicizing his forthcoming club, "Kiley, then Kleagle of a Kabaret," promised Christmas Eve receipts "to the needy barflies of Harry's, Frank's Ritz Bar, and other charitable institutions."[43] This led the New York Bar's owner, Harry McElhone, to create the I.B.F., with McIntyre as Big Blue Bottlefly and himself as Little Blue Bottlefly. Billy Arnold, Bill Henley, and Billy Trittle were installed as Gadflies, and emblems were created from sugar cubes decorated with dead flies.

One might deem this organization a harmless if inane invention, were it not for the toxicity of what Woon termed "the Ritz-New York Bar-Luigi's [sic] struggle," engaged in by the chronic American drinkers one sees "at Zelli's at 3 o'clock in the morning."⁴⁴ A prime victim of this poison was Franco-Senegalese boxer Louis Phal, known as "Battlin' Siki," winner of a light heavyweight championship bout with world titleholder Georges Carpentier. After describing Siki as a "jungle mauler, . . . a wooly head closely resembling a fire alarm box," Woon shamelessly relates how one day Siki "wandered late into the New York Bar, run [in 1923] by . . . sportsman, Charley Herrick . . . and the bartender declined to serve him. Siki protested that in France Blacks are on an equal footing with whites. 'This ain't France—it's New York,' answered Herrick. Siki grumbled darkly but left. At Lougi's [sic] Elmano Bar, also run for Americans, he was confronted with a sign: 'We don't serve colored men—not even Siki.' Here his party broke a few glasses by way of argument."⁴⁵

This is the insidious and long-standing world of white privilege denoted by the name I.B.F. Beneath the frat boy antics lay a racist bias, evident in several loaded terms of Moss' account, linked to the I.B.F. in the name of wit. But none of this humor is innocent. The expression "Kleagle" denotes a high-ranking officer in the hierarchy of the Ku Klux Klan (Kl [an] + eagle) whose vigilantes were idealized in D. W. Griffith's controversial *Birth of a Nation* as the chivalric rescuers of white women threatened by demonized Black scoundrels, intent on rape and the creation of a mongrel race. The film would have been present in the minds of Parisians. Having been refused an exploitation visa in 1916, it was released in mid-1923 only to be banned by the government of French President Raymond Poincaré. The second birth mentioned in Moss' mock chronicle concerns the quintuplets of the Slovak woman from Pennsylvania. The Keystone State was a favored destination of Slovakian émigrés, and the extravagant fertility of the Slovak "society" woman suggests a Nativist, anti-immigration slur. Even more egregious is the placement of the hit song "Birth of the Blues" (1926) in parallel with the Ku Klux Klan. Although written by white songwriters, it invoked a uniquely Black genre, one of the essential constituents of jazz.⁴⁶

The I.B.F. was basically an old boys' club, even if prominent women like Marlene Dietrich and Elsa Maxwell were inducted after 1925. However, this hospitality did not extend to Black people. When Woon declares that "the score or so of American musicians in Paris make the place their headquarters," one senses a smug racial insularity.⁴⁷ There is no evidence that in 1924 Mitchell or any of Montmartre's Black musicians ever set foot in Harry's. Furthermore, ignoring the contributions of James Reese Europe and Louis Mitchell, Woon asserts that the "first of the jazz bands here [in Paris] was that organized by Bill Henley from American soldiers stationed in Paris just after the armistice. . . .

Following Henley came Mitchell."[48] As we know, these declarations are either misinformed or in bad faith.

Reexamining the nimble dancer of Zito's drawing who so oddly resembles Kiley, if we imagine the top-hatted reveler to be exercising the skills that had earned Jed the sympathy of the young Princess Rospigliosi, it is tempting to envision the personage as figuring his relation to the two poles of his existence, an allegory of his dilemma: dancing desperately between two worlds, the confraternity of bigoted, white American barflies who haunted alcohol-soaked retreats like the Ritz, Louigi's, or Harry's New York Bar and the community of Black entertainers that had assured his success in the more diverse cabarets of the rue Fontaine.

For reasons unknown, on October 7, 1925, Shanley's became the Palermo. A few months later Paul Santolini, aka Paul Santo, was appointed artistic director.[49] Totally absent from modern histories of the Butte, by 1929 he came to dominate Montmartre night life. A debonair gentleman of Corsican ancestry, he sported Mediterranean looks and an Adolphe Menjou moustache—similar to those of Zito and Pepito— in keeping with his past as a gigolo "whose services could be had for a price when a visiting lady at the cabaret where he was employed wished to have a capable and picturesque partner."[50] A year after the Palermo's inauguration, Santo became codirector.[51] The former gigolo had begun his ascension.

Before granting the title to Zelli, Arthur Moss had described Jed as "the ex-Mogul of Montmartre, Old King Kiley."[52] Yet, reporter Henry Wales, who knew him well, recounts that on the day before Charles Lindbergh's historic solo flight landed (May 20, 1927), he stopped in at Kiley's club in the rue Fontaine and found him in a Cossack costume doing the sword dance.[53] In the midst of constant transformations, did the Dance-Hall King somehow reenter the picture? This appears unlikely. Kiley was then on the verge of launching a new cabaret in Montparnasse, and Wales' testimony was proffered ten years after the fact.[54] This period represents a puzzling chapter in an extraordinary biography where truth and fiction are equally strange.

Lured by dreams of literary glory, in March 1927 Kiley wrote his first piece for the *Boulevardier*, a satirical review on the order of the *New Yorker*, financed by his friend Erskine Gwynne and edited by I.B.F. historian Arthur Moss. Constantly divided between two vocations (in his own words "literary in the daytime and mercenary at night"), six months later he opened the College Inn in Montparnasse.[55] However, that is not how Kiley tells the story. He contends that "in November of 1929 the big Depression bounced off of Wall Street and hit Paris hard.... Lost the place in Montmartre and the *Boulevardier* folded for want of readers."[56] Yet, as we shall see, all his Montmartre clubs had been "lost" by May 1925, and even the College Inn was misplaced before February 1929.[57] As for the *Boulevardier*, it didn't "fold" until 1932. It was convenient to blame everything on the Crash but, in fact, Kiley had sailed for Hollywood a month before the great financial debacle, hired as a scriptwriter for the new talking pictures and, incidentally, as technical director for the film adaptation of Cole Porter's *Fifty Million Frenchmen*.

There is another province of Kiley's unstable mini kingdom that is elided in his assertion, one that has escaped the notice of Montmartre historians. After commenting on the loss of the fatal man's first Pigalle cabaret, Woon adds that "just before Christmas 1924 a new 'Kiley's' opened on the rue Fontaine"—the unspecified cabaret whose proceeds were to benefit the barflies of the I.B.F.[58] Nevill confirms the existence of the elusive *dancing* but again offers few details.[59] For contemporaries, the subject was less opaque. A classified ad by colorful *Herald* sports reporter Sparrow Robertson dated January 25, 1925, saw fit to warn the public, "My wife having left my bed and board I will not be responsible for any bills run up at Kiley's, 25 rue Fontaine, Montmartre."[60] (See gallery 2.)

Louis Aragon was also familiar with the establishment, a stop on the round of jazz and champagne palaces that constituted a standard tourist itinerary of "Montmartre by Night." One evening in 1925, Aragon and his friends ended up at "Kiley's, a club that no longer exists, in the basement of the *Gaity*, the little music hall in the rue Fontaine.[61] A vast room, always empty, with a very good orchestra, and the place where one danced looked like the ring of a circus. The die-hards came to drink at the little bar where Mme Kiley played at dice with the customers. And Kiley, a badly disillusioned man who so often had suffered bankruptcy, caressed his great police dog."[62]

The "die-hards" in question were the young Surrealist writers who frequented the quarter. For Aragon, the mystery of those nights was personified by an imposing woman who materialized in the early mornings at the crossroads of the rue Pigalle and the rue Fontaine, dressed "in an evening gown, with a cape of black silk, or one of those orange or pink cloaks with ruffled collars that since the war have become the fashion. Décolleté. Opulent, awe-inspiring breasts." The young Frenchmen were dazzled by this "diamond draped statue" looming at the end of the bar, "straight as a rod. Inebriated. Waiting for one of us to fall down drunk and to take him to God knows where"—an arresting and enigmatic vision given to humming the blues and raising her skirts to Charleston, incarnation of the voracious carnal appetites of Montmartre.[63]

The club was indeed "vast"—two stories with a mezzanine balcony—and during the evanescent spring of Kiley's Gaity the "very good orchestra" included excellent blues pianist Danny Wilson, who since the beginning of the year had been playing at Mitchell's, around the corner in the rue Blanche.[64] But notwithstanding his invaluable testimony, Aragon makes two errors. The first involves the "great police dog." McIntyre informed his readers that "everybody in Montmartre knows M'soo Kee-lay and his snow-white Russian wolfhound."[65] Wolfhounds, or "borzoi," are indeed large, but unreliable as watchdogs, being of a tranquil temperament and friendly toward strangers. Kiley's four-legged friend was Countess Arabella von Frankenstein, from the kennels of a Russian grand duke. And that was the least of the pooch's aristocratic connections. In search of financing after losing 6 rue Fontaine, "M'soo Kee-lay" and his dog were refused entry to the Deauville Casino. However, when the Prince of Wales laced his arm through that of his "old friend" and proceeded to enter, Countess Arabella trailing in their wake, no one dared to stop them. As for the blue-blooded canine, according to wag Arthur Moss, she declared in dog language, "I came; I saw; and I'm not coming back. Those chips are not real bones!"[66]

The second error is more consequential and concerns the woman behind the bar. Following a traditional social model exemplified by the Zellis, Aragon assumes that she is Mme Kiley, even though one of Jed's well-known traits was his aversion to matrimony! If one consults Dick Carlish's autobiography, the true identity of "Mme Kiley" is revealed. After his gig with the Southern Syncopated Orchestra in 1922, Carlish performed at various Parisian nightspots with Harry Wellmon. But by 1925 he was back home managing the infamous 43 Club for Kate Meyrick, "Night Club Queen" of London.[67] At Kate's request, he crossed the Channel to scout sites for a cabaret. "Sunshine filtering through the trees and the birds and the bees and the flowers galloping into action all over the place."[68] If all that is not just literary decoration, he would appear to have arrived in April. Thanks to his connections, he eventually found a locale and alerted Kate, who sent him home and opened "Merrick's Gaity" herself.[69]

The lady in question appears to propose a different story in her memoir, *Secrets of the 43*. She makes no reference to Carlish or a manager, recounting that in late April, newly released from Holloway Prison after serving time for selling liquor after hours and threatened by "drastic police intervention," she was advised by friends "to lie low until the storm blew over." In June, she took their advice and sagely decamped to Paris. Kate further asserts that after a frustrating search she "purchased an empty cabaret" from "Monsieur Bergère."[70] Manifestly, she is referring to Gaity owner Léo Berryer, but what did she really purchase? Certainly not the cabaret; more probably she obtained a lease, available due to Kiley's insolvency. However, the dissonance is only apparent. Carlish adds that "as soon as she [Kate] felt that the Gaity had been suitably launched, she wired me to come over and run it." This occurred in mid-November.[71] Therefore, aside from Kate's silence about her associates, there is no contradiction.

Even though Kate's name is absent from Montmartre annals, she was well known to contemporaries like Joe Zelli, whom she describes as having a "big, generous heart." His terse greeting the day before she and Kiley were to open was, "Welcome, Mrs. Meyrick, and—goodbye!... Please go back. You do not know Paris; I do."[72] Zelli was not discouraging an unwelcome rival; rather, he was offering a friendly warning about "the dark side" of the cabaret trade, a subject with which he was intimately familiar. What he perhaps ignored is that she had already braved the proximity of Soho drug dealers and was "absolutely determined to succeed at all costs."[73]

While Kate's project clearly involved Kiley, the nature of their relation remains ambiguous.[74] By May, Jed had run through the $40,000 won at the Bellevue Casino in Biarritz the previous October and was obliged to declare bankruptcy.[75] Kate refers to him as "manager," but there was already a manager (former silent film star Bertram Burleigh).[76] Therefore, Kate is most likely referring to a partnership involving an infusion of cash—she speaks of paying off "outstanding bills" and counting up receipts and expresses her delight in "the services of so popular a man."[77] In any case, if the exact nature of their alliance remains uncertain, it is evident that she is the anonymous woman behind the bar in Aragon's text.

The poet wrote, "And Kiley, a badly disillusioned man who so often had suffered bankruptcy, caressed his great police dog." Aragon may have been unaware of Jed's romantic difficulties; even so, this comment on his financial failures is equally applicable to the sentimental realm. At the time when he glimpsed him fondling the faithful canine, Kiley's business and personal affairs were at an equal low. A rumored engagement to opera singer Suzanne Gautier seems to have come to nothing, and shortly after, under the shocked gaze of Kate and the staff, a distraught American inamorata would savagely attack him before being rapidly ejected.[78]

But the most serious of his emotional troubles concerned his breakup with dancer Marion Forde. Their engagement was announced on February 2 of that year. Prudently insisting on a pause, Marion left for New York to put "her heart to the test."[79] The results were clearly negative. By the end of March she was back in Paris pursuing a blossoming career. Though insufficient to save their relationship, they shared a common passion: Marion's debut at the Casino with Mitchell's Jazz Kings had made her a star.[80] Writer Mac Orlan for one was greatly impressed: "She dances powerfully and with joy under the gaze of the Black musicians who follow her, intent on the rhythm that the slide trombone [Frank Withers] presides over with paternal goodwill."[81]

If Kiley's amours with the ebullient Miss Forde were ill-starred, he gave no appearance of pining away. A few months later he rebounded at the races with tainted San Francisco heiress Muriel Buell Caples, rumored to be his fiancée.[82] Bad girl Muriel was not as prestigious a catch as Marion, but her tawdry adventures with "Ketchup King" Jefferson Livingston had received much publicity when she sued him for breach of promise, alleging that he had guaranteed her a $1750 monthly allowance for life. The engagement with Kiley was probably newspaper gossip, but the excitable Mrs. Caples took it more seriously. The following year she vied to become the fatal man's eighth amorous casualty. After three attempted suicides with veronal, she hysterically proclaimed that her love affair had been shattered when Kiley abandoned her for another. Moreover, she alleged that at the time of his bankruptcy he had fooled her into believing they were married and proceeded to squander her wealth in the gambling rooms of Vichy and Nice.[83] Could Muriel be the overwrought young woman who assaulted the restaurateur at Merrick's Gaity? If so, her aborted suicides may have caused a chill to run down Jed's spine; in the *Pittsburgh Press'* apocryphal story Princess Rospigliosi had died of a veronal overdose!

Kiley's book on Hemingway inadvertently suggests that the sum of these turbulent affairs had soured him on love. The last of its four Parisian sequences develops the theme of frustrated passion—literary and amorous—triggered by the presence of a man whom Jed perceived as his rival both in literature and love.[84] After a violent row during the boxing matches at the Vélodrome d'Hiver in which Ernest Hemingway took his side, Kiley offers to drive the novelist home, accompanied by two American girls he has been squiring. He is annoyed when they gush over the newly famous author like "a couple of bobbysoxers," causing him to remark callously, "I didn't mind too much about the brunette [raven-haired like Marion]. She was a spare. But the redhead was putting it on too thick to suit me." When Hemingway announces that he is working on a short story collection titled *Men Without Women*, Kiley acidly comments, "Did you ever see a man without a woman in Paris? You are in

Paris, France, now, kid, not Paris, Illinois. There are no men without women here and no women without men outside of Lady Brett perhaps."[85]

In this ostensibly literary discussion, Kiley's disenchanted attitude toward matters of the heart bubbles to the surface. Claiming never to have read *The Sun Also Rises*, he nevertheless gathers from the girls' chatter that the heroine, Lady Brett Ashley, was keeping the hero and perfidiously intimates to the redhead that Hemingway is the original of the sexually wounded Jake. ("All's fair in love and war," he rationalizes.) Then, carelessly conflating Lady Duff Twysden and her fictional double, he reflects, "All that baby ever kept was the change when somebody gave her over two dollars"; and, in a naked self-confession, he admits, "She was no more capable of spiritual love than I was."[86]

Apparently, his tragic romance with Dora, the ice-skating queen of Berlin, had fouled his dreams. Sometime between returning from Berlin in the first week of May 1921 and Jeanne Darcy's closure of Chez Harry Pilcer on the tenth, Kiley was observed in the dancer's shimmy salon gazing longingly at a photo of Dora, "the Mary Pickford of Germany . . . of an almost spiritual beauty."[87] He told a friend that "it was the first time he had believed in the sensation that is called love at first sight."[88] Years later in Key West, the sight of a shark cannibalizing her dying mate prompted this disabused observation: "That's the female of the species for you. . . . A minute before she had been swimming lovingly by his side and now she was eating the guy alive."[89]

On one occasion Kiley assured the P.O.W. that he had never married and never would. Employing one of the Americanisms he affected, the latter replied, "Shake brother! After all, England had a virgin queen, didn't she?"[90] The "virginal" Edward would marry the somewhat tarnished American divorcée Wallis Simpson. At age fifty-four Kiley would also wed—Joan Sawyer Rentschler, a fifty-six-year-old former dancer and vaudeville star, one of Maurice Mouvet's ex-partners and fiancées. He may have known her from the glory days of the Aladdin's Lamp Club, of which she was a charter member, and they shared a taste for Black music. As with Marion Forde, musical harmony was insufficient. From a hospital bed in Miami, where he was recovering from an encounter with a drunk driver, Kiley wryly commented, "Two years ago I was married in this town. One year ago I was divorced here. This year I was only run over."[91]

By way of explaining Emma Bovary's sad destiny, Flaubert states that she was not an artist, that her artistic aspirations outstripped her capacity to realize them. A glance at Kiley's scant literary production suggests a similar analysis. At the time of his flight to Hollywood, his purported friend O. O. McIntyre bemoaned the fact that he had "been sold down the river."[92] In fact, was there anything to sell? Before leaving for Europe, he had worked briefly for the *Chicago Examiner* and after the war done a short stint at the Paris *Herald*, but his journalistic career was hardly distinguished. Clearly chastened by the failure of the Gaity, in 1926 Kiley's thoughts turned increasingly to literature. Perhaps inspired by his former neighbor Omar Khayyâm's *Dancing*, he penned a clumsy pastiche of Edward Fitzgerald's widely known 1859 translation of the Persian poet's *Rubaiyat of Omar Khayam*. He called it the "Boobyat of Montmartre Kiley." I will cite the first quatrain and ignore the rest.

> Awake! for the Chasseur in the Paris night
> Has called the cab which starts the party right;
> And lo! the hunters of the franc have caught
> The hill of Montmartre in a noose of light.[93]

Unsurprisingly, this effort did not earn a Nobel Prize. His chief claim to literary eminence would lie in his association with the *Boulevardier*, according to Woon a "mixture of amateurism and cleverness," a critique that might apply to his friend's productions.[94] Kiley's self-image is more flattering. He does not hesitate to insert himself into a distinguished pantheon, referring to "Sinclair Lewis, Scott Fitzgerald, and the rest of us" and adopting a particularly condescending attitude toward the author of *Main Street*, the celebrated satire of provincial life. He declares that, unlike Hemingway, Lewis was a "nice guy. You don't mind helping out a writer like that."[95]

In truth though, what had Kiley written—the "Boobyat"? At best, his contributions to the *Boulevardier* had some success: a piece entitled "My Daily Life and Work" by "Bonita Mustardini," described as an "intimate story of how the Duce spends his twenty-four hours," and another called "Ladies Prefer Argentines" by "Senor Jed Kiley de Chili."[96] But as literary creations they were distinctly minor. One of his best sketches was "The Boat Train Girl," based on his Parisian experiences. It was published on the verge of his depart for Hollywood where, whatever their value, his scripts would be butchered, a fate that Fitzgerald and writers better than he did not escape.

In 1934 he moved to Florida. Subsequently, detective stories such as "Three of a Kind," a trifling tale of "clever Chinese" with an O. Henry–like ending, constituted the essence of his literary work. Its chief virtue was a laudable sympathy for the plight of Chinese immigrants.[97] In the thirties and forties newspaper readers were no longer interested in his hoary Parisian adventures. His reputation was kept alive largely by O. O. McIntyre and, after the latter's death, by his heir Charles B. Driscoll. By the time Kiley wrote the *Playboy* articles that make up his book on Hemingway, he was running out of time. His final publication was a pathetic memento of his illustrious past: a recipe for the Aga Khan's favorite dessert, chocolate à la maison. In May 1962 he declared, "I once stole a gal from Rudolph Valentino. I've had people chase me with guns and knives because of women. Now I'm writing a book about myself: I'm calling it *I've Had It.*"[98] Five months later he was dead.

Aragon may have been less well-informed about Kiley's artistic and sentimental problems than readers of American Sunday supplements, and he could not have foreseen the Dance Hall King's dismal future, but he sensed the vulnerability and dismay concealed by the streetwise carapace, capturing him in a moment of intense solitude. The most glaring discrepancy in Kiley's account of his career is his leap from the loss of "the place in Montmartre" to his 1929 departure for Hollywood, totally ignoring ownership of the College Inn. Allegedly, the name of that night resort was inspired by a Chicago night club, but one should note that his partner in the venture was James "Jimmy" Cossitt, an ex–University of Michigan athlete.[99] The designation smacks of nostalgia for those distant, sun-glazed afternoons when as a star halfback at the University of Wisconsin Jed had first tasted the adulation of the crowds, a moment when reality meshed with desire.

Torn between conflicting aspirations, he ardently longed for literary recognition, yet constantly wavered between art and commerce, his writing and the tawdry fame of the dance halls. All evidence points to a real sympathy for Black artists, yet he befriended averred racists such as Basil Woon and frequented institutions that fostered bigotry. Cynical about sentimental relations, he nonetheless engaged in a series of desperate love affairs. Conceivably, these conflicting desires sprang from the same source, an inordinate need for affection and admiration. He had been a college football star, earned $100,000 in the clandestine *dancings*, been crowned and deposed as Foxtrot King, Ice Cream King, and Mogul, credited with the love of seven fatal beauties, befriended by the heir to the British throne, affianced to and separated from one of the most beautiful dancers in Paris. Yet, in Aragon's prophetic image he stands alone in the basement of the Gaity attended only by the devoted Countess Arabella von Frankenstein.

His vacillating but indisputable empathy with Black musicians contrasted with Kate Meyrick's unambiguous racist streak; she railed against "the association of white girls with men of colour," replacing the latter with the sonorous Kalada de Pestchansky and his Russian jazz band, or the University of Alabama Capstone Orchestra (white of course, there were no Black students at the University until 1963).[100] By April Danny Wilson had returned to Mitchell's, but one cannot help imagining the eloquent blues piano of the man who composed "With Someone Like You Around Me, How Could I Feel Blue" still echoing in the immense, deserted hall. The "fatal man" had won many colorful battles, but in the end, he would lose the war.

PART III

AROUND THE RUE PIGALLE

Triumph and Failure on the "Great Black Way"

CHAPTER EIGHT

"AN OSTRICH FEDDAH SUIT O' CAT'S PAJAMAS"

Louis, Flo, and the Prancing Princes

Florence, stamping her small right foot for quiet, awarded to His Royal Highness the first prize, held it aloft before the crowd, explained in mock Negro dialect: "Dis y'ere fust prize am an ostrich feddah suit o' cat's pajamas!"

In a Montmartre with no dearth of would-be monarchs, Louis Mitchell and Florence Jones were unique. However, their rule did not go unchallenged; though inhibited by legal restraints and tolerant French attitudes, racist Americans mounted a thinly veiled resistance. Mitchell had extolled to Eubie Blake the freedom provided by the Montmartre Utopia. This sense of self-confidence and access to economic opportunity explains why after four and a half years at the Casino de Paris he decided to go out on his own. Many situate his first cabaret at 36 rue Pigalle, but, in fact, his club debut was the Grand Duc at number 52, an unpretentious nightspot owned by Georges Jamerson, a Frenchman from an important family with alleged mob connections.

Pernet and Rye acknowledge this but, relying on the Cooke interviews, place the supposed inauguration of the Grand Duc on Thanksgiving Day 1923.[1] Cooke details a glittering roster of "first nighters," studded with the names of Jardin regulars: the Marquis and Marquise de Polignac, Grand Duchess Marie of Russia, Princess Cystria, Deering Davis, Fanny Ward, even Jardin co-founder Elsa Maxwell.[2] To support her narrative, Cooke cites an undated article by *Vogue* society writer John McMullin, implying that it appeared after the Thanksgiving opening: "Mitchell's is a new kind of place for Paris. It is a little bit of Harlem-on-the-Hudson, with its 'darkies' brought to the Place Pigalle (see gallery 2)."[3] However, the piece was actually published on June 15! And Mitchell had not waited until then to realize his dream.

It is no coincidence that rumors of Mitchell launching a night café surfaced at the same time as his frequentation of the Tempo Club, for despite his success at the Casino, he was only hired help. Cooke transcribes his thoughts: "Look here, Mitch... you're being a damn fool. Look at these folks jamming into the Perroquet every night because they like your brand of entertainment. Paris is ripe for a Negro club featuring colored entertainers and you're the little boy to give it to them."[4] Perhaps imaginary, this interior monologue nevertheless exposes his state of mind. The Tempo Club provided him with a vision that became reality in January 1923. At that time, he took over the Grand Duc in collaboration with clarinetist/violinist Paul Wyer, known as "the Pensacola Kid."[5] Their alliance was brief. Wyer accepted a South American tour in a revue starring Mistinguett and sailed for Buenos Aires in May, leaving Mitchell alone to manage the Grand Duc, where he was spotted by McMullin.[6]

Even more surprising than Mitchell's early presence is that of another habitué of the Tempo Club, Florence. The doxa maintains that Gene Bullard hired her in 1924, but that date is contradicted by a hostile witness, none other than Ernest Hemingway.[7] Buried among the short texts that he wrote for the *Toronto Star* is his account of seeing Florence at the Grand Duc in the summer of 1923, a presence confirmed by surrealist poet and writer René Crevel, who wrote of "skin color of black pearl, poured into a sheath of white satin, fresh in rhinestones and pink feathers at two in the morning."[8] Hemingway insists on her growing vogue among the nobility and implicitly contrasts the modest surroundings with the "very dressy *dancings* in the rue Caumartin, where one would find Peggy Joyce and other famous ladies of the front page." He then declares with disdain that Florence "was a [stereo] typical Negro dancer, jolly, funny and wonderful on her feet," reducing her to what Black feminist scholar Marina Magloire characterizes as "servile jolliness."[9] Furthermore, Florence was a singer, she did not dance!

After Mitchell ceded the direction of the Grand Duc to Bullard in December, Florence lingered for a time but soon followed him to 36 rue Pigalle.[10] The stage was set for the Prince of Wales' "revolution." Before a dozen or so tables and a minuscule dance floor, Florence was discovered by the foxtrotting prince.[11] In an offhand remark, Bertelli states that the P.O.W. "was enthralled by Florence, the colored queen of Montmartre, who sings jazz as they used to sing it down in Alabama before the war." It is not clear what the journalist knew about the lyric styles of antebellum Alabama, but he reflects the complacent, bigoted attitudes subjacent to such seemingly anodyne comments. Nor is the citing of Alabama incidental. "The Cotton State" had been home to many large, slaveholding plantations, a racist history of segregation and Black disenfranchisement that would later culminate in the Montgomery bus boycott of 1955–56 and the 1963 Birmingham civil rights protests led by Martin Luther King Jr.

In Montmartre, the chorus of racist disinformation began early on. O. O. McIntyre had already dismissed the Jazz Kings performances at Harry Pilcer's *Dancing*: "A Negro crew of jazzers from Birmingham furnish the whiny syncopated notes."[12] And shortly after the prince's consecration, John O'Brien commented maliciously, "Or perhaps he [a nightbird] wants 'a stack of wheats' or 'sausages and bacon.' Nothing is too much for Montmartre. Mitchel [*sic*]— Mitchel from Alabama—will serve them just as his mammy or somebody else's mammy made 'em."[13] Aside from O'Brien's condescension, one should note that Mitchell was born in New York; and the journalist surely knew that, aside from wheat cakes and sausages, "his stock of 1911 Cordon Rouge would make even Caspar at Ciro's envious."[14] As for Florence, she was a native of Bridgeport, Connecticut. Nor did the colored queen of Montmartre sing what were known as "plantation songs," sneeringly labeled "the syncopated cornfield melodies of our mammy days."[15] Without being connoisseurs, clubgoers knew they were not dancing to "cornfield melodies"; Florence sang, in Goffin's words, "sorrowful blues which enchanted the heart of Paris."[16] If white journalists characterized them as "plantation songs," it was only to relegate the singer to the sphere of "the old plantation," a devalorized social space designated by the code word "Alabama."

This false debate about origins and musical genres conceals the fundamental issue raised by the Prince of Wales' visits: race-mixing. One journal, the *Hartford Courant*, posed a valid question: "How are they going to keep him down on Windsor farm, after he's seen Paris?"[17] This was an allusion to a song recorded by James Reese Europe, among others: "How 'Ya Gonna Keep 'em Down on the Farm (After They've Seen Paree)?"[18] The lyrics evoke American soldiers coming home to a rural environment, but in retrospect Europe's performance takes on a singular resonance given the race riots of the "Red Summer" of 1919 and the hostile if not lethal reception accorded returning Black soldiers. In contrast, the article in the *Courant* focuses on a parallel between Black "doughboys" discovering the relatively unbiased world of Paris and the foxtrotting prince, liberated from the constraints of protocol and seduced by the neon dazzle of Pigalle.

This aspect was stressed by correspondent Lawrence Martin in his description of the prince's Good Friday stop at Mitchell's. Unlike Harlem nightspots such as the Cotton Club, where entertainment was Black but audiences white, at Mitchell's "Blacks and whites mingled freely, Negroes dancing with white women, and the principal entertainer was a negress from New York. Crowds stormed the doors of the negro cabaret when the word went around Montmartre that 'Le Prince de Galles' was there. White folks waved 500-franc notes, trying to bribe the doorman to let them in."[19]

Cited by Cooke without attribution, the *Daily News*' version of Martin's text was titled "Wales Knee Lobs Where Races Mix and Night's Long"—an enigmatic headline if one ignores the invention of the "Prince de Galles Trott." Even so, the challenging syntax is clear. Many denizens of the rue Caumartin had emigrated to Pigalle; now "grand duchesses could rub elbows with cocottes."[20] The concomitant of this social fluidity was the racial mixing highlighted by the headline and underscored by divergences between the *Daily News*' text and other versions of the story. The former is the one conserved by Mitchell and passed on to Cooke. It presents small but telling variations from the text bearing Martin's byline, notably the substitution of "colored" for "Negro," and a telling emphasis on the social activism of the female patrons: "white women choosing colored partners" rather than "Negroes dancing with white women."[21]

The subtitle of another variant proclaimed, "Blacks and Whites Mingling Freely in Montmartre Shown to Prince," as if Mitchell were conducting a scientific experiment for curious royal eyes.[22] Quite the opposite; far from a passive spectator, the prince caused Black newspapers to contemplate the unimaginable: "The Prince of Wales . . . often danced with her [Florence] and drank coffee from her cup."[23] Inconceivable indeed for those who considered it an unnatural union. If the Black press envisioned this symbolic miscegenation with wonder, it was exactly the point that galled many American clubgoers and religious reformers. Holy crusaders often spread the good word in Montmartre—on a "sin tour," evangelist Aimée Semple McPherson sought, vainly, to convert Bricktop's staff from their wicked ways.[24] Many white Americans ranked race-mixing among such sinful pursuits, like the Southerner who, less hypocritical than Lady Cunard, "tried to snatch an English lady from the arms of an Indian prince on the grounds that she was 'a white gal dancin' with a black.'"[25]

Although many minority newspapers approved of this promiscuous racial atmosphere, the sentiment was not universal. J. A. Rogers reports that Black political activist Marcus Garvey attended a reception and dance in his honor organized by *La Dépêche Africaine*, a moderate, assimilationist revue. After the musical program, Garvey prepared to leave, but Rogers attempted slyly to lure him into the ballroom. Unsuccessfully. "Inside was taking place that which was the reverse of his theories. African Negroes, the color of ink, almost, and with hair that was at least 3,000 miles as the crow flies from the nearest hair-straightening parlor, were dancing with white women, some of them pronounced blondes, while the few Negro women, also with hair quite innocent of kink-no-more, were with the exception of one or two monopolized by white men."[26] For Garvey, as well as many white Americans, such a situation was anathema.

At this point French colonial politics intersect with the concerns of the Black expatriate community. Eight months before the Embassy gala, President Poincaré had issued a firm diplomatic note: "Foreign tourists, forgetting that they are our guests and therefore bound to respect our laws and customs, on several recent occasions have violently manifested their aversion to seeing colored people from the French colonies seated by their side in public places. They have even gone so far as to demand their eviction in insulting terms. If such incidents are repeated, punishment will be exacted."[27] He referred here to the American reaction to Senegalese passengers on a bus tour of the battlefields where both groups had lost loved ones, but clashes such as Bullard's melee with Kiley and the Californian lawyer also fed the fire in this explosive atmosphere. Coming three days later, Prince Tovalou's highly mediatized expulsion from the tango palace El Garrón by angry Americans and a complicit French manager was seen as a defiant challenge to Poincaré's note.[28] Ironically, the prince's exclusion coincided with McMullin's revelation of Mitchell's Grand Duc to *Vogue*'s fashionable readership. Relevant both to a seat on a bus or racial mixing on a dance floor, Poincaré's message made no distinction between the civil rights of "colored people from the French colonies" and those of Black Americans, causing his condemnation to resonate in the *dancings* of Montmartre.

Not that the president's purpose was entirely altruistic. Poincaré was motivated as much by politics as a concern for universal human rights. His right-wing government was committed to social stability, which meant pacified Black colonies. "The power of France in Europe," he acknowledged, "is enormously increased by the possession of an African empire of 40,000,000 inhabitants in close proximity to the home country . . . we must leave nothing undone that will help to bind our African colonies to us by ties of affection and self-interest."[29] Like the venal manager of El Garrón, he was obliged to walk a tightrope between the demands of African citizens for equality and the financial might of invading Americans. Faced with his firm attitude, biased American journalists could not voice their opposition too openly; nevertheless, it surfaced in sarcastic formulations such as the "Great Black Way."

After Florence and Mitchell parted ways in November 1924, both cabarets flourished. However, this did not halt Woon and company's insidious sniping. His terse treatment of the pair in *The Paris That's Not in the Guide Books* makes silence seem a virtue; the syndicated pieces are more prolix and malicious. Obliged to mention Black clubs, he cannot disguise his contempt. In an astonishing passage on Chez Florence, he advances a degrading analogy with the "Scopes Monkey Trial," the highly mediatized case of a high school teacher prosecuted for teaching the theory of human development from a lower order of animals: "With the evolution of mankind holding the center of the stage in the Tennessee mountains, society's own small problem of evolution is exciting the spendthrift world on Montmartre hill. Society's effort to uphold the Biblical teaching that all races and creeds are brothers has a startling demonstration nightly on rue Pigalle. . . . In a tiny room chockful of tobacco smoke and champagne fumes, 'fashionable' people . . . are guests of an American negress whose sumptuous mode of living has amazed even the French."[30]

Nine months later he returned to the charge, asserting that "Florence's is a Negro place, run by, but not for, Negroes. The entertainer is Florence, a mulatto; the jazz band is Black, the waiters are Black and the cook is Black. As for the patrons, they, as might be expected, are the 'cream' of Paris society. The African craze among alleged blue-bloods seems to be stronger than ever."[31] His implicit critique aims at restoring the racial hierarchy between customers and entertainers current in Harlem night clubs, a system that excluded "color fraternizing." He then mocks the white clientele that followed the lead of the Prince of Wales (the same whose antics provided his bread and butter), questioning their pedigrees and decrying their patronage of "the Great Black Way, run by former residents of Birmingham and Harlem."[32]

Again the fixation on Alabama! McIntyre contributed a similarly disparaging reflection: "Florence and Palmer Jones are two southern darkies who run The Rendezvous Florence at 36 rue Pigalle. . . . They sing Negro songs, the 'mammy' craze having swept Montmartre."[33] Nothing was further from a head-wrapped Aunt Jemima than the stylish Florence. Praising her elegance, Langston Hughes evoked the specter of Alabama, but to different effect. He declared that she would arrive looking "as fresh and lovely as a black-eyed Susan from some unheard-of Alabama *jardin de luxe*, where sophisticated darkies grow."[34] Presumably, Hughes knew her true origins. However, his Southern reference is not employed in the sneering manner of O'Brien, Woon, and McIntyre. Rather, Hughes exploits the "Cotton State" as part of an ironic poetic trope designed to subvert such bias.

"Where the Black-Eyed Susans Grow" was a popular foxtrot, sung in blackface by Al Jolson and favored by Zelli at Cadet Rousselle.[35] Nothing specifies the locale or the heroine's race, but set in fields of golden grain, the text's rustic shack evokes the South, and the lovely black-eyed Susan is lauded as superior to "your snow white lilies." Moreover, the song's association with the blackface singer renders the subtext unambiguous. However, Hughes mobilizes the regressive plantation image only to disrupt it, turning its bucolic fields into an "unheard-of *jardin de luxe*"—a utopian garden unheard-of in Alabama—and its rustic maiden into a "sophisticated darkie," canceling the term's negative tenor by an adjective that McIntyre might have considered oxymoronic.

Racist journalism took myriad forms, including an attempt to reduce Montmartre's multicultural richness to a Manichean opposition pitting Black Americans against "White Russians." Aragon exposes the context for this when he notes that "the search for female company reaches its apogee in the portion of the rue Pigalle that stretches from the square [Place Pigalle] to the rue Fontaine. Thus, it begins under the aegis of prewar Paris, traverses a small Russian island, and finishes in front of the oriental Harem, in the heart of the Negro quarter."[36] With the emigration occasioned by the downfall of the czar, Russians became a key element of the quarter's ethnic diversity. Aragon's "Russian island" consisted of the Château et Caveau caucasiens at 54 rue Pigalle and Le Yar on the opposite southwest corner. More properly an archipelago, it was peopled by the ruined émigrés who had washed up on its shores—further up the rue de Douai, where it crosses the rue Fontaine, lay outlying islands, the Troïka and the Normandy, along with numerous islets (such as the Samovar), which regularly rose and sank in the turbulent Montmartre seas.

Seizing upon Russian popularity, one journalist used it to rewrite history for an American audience predisposed to a jaundiced narrative. "The Ethiopian dynasty," he claimed, "has been snuffed out.... Popularity, that fickle jade of the night, has turned her smiles in another direction; towards the sons and daughters of Russia, the fair people of the Caucasus.... The invasion of Montmartre by these whites... has swept everything before it, and driven the Negro cooks, the Negro jazz bands, the Negro barkeepers and the Negro singers and dancers down the slopes of the great little hill into memory." He then advanced the baseless assertion that Black expatriates were "perhaps A. W. O. L.'s" from the AEF.[37]

An overlooked deposition throws an interesting light on the alleged Russian conquest. With Florence on her own, Louis needed a new attraction. It came in the person of New Orleans vocalist Lizzie Miles. Accompanied by Danny

Wilson and saxophonist-violinist Oliver (Ollie) Legare, her presentations were well received, as she was able to perform pop ballads, standards, and blues in her first language, French. Fortune beamed until visa problems threatened her with expulsion.[38] She obtained the necessary labor permit, but the contretemps elicited an angry letter in which she proclaimed, "Say in big letters that Lizzie Miles will stay in Paris indefinitely, as also will Danny Wilson and Mr. Legare."[39] (There is no further trace of Legare, but on March 5, Wilson was at Kiley's Gaity supplying background music for his calamitous loves.)[40]

The first noteworthy revelation of Lizzie's letter is that Mitchell's partner was Mme Regina "Bouglor" [Bouquin], a somewhat larcenous Frenchwoman.[41] This was not her first flyer in the night club trade. In April of 1924 she had launched the Ver luisant (The Glow-Worm), a restaurant-*dancing*, in her hotel at 61 rue Blanche.[42] Its existence was brief, but in late November Mitchell revived the defunct club under his own name. Lizzie states that Mme Regina owned it, but presumably there was some financial investment by the drummer. Lizzie's second surprise is that Mitchell's "is now operated by Alexander Schaifinsky [*sic*] and uses nine Russian entertainers and Lizzie Miles and Jazz Band."[43] In a play on words, Skarjinsky christened her "La Rose noire de la rue Blanche," distributing black satin flowers and introducing Russian cuisine.[44] This appears to confirm the Russian victory, but why does Lizzie claim that Mitchell was no longer in command? In a letter to the *Defender*, Gene Bullard echoes her allegation, but it is not immediately clear what impelled his support.[45] Skarjinsky's cabaret had debuted in the setting of Mitchell's club.[46] Was there a subsequent dispute with Mme Regina? An ad for Mitchell's dated April 11 announces a "reopening," with an "all American cabaret" headlined by Lizzie and her band.[47] Even if Bullard and the singer were correct, it is obvious that the drummer's eclipse was only temporary, and that the Russian invasion had inexplicably ended.

Nevertheless, something was amiss; in July either Mitchell or Mme Regina sought an investor.[48] Could Florence and Palmer be the new associates they were seeking? In October 1925 the couple relocated to the rue Blanche. From that point on, the names Mitchell's and Chez Florence appear at the same address and evidence attests that this curious consubstantiation lasted until at least August 1926.[49] Wiggins' 1971 article provides a garbled account of the musical scene in the twenties but one statement merits consideration: Florence was "in partnership with Louis Mitchell and Mme Regina."[50] Whatever the case, in the fall of 1925, far from having been swept down the gentle incline of Montmartre's hill, Mitchell's "Negro cooks" were still producing stacks of wheat cakes and sausages, and syncopated rhythms continued to resound in the rue Blanche.⁵¹

The most ostentatious evidence of this fact is the popularity contest of the "Diamond Queens," staged chiefly at Mitchell's. Among the refugees of the society *dancings* who haunted the "Great Black Way" figured Peggy Joyce (now Countess Gösta Mörner). Busy in New York acquiring her title, she had missed the famous Embassy gala. In October 1925 she was back and, like many, had abandoned the expiring Jardin for the "noise, . . . thick atmosphere and . . . general letdown" of Mitchell's.⁵² The Jazz Baby's rivals were the much-married Jean Nash and extravagant socialite Mabel Boll. Known as the "Diamond Queens" for their eye-popping jewels, the three women had another point in common: serial matrimony.⁵³ Mabel was on the second husband of four; Peggy on the fourth of six and in pursuit of that goal had returned to Paris to divorce Count Mörner. Jean outclassed them both, having already disposed of four spouses.

In this extravagant rivalry, Peggy had provisionally won "the devotion of Duke de Medici, one of the richest of Spanish noblemen"—more accurately, the Marquis di Medici, scion of the Italian family noted for its partiality to poisoned rings and needle-pointed stilettos.⁵⁴ The Marquis' less lethal hobbies focused on American ladies. He had competed with Carlos Basualdo for the favors of Leonora Hughes and courted Jean Nash after her divorce from an Egyptian prince. Jean was thus understandably jealous when, dancing by their table at Mitchell's, an English girl tenderly kissed the Marquis' head. Seizing a bottle of champagne in her diamond-encrusted hand, Jean launched the bubbly missile across the room, destroying the English girl's slipper. Another morning at Mitchell's, Jean overheard the Marquis crooning "I love you" in Peggy's ear. His disingenuous defense was that he was "mouthing the words of the latest Charleston." This time Jean forswore champagne bottles: she ended their engagement and took solace one-stepping with Rudolph Valentino, again at Mitchell's.⁵⁵ Ultimately the Marquis wedded none of the ladies, being already married. He envisioned the possibility of a papal dispensation, but the Vatican had advised him, "Rome does not consent to the marriage of a person who has one husband living, much less a regular collection."⁵⁶

Instead of giving Mitchell's a black eye, the romantic rivalries and bottle throwing caused "thrill seekers to storm the place"; yet one wonders what Mitchell thought of this libidinal circus.⁵⁷ Since 1912 he had been happily married to Antoinette Brooks, a pastor's daughter, and devoted to their son Jack. His chief vice was a passion for gambling. Beyond that we have little evidence of his moral or political convictions, but promoting the mode for humble wheat cakes might be seen as a subtle revenge on the pretensions of his clientele, even if Jean Nash focused on their therapeutic powers.[58] At Mitchell's, she reflected, "you can enjoy all sorts of simple, old-fashioned American food, including hot griddle cakes, and listen to Southern songs rendered by colored men from Dixie. . . . Ham and eggs and hot griddle cakes have a remarkably stimulating and restorative effect after a long night spent in all forms of dissipation."[59] If Mrs. Nash persists in racist stereotypes, they take a more benign form and stop short of false birth certificates.

But Mitchell's boisterous fame was not without cost. How much was due to personal failings and how much to external pressures is impossible to measure. Montmartre offered greater social freedom and economic opportunity than America, but in return it required conformity to a clichéd vision of Black culture cultivated by even relatively enlightened members of a white audience more interested in dancing and romancing than appreciating the artistry on offer.

Though plagued by bias, Mitchell and Florence's alliance dominated the Montmartre scene until the fall of 1926, when it underwent a sea change. Bricktop declares, "When I was looking for a place . . . Louis had a closed-up club."[60] That "place" would be the first Music Box, in the Trinité Palace, a hotel and entertainment center at 41 rue Pigalle. Mitchell acted as director, with Bricktop as the chief attraction. Concerning its creation, she is unusually precise. On "October 29, 1926" she was invited to entertain at the home of an American millionaire where the Prince of Wales had sought refuge after a boring embassy dinner. She was asked to teach him the latest dance, the Black Bottom. This lesson led to the prince giving a party at the Music Box, thus granting his imprimatur to the new club.[61]

The unanswered question is this: Why did Mitchell terminate his partnership with Florence? Perhaps Bricktop knew more than she tells but she confines herself to speculation: "He was kind of down and out at the time [and] forced to close his place. I never found out exactly why. It may have been because Florence left. Also, Louis was a big gambler, and he probably got in so deep he lost the club."[62] Memory plays her false—in the fall of 1926, Florence was still in the rue Blanche.[63] Gambling is a more plausible explanation. In any case, there was no bad blood between Florence and Mitchell. After the rapid failure of the Music Box (ca, February 1927), he opened a "Quick Lunch" at 35 rue Pigalle. Florence, and Palmer, were among the first to perform.[64]

It is common knowledge that, before opening the Music Box, Bricktop spent the summer in Venice at Cole Porter's invitation. It is less well-known that, propelled by their growing notoriety, Florence and Palmer had preceded her at Chez Vous, the exclusive terrace night club of the Excelsior Hotel on the Lido.[65] Back in Paris, they assumed the sole direction of 61 rue Blanche, catering to a stellar clientele. Due to our incomplete knowledge of the musical scene, her success is often underestimated. It has been said that "[Josephine] Baker's jungle aesthetic supplanted Jones's sophisticated sleekness," or that "by 1929, Bricktop had eclipsed Embry Jones to become reigning queen of the jazz cabaret."[66] A comparison of their relative fame is unwarranted. Aside from a brief period between the inauguration of Josephine's club in December 1926 and Florence's departure in October for a six-month stay in New York, the three artists were never in competition and, as we shall see, Florence's "eclipse" had nothing to do with Bricktop.

More significantly, Florence's prominence once more raises questions about the relationship between performer and audience. We could only speculate about Mitchell but in her case two revelatory texts exist: the memoirs of Langston Hughes and a *Time* magazine article from 1927. The latter records an unforgettable dance contest. It is usually treated as a trivial news item or another example of Florence's arrogance; however, I would like to read it more closely.[67] Established in the rue Blanche, Chez Florence became the headquarters of the Charleston, the knee-bending, syncopated exercise that, as Nevill notes, "visitors willing or unwilling are sometimes made to dance, a gigantic nigger [probably Frisco, known as Professor Jocelyn A. Bingham] tapping people on the shoulders to remind them that participation in the dance is one of the rules laid down by Florence, the half-caste who gives her name to the place. Such compulsory dancing, of course, produces ludicrous effects, the sight of an old gentlemen in spectacles or a fat old South American lady covered with jewelry executing the Charleston, sending everyone into fits of laughter."[68]

A dance critic had proclaimed, "The Fox is dead ... the Charleston arrived and wolfed it down like a vulgar rabbit."[69] In its turn the Charleston was devoured by the Black Bottom, the dance à la mode Chez Florence on the night of June 7, 1927.[70] Her "visitors" that evening were not bespectacled seniors or aging, overweight Latinas but some of the most faithful devotees of the society *dancings*. Two weeks earlier Maurice's funeral had been held at the American Church. On his deathbed he had optimistically declared, "After a while I shall be strong again and return to the dance floor. Not to America, where they want nothing now but the Black Bottom."[71]

Too late! The parquets of Montmartre were already infested, and Maurice's onetime admirers had thrown off the restraints of "polite" society. Therefore, "when His Royal Highness, 27-year-old Prince Henry of Britain, strolled into Chez Florence, atop Montmartre, at 3 a.m., with a highly unofficial entourage, habitués, such as the Princess Murat, and Sem, famed cartoonist, were unsurprised."[72] The latter was an assiduous client of the *dancings*, and the decadent Princess Violette Murat—descended from Napoleonic nobility by marriage and birth—was exactly the sort of highly colored game that he pursued. The young prince was not one of them. He was known as a nondescript soldier, always trailing after his charismatic older brother. On that night, however (perhaps to celebrate his recent promotion to captain in the 10th Hussars), Henry would accept Florence's challenge to perform the Black Bottom.[73]

Nested inside the main narrative (like a set of Chinese boxes) lies a second that explains the sangfroid of the princess and the satirist: "They recalled how once the King-Emperor's eldest son, on a memorable visit . . . called across to her: 'Hey, Florence! How many *poules* do you know in Montmartre?'[74] Replied Florence: '*Poules*? chickens, your Royal Highness?' Then, dropping into Harlemese, as she seldom does, Miss Jones addressed the crowd, pointing at Edward of Wales: '*Poules*! He as' me 'bout *poules*! Hey-ho! Haah! Jus' look who's askin'!' Edward, fairly caught, laughed among the first."[75]

This exchange invites us to reconsider the legend of Florence's arrogance. Shortly after Prince Henry's outing, Woon attacked again with faint praise and vitriolic scorn. While reluctantly allowing that Florence's was "the smartest establishment in Montmartre," he reproached her, in effect, with being an "uppity nigger": "Florence is an American negress of insufferable conceit which may perhaps be pardoned her because she was 'launched' into her present amazing vogue by no less an all-nighter than the Prince of Wales."[76] Woon was scoffing at a key moment in the evolution of Montmartre, the utopian possibility of a more egalitarian relation between artists and audience than the impermeable social order of the society *dancings*.

Langston Hughes conceded that a measure of Florence's reputation was based on haughtiness, "no doubt, a professional snobbishness which she deliberately cultivated, because outside the club she was as kind and sociable a person as you would ever wish to find. And those who worked with her, from musicians to waiters, loved her. But to the patrons she adopted an air of unattainable aloofness. She would sing a requested song with only the most casual glance at the table she was singing for—unless a duke, or a steel magnate, or a world celebrity sat there." Enlarging on the idea that this was not a negative character trait, he added, "it was the first time I had ever seen a colored person deliberately and openly snubbing white people, so it always amused me no end to watch Florence move away from a table of money-spending Americans, who wanted in the world nothing so much as to have her sit down with them."[77]

By 1927 Florence had fully assumed this proud demeanor, amplified by the sardonic sense of humor evident in her quip about "poules"—the ladies of easy virtue who decorated the Montmartre *dancings*. There is no evidence that Edward patronized common prostitutes, but even if the number of Kiley's hostesses did not approach Zelli's industrial levels, he admits to about ten, and the P.O.W. had certainly met a few at his club.[78] Moreover, it should be remarked that the prince does not refute the teasing indictment.

Woon tells a similar story involving Stephen "Laddie" Sanford, heir to the Bigelow-Sanford carpet fortune, an infamous Don Juan and frequent companion of the Prince of Wales. Woon writes, "According to a yarn I heard, the Prince of Wales said to him one day in Lunnon [London in Scots]: 'Laddie, how many girls do you know anyway?' 'Look who's asking,' returned Laddie."[79] Is the prince repeating himself, or is Florence taking up a familiar story for her own purposes? Regardless, those aware of Edward's liaison with Princess Fahmy Bey certainly appreciated the irony, his ex-mistress being a "poule de luxe," a high-class call girl.

If the play on the word "poule" furnishes the content of Florence's retort, the more subversive aspect lies in its form: the mock "Harlemese" that she assumes as a kind of "aural blackface." Born in nineteenth-century minstrel shows, blackface was espoused by white performers who applied burnt cork to their faces and painted on exaggerated white lips in order to mock Black entertainers while at the same time exploiting their music. Although unacceptable today, this maquillage served as an integral part of the panoply of popular white vaudevillians such as Al Jolson and Nora Bayes.

As might be expected, Hemingway was a literary heir to this tradition. During his 1923 visit to the Grand Duc he claimed that Florence's endorsement by French nobility had caused her to assume an upper-class British accent and a languid manner: "'Oh. Hulloa,' she said. 'Yes, I'm dawncing private now. But do drop in on us sometime heah. So jolly to see you again.' It wasn't jolly at all. Another of the really amusing after-midnight places had been ruined by prosperity." Like Woon, Hemingway contends that Florence had been spoiled by the adulation of her betters and was acting above her station. This criticism is developed in the purported comments of one of the waiters at the Grand Duc: "Miss Flawnce she ain't a Niggah no mo. No suh. She done tell customahs mammy's an Indian lady fum Canada. . . . Ah'm luhnin' to talk that

English way, too. Ah'm goin' tuh tell people my mammy's an Indian lady fuhm Noble Scotia. Yes, suh. We'll all be Indiums this tahm nex' yeah."[80]

Need one insist on the stereotypical character of the waiter's minstrel show dialect? His vernacular is as false as Florence's alleged British enunciation and more indicative of the writer's heavy-handed humor than anything the waiter might have said. The anecdote is also dubious, not only because of the parodied Black speech but because the reference to Indians is, in fact, a timeworn joke.[81] Of course, the transcription of dialect is always to some extent a literary invention. The question is one of intent. Hemingway's aim is to demean. It is no wonder that Bricktop "never took to him. I wasn't the only one," she wrote. "He just wanted to bring people down."[82]

It is in this context that Florence performed her aural blackface, one of Magloire's "act[s] of resistance."[83] Even *Time* admits that her "Harlemese" was a "mock Negro dialect." After all, she and Palmer were hardly "peasants." He was a graduate of Fisk University, and the couple frequented the elite of the Harlem Renaissance, so one must presume that her use of the putative Harlem patois was a calculated irony. She was implementing in auditory fashion a strategy often employed by Black performers: reappropriating the overstated Black makeup of white minstrels and turning it into a subversive parody of their derisive caricatures. For if it perpetuated racial stereotypes, it also poked subtle fun at racist expectations. Trapped in the prejudiced conventions of the time, Black entertainers were compelled to use these constraints to create their art, fashioning a silk purse out of a sow's ear.

Florence's travesty exposes the absurd preconceptions nourished by many white Americans in her audience, not by direct opposition but by subtle mockery. The exercise is particularly potent in that it was not directed at the prince's person—after all, she owed him her renown—but at his function as a symbol of Nordic privilege. Some guests may have been shocked by her impudent response, but to his credit the heir to the throne laughed with good grace, recognizing the extent to which he had been fairly "caught." The text then returns to the morning of June 7:

> Prince Henry was not irked when Miss Jones sought to draft him as a contestant in an impromptu Black Bottom contest. Florence's chic ankles twinkled towards him. Her figure is svelte, lithe—though she does not dance. . . . Prince Henry hesitated, then rose, followed Florence out on the floor and black bottomed. "Hey! Hey!" she cried. "Give the little boy a hand! Hey! Hey!" Then to pace His Royal Highness at black bottoming, she called up from the crowd Nora Bayes,

Georges Carpentier and Florence Walton. . . . To some present it seemed that Nora Bayes black bottomed better than Prince Henry; but when the moment of judging came they "gave the little boy a hand." Florence, stamping her small right foot for quiet, awarded to His Royal Highness the first prize, held it aloft before the crowd, explained in mock Negro dialect: "Dis y'ere fust prize am an ostrich feddah suit o' cat's pajamas!"[84]

The presence of Florence Walton and Georges Carpentier was not unusual. Both were used to the limelight; she the ex-wife and dancing partner of the late Maurice; he the champion who had floored Blink McCloskey and famously lost his title to "Battlin' Siki." However, Florence's choice of these contenders was not innocent. They were all professionals, even Carpentier. Retired from the ring, he had profited from Harry Pilcer's coaching to costar with Miss Walton in a Palace Theater revue, *Femmes et Sports*, a surreal farrago involving an ostrich farm, naked dancers, and a boxing match.

But from our viewpoint the most interesting of the *black bottomiers* is Nora Bayes. She was well-placed to appreciate Florence's ironic use of blackface. She had begun her career impersonating a mammy in a song titled "Beautiful Coon" and was known for "Regretful Blues," also sung in the persona of a Black woman—a cultural appropriation one might also call aural blackface. Predictably, some thought Nora had won. Prince Henry was perhaps better at cricket than dancing; he certainly could not compete with Nora and Florence Walton, or even amateur Mabel Boll, who had honed her skills on the very same dance floor. Nevertheless, with a calculated mix of familiarity and affectionate ridicule, Florence proclaimed Henry the winner. Echoing the subversive use of Black dialect that she had utilized with Edward, she referred to the king's third son as "boy" (a demeaning address used by whites to designate Black men of any age) while at the same time awarding him the prize.

Though she is visibly sending the prince up, the terms remain puzzling. It is unnecessary to gloss on the expression "cat's pajamas"—jazz age slang for up-to-date and extremely desirable. But, unlike his suave older brother, Henry was hardly an icon of modernity, so the expression's use must be attributed again to a combination of scorn and flattery. However, there remains the peculiar "ostrich feddah suit." Ostrich feathers had long been an element of fashionable dress, although the market slumped after the war. At risk of overinterpretation, might one not see in the once-precious suit of ostrich feathers an ironic allusion to the ritual of tar and feathering, conceived as a means of public retribution, notably against Ku Klux Klan victims in the southern United States? On this disquieting note, the exploits of the King-Emperor's progeny in the rue Blanche come to an end.

The reiterated support of the two princes consecrated Florence and Palmer's reputation. On the strength of this prestige the couple recrossed the Atlantic in early October.[85] They were welcomed back to the select artistic milieu they had previously frequented and headlined at Chez Florence, a nitery managed by Tommy Guinan, disreputable brother of the incendiary "Queen of New York night clubs" Texas Guinan.[86] To celebrate the couple's success, A'lelia Walker, the Black hair-care heiress, even threw a party in her legendary Harlem "studio."[87]

Upon their return to Paris in April 1928, ads proclaimed their intercontinental celebrity, citing Florence's "triumph at her own club."[88] Four months later, a young Vincent Price, not yet the Master of Horror, walked through the blue draped door in the rue Blanche. Struck with admiration, he wrote in his diary, "We went to a place called Florence's entirely run by Nigros [sic] ... and Florence herself came and sang to us *Just Bill* ['He isn't tall ... or slim ... I love him because ... he's just my Bill']."[89] Was she thinking of her corpulent husband? They had agreed to return to New York to appear again at Guinan's Chez Florence, but misfortune struck.[90] Five days after Price's visit, Palmer died of acute indigestion. An elaborate service similar to Maurice's was held at the American Church. He was forty years old.[91]

After Palmer's death, Opal Cooper soldiered on as the leader of the International Five, but Florence's heart was no longer in it. Blues singer Edith Wilson, also a recent widow, replaced her in December, and in January the new management closed for "transformations." The club reopened in February as "Le Florence," but the eponymous star had already returned to New York.[92] Plans to appear at Guinan's club fell through when she found him facing jail for prohibition offenses. Encouraged by backers, the Montmartre nightingale quickly bounced back with a cabaret near Broadway.[93] International Five regulars Opal Cooper and Sammy Richardson were imported for a sixteen-week engagement and the new night café was acclaimed as "quite the ritz in ofay Broadway clubs with sepia revues."[94]

Sadly, in May 1931 her flourishing career was halted by a "mental illness" that led to her hospitalization with a nervous breakdown.[95] Snelson speculates that her beauty and radiance were disrupted by temperamental anguish. "Narcotics that pretended to soothe her heartbroken soul undermined her into oblivion."[96] This seems to echo a claim that she had been interned in the narcotics ward at Welfare Island, but it is at variance with stories placing her at

Harlem Hospital, and Snelson's histrionic tone inclines me to discount it.[97] What we do know is that she was high-strung, and the death of Palmer, to whom she was deeply attached, must have severely affected her psychological state. A story from Bricktop is indicative of Florence's dependence on an oft-unfaithful husband: "I once asked her why she paid so much attention to clothes. She answered simply, 'Because my husband fools around quite a bit and when he comes home, I have to look pretty and chic.'"[98] These suggestions of a vulnerability hidden behind the mask of confident superiority illuminate Langston Hughes' tale of a riotous fight at the Grand Duc that left Florence "in the midst of the wreckage, hair awry, orchids gone, tears of triumph in her eyes and a run of golden sequins dripping from her dress." A pregnant hostess had quarreled with the owner, resulting in her being slapped to the floor. Florence leapt to her defense: "Don't touch that woman!" she cried, "She's a woman and I'm a woman, and can't nobody hit a woman in any place where I work!"[99] Doubtless she was projecting her own marital frustrations.

Early on January 1, 1932, a few weeks after her return from Harlem Hospital, the imperious colored queen of Montmartre suffered a fatal heart attack.[100] Chez Florence continued under the redoubtable Mme Regina Bouquin until her own death in 1959, making it the most lasting of the Montmartre clubs. Thanks to her, the name continued to symbolize style and excitement for generations who preserved only a tenuous image of the real "Florence." Mitchell left that excitement behind, returning to New York in September 1930. In the intimate theatrical world of Black New York, it was inevitable that their paths cross again; the *Afro-American* confirmed their joint presence at a party on October 1 honoring Black performers returning from Europe.[101] Thus, one can only imagine his pain at hearing the news of her death. Professional partners, at times sibling rivals, armed only with their talent, the "Colored Gentleman" and his "Sister" had reigned over their nocturnal kingdoms. Braving economic obstacles and racist invective, these utopian dreamers inscribed African American culture in the European landscape and offered an aspirational model for future generations.

CHAPTER NINE

BRICKTOP AND BUDDIE AT THE GRAND DUC

"Black and Laughing, Heart-Breaking
Blues in the Paris Dawn"

[Bricktop] was one of those Black Americans who discovered in
Paris a way of being that they could not experience in their
native land and that allowed them to highlight, without arrière-
pensée, their finest qualities.
—Jacques Baron

A year before the publication of Gwendolyn Bennett's well-known story "Wedding Day," Aragon had proposed the analogy between Harlem and Montmartre. He contended that the quest for feminine company finished "*before the oriental* Harem, *in the heart of the Negro quarter*," but why a "*Negro quarter*?" As he reasoned in 1975, it was because "at this '*crossroads of the rue Fontaine*' is located the *Grand Duc*, the cabaret of so many nostalgic memories, where after their gigs here and there in Paris the Black musicians came late at night to repeat their numbers, a question of gathering among themselves. But how can the idea of seeing there a '*Negro quarter*' be disassociated from a purely mental association of ideas, based on a single letter more or less, the *Harem* automatically evoking the memory of the Negro quarter of New York, Harlem?"[1]

The poet was suggesting a parallel, but the comparison was only imagined. He had never visited Harlem; for him the name evoked merely a glamourous elsewhere, an illusory lost Eden. This utopian vision of the "Negro quarter of New York" was nourished by his experiences at the Grand Duc, hosted in 1925 by Ada Beatrice Queen Victoria Louise Virginia Smith, familiarly known as "Bricktop," a Black entertainer with a successful Harlem career who owed her sobriquet to the freckles and red hair inherited from Scottish-Irish antecedents. Gene Bullard had sent Sammy Richardson to New York with the offer of a job as replacement for diva Florence Jones, who had moved to Mitchell's. Arriving less than a month after the P.O.W.'s discovery of the "Great Black Way," she followed the path laid out by Florence and Louis Mitchell.

Using a patronizing tone, Leiris describes Bullard as greeting clients "with the attentive cordiality of an old-fashioned steward receiving the most intimate friends of the family in his lord's château."[2] This obsequious amiability causes Lloyd to speculate that, while Langston Hughes believed the talent of Florence Jones had beguiled Jardin de ma Soeur stalwarts like Fanny Ward, Bullard's social relations with the actress may have already brought her to the club. Based on Bullard's at times unreliable memoir, he also gives him credit for attracting Elsa Maxwell.[3] Lloyd's conjectures are based on inaccurate assumptions and cause him to misjudge social dynamics. Accepting the received chronology, Lloyd ignores the fact that Florence was entertaining both Ward and Maxwell at the Grand Duc before Bullard's arrival in December 1923, and his 1924 collaboration with Bricktop lasted only a little over three months.

After his departure in August, she took over the club and, exploiting Buddie Gilmore's equally impressive contacts in high society, embarked on a loose partnership with the drummer.[4] Faced with a meagre clientele, they initiated an ad campaign in which the name "Miss Bricktop" alternated with announcements of Gilmore's nightly presence at "Buddie's A.M. Café."[5] Strangely, but in keeping with a certain self-absorbed tendency, in her autobiography Bricktop only mentions Gilmore once, in the context of her meeting with Cole Porter. She says nothing about her partnership with him, even though Gravigny acclaimed the duo as a distillation of early morning jam sessions at the Grand Duc: "Buddie Gilmore, the King of Jazz [and] Bricktop, the creole singer with auburn hair."[6]

At the moment when the cabaret had begun what Fitzgerald calls "its slow, rattling gasp for life in the inertness of the weakest hour," Buddie would come in "looking cheerfully insinuating. He insinuated he wanted a gin and had it and sat down to his drums to play, and sing *I'm in love again, and I can't rise above it*. Buddie could get more music out of a drum than most orchestras do out of all their instruments. An Englishman walked over to Buddie with a half-bottle of champagne. Back went Buddie's black head, his eyes glistened. The man lifted the bottle to pour champagne down his eager throat and as he gulped, he beat the drums into a madder rhythm."[7]

Gowned in Schiaparelli, or something by Elsa's partner Molyneux, Bricktop would then take her place beside him on the miniscule bandstand, her urbane composure complementing his joyous abandon. Even wine did not seem to trouble her serene self-mastery. Like Socrates, who, Plato informs us, "will drink whatever you put in front of him, but no one yet has seen him intoxicated," Bricktop "drank without ever appearing inebriated. She held long conversations with the Black intellectual Jackson, who accompanied her on the piano. From time to time it amused her to sing the duo *I am in love again* with Buddie Gilmore, a small Negro round as a ball, full of imagination and fantasy":[8]

> I'm in love again, and the spring is comin'
> I'm in love again, hear my heart strings strummin'
> I'm in love again, and the hymn I'm hummin'
> Is the "Huddle Up, Cuddle Up Blues"

Ever since his arrival in 1921 and his appearances at Poiret's Clover, the genial Buddie had been assiduously cultivating his relations with Paris' elite. Claude Hopkins, leader of the *Revue nègre*'s Charleston Jazz Band, claimed that Gilmore "had four or five jobs a night. He used to do fifteen minutes here on the drums and then ten minutes somewhere else": Kiley's; sessions at Zelli's; or playing with his wife Mattie for assorted sovereigns, aristocrats, and members of New York's Four Hundred, notably at the Sunday night dinner-dances of that bastion of white privilege, the Ritz Hotel.[9] A millionaire he met at the Grand Duc had even gifted him with a Long Island estate for Christmas.[10] The climax of his public prestige was a photograph by Man Ray's assistant Berenice Abbott, titled "Buddie Gilmore at Zelly's" [*sic*] (see gallery 2). His vogue among the smart set had led her to include him in a gallery of celebrated Parisian personalities that included James Joyce, Jean Cocteau, and Princess Violette Murat. He poses with drumsticks suspended above a drum set, his broadly grinning face angled toward the camera. By 1928 this image had become iconic. It appeared on the first panel of a mirrored and painted screen titled *Le Jazz*, exhibiting a group of Black musicians energetically exploiting their instruments. Conceived by art deco designer Etienne Drian, it was commissioned by the young Maharajah of Indore for the music room of his modernist palace, Manik Bagh.[11]

The images are similar and, given their respective dates, the drummer on the screen is generally thought to have been copied from Abbott's print, but the resemblance is more readily explained by their common source: a publicity photo for the Grand Duc that appeared in October 1924, at the moment of Gilmore's new partnership with Bricktop, patronizingly billing him as the "Mascot of Society."[12] This in itself was a replica of an even older advertisement for Gilmore's 1921 appearances with the Southern Syncopated Orchestra.[13] Indeed, Drian's image circumvents Abbott and hews closer to the original, linking it to the heyday of the Tempo Club.

The list of the drummer's accomplishments demonstrates that they were based on the cultivation of white patrons. As 1924 neared its end, the *Chicago Defender* took stock of the situation: "Montmartre now boasts of two Race women as managers. Miss Ada (Bricktop) Smith at La Grand Duc [*sic*] ... and Chez Florence ... managed by Mrs. Palmer Jones. ... Mr. Mitchell opened his new place on rue Fountain [Blanche] Dec. 1. This makes three places altogether run by members of our group."[14] The note of triumphalism was understandable, but it ignores the fact that even though an increasing number of clubs were owned or managed by Black entrepreneurs, their triumph depended on the good will of a white clientele.

For Bricktop, her foremost white benefactors were Cole Porter and F. Scott Fitzgerald. The latter is said to have quipped, "My greatest claim to fame is that I discovered Bricktop before Cole Porter." The story is perhaps apocryphal.[15] In any case, Fitzgerald's witticism is deceptive as to their relative importance. Porter ensured the entertainer's material success by introducing her to influential members of Parisian society, but Fitzgerald's discovery was pivotal in other ways. It is thanks to him that Bricktop gained her place in English literature; she was immortalized in one of his best short stories, "Babylon Revisited."[16] Putting such weighty questions aside, Fitzgerald's boast of discovering Bricktop before her other celebrated patron is not just an idle jest. Scott and Zelda found her singing at Le Grand Duc in October 1925, whereas Cole Porter did not frequent the club until he came back from New York sometime in early 1926.[17] One cannot overstate Porter's allegiance to the rituals of the society *dancings*. He was present at many of its key ceremonials: the inauguration of the Acacias, Howard Sturges' flamboyant gala at the Jardin de ma Soeur, and the opening of the club's final season. His only infidelity was the Jardin's New Year's closing, as faithful regulars charlestoned awkwardly into the night. Upon his return from New York, the author of the "Colored Gentleman's" ragtime step discovered the pedestrian "Palais du Billard" in place of the extinct Jardin, and despite a nostalgic visit to of one of Maurice's final performances, he quickly transferred his affections to the rue Pigalle.[18]

Bricktop describes their first encounter: "One morning ... a slight, immaculately dressed man came in [and] sat down at one of the tables. ... I got up to sing and could sense that the man was watching and listening with more than ordinary interest. He applauded when I finished the set

... and got up to leave. Just then Buddy Gilmore came through the door. ... He grabbed the stranger and started hugging him. 'Who was that?' I asked Buddy later. 'That was Cole Porter,' he said. [The drummer's social prestige and ubiquity positioned him as an intermediary between the diverse elements of the Grand Duc's clientele.] 'Oh, my God!' I said. 'I've just been singing one of his songs!'"[19]

The tune was "I'm in Love Again," written for the Greenwich Village Follies of 1924, where it was sung by the Dolly Sisters. It was quickly cut but achieved underground notoriety. Porter had the impression of hearing it everywhere. In a letter to his mother, he humorously observed, "Last year, in New York [1926], I heard it at Maurice's cabaret.... I went to the band leader and asked him who wrote it, and he said, 'Oh a Harlem nigger wrote it.'"[20] In *Within the Quota*, Porter had acknowledged the "Colored Gentleman's" role in a gradually evolving American culture, and he seems to take the bandleader's offensive designation as a compliment. On that winter night, Bricktop was in the same position as the bandleader; she ignored the identity of the "slight, immaculately dressed man" in her audience, but she knew that the song had not been written by a "nigger" from Harlem!

However, it was not really her singing that interested Cole. He had appreciated the *Revue nègre*'s Charleston Jazz Band at the Jardin de ma Soeur, and he wanted her to give lessons in the dance at his luxurious residence. A few nights later he brought his old friend Elsa Maxwell to the Grand Duc. According to Bricktop, "she clapped and shrieked. ... If anything pleased her, her enthusiasm was boundless."[21] It should be noted that this choreographic consultation followed Elsa's attempts to import the dance to the Jardin de ma Soeur, and the society maven was not, as Bricktop appears to believe, a stranger to the Grand Duc. Her empathy with Black performers explains her readiness to embrace the Charleston, as she would the next sensation, the Black Bottom.

Woon's book completely ignores Bricktop's role in popularizing these dances. He even feigns to ignore her sobriquet, declaring that "'Mitchell's,' across the street, features 'Brickbat' [sic], a mottled lady of disturbing charms who has been a Paris character for years."[22] One might find this error amusing were it not symptomatic of his ingrained racism. Predictably, he also labels the Charleston "the latest atrocity from the new world," directing his venom against both Elsa and Black people: "One of the funniest pictures I have had in recent years was that at the Ritz the other night when plump little Elsa Maxwell, guide to society, danced her version of the Negro contortion."[23] (See gallery 2.) Woon had not mistaken his target. Despite the ambiguities of her stance, the woman who had helped to codify the protocols of the society *dancing* was willing to make a hesitant step across the sacrosanct color line, even if only with a limited visa.

Even so, Elsa is not one of the white patrons to whom Bricktop attributes her celebrity. "I could have gotten into a feud with her if I'd called her on her claim that she was responsible for my success," she declares, claiming to fear her sharp tongue.[24] On the contrary, the doyenne to whom Bricktop ostentatiously and falsely credits the revival of her flagging fortunes was another Jardin regular, the eternal ingénue, Fanny Ward. According to Bricktop, for months after her arrival in Paris she languished at the Grand Duc, disturbed only by an occasional admirer seeking the absent Florence.[25] One warm spring evening of 1925, a gentleman fleeing the crowds at Chez Florence entered, Fanny's husband Jack Dean, wearing the same never-ending grin, a consequence of plastic surgery. Dean promised to bring in his wife. She came. With her "strange, fixed smile" she demanded, "Can you stand success?" "Nothing excites me," Bricktop replied. "Florence Jones got excited," challenged Fanny. Defiantly, Bricktop responded, "Her name is Florence. My name is Bricktop." Fanny ignored this rejoinder and vowed "to pack" the place—Florence needed a lesson, she was "too spoiled."[26] Toward the end of the season, Fanny and her crowd "gradually drifted away," to be replaced in October by F. Scott Fitzgerald and "the Montparnasse crowd."[27]

This is inexact. Montparnasse icons like McAlmon, Man Ray, and Hemingway had already visited the club. Nevertheless, the real difficulty with Bricktop's story is that between February and late June of 1925 Fanny was absent—visiting America![28] If there is any truth in Bricktop's narrative, Fanny's visit would have to have taken place between October 1924 and February 1925. In any case, in June the actress resumed her patronage of Florence's, where Woon glimpsed "the girlish grandmother and her effervescent husband."[29]

Is this a case of faulty memory? (Bricktop was writing almost sixty years after the event.) Or did she consciously falsify the facts?[30] And what might be her motive? It is likely that Fanny frequented Bricktop's Grand Duc at some point, but the redhead's attribution of her sudden prosperity to the fading star lies somewhere between history and myth. The lesson to be drawn from the story lies not in the veracity of Bricktop's musings but in Fanny's condescending attitude and her not unreasonable assumption that, despite Bricktop's proud retort, she retained the power to make or break her.

According to Bricktop, Fanny and Elsa were rivals for the position of most popular hostess in Paris.[31] But this was more than a struggle for social prominence: the two women represented fundamentally differing attitudes toward the emergence of the Great Black Way. Ascribing her triumph to this unsympathetic personage—to whose arrogance she claims to have opposed a proud resistance—allows Bricktop to reserve more sympathetic roles for patrons like Porter, whom she fulsomely praises, and Elsa, to whom, while denying any role in her rise to fame, she still accords the status of "casual friend."[32]

Bricktop's shifting perspectives tend to obscure the fact that the world of white privilege represented by the society *dancings* had not ceased to exist; it had simply been restructured. Minority presence in clubs like the Grand Duc was not limited by racist restrictions but by the relatively small number of Black expatriates in Paris. The principal problem lay in the hierarchical relation of white patrons and Black performers. As I have pointed out, many Black artistes had begun their careers on the rue Caumartin, but only as employees who were forbidden to cross the footlights. Now they were managers, owners, and even guests at the smart parties where they performed, and the old guard of the society *dancings* was convoked, not just to be entertained, but to interact on an intimate basis with a diverse, multiethnic throng.

Fitzgerald's importance lies in his evocation of these interactions, but its most direct expression is not to be found in the celebrated *Babylon Revisited*. It lies buried in the manuscript pages of his expatriate novel *Tender Is the Night*. Stovall castigates its "notoriously racist passages about blacks."[33] But he is evidently not familiar with the drafts where Fitzgerald makes it clear that he was not unaware of "the laughing stoicism which has enabled the American Negro to endure the intolerable conditions of his existence."[34] Behind the mask of frivolous jazz age chronicler, he was too keen an observer of the historical and societal forces that underlay the gaieties of the Jazz Age not to have perceived the violence and racial paranoia that were regrettable traits of the American psyche, thrown into relief by the microcosm of postwar Montmartre.

This is particularly manifest in the fourth draft of *Tender Is the Night*. Unlike the printed novel where the hero and his friends go on a vague enchanted "odyssey" across nighttime Paris, the draft reveals the sublimated reality of Montmartre.[35] There the group encounters a gay Native American, George T. Horseprotection, at the Ritz Hotel. Surviving in the novel only as a comical name, the "large, brown, splendidly dressed oil-Indian" plays a key role in the manuscript text.[36] In Montmartre, the term miscegenation took on a broader signification: an "inappropriate" mingling of categories, be they racial, social, or sexual. With his dusky skin and alternate sexuality, Horseprotection conflates the roles of racial, social, and sexual outsider.

This unusual tour guide leads the party to 52 rue Pigalle, where the Grand Duc squats on the blunted triangle formed by a junction with the rue de La Rochefoucauld.[37] A year earlier Woon had presented a roll call of the Embassy gala's guests, his bleached conception of "Society with a big S." Now the tide has turned, and a more heterogeneous group congregates in the rue Pigalle amid a haze of smoke and endless rounds of champagne. Fitzgerald details the diverse clientele crammed into the minuscule space: "The Grand Duc was closing. Among others discernable through the yellow smoke of dawn there were Josephine Baker, the Grand Duc Boris, [an?] Eskimo, Pepy, a manufacturer of dolls' voices from Newark, Albert McKiscoe, unhappily able to walk [sic], and the King of Sweden. In the corner was a big black buck with his arms around a French girl, roaring a song to her in a deep beautiful voice."[38]

If the personalities dimly emerging from an accumulation of long nights of stale cigarette smoke seem an improbable group, they are nevertheless a faithful reflection of the club's diverse clientele. Josephine was a frequent guest. In the fall of 1926, she was performing across the street at the nearby Impérial (renamed "Joséphine Baker's Impérial" to capitalize on her popularity) and often stopped by after dancing at the rival club.[39] At her side is her boyfriend/manager, the self-styled "Count" Pepito di Abatino. Mingling with Josephine and "Pepy," the Grand Duke Boris is a living souvenir of prewar days when the visits of Russian aristocrats to the sordid haunts of the quarter were known as "la Tournée des Grands Ducs," rechristened "la Tournée des Américains" in honor of the Yankees' spendthrift ways.[40] His mingling with Josephine brings to mind Fitzgerald's reminiscence of "living with the insouciance of grand ducs and the casualness of chorus girls," implying that in Montmartre the two social categories were not incompatible.[41]

Then, there is the King of Sweden. Although it might seem unlikely that the sixty-seven-year-old Gustaf V would be out prancing at the Grand Duc, the words "King of Sweden" figure alongside the first mention of Bricktop's name in Fitzgerald's *Ledger*.[42] In fact, the king was an eminent Francophile and well known in Montmartre circles. What is more, as Nevill observes, one of the innovations of postwar life was a generational intermingling that paralleled the easing of racial and social barriers. In support of his assertion of the unnatural intrusion of the aged into precincts previously reserved to youth, he cites humorist and law reform activist A. P. Herbert:

> Night clubs now are simply spas
> For our young Methuselahs,

> So don't let's go to the dogs to-night
> In case my granny's there.[43]

However, there is a more profound reason for this royal presence. Downgraded in the novel to an "heir to a Scandinavian throne," the king represents a clientele of aristocrats and royals such as the Grand Duke Boris and the Prince of Wales, referred to in the manuscript as "the most famous young Englishman in the world," not merely a celebrity, but an incarnation of "the British Empire."[44] In effect, like the Nordic monarch, the prince is an emblem of a contested white privilege that belies the more relaxed social order of the Black *dancings*, the specter that, in one form or another, threatens the utopian dream of Montmartre.

As an essential component of this potential new order, we should imagine the habitués noted by Jacques Baron. Echoing Aragon, he wrote that "in the early morning the Black Americans, singers, dancers or musicians who had finished their shows debarked at Bricktop's, joyous and handsome in their elegant finery, and having a marvelous time"—a resumé of the jazz scene that had developed a few yards north of the crossroads of the rue Fontaine and the rue Pigalle.[45] Under Bricktop's sway, a romantic nostalgia for the brief, intense flowering of the Tempo Club floated over the cabaret. Many of its former devotees now congregated at the Grand Duc (Joseph Hall, present during Mazie Mullins fatal malaise, was leading the club's band when Bricktop arrived in May 1924).[46] Even those who ignored those halcyon days discovered the rare pleasure of being, according to Langston Hughes, "professional merrymakers no longer being professionally merry—but just themselves."[47] "Being themselves" may seem fundamental in a free society, but it was a possibility often denied to these victims of American racism. For Baron, Bricktop "was one of those Black Americans who discovered in Paris a way of being that they could not experience in their native land and that allowed them to highlight, without arrière-pensée, their finest qualities." That "way of being" was quite simply a sense of freedom.

All those who had the good fortune to participate in this exceptional moment insist on the select yet informal character of early mornings at the Grand Duc. The unique atmosphere was that of an intimate family gathering; "one never had the impression of finding oneself in a night resort, but rather in a sort of small, private social club where one enjoyed oneself in a harmlessly puerile manner."[48] Like the sheltered mezzanine above Zelli's, it was a tacitly closed circle whose members were largely Black entertainers, but again like the

Tempo Club it did not exclude white guests (one journal even described it as "a black and tan rendezvous").[49] It represented, as Magloire emphasizes, an attempt at "construction of a [new] social space."[50]

Reflective of a loosely formulated dream of harmony between races and classes, the Grand Duc was the rightful heir to Mazie Mullins' lamented club. It served a unifying function, embracing the community of Black musicians, expatriate American writers like Fitzgerald and McAlmon, French surrealists like Aragon, Leiris, and Baron, while also serving as a fashionable gathering place for Elsa Maxwell, Fanny Ward, and other refugees of the Jardin de ma Soeur. Bricktop's social and racial ecumenism even extended to former White Lyres' bandleader Bill Henley, who manned the barbecue pit for parties at her country estate in Bougival, a posh Parisian suburb.[51] Indicative of this cosmopolitan climate is a photo of Gene Bullard, taken either in spring 1924 or 1926. Resplendent in impeccable evening dress, he is seated casually on a bar stool with a *coupe* of champagne in his hand. Gathered around him are his old boxing pal "Blink" McCloskey, "eccentric dancer" Fernando Jones (a close friend from their days with Belle Davis' Pickaninnies), a young white barman, possibly one of the two Italians, Luigi and Romeo, a white doorman, and assorted clients, Black and white.[52]

Leon Crutcher's partner, George Evans, wrote to the *Chicago Defender* that "our hanging out place for the wee hours of the morn will find us taking a little whisky and soda with Ada Brick-top Smith ... who is still director of the famous Grand Duc night club, which really should be named the Entertainers' café, as you may find every artist in Paris there after 4 a.m. doing his or her stuff. This means artists of both races."[53] In a news story concerning the threatened expulsion of singer Lizzie Miles, the *Afro-American*'s correspondent felt obliged to note that in France, "contrary to opinion, the laws are just and equitable for all. No color discrimination enters." Demonstrating the point, eight months earlier twenty-five American musicians had been ordered to leave France, among them Palmer Jones' International Five and Billy Arnold's white band.[54]

Studies like those of Stovall and Shack have been accused of seeing the world of Black Montmartre in Evans' terms, through rose-tinted spectacles.[55] Evidently the multicultural dream narrative presents problems. If we characterize it as utopian, we must also recognize that the term may carry negative connotations: chimera, illusion, unrealistic dream. French culture in its ideal formulation as a universal moral value was not perfect, above all in its censurable treatment of its colonial subjects. There is also something troubling in Leiris' paternalistic depiction of Bullard (officiating "with the attentive cordiality of an old-fashioned steward") that recalls his acknowledged use of Black stereotypes ("sensual," "illogical," etc.). Nonetheless, as Stovall points out, the biased images of the French were "overwhelmingly positive, however demeaning they may seem from present-day perspectives."[56] If the Black denizens of Montmartre subscribed to the utopian phantasm of a liberal government reigning over a pacified, multiracial people, it was because they wanted desperately to believe in it and fought bravely against the encroachments of an old order that assumed the form of viperish white journalists, perhaps biased manufacturers of dolls' voices from Newark, and intolerant American tourists drawn to Montmartre by its sulfurous reputation and free-flowing champagne.

The dithyrambic praise of French society voiced by Black expatriates in the Black press was utopian in that it could be seen as "an economic, political, or social view that ignores reality." But, exactly as More's *Utopia* responded to the real communal structures of sixteenth-century England, their Utopia was "in dialogue with the varied forms of segregation" of twentieth century America: discrimination and poor working conditions (T.O.B.A, "The Theatre Owners Booking Association," which booked the African American vaudeville circuit in the twenties, was referred to as "Tough On Black Asses").[57] Even Bricktop, whose tone is largely upbeat, could not forget the toxic racial climate she had left behind. Despite a nonmilitant stance, her repertoire was composed of more than lightweight trifles like "I'm in Love Again"; certain songs had a more political bite, such as "Insufficient Sweetie," one of her hits, a seemingly innocuous number from Gershwin's *Lady Be Good*: "You claim the day will come when I will hold your hand. / That's when a rabbi will be the Kleagle of the Ku Klux Klan!"[58]

The question is not whether the myth of a color-free France propagated by Black expatriates was unqualifiedly true. If America was the standard against which French society was to be judged, the latter was undeniably "utopian." The Black expatriates of Montmartre were all too familiar with the truth of racism, but France offered them a more clement vision of those verities, one which they were eager to seize upon as an ideal. And if Montmartre's dream narrative reflected its residents' hopes for a world of utopian race relations, it was nevertheless based on certain positive realities: unrestricted entry into shops, clubs, and restaurants, greater economic opportunities, and interracial mixing.

In response to this last point, one might object, as does Stovall, that while some white expatriates "occasionally crossed the color line, they never tore it down," an argument that rightfully raises the issue of social equality.[59] Yet, I question his emphatic assertion that "although Bricktop may have admired Fitzgerald and Porter, she came to their homes as a hired musician, not as a friend and equal."[60] Unlike the wealthy composer, Fitzgerald never hired musicians at his residence, although Bricktop acknowledges that their home was one of the few that she visited as a simple friend.[61]

However, to respond to the substance of Stovall's comment, entry to the residences of white patrons was one of the key differences between France and the States. "When I was going through the front doors of the most elegant homes in Paris," Bricktop writes, "entertainers working private affairs in America went in the back door and ate in a separate room. . . . That never happened in Paris. Even though we were being paid, we ate and drank at the buffet and mingled with the other guests."[62] An anecdote involving the spirited Buddie Gilmore supports Bricktop's claim. One night he and his band were performing at one of the charity costume balls of which high society was so fond. The group refused to don any sort of masquerade. To convince them to do so, the host explained that their tuxedos would be noticed when they went to the buffet where everyone was in fancy dress, at which Buddie declared with his usual bantering wit: "In that case, go ahead and disguise me!"[63]

A change of status had taken place. But if Black entertainers were treated with more respect, does this signify that they were considered friends or does Stovall correctly maintain that there was "no true equalization of relations between Black and white Americans?"[64] The assertion that Bricktop was not really an intimate of the white patrons of the Grand Duc should be nuanced. She clearly considered Porter "one of the best friends I've ever had."[65] In the summer of 1926 he arranged for her to give dance lessons at the Excelsior Hotel in Venice, and this invitation decisively launched her with the international set.

From mid-August to mid-September, Venice turned into a southern colony of Montmartre. On the dance floor of the hotel's "Chez Vous" a familiar cast—Porter, Peggy Joyce, the Maharajah of Kapurthala, etc.—perpetuated some of the codes of the society *dancings*, but there was a difference. That summer, on the night of her of birthday, Bricktop staged the dances for a charity gala, featuring a distinguished chorus of society ladies dancing the Charleston and Elsa Maxwell in a bathing suit and curly blond wig warbling "Just a Lonely Little Lady on the Lido."[66] After the show a Venetian count emerged from the audience, carrying a cake. One by one the distinguished guests wished her happy birthday, bringing the entertainer to tears.[67] In effect, such an event would have been unthinkable at the quintessential society *dancing*, the Jardin de ma Soeur, where Maurice and his brother were incapable of imagining anything other than the demeaning "Plantation Night" organized for the widow of banjoist Usher Watts.

The same warm relations are evident in Bricktop's interactions with the Marquise de Polignac. On July 1, 1926, the latter wrote in a distinctly cordial tone, "Dear Bricktop, if Monsieur Sem, the famous French caricaturist, writes to you or goes to see you, be sure to pose for his drawings of Charleston steps if he asks you to, as it will bring you the best publicity. I gave him your name and address last night. Wishing you every success."[68] Nor was this the only amicable service rendered by Mme de Polignac. She was responsible for Bricktop's crucial introduction to the Prince of Wales.[69] If friends may be defined as those who rally round in time of need, then prominent white patrons such as the marquise would certainly qualify.

Similarly, on the eve of World War II, it was thanks to the efforts of the Duchess of Windsor and Elsie de Wolfe (Lady Mendl), American wife of a British diplomat, that Bricktop escaped the advancing Nazis, installed in a private cabin on the Cunard liner *Washington*.[70] Yet, in another passage of her memoirs, Bricktop tempers her enthusiasm: "In those days we entertainers were treated as acquaintances," she maintains, "not friends, but good acquaintances," further stating that she was her clients' "friend in Bricktop's, but I usually didn't see them outside the club—and didn't want to."[71] Bricktop walks a fine line, conforming to the behavioral codes that had made her another "Mascot of Society" (with all that connotes of condescension and objectification) but never hesitating to assert her independence.[72]

The unstated fear of these free interactions between the races was that they might lead to taboo sexual relations. As Fitzgerald's manuscript draft suggests, Montmartre was a paradise of miscegenation. Interracial liaisons were common (at times between same-sex couples like Cole Porter and pianist/singer Leslie Hutchinson, a colleague of Bricktop), from the casual affairs to which Bricktop freely admitted to the more or less happy marriages of Gene Bullard, Joe Boyd, Joe Caulk, and Bobby Jones. Some mixed-race relationships, like Bullard's, ended in divorce. A few terminated violently, as in the homicidal farewells of Leon Crutcher and Marie Boyard. Although some Black expatriates had internalized the prohibition against interracial unions or, like Marcus Garvey, rejected them for ideological reasons, for the majority, forays across the color line posed no serious difficulties. In *Nightinghouls of Paris*, McAlmon has Crackerjack Joe Caulk sanguinely reflecting on the consequences: "People get it in the neck one way or the other, and it's as interesting being mixed blood as not if you're going to amount to anything."[73] It was chiefly in the eyes of their white compatriots that such interactions became problematic.

Bricktop was an exception. Socially liberal, in the sentimental realm she was extremely conservative: "I had my own strong feelings on that issue of interracial marriage. Sure, I'd had white men, but I certainly never intended to marry one."[74] Bricktop's attitude toward her romantic relations is typical of this clear-eyed lucidity. A woman alone (most Black female entertainers—Mazie Mullins, Florence Jones, Mattie Gilmore, Tony Mitchell—benefited from the security of husbands), only as puritanical as she needed to be, Bricktop admits to having several white lovers but recognizes the limitations of interracial unions. Asked to intervene in a scandal over Paul Robeson's sexual involvement with a white woman in London, her objection is overdetermined. She advances two reasons, both economic and social, which she applies to her own case.[75] "It wasn't in my best interests to mix business with pleasure, or to be some sort of threat to wives and girlfriends of my clients," she declares; at the same time she "didn't want to be a back-street mistress . . . and that's all I could have been." Having offered the latter comment, she dismisses the problem with a flippant aside: "What would we have talked about when we got out of bed? I don't know nothing about polo!"[76]

Stovall writes that Bricktop's memoirs "provide a disturbing example of the limits to interracial tolerance in the interwar years."[77] This is true to the extent that the ambiguities and hesitations of her autobiography and interviews (close, but not too close; casual lovers, but not a committed relationship) reveal both the influence of her conventional middle-class upbringing and the constraints that the era imposed on Black/white relations. But ultimately her irresolution reflects a doubt that conditions were ripe to realize the utopian dream that had begun to take form in the dim-lit precincts of the Tempo Club. Following in the footsteps of Mazie Mullins, Bricktop "created a fantasy world, a vision of America as it could and should be."[78] Should, certainly; could, perhaps not yet. While based on concrete experiences, this vision was of necessity subjective, utopian, and illusory, mirroring neither an American nor a French reality. Fredric Jameson suggests that, as on More's island, we are faced with "the ideological difficulty of reconciling a hierarchical social order . . . with the ideal of absolute equality that is supposed to govern the organization of Utopia."[79] Evidently, a hierarchical system cannot create total parity; nevertheless, if not quite a melting pot, by the potency of their vision the entertainers, artists, and crowned heads who jammed with Bricktop and Buddie at the Grand Duc produced a very fragrant stew.

Canadian writer John Glassco's physical portrait of Bricktop is unflattering, and incorrect—a "plump, glowing negress with a bush of dyed red hair"— but his appraisal of her singing is perhaps the most lyrical ever penned: "Her voice, small but beautifully true, tracing a vague pattern between song and speech ... seemed to compose all by itself a sentiment at once nostalgic and fleeting, anonymous and personal, inside the song itself; her voice followed rather than obeyed the music, wreathing an audible arabesque around her; the melody, something banal by Berlin or Porter, was transformed and carried into a region where the heard became the overheard and the message one of enchanting sweetness and intimacy."[80]

Undoubtedly, the redhead put her own stamp on "I'm in Love Again." We can imagine her cool, disabused rendering (perhaps a medium-slow, blues-inflected foxtrot). "Something banal by Berlin or Porter," wrote Glassco, "a silly refrain ... Its composer conceded the triviality of the languorous fox-trot," but Porter shared with Bricktop a talent for rendering the serious frivolous and the frivolous profound.[81] Though separated by layers of class, color, and experience, this was perhaps one of the sources of Porter's profound admiration for the mistress of the Grand Duc.

The Surrealists were in a different category than her other white enthusiasts. They did not suffer from the severe handicap of a violent American racism, and they had never been tempted by the paper-thin joys of the rue Caumartin. Seated in the Grand Duc's triangular room, "a strange, narrow place, a sort of corridor leading to a crypt ... from which the guttural chant of Bricktop rose up, like the voice of happiness commenting the distress of human passions," these *âmes sensibles* (sensitive souls) responded to the entertainment in a different manner than many other white guests.[82] On hearing Bricktop's interpretations of "All Alone (By the Telephone)" or the haunting "Sweet Creola," the poetic musketeers extracted from her fragile instrument a metaphysical principle. Leiris conjured up "a voice such as I've never heard, a voice comparable to a heavy embroidered cloth slashed by the blows of an axe, or a flight of sparrows troubled by eagles, or the ruins of the grand hotels of Palm Beach and Los Angeles after an earthquake."[83] For these Frenchman, Bricktop's renditions of classic blues like "Saint James Infirmary" or modest Broadway ballads such as "I'm in Love Again" "spoke of almost nothing other than Paradise, of naïve love, and at times of exile."[84] The Black artists who deployed their talents in Aragon's round of Pigalle cafés—"*Shanley* [sic], today's *Palermo, Zelli's ... La Perle ... the Grand Duc*"— afforded them a glimpse of the purity and spiritual depth perceived by Soupault in "Mily's" solitary dance.[85]

Like the Black American experience of Montmartre, Bricktop's vocals presented a dual face, a celebration of the utopian dream, a cruel recognition of its limits—the note of mingled joy and sorrow that is evident in Baron and Leiris' evocations and that may also be found in the soi-disant "frivolous" Fitzgerald's appreciation of jazz, a music he relished not only as the soundtrack of a unique historical moment but for its essence. Witness this passage on Black musicians from a 1920 short story: "In single file they marched, weaving in concentric circles, now with their heads thrown back, now bent over their instruments like piping fawns. And from trombone and saxophone ceaselessly whined a blended melody, sometimes riotous and jubilant, sometimes haunting and plaintive as a death-dance from the Congo's heart."[86] Or as Langston Hughes wrote of the Grand Duc, in a comparable vein of rueful and joyous recollection: "Blues in the rue Pigalle. Black and laughing, heart-breaking blues in the Paris dawn."[87]

Gerald "Jed" Kiley.
Chicago Tribune, August 10, 1919.

"Le Palermo, façade," Séeberger frères (1925). © Ministère de la Culture / Médiathèque du patrimoine, Dist. RMN-Grand Palais / Art Resource, N.Y.

"Le Palermo, rue Fontaine," Jean Dulac, 1927. From *Montmartre: Album descriptif de Montmartre en 1927*.

Kiley's Gaity, corner of rue Fontaine and rue Mansart, 1925. Courtesy of the author.

et Rue de Douai

Le Grand Duc / Mitchell's, Pierre Brissard.
Vogue (New York ed.), June 1923.

"Buddie Gilmore at Zelly's," Berenice Abbott, 1926–27. Getty Images.

"Ada Smith, aka Bricktop," Man Ray, 1928.
Digital Image © CNAC/MNAM, Dist. RMN-Grand Palais / Art Resource, N.Y. © Man Ray 2015 Trust / Artists Rights Society (ARS), N.Y. / ADAGP, Paris 2024.

Elsa Maxwell doing the Black Bottom, Sem (Georges Goursat), 1927. From *White Bottoms*. PWB Images / Alamy Stock Photo.

Advertisement for Mitchell's La Plantation.
Comœdia, December 11, 1929.

Josephine Baker in the "Plantation"
tableau from *Un vent de folie*, 1927.
Historic Images / Alamy Stock Photo.

"Josephine Baker," Studio Harcourt, ca. 1940.
© Ministère de la Culture / Médiathèque du patrimoine,
Dist. RMN-Grand Palais / Art Resource, N.Y.

CHAPTER TEN

"STILL LONGING FOR DE OLD PLANTATION"

Miscegenation, Violence, and the Collapse of a Utopian Dream

All up and down de whole creation
Sadly I roam,
Still longing for de old plantation
And for de old folks at home.
    —Stephen Foster, "Swanee River" or
    "Old Folks at Home," 1851

La Plantation, the penultimate *dancing* initiated by Louis Mitchell in December 1929, only to close seven weeks later, was situated at a historic location, 58 rue Notre-Dame de Lorette, a southeastern extension of the rue Fontaine. In the nineteenth century it had housed the studio of the painter Degas and a famous cabaret, Le Jockey Club de Montmartre. After the war, the two-story edifice became Jules Volterra's Capitole, a welcome last stop after a night of dissipation. Given the club's vital role in Montmartre nightlife, it is not unusual that two scandals illustrative of the flaws of jazz age Montmartre (an ever-present fear of miscegenation, an excess of violence, and a stubborn racism) were linked to its successor, the Plantation: the interracial romance of English heiress, Nancy Cunard and jazzman Henry Crowder, and the infamous shootout between Black musicians Mike McKendrick and Sidney Bechet.

Mitchell's utopian dream was built on the ashes of these two affairs. However, he had not created the emblematic cabaret. The ambitious Paul Santo acquired the Capitole in the fall of 1928, at a moment when he was consolidating his grip on Montmartre. In allusion to his origins, Santo was likened to another conquering Corsican and dubbed "the Napoleon of the Night Clubs." Montmartre had always varied its pleasures, but Santo recognized that after a decade of feverish dancing a fickle public demanded an even broader range of exotic settings, and he raised this perception to the level of a philosophy. He was unconcerned with the authenticity of Black music posited by Soupault; it was simply an element of the ethnic exoticism at the core of his business model. Guy Hickok explained, "Santo knows that cabaret addicts like variety. He makes a genuine effort to make each of his dance paradises unlike the others, at least on the surface. He may have a standard champagne, and a standard price for it, and he certainly takes his reward in a standard currency. But he tries to provide a diversified diversion."[1]

Thus, in addition to the Palermo, temple of the tango, Santo's empire encompassed the Florida, heir to the Apollo *Dancing*; three night cafés (the classic French Rat mort, Le Floresco, initiated as a Russian cabaret, Le Narguileh, for devotees of middle eastern dancing); and in 1929, the crown jewel of Montmartre, Le Perroquet.[2] Flushed with these conquests, he created the Plantation, catering to revelers seeking "picturesque, violent, thrilling Black jazz, in a strange, exotic setting."[3] For the ground floor restaurant, he preserved the name Le Capitole—music floated down from the *dancing* as one dined— and as manager he chose a close friend, Gaëtan Lherbon de Lussats, aka "the Baron." An advertisement for the opening of the restaurant promised a return to the "joyous gatherings of yesteryear," but by hiring this suave gangster, Paul Santo encouraged Le Capitole's implication in an endemic savagery.[4]

Not some faux underworld nobility but a genuine baron with a rap sheet including robbery, jewel theft, and a drug conviction, de Lussats was also guilty of murdering a man during a card game.[5] Acquitted on grounds of self-defense, he acquired a palatial Montmartre apartment and, parading the doleful face that had earned him the moniker "Le Croque-mort" ("The Undertaker"), embarked on a career of protection, drug dealing, and prostitution. Among his intimates featured the predatory Alexandre Stavisky, whom he had first known as a petty swindler in the Faubourg Saint-Martin and the rue Caumartin.[6] The baron was regarded as one of his chief henchman, so it is unsurprising that after Stavisky's "suicide" in 1934 he was a suspect in the murder of an examining judge of the "Affaire."[7] This was the delightful gentleman chosen by the Corsican to run the Capitole, situated below the Plantation with its "violent, thrilling" jazz.

Apparently, Santo left the décor unchanged—satiric scenes of the Capitoline Hill, ancient and contemporary, unlike the upstairs cabaret, described as "modern cabaretty" [*sic*]."[8] Were it not for Nancy Cunard's friend Richard Aldington, we would have only this cryptic description. The British poet and novelist thought it "a most amusing nigger cabaret . . . the dancing room was decorated in *style moderne* with fanciful patterns in blue and silver of no particular shape or meaning; there was an alcove with a large picture of a Mississippi steamboat seen in oblique perspective from the prow; the walls had a number of black panels rather like school blackboards, with very clever sketches of Negroes in white outline. There were wall seats of pinkish velvet, and tables with red and white check tablecloths."[9] Santo had realized a gaudy synthesis of two seemingly contradictory elements, rustic echoes combined with the up-to-date abstractions of art deco.

The hybrid décor had a precedent, Lew Leslie's Plantation Room, opened on Broadway in early 1922 with an all-Black revue led by the scintillating Florence Mills. As its name implies, Leslie's club exploited plantation tropes. Among other scenic novelties there was a simulated log cabin, a bandanna-coiffed "Mammy" flipping flapjacks, and a "large electric chandelier in the shape of a watermelon" hanging over the dance floor, with seeds figured by electric lights, a signpost of modernity in this staged rurality.[10] The orchestra performed in front of a papier-mâché steamboat, seen in oblique perspective cruising on the Suwannee (Swanee) River. Attended by the "Six Dixie Vamps," Edith Wilson sang "Robert E. Lee" and, in an obligatory reference to Alabama, a performer crooned "Swanee River" in the guise of a "Ham from Birmingham."[11]

Although Santo's steamboat openly references Leslie's décor, Aldington's cursory text renders it difficult to judge if the influence was direct or filtered through a series of mediations. The "Mississippi Steamboat Race" tableau in the *Revue nègre* had featured Josephine Baker dancing before a backdrop of river boats, but the plantation theme goes back to Elsa Maxwell's Acacias: a Southern plantation on the Mississippi "with a Negro mammy to cook Southern dishes and pickaninnies to serve them."[12] Directly or indirectly, Santo inherited the schema from Leslie, along with the aspiration to satisfy a white clientele seeking "Black jazz, in a strange, exotic setting." To this end Santo brought in a bona fide Black entertainer ("The irresistible Frisco will receive you and recreate for you the gay night life of New York's Harlem").[13] "Professor" Bingham's Charleston lessons had granted him an unquestioned legitimacy, even if Santo saw no inconsistency between a Mississippi steamboat and the night life of Harlem.

The club opened on October 5, 1928, but Frisco withdrew two weeks later, replaced by a white dancer.[14] On November 10 a new revue was unveiled. Again, Aldington enlightens us: "The nigger orchestra was good, but I didn't think it very extra; but I was introduced to 'Henry,' the nigger pianist & he turned out to be one of Jelly Roll Morton's Red Hot Peppers! Such a thrill!

There were some tunes, a nigger songstress whom Nancy thought marvellous & I thought rather bad, a nigger lady, clothed only in a red cache-sex & silver breast containers, who danced with remarkable undulations of her lumbar regions; & a Negro man who cut double shuffles with unusual celerity."[15]

Although Aldington does not deign to communicate the artists' names, a *Journal* advertisement identifies them: "the elegant hostess June Day . . . Wilkins and Riley [and] Louise Waner [Warner]."[16] Day, a white American, was a survivor of the dance wars. She had partnered Harry Pilcer at the Alhambra in 1922 and appeared with his brother Murray, suggesting an affinity for jazz, even if questionable musical taste. It may be that Aldington omits her because she does not fit the category of a "nigger" cabaret. However, his "Negro man who cut double shuffles" is certainly half of the well-liked duo Wilkins and Riley, practitioners of "eccentric dancing," who had appeared that spring with Miss Day at the Abbaye. About Louise Warner, little is known other than that she was another example of Black cosmopolitanism, a young British dancer who had toured Italy and Germany before signing a three-month contract with Santo.[17] Visibly, she is the "nigger lady" who swayed with "remarkable undulations," in an outfit recalling the costumes of the "Dixie Vamps."

Lastly, there is the nameless "nigger orchestra." Despite Aldington's disparagement, the band was considered to be an ensemble of gifted artists and lauded in the *Journal* ad as "the marvelous colored quartet, Eddie South and his Alabamians." South, a musical prodigy whose classical career was thwarted by the dearth of opportunities for Black musicians, had just returned from Venice, where a tale of jealousy and miscegenation involving Nancy Cunard and the talented Henry Crowder had begun to unfold.

Crowder was born in Georgia, son of a Black workingman and a half-Indian mother. Having begun as pianist in a Washington brothel, he married a young Atlanta woman and gained respectability managing bands. After the war, he tried his luck with the Alabamians. The group had no connection to the Cotton State, yet exploited the racist image, appearing in publicity photos costumed in overalls and broad-brimmed straw hats. They enjoyed considerable success until January 1928, when their leader encountered Ziegfeld beauty "Bee" Palmer. On the verge of a divorce, she hired the band to accompany her at the College Inn in Chicago. Eddie was soon smitten; he insisted on relocating to New York to be closer to his pale inamorata. Reluctantly, the band followed, but Bee "could not or would not do a thing for" Eddie, and the affair collapsed. One night the audience at the Fifty-Fourth Street Club, where the band was playing, included a "sugar daddy" and his girlfriend. The daddy had plans to open a Paris cabaret for his lady and offered the Alabamians a contract as her backup band.[18]

Filled with enthusiasm, Henry embarked: "France! No color bar there. No discriminations! Freedom! A chance to live as every other man lived regardless of color."[19] However, chilled by South's example and armed with a bitter wisdom acquired in America, where interracial unions led only to disaster, he resolved to have nothing to do with white women. The manager who had lured them across the Atlantic quickly disappeared. When finally located, he revealed that the night club deal had aborted and promptly returned to America, stranding the band.[20] Fortunately, they were able to obtain a few short engagements, most fatefully, the contract in Venice.

After a sweltering twenty-four-hour train journey, they arrived on a late August evening. The band was booked into the café-restaurant of the Grand Hotel Luna, near Saint Mark's Square—a fashionable rendezvous frequented by Bricktop in 1926. As South later reminisced, "Enhanced with gilded stucco and antique oil paintings . . . they called it the Embassy because of its beautiful decoration. . . . Old Italian popular songs sung by Venetian boys and girls rose up from the lagoon and the gondolas to mix with the sound of my violin."[21]

As usual, Nancy was in Venice for the season, escorted by Louis Aragon. For two years the *dancings* had fueled their passion. Recalling Bricktop for another love he wrote, "We went to Montmartre to forget we would cry . . . Remember the songs the light-skinned Negress sang to please us, that powdered midnight."[22] The poem could have been composed for Nancy. Their relationship was near its end. They quarreled constantly, and Aragon attempted suicide. He survived and retreated to Paris, pausing in Milan to listen six times to Verdi's *Otello*![23] Nancy was ready for a new adventure. One night she entered the Embassy Room with her cousins Edward and Victor Cunard—"so thin, so white and so fragile."[24] On that evening (across the Grand Canal an early autumn moon sick with color, hanging over the domes of Santa Maria della Salute), the romance of Nancy Cunard and Henry Crowder was born. Her life had not been mundane: T. S. Eliot limned her in an early draft of *The Waste Land*, Samuel Beckett praised her courage and verve, and her lovers included Aldous Huxley and Ezra Pound. But at the Embassy she experienced a new thrill: the electrifying jazz of the "charming, elegant American musicians . . . Eddie, 'the dark angel of the violin,' Mike, the huge Black guitarist, Romie, the drummer [Jerome Bourke]."[25] Several nights later, Mike McKendrick was seated with Nancy's party. As Crowder passed, a female voice invited him for a drink. Initially, Nancy favored the handsome guitarist, but it was Henry who finally retained her attention.

Returning to Paris in mid-October, the Alabamians secured a gig at the newly opened Plantation.[26] All the protagonists were back from the Italian interlude: Nancy, Henry, Aragon, the Cunards, and an allegedly impartial observer, Richard Aldington. He denied having a romance with Nancy but had reasons to tolerate the gossip. Involved as he was with a married woman, it suited him to use Nancy as a smokescreen.[27] Though not present in Venice (he met Nancy in Rome in October), his new friendship made him a privileged witness to Nancy and Henry's affair.

Their interracial liaison flourished in the "violent, thrilling" atmosphere of La Plantation, but from the start it was subject to internal and external pressures. The most notable of the former was the green-eyed monster: jealousy. In a curious inversion of roles, their story echoed the Venetian triangle of Shakespeare's *Othello*. The jazz age moor claimed to be devoid of jealousy and not really in love, lured only by "an indefinable attraction," while the modern Desdemona was conspicuously lacking in maidenly fidelity.[28] As for Othello's falsely accused rival, Cassio, his contemporary counterpart, Aragon, was the most possessive of the three. Exchanges with Henry were polite but strained. In a letter to his mistress dated December 3, Aldington described a supper at the Plantation: "We met Aragon, Dolly Wilde, 'Victor' & 'Edward' (?Cunardiers?) and Nancy danced with Victor & Dolly with Edward while I watched or talked to Henry & Aragon. I like Aragon very much, he has a very beautiful and sensitive face, and a charming manner. But he is jealous as a million devils & made a frightful scene with Nancy about 3 a.m. apropos a girl whom he said Nancy had taken away from him, and also apropos the 'Henry.'"[29]

The "Negroes," who Aragon had imagined spreading "like an ink blot in the environs of the Place Saint-Georges," had seeped into his private life. Despite Crowder's avowed indifference, he was subjected to a similar fate. Nancy began frequenting other Black lovers, among them pugilist Bob Scanlon ("boxing lessons," she explained). "I was not jealous," Henry wrote, "but I had a great deal of pride and to have people laughing at me and considering me a fool was not pleasant."[30] The greatest affront was Nancy's liaison with rival pianist and ex–Jazz King Dan Parrish, a fixture at Le Grand Ecart.[31] Parrish was roly-poly, with a receding hairline, and very dark, as dark as the glossy black oilcloth lining the walls of his club. This surely pleased Nancy, who often told Crowder that she wished he were darker.[32]

If jealousy was the chief internal pressure on this cabaret Othello and Desdemona, the tangled threads of economics, class, and race also complicated matters. Nancy's fierce sexual independence, bolstered by the economic freedom inherent to her class position, allied her with the New Woman—an intellectual, socially progressive Peggy Joyce—but inevitably these factors undermined their relationship. From the very beginning she imposed financial dominance, buying costly rings for the band, including one for Henry in jade, lined with gold.[33] To compensate for this financial inequality, he traded his artistic talents and knowledge of a world whose injustices she ignored. Nancy learned what lay behind the picturesque steamboats and laughing "darkies" decorating the walls of the Plantation: bias, segregation, lynchings, a social violence with which Henry was personally familiar.[34]

Combined with the issue of race, these economic and social disparities proved toxic. French society folk, such as Nancy's friend Princess Violette Murat, were not shocked, and even some Americans like Elsa Maxwell or Ezra Pound may have been sympathetic—dancing at the Plantation with her ex-lover, Nancy thanked him for his "charming and appreciative ways with Henry," and in Venice Elsa invited the Alabamians to play for her select barge parties on the "Garden of the Hesperides," with its golden apples glowing in electric lights.[35] But despite the approbation of French law and Montmartre mores, many Americans and upper-class Brits harbored unfavorable judgements. As Robert L. Allen comments in his epilogue to Crowder's memoirs, Nancy and Henry must "have also sensed the patronizing attitude of friends who might smile when they met but then made racist remarks behind their backs."[36]

Typical of this mentality is Aldington. He did not faint at the sight of Black entertainers, but his correspondence is filled with negative observations, such as the "nigger songstress whom Nancy thought marvellous." Nor did Henry escape his disdain. Nancy recalls the two men laughing together "about the ironies of the race and color question."[37] Yet the poet consistently favored Aragon and, with the social and racial snobbery of his upper-class British education, wryly confided to his mistress, "I deduce that Nancy has now passed to the *culte des nègres* and is no longer interested in poor white trash."[38]

For over two months, Montmartre regulars had been titillated by gossip about the interracial couple. But hardly had they digested the scandal than they woke to shocking news of a shootout in the rue Fontaine, an incident that exposed another major problem of Montmartre life: pervasive violence. Members of the quarter's leading bands were involved. Saxophonist Sidney Bechet and banjoist Mike McKendrick were the trigger-happy gunmen, and pianist Glover Compton a not-so-innocent bystander. Bechet was playing with the

International Five at a Chez Florence still under the pall cast by Palmer Jones' death; Compton was, as we know, a prominent member of Zelli's Royal Box Band, and since their return the Alabamians had solidified their reputation at the Plantation.

Crowder's account is the most detailed:

> Mike, our banjo player, had been on a spree for some days and though he always turned up for work he was usually in a pretty drunken condition. One night he came to work particularly drunk and expressed his intention of shooting anyone who interfered with him. I cautioned him against doing anything foolhardy but he seemed to grow more and more determined as the night wore on. At 5 a.m. we finished work and Mike and I left the Plantation together. He invited me into the Costa Bar to have a drink. I refused and left him. The last I saw of him that morning he was staggering noisily into the door of the Costa Bar Café. The same evening I came down the rue Fontaine about seven o'clock and someone asked if I knew that Mike was in jail. I said I did not and then heard for the first time an account of what happened. After I left Mike, he went to Brick-Top's place [Le Grand Duc] just around the corner from the Costa Bar. There he met Sidney Bechet.... An altercation arose between the two about the musical qualifications of the members of our band and especially about myself. Bechet made some particularly nasty remarks and Mike struck him in the face. When Bechet attempted to retaliate Mike drew his pistol and threatened to let daylight into Bechet's body. ... Bechet, in great anger, left Brick-Top's, went home and got his pistol and came back looking for Mike. By this time Mike had returned to the Costa Bar. When Mike appeared someone told him that Bechet was outside waiting for him with a gun.... As soon as Mike appeared in the doorway bullets began to fly.[39]

The exact date of the Costa Bar's foundation is unknown, but by 1925 it was already an institution. The owner was a diminutive Italian American who, unlike his convivial compatriot Joe Zelli, was said to be uncouth and unfriendly. Though he owed his prosperity to the Black musicians who made the bar their rendezvous, his meanness often caused them to desert. Inexplicably, they always drifted back, rejoining what Aragon described as "floating populations of taxi drivers, street girls, queers, doormen, Black jazz musicians, and drunkards who lack the courage to go any further."[40] This description is documented by the only known photo of the bar. Groups of nattily dressed Black people, male except for a lone woman, lounge outside glass doors set in an angular art deco facade, with the name Costa-Bar inscribed in bold letters above.[41]

This was the scene of the early morning skirmish. The weapons of choice were, as usual, Brownings. McKendrick fired and Bechet replied with over ten shots. The latter was unharmed, but a bullet grazed Mike's forehead.[42] Unfortunately, that was not the only injury. Three others were wounded; an aged charwoman was hit by a ricocheting bullet, and a young Australian dancer received two bullets in the chest, apparently as she exited behind Compton, causing her to cough up quantities of blood. The pianist was also badly injured in the knee and had to be taken to the American Hospital.[43] Bechet accused him of instigating the quarrel: "He was always acting like he wanted to stir up trouble, like he wanted to be known as a place where trouble started."[44]

Bechet and McKendrick were arrested. Crowder was aware of Nancy's susceptibility to the banjoist's brooding good looks—one night after a dinner party in Venice he had witnessed stolen kisses.[45] There is no evidence that they were lovers, but upon hearing of the events she immediately sought a lawyer to defend him. Since early November, Aragon had been invested in a new relationship, but he was still bound to Nancy by a lingering fascination. Thanks to his contacts she was able to engage famed criminal attorney and politician Henry Torrès, champion of "small time gangsters and the kings of the underworld," whose campaign aide and official bodyguard was none other than the sinister de Lussats.[46]

Torrès' selection was overdetermined. Aragon was acquainted with his associate, Gérard Rosenthal, a young lawyer and poet linked to the Surrealist movement. At the same time, Mike's employer, Paul Santo, was a member of Torrès' inner circle and a habitué of Chez Nine, a restaurant off the rue Pigalle where leaders of organized crime mingled with the social and political elite. The proprietors were Louis, a retired safecracker, and his wife, the eponymous Nine. Through the ex-thief, Santo met two of his former confreres, de Lussats and his murderous liege man, Albert Aflalo, known as Gros Albert (Fat Albert).[47] Torrès and the latter three were part of a disreputable band that congregated at Santo's Palermo, or at the Cloche d'Or (formerly Arsène's), testifying to the imbrication of gang and club cultures.[48]

Winter set in. It was bitter cold, and the musicians had been placed in a freezing cell, clad only in thin tuxedos and bloodied dress shirts. Nancy and Victor Cunard arranged to supply them with clothes, cigarettes, and pocket money.[49] Aragon agreed to testify as a character witness, as did Gene Bullard, who had procured for Bechet the services of Maître Raymond Hubert, defender of the homicidal Mme Crutcher. Bullard's solicitude might seem odd; after all, Compton was his bandmate and Bechet's nemesis. However, Gene and the saxophonist shared a history. When Lloyd wrote "sometime in this heady period, Bechet and Bullard became friends," he was unaware of the origin of their camaraderie.[50] Shortly after the former's arrival in January, they had taken part in two scuffles at the Capitole. The first ended with plates and glasses flying, wounding then-owner Jules Volterra when he tried to intervene. Barely had the dining resumed than a group of "fascist" Southerners objected to the presence of Black clients, calling Bullard a "nigger." "I'm a French citizen," declared the ex-boxer, saying, "If you don't like it here, leave!" The white men's vehement response triggered a second brawl. Abruptly, two shots rang out, fired by an anonymous gunman (according to Gérard Rosenthal the lethal Baron de Lussats), piercing the wrist of a female patron and striking Bechet in the chest.[51]

Thus, even before assuming the direction of the Capitole, the baron was a catalyst of violence. Perhaps one of Georges Jamerson's mob connections, he first ran afoul of Bricktop over his unwelcome advances. "No one in the saloon business can avoid gangsters, hoods, petty crooks, and other types of criminals," she remarks philosophically. That was most likely in 1927, but it was only in January 1932 that "the Baron" sought to introduce "poules" into Bricktop's Monico, and she was obliged to begin carrying her own Browning.[52] These episodes were symptomatic of a uniquely American savagery that Fitzgerald sardonically labeled "the honorable, the traditional resource of his [the American hero's] land."[53] Discussing mobsters like Jack "Legs" Diamond, whom she had known in Harlem, Bricktop noted that "the Baron" and his colleagues were "beginning to take some cues from American gangsters. . . . [They] started organizing protection rackets. . . . When the gangsters decided to get nasty, those who protested found themselves at the wrong end of a bullet or a switchblade."[54] In effect, while Diamond was visiting Montmartre with a view to expanding the scope of his operations, a colleague remarked that "next to Chicago gangsters, the Pigalle clowns were like little boys, their imitations of Al Capone went no further than their Borsalino hats."[55] For all its frantic gaiety, the culture of the night clubs was a dangerous milieu. As Aragon opined, "When the maître d' bends over the champagne buckets, the revolver is never very far."[56]

Notwithstanding his violent past, Bullard sought to play the peacemaker.[57] Sensing a negative verdict, at the trial he launched into a wild diatribe as to what had "really happened."[58] To no avail. Both men received fifteen-month sentences and fines of 10,000 francs. As to the real cause of the fracas, witnesses agree that it began with a quarrel over artistic credentials. This reflected a rift between musicians like Bechet, a son of New Orleans, and Chicago musicians like McKendrick and Compton (even though the latter were both born in the South). At the same time, one American report recast the incident as a parable of the evils of interracial affairs, thus linking the theme of violence to the dread of miscegenation. It was alleged that the dispute was over the favors of a blonde Belgian dancer, though no French sources support this.[59] Bechet mentions a girl he wrongly believed to be Compton's companion, perhaps the Australian dancer, but the elusive Belgian beauty was a chimera.[60]

The *Chicago Defender* and some other Black papers bought into this fable, while claiming that the ugly publicity was fomented by white Americans to promote hatred against Black performers.[61] To its credit, the *Defender* ultimately published Compton's testimony. According to him, the story was "hatched in the *Chicago Tribune*'s incubator of prejudice." His self-serving comments minimize his role, but on one point he concurs with Bechet and Crowder: "There is absolutely no truth in the statement that a blond Belgian girl was the cause."[62] Journalist Geo London corroborates that the fight was "not at all for the love of a belle, black, white, or rose, but because of an artistic disagreement."[63]

Bechet's account is subjective and full of holes; its value lies in the insight it offers into his violent and confused mental state: "It was something the way it happened... something hard to make it clear. It's like there's somebody else inside a man, somebody that's not really that man, and when a thing happens, an anger like I had then, that other person takes over. That's not to make excuses. ... That's just to try to tell you what feeling there was to it standing there on the street, not even giving a goddamn how many shots they're sending back at me... just standing there pumping my gun and wanting to see everyone [*sic*] of them dead."[64]

In the end, the issue of artistic supremacy was no more the underlying cause of the shootout than the romantic rivalry invented by biased journalists. Both men possessed fiery tempers; however, beyond personalities they were victims of an omnipresent atmosphere of violence, an imported American aggressivity. Introduced by Gérard Rosenthal as a witness for McKendrick, Aragon plead in favor of the errant musicians ("homage of a jazz aficionado"). The judge caustically replied, "It is nonetheless true that they transformed the rue Fontaine into a scene from the Far West."[65]

The viciousness of this confrontation convinced Crowder to accept Nancy's proposal to work at her small press in Normandy. He maintains that the band then broke up.[66] In reality, it continued until the ensuing summer.[67] After that, Santo was reduced to presenting an obscure singer, Ivia Perrene, the insipid Gay Brummel Band, and Brodmann-Alfaro, a recently formed tango orchestra that, whatever its virtues, was hardly the "thrilling Black jazz" he had promised.[68] In the end, he capitulated, leasing the club to the dynamic Louis Mitchell.

Even lacking detailed records, it is evident that in the period preceding the takeover, the "Colored Gentleman" was seriously "overextended." A brief glance at his finances from the failure of the first Music Box to the opening of the Plantation gives an impression of flailing about; his oft-cited geniality perhaps hid the face of a man near the end of his rope. All was not negative; the Quick Lunch was a success. Then again, other projects were less profitable. Take, for example, the Pile ou Face (Heads or Tails) on rue Pigalle. In the closed ecosystem of Montmartre, Josephine's abandonment of the Impérial led indirectly to this venture. Since the last years of the war, the Impérial had flourished under J.-B. Pagès, one of the traditional Auvergnat innkeepers of Paris. In early 1926 ownership passed to Harot and Léonard, two Frenchmen who gave the cabaret a Yankee flavor, complete with a new barman and artistic director, both American. Following this strategy, they engaged Crickett Smith's Jazz Kings, recently returned from Russia. But as an American star, who better than the latest sensation Josephine Baker! Alas, her precipitous defection left the Impérial foundering.[69] Desperate, the owners turned to Bricktop, but after she severed ties in mid-May of 1928, the Impérial folded.

In the fall, the Pile ou Face opened at the same address, with the ubiquitous Mitchell as manager, but he quickly moved on.[70] Considering its brevity, Mitchell's tenure could not have been very lucrative, and there were other disquieting signs. In January 1929 he was seeking an investment partner for the Quick Lunch; by June it was operating under white management.[71] Sandwiched between these dates was a short run at El Garrón with a revamped Jazz Kings. Given the large personnel, ten musicians, it was perhaps more prestigious than cost-effective, and in June he accepted the direction of the second Music Box.[72] These financial problems were aggravated by his gambling addiction and a ruinously expensive move. Prompted by hubris or folly, he relocated to a villa in the smart western suburb of Saint-Cloud, where he and his wife entertained at lunches and teas on the beautiful grounds and, like Zelli, he enjoyed the life of a rural squire. "Country woman at last!" Tony wrote to her brother—a pastoral Gallic version of the American Dream rarely accessible to Black citizens back home.[73]

In this economically fragile situation, Mitchell hired forty-five employees and sank $126,000 into La Plantation.[74] The moment for a costly new venture was ill-chosen: December 7, five weeks after the Wall Street financial disaster that sent droves of wealthy club-goers fleeing back to America. Equally flawed was his adoption of Santo's original concept. This was fatally clear in his advertisement announcing an "authentic Negro Revue."[75] Well and good, but the ad was illustrated by a crude graphic that might have troubled even the most insouciant of his contemporaries. In an idyllic landscape of rolling fields stands a group of "darkies": a young "buck" in overalls, a "pickaninny" in ragged cut-offs, a benign "Uncle Tom" with a lavish white beard, and a matronly "Aunt Jemima" in apron and headwrap![76] Posed before a radiant sky they cheerfully vocalize (see gallery 2).

Mitchell's musical choices were less ideologically charged but equally misguided. Renowned singer Ethel Waters was rumored to appear. After a throat operation with a specialist recommended by Gene Bullard, she relocated to Mitchell's Saint-Cloud villa in early October. However, she never sang at the Plantation.[77] This was unfortunate; her classic blues might have lent legitimacy to the revue, but in December she was performing in London.[78] Cornered, Mitchell fell back on a mix of newcomers and veterans, the Versatile Four and the duo of Marino and Norris.[79] The twenty-two-year-old Cuban Marino Barreto had played in American dance orchestras, but he was known as an exponent of Afro-Cuban music—the rumba and the beguine. At his age, the forty-six-year-old Norris Smith was touring Central Europe with the Black Diamonds, a quartet who danced the Cakewalk, sang ragtime tunes, and even assayed some Tyrolean yodeling! Thus, though Marino was refreshingly young, Norris was clearly an old timer, even, as implied by Rainer Lotz, "prehistoric."[80]

The other headliners, the Versatile Four, were advertised as providing "Negro folksongs." In effect, the then twenty-four-year-old Polish pianist Alain Romans remembered it as "a singing group mainly but it was also jazz because we used to take choruses—we would scat them."[81] Their credentials were impeccable: one of the first ragtime ensembles to tour England in the teens (though fifty-year-old banjoist Anthony [Tony] Tuck was the only original member). Their drummer was old-hand Charlie Clarke, and the fourth member Bobbie Jones. If Jones had not followed the Crackerjacks to Cannes in September, it was undoubtedly because he had married a Frenchwoman, and she had just given birth. The racial, national, and generational diversity was admirable, but it was hardly cutting-edge jazz.

Miller deems that "Mitchell's choice of music . . . was no less passé than his choice of décor."[82] Despite modernist elements, the furnishings were also conceptually outdated. Mitchell's sole excuse was that he inherited them. With little time for renovations, he likely confined himself to the street level: a quick lunch, with a log-cabin window display and a Black mammy operating the kitchen—a patent reference to Leslie's Plantation Room.[83] Serving pancakes and sausages in the rue Blanche might have been seen as an attack on the pretentiousness of the Prince of Wales and his cohorts, but a live "Aunt Jemima" catered to O'Brien's worst fantasies about the Alabamian origins of Mitchell's mother. Leslie's club was seminal in the evolution of the Black revue, but by 1929 the formula was a reactionary chestnut. Yielding to Montmartre's insatiable thirst for plantation echoes, the "Colored Gentleman" embraced a retrograde formula.

Seven weeks was not enough to amortize his investment. The ideological reasons for his failure were echoed in a March 1930 concert for flood victims that he presided as stage manager. Bricktop performed; Bullard participated in a comic boxing match umpired by Bob Scanlon; Frisco sang in three languages, the event drew Noble Sissle, Henry Crowder, a Hawaiian banjo band...all the Black artists of Montmartre had answered the call. Rife with reminiscences of "the old plantation" (Crickett led a minstrel band; Harvey White sang his 1929 success, "Ol' Man River"; and Joe Boyd rendered the archetypal plantation melody, "Swanee River"), the concert ushered in the end of an era.[84]

In August 1930 Mitchell made his last public appearance. A group of Gold Star mothers had been brought to France by the U.S. government to visit the graves of their slain children. In a familiar pattern of discrimination, the Black mothers were segregated and obliged to travel in cramped berths below decks while the more comfortable cabins above remained largely empty. Paris showed greater respect. Along with Bricktop and a host of Montmartre performers, Mitchell entertained the grieving women at the Casino de Paris, bringing his Parisian adventure full circle with a characteristic display of generosity.[85]

But shortly before that Mitchell had made a desperate throw of the dice with his ultimate club, L'Esperanto.[86] Did the name refer to the universal language or to its root meaning: "hopeful?" If the latter, it was to no avail. Mitchell had naively declared he would remain in Paris for the rest of his life, but now he was forced to avow, "I tried to keep up for a while, but I was facing impossible odds. Ruin and jail stared me in the face." The intervention of an American multimillionaire, Victor Emanuel, saved him from disaster; however, the elegant lawn parties at Saint-Cloud were a thing of the past.[87] In September, he and Tony were obliged to return to New York.

We ignore Mitchell and Santo's financial arrangements, but no doubt the Corsican was also overextended. His rise to the imperial throne had been swift;

his fall even swifter. In April 1930 he was spotted at the bicycle races. Amid countesses, prize fight managers, and "solemn members of the French Academy," a reporter identified him for a public with a short memory: "Paul Santo, who used to run a whole chain of Montmartre cabarets."[88] Without fully charting the dissolution of his empire, we should note the cession of the Floresco to Bricktop and the surrender of the brightest jewel in his crown, Le Perroquet. But all was not lost. Once again, he called on Eddie South's Alabamians to confer an illusion of life, this time on the transient, 1931 resurrection-in-exile of La Plantation, a pathetic echo of that factitious southern world, now rotting gently under the genuine Mediterranean palms of Monte Carlo.[89]

Along with violence and an obsessive anxiety about miscegenation, the deceptively utopian fiction of "the old plantation" was the third serpent in the earthly paradise of Montmartre. As codified by Lew Leslie and relayed by Elsa Maxwell and others, it had never been merely innocent nostalgia for a pre-industrial past. "Some Sunny Day," an Irving Berlin song featured in Leslie's revue, betrays an alarming indulgence in the clichés of the plantation topos. The tune was introduced at Elsa's Acacias by Jenny Dolly in 1922 and widely recorded, notably by the Jazz Kings. As in "Where the Black-Eyed Susans Grow," the lyrics lack a specific Black content, but they belong to the category of "carry-me-backs," a genre exemplified by "Swanee River." "Carry-me-backs" encode a theme of nostalgic yearning for the security and solace of the old plantation (in the mawkish lyrics of "Some Sunny Day": "Alabam' my home . . . that cabin door . . . never more to roam").[90]

The following year, another Berlin "carry-me-back," "Homesick," received an unsettling interpretation in the Dolly Sisters' revue, *Paris sans voiles* (*Paris unveiled*). Once again one observes a longing for return to an idealized *locus amoenus*. "Grave and sweet, a little melancholy song," the lyrics evoke a generic bucolic scene ("cozy little shack . . . funny old mule . . ."), but the staging exposed the Black subtext.[91] Surrounded by agricultural equipment, the glamourous Dollys sang and danced in blackface! This romanticized image of life on a coffee plantation as a regretted golden age was echoed by a French critic who enthused about "the beautiful warm-toned vision, from straw yellow to orange and fiery red, seen in the tropical sketch *Plantation Days*, [and the negresses] whose peculiarity is to have a golden skin, shadowed with pale ochre, and the charming face of the Dolly Sisters."[92] If these comments seem to express an innocuous French desire for escapist entertainment, they take on more disquieting undertones in an American context. Murals in Leslie's Plantation Room, a "costly replica of the south before the war," represented an antebellum mansion, outbuildings, and a barn. However, with nonchalance, the artist had not hesitated to include the squalid slave quarters.[93] That a sentimental and essentially racist vision recast the lives of these enslaved laborers as one of blithe, rustic simplicity occulted a cruel reality: the violence and constraint required to support such a social system.

Jenny Dolly's spectacular presentation at the Acacias exposed similar ambiguities. Elsa is unforthcoming about the plantation framework. She recalled only that the star entered in a cape of fresh gardenias designed by Molyneux—a flower linked to the mythos of the old South.[94] Grace Moore expanded on her memories: "Jenny would pluck and toss [the gardenias] out to the men as she danced around with Clifton during the introduction music. Webb had two little Black boys, like nineteenth century Nubian figurines, who waltzed around with him, holding two baskets filled with corsages which Webb handed out to the ladies as he danced."[95] Elsa's omission may have stemmed from a certain unease but apparently Moore, a Southerner, found the appalling "pickaninnies" unobjectionable.

Though the term "pickaninny" was considered an offensive racist slur, like "darky" and "nigger," its use was widespread.[96] In 1935 a *Vanity Fair* journalist queried, "Does the Countess Pepito Abatino ever pause to dwell once more in memory on her pickaninny days in America?" jeeringly linking the term to the aristocratic title that Josephine herself had long since debunked.[97] The "pickaninny" image clung to her even after she outgrew the demeaning persona of her early comic performances—in *Chocolate Dandies* (1924) she had "exploited the stereotypes of minstrelsy," performing in blackface, eyes crossed in ironic self-mockery, in a solo titled "Land of the Dancing Pickaninnies!"[98]

At this point (suggested by the work of Jennifer Anne Boittin among others), one discerns another junction between Black French and Montmartre's Black expatriates. The mythic image of "exotic" island sisters proposed by the Dollys' performance in *Plantation Days* became a reality in jazz age Paris: the brilliant Nardals from Martinique (there were seven). Paulette, the eldest, arrived in 1920, the first Black woman to study at the Sorbonne, followed in 1923 by her younger sister Jane. They settled in Clamart, a southern suburb of Paris, where in the late twenties and thirties they hosted a literary salon uniting African, Caribbean, and American segments of the diaspora (Alain Locke, Langston Hughes, and Marcus Garvey visited), an initiative that was influential in the development of the nascent negritude movement.[99]

The adjacent train station (fifteen minutes from the Montparnasse cafés) allowed the Nardals to pursue an active social life that apparently included visiting the Folies Bergère, where Parisians were all agog over Josephine's appearances. As well-brought-up Catholic bourgeoises, they may have been shocked by the exuberant nudity of the infamous "banana skirt" tableau, but their intellectual acuity allowed them to extract deeper lessons. One consequence was Jane's 1928 essay "Pantins exotiques" ("Exotic Puppets").

At that time, the Black star was on a world tour, but the souvenir of her mesmerizing performance was a catalyst for Jane's exercise in awakened race consciousness. Published in *La Dépêche Africaine*, she deplored Parisians' fascination with exoticized and eroticized Black women, a trend whose objectifying effect was reinforced by the "public performance expected of women of color."[100] Nardal surveys the exotic imagery of French writers, from the idyllic landscapes of Bernardin de Saint-Pierre (akin to the "warm-toned vision" of the Dolly Sisters' sketch) to the "violent urban primitivism" of Soupault's *Le Nègre*.[101] "But," she announces dramatically, "Josephine arrived . . . , breaking through Bernardin's painted stage décor. . . . Even though still dressed in feathers or banana leaves, she brings to Parisians the latest products of Broadway (Charleston, jazz, etc.). The transition between past and present, the fusion of virgin forest and modernism, is consummated and rendered palpable by Black Americans . . . the delightfully spicy contrast of primitive beings in an ultra-modern setting, of African frenzy deployed in the cubist décor of a night club."[102] Jane Nardal had grasped "the manner in which [Josephine] linked the discourses of the primitive and the modern, the colonial and the Parisian."[103]

However, one should note that Nardal's critique of this alienating exoticization is directed at white authors rather than at Josephine herself—half of her essay is devoted to Paul Morand's collection of short stories, *Magie noire* (*Black Magic*, 1928), with its tragic, atavistic heroines, such as the African American dancer, Congo, clearly inspired by Josephine.[104] Even so, the Martinican did not appear to recognize the extent to which Josephine had assumed the exotic label imposed on her and turned it on its head through a conscious manipulation of this hypersexual image. Bennetta Jules-Rosette convincingly argues for a high degree of self-agency, on and offstage. "She became an artifact, and she did so thru her own artifice as a performer."[105]

Josephine's second Folies revue, *Un Vent de Folie*, exploited this play with cultural representations. In the "Plantation" tableau she wore an outfit identical to her *Revue nègre* costume: cutoff coveralls, a raggedy blouse, and black MaryJanes (see gallery 2). Though she later refused to perform "mammy songs," here she sang "I'm A Leavin' for Alabamy" backed by the Thomson Jazz Band, dressed as "darkies" in overalls and straw hats—another carry-me-back extoling a fantasy world of perpetual sunshine.¹⁰⁶ Her persona had always contained an implicit duality. Juxtaposed with her Topsy impersonation in *Chocolate Dandies* there was the elegant rigout of her comic turn as "A Deserted Female."¹⁰⁷ That show elicited mixed reviews from white critics who demanded more conventionally primitive plantation scenes. "Too much so-called politeness," one wrote, "too much platitudinous refinement and not enough of the racy and the razor-edged. There is, in a word, too much art and not enough 'Africa.'"¹⁰⁸

Un vent de Folie espoused the American topos in the name of an equally conventional but more romantic union of instinct and civilization, one distinct from the slave-haunted image of the old Plantation. Black French like Paulette and Jane Nardal had access to French society on condition that they accept the language and norms of Gallic culture. Thus, while the French enslaved and colonized without restraint, slavery never traumatized its white citizens as it did in America during the post-slavery period. Lucidly, Paulette Nardal attributed the Antilleans' slow awakening to race consciousness to the absence of the more extreme and violent oppression of American racism.¹⁰⁹

As with the Dollys' agricultural estate, the Folies did not represent a real Dixie plantation. On the contrary, palm trees, flowered trellises, and a bamboo hut evoked a tropical Eden, and like the eighteenth-century French shepherds of pastoral whose beribboned costumes only mimed peasant garb, Josephine's cutoffs were of black satin, suggesting, as Jane Nardal understood, the synthesis of primitive and sophisticated inherent to her persona. In the *Vogue* article that accompanies a photo of the "Plantation" tableau, McMullin extols her elegance: "This woman is like a living drawing by Aubrey Beardsley or Picasso."¹¹⁰ The Beardsley analogy frames her as an urbane and decadent artifact, and the reference to Picasso positions her at the pinnacle of modernity. The metamorphosis is evident in an exquisite Harcourt photo (ca. 1940). Minus the provocative *garçonne* hairdo, face burnished to serene, classical perfection by the studio's hallmark lighting, she rests her head against a Roman vase. The only reference to her "primitive" character is the tongue-in-cheek image of a satyr, barely visible in relief on the side of the urn (see gallery 2).

What was known as jazz undermined traditional values. For the French this was part of a liberation from prewar cultural practices, but for Black Americans it assumed a character I have chosen to call utopian. The Greek etymology of the word *utopia* [Ou (non) + topos (place)] necessitates seeing it as a nonplace whose nonexistence maps a real world of which it offers a negative image. For provincial American readers of the syndicated press Montmartre was indeed unreal, a fantasy savored over cups of coffee in their small-town kitchens. Regrettably, this Utopia was situated in Montmartre, and a majority of its clubgoers consisted of white Americans of two sorts: those who dared a cautious step across the color line, and the large number who were revolted by what they regarded as utopian reveries contrary to natural law. This brings us to the visions of the old plantation inherent to the concept of Utopia, one a bucolic dream, the other Billie Holiday's sardonic "pastoral scene of the gallant south." Poet and aesthetician Friedrich Schiller's category of "elegiac poetry" encompasses these opposing discourses: "the broadly elegiac," a reactionary nostalgia for the lost golden age of the "carry-me-backs" (a vision at variance with both industrialization and an ideal of racial equality) or conversely, the as-yet-unrealized "idyll," a progressive opening towards a utopian future that might reconcile the real and the ideal. As Schiller wrote, "That [the idyll] would lead man, who cannot now return to Arcadia, forward to Elysium."[111]

Symptomatic of the double bind in which Black artists found themselves, Mitchell was unable to resolve the contradictions of the two utopian visions. At the Plantation he adopted the threadbare clichés of a theatrical genre that persisted in the popular songs of the Montmartre *dancings*; what, in a doubly racist formula, Dashiell called "those cornpone, cabin door and coal black rose melodies, written on Broadway by a one-fingered pianist who never saw an old cabin door, and who would fall ill if he ever ate cornpone."[112] Rhapsodic images of the antebellum South had infiltrated the collective memory, and Mitchell's clientele was ready to believe that his more "authentic" performers "might actually be gathered informally around the old cabin door, singing in the moonlight."[113] By perpetuating these stereotypes, the man who had played a major role in the emergence of "the Great Black Way" ended his Parisian career a willing victim of an insidious myth.

When, in *Fifty Million Frenchmen*, Cole Porter celebrated the "Happy Heaven of Harlem," he was not referring to the Black district of New York but rather voicing nostalgia for the champagne nights of Le Grand Duc—a celestial reward for sufferings endured in the dystopian Harlem streets:

> There's a happy heaven of Harlem
> In a country over the sea
> Where there ain't no rule
> Against white mule
> And all lovin' is free.[114]

This prospective Utopia of racial harmony was sabotaged by the false Utopia embodied in the spurious myth of the old plantation. The authenticity of the Tempo Club was traded for a hollow stereotype. Like Mitchell, Montmartre was caught between these two visions, proposing a progressive model of social interaction, yet mired in the formulas of a fictive Arcadian past—the regressive image that fueled Woon and his confreres' incessant harping on Alabama. Because some white Americans refused a redefinition of race relations (abetted by certain French club owners more concerned with profits than social equality), Montmartre's Utopia was stillborn.

Wasn't this inevitable? Montmartre was only a virtual Utopia; it could not provide a solution to the problem posed by French philosopher Louis Marin: "Utopian discourse is the one form of ideological discourse that has anticipatory value of a theoretical kind: but it is a value that can only appear as such *after* theory itself has been elaborated, that is to say, subsequent to the emergence of the material conditions for the new productive forces."[115] The boisterous, multicultural landscape of Pigalle made visible the fragile, experimental space of an ideal world, a future horizon that has still to become our present. Perhaps the material conditions have not yet been fully realized, but in lieu of a flawless, utopian society, frozen in its perfection, Montmartre may be envisioned as an evolving social movement, "a type of *praxis* ... that has less to do with the construction and perfection of someone's 'idea' of a 'perfect society' than it does with a concrete set of mental operations to be performed on a determinate type of raw material given in advance, which is contemporary society itself": Montmartre as a disorderly prelude to Utopia![116]

EPILOGUE

"NO DOUBT ONE MUST BID THEM ADIEU"

Therefore, au revoir. This is what I am compelled to say to luxury, to the superfluous, to my deepest self. And as for the personages of that happy time of opulence, no doubt one must bid them adieu.
—Maurice Sachs

Jean Cocteau's secretary, Maurice Sachs, was bidding a succinct farewell to the actors of an lavish and extravagant epoch. Although not American (the family fortune was managed by a Yankee uncle), he was a victim of the Wall Street crash, the financial disaster that weakened the commercial underpinnings of the pleasure fair that was Montmartre. Along with drugs, xenophobic French labor laws, and increasing gang violence, the 1929 debacle announced the beginning of the end of frenetic pleasures. Rich Yankee expatriates grew scarce, and the flight of American dollars cast a cloud over the dance palaces of Montmartre. It is difficult to consign history to neat little boxes, but coming hard on the heels of the economic catastrophe, 1930 seemed to initiate the fading of a golden age. Not an abrupt conclusion (as Bricktop defiantly wrote, "we all played on"), nevertheless, Hitler was waiting in the wings, and the occupation of Paris in 1940 would be only the final coup de grace to what had been an unreal, utopian vision, an enchanted parenthesis undermined by its social and ideological conflicts.[1] Those who had lived through the twenties—illumined by the last flames of hellfire and the radiant glow of an imagined Eden—were faced with the realities of the depression and the loss not only of personal dreams but of the implicit utopian dream of Montmartre.

Returning to our list of influential Americans, we see that, except for Bricktop and Josephine, who were relative latecomers, the dawn of the decade had filled them with a desire for something new to replace the ruins of an exhausted civilization. Yet, apart from a handful, by 1930 they were gone. Some of these larger-than-life figures died—a fate for which the acknowledged vices of Montmartre, drugs, gangs, endemic violence, could not be blamed. On the threshold of the new decade, Oscar Mouvet followed in the footsteps of his late brother, expiring in a Pyrenees clinic from lung injuries incurred during the war.[2] Three years after Palmer's sudden demise and her abandonment of Paris, Florence succumbed to a heart attack in New York, leaving behind only a half-remembered legend.

Others, like Buddie Gilmore, had already moved on. After the giddy nights of 1924 and '25, and the spring of 1926, he spent much of his time touring and eventually returned to the States. For the rest, the end of the decade marked a turning point. Joe Zelli and Louis Mitchell were direct victims of the Crash. Before departing for New York and his triumphant cameo appearance in *Fifty Million Frenchmen*, even the normally ebullient Zelli was obliged to acknowledge a dire situation: "Unless the market comes back sharply, we are going to have the worst season next year than of any years since the war . . . I am afraid the old Royal Box will be vacant many a night next summer."[3] His prediction was cruelly accurate. In the early thirties he crisscrossed the Atlantic several times, but after the failure of the Club des Lapins in 1934 he would abandon Paris.

With the closing of the Plantation, Louis Mitchell also found himself in financial straits. Only an intervention of the wealthy Victor Emanuel kept him from total ruin, and in 1930 his Parisian sojourn came to a regretted close. Commenting on an encounter with Mitchell in front of a Harlem bar in the early forties, Goffin wrote, "He earned millions in Paris, but he liked to play the horses and shoot dice. Today he passes unnoticed, a member of the anonymous throng, and nobody knows that this still elegant man . . . was once the idol of Paris, the man who introduced jazz to Europe."[4]

Where Jed Kiley is concerned, the Crash provided a convenient excuse for personal failings; in reality, he had decamped a month before the Wall Street cataclysm. The irrepressible Elsa Maxwell also arrived in New York before Black Tuesday but, unlike Kiley, she wittily argued for the absence of any adverse effects: She had never had any money! As to her reasons for leaving Europe, she wrote, "I was homesick after living abroad for ten years. I was tired of being a foreigner everywhere I went, fed up hearing myself speak French, Italian and German with abominable accents."[5] Elsa's departure was not definitive. In the thirties she continued to traverse the ocean and profit from her many society connections, the latter mostly on the western shores of the Atlantic. Eventually, like Montmartre expats Kiley, Woon, and Vauchant, she ended up in Hollywood, in her case becoming a successful gossip columnist.

Harry Pilcer survived the thirties, but with the advent of the war he also hied himself to Hollywood. Léo Vauchant recounts meeting him one brilliant California afternoon, forlornly waiting for a bus on Sunset Boulevard. Upset that he hadn't been hired as technical advisor for the film biography of his old friends Jenny and Rosie, he grumbled, "Can you imagine? They do a picture about the Dolly Sisters and nobody wants to hear from me."[6] After the war he returned to France and worked as a host in the Casinos of Deauville and Cannes until his 1961 passing in a Riviera resort at the age of seventy-five, dying as he had lived, on a night club dance floor.[7]

In the early thirties Gene Bullard opened L'Escadrille at 15 rue Fontaine, almost directly across the street from the lost kingdom of his onetime boss, Joe Zelli. As war clouds gathered, he began to spy on German patrons for the benefit of French counterintelligence, but in the spring of 1940, he was obliged to flee, eventually making his way to New York, where he lived in virtual obscurity until his death in the same year as Harry Pilcer, surrounded by largely indifferent compatriots of both races who ignored his dazzling past.

Like her protégé Josephine, who navigated the thirties with success and achieved a lengthy career, Bricktop was a fighter. Her Montmartre projects prospered until 1936, when she was obliged to give up her club and work for others as a paid hostess. As with many American musicians, the arrival of the Nazis (who were, among other faults, violently opposed to "degenerate black jazz") compelled her to take ship for America, aided by Lady Mendl and the Duchess of Windsor. Following other Montmartre fixtures (Frank Withers and Mike McKendrick had sailed a few weeks earlier), on October 26, 1939, Bricktop left her beloved Paris behind under a driving rain.[8] Nevertheless, she continued her extraordinary career in the postwar period, running profitable clubs in Mexico City and Rome. In August of the following year, Parisians would be treated to the spectacle of sightseeing Nazi soldiers crowding the steps of Sacré Cœur, on the crest of the "Mountain of Martyrs," jostling each other for a breathtaking view of the vanquished city.[9]

Varied were the fates of these erstwhile kings, queens, moguls, and emperors, some less fatal than others but even the most auspicious far from equal to "that happy time of opulence" lived out on a few contiguous streets of the Parisian quarter known as Montmartre. With the coming of the war, those burnished utopian dreams gradually became, even for their protagonists, merely a distant and frivolous memory.

APPENDIX

BARS, CABARETS, *DANCINGS*, RESTAURANTS, AND THEATERS CITED IN THE TEXT

The numbers following the addresses refer to the Parisian *arrondissements*.

L'Abbaye de Thélème (1 place Pigalle, 9ᵉ)

Les Acacias (47 rue des Acacias, 17ᵉ)

The Aladdin's Lamp Club (21 boulevard de la Seine, Neuilly)

L'Alhambra Theatre (40 rue de Malte, 11ᵉ)

The American Foxtrot Club (15 avenue Montaigne, 8ᵉ)

Apollo Theatre (20 rue de Clichy, 9ᵉ)

Arsène's (3 rue Mansart, 9ᵉ)

The Author's Club (Auteuil?)

The Blue Room (17 rue Caumartin, 9ᵉ)

Bricktop's (59 bis-61 rue Pigalle, 9ᵉ)

Bricktop's [Harem] (53 rue Pigalle, 9ᵉ)

Bricktop's Impérial (59 rue Pigalle, first floor, 9ᵉ)

Bricktop's Monico (66 rue Pigalle, 9ᵉ)

Cadet Rousselle (17 rue Caumartin, 9ᵉ)

Le Capitole (58 rue Notre-Dame de Lorette, 9ᵉ)

Le Casino de Paris (16 rue de Clichy, 9ᵉ)

Château et Caveau caucasiens (54 rue Pigalle, 9ᵉ)

Chez Florence (36 rue Pigalle, 9ᵉ)

Chez Florence (61 rue Blanche, 9ᵉ)

Chez Harry Pilcer (17 rue Caumartin, 9ᵉ)

Chez Harry Pilcer [L'Oasis] (26 avenue Victor Emmanuel III, now avenue Franklin D. Roosevelt, 8ᵉ)

Chez Henri (Place Gaillon, 2ᵉ)

Chez Jane Darcy (17 rue Caumartin, 9ᵉ)

Chez Joséphine (40 rue Fontaine, 9ᵉ)
Chez Nine (34 rue Victor Massé, 9ᵉ)
Ciro's (6 rue Daunou, 2ᵉ)
La Cloche d'Or (3 rue Mansart, 9ᵉ)
The Clover Club (25 rue Caumartin, 9ᵉ)
Le Club des Lapins (16 rue Caumartin, 9ᵉ)
The College Inn (28 rue Vavin, 6ᵉ)
The Comedy Club (25 rue Fontaine, in the basement of the Gaity Theatre, 9ᵉ)
Costa Bar (1 rue Fontaine, 9ᵉ)
The Dixie Club (199 rue Saint-Martin, 3ᵉ)
El Garrón (6 rue Fontaine, first floor, 9ᵉ)
El Garrón [Le Nouvel] (10 rue Fontaine, 9ᵉ)
The Embassy Club [Le Jardin de ma Soeur] (17 rue Caumartin, 9ᵉ)
L'Escadrille (15 rue Fontaine, 9ᵉ)
L'Esperanto (16 rue Frochot, 9ᵉ)
La Féria (16 bis rue Fontaine, ground floor, 9ᵉ)
The Flirting Club (Auteuil)
Le Floresco (59 bis-61 rue Pigalle, 9ᵉ)
Florida (20 rue de Clichy, in the Apollo Theatre, 9ᵉ)
Les Folies-bergère (32 rue Richer, 9ᵉ)
Frolics (30 rue de Gramont, 2ᵉ)
Gaity Theatre (25 rue Fontaine, 9ᵉ)
Le Grand Duc (52 rue Pigalle, 9ᵉ)
Le Grand Ecart (7 rue Fromentin, 9ᵉ)
Le Grand Teddy [So-Different] (24 rue Caumartin, 9ᵉ)
Le Harem (53 rue Pigalle, 9ᵉ)
Harlem (53 rue Pigalle, 9ᵉ)
Harry Pilcer's Acacias (47–49 rue des Acacias, 17ᵉ)
Harry Pilcer's *Dancing*, (20 rue de Clichy, in the Apollo Theatre 9ᵉ)
Harry's New York Bar (5 rue Daunou, 2ᵉ)
L'Impérial (59 rue Pigalle, first floor, 9ᵉ)
Le Jardin de ma Soeur [The Embassy Club] (17 rue Caumartin, 9ᵉ)
Joséphine Baker's Impérial (59 rue Pigalle, first floor, 9ᵉ)
Kiley's (6 rue Fontaine, ground floor, 9ᵉ)
Kiley's Gaity (25 rue Fontaine, in the basement of the Gaity Theatre, 9ᵉ)

Louigi's Elmano Bar (4 rue Edouard VII, 9ᵉ)
Maurice and Eleanora's Club (47–49 rue des Acacias, 17ᵉ)
Maurice's Club (14 rue Caumartin, at Le Romano, in the Hotel Grande Bretagne, 9ᵉ)
Maurice's Club (25 rue Caumartin, 9ᵉ)
Merrick's Gaity (25 rue Fontaine, in the basement of the Gaity Theatre, 9ᵉ)
Mitchell's (36 rue Pigalle, 9ᵉ)
Mitchell's (61 rue Blanche, 9ᵉ)
Mitchell's Quick Lunch (35 rue Pigalle, 9ᵉ)
Le Monico [New Monico] (66 rue Pigalle, 9ᵉ)
Morgan's *Dancing* (46 ter rue Saint-Didier, 16ᵉ)
Le Moulin Rouge (82 boulevard de Clichy, 18ᵉ)
The Mr. Will-Stay-Up Late Club (Auteuil)
The Music Box 1 (41 rue Pigalle, 9ᵉ)
The Music Box 2 (53 rue Pigalle, 9ᵉ)
Le Narguileh (Place Pigalle and rue Frochot, 9ᵉ)
Le Normandy (26 rue Fontaine, 9ᵉ)
L'Oasis [Chez Harry Pilcer] (26 avenue Victor Emmanuel III, now avenue Franklin D. Roosevelt, 8ᵉ)
L'Olympia (28 boulevard des Capucines, 9ᵉ)
Omar Khayyâm, *Dancing* Persan (16 bis rue Fontaine, mezzanine, 9ᵉ)
Le Palace Music-Hall (8 rue du Faubourg-Montmartre, 9ᵉ)
Le Palermo (6 rue Fontaine, ground floor, 9ᵉ)
La Perle (59 bis-61 rue Pigalle, 9ᵉ)
Le Perroquet (16 rue de Clichy, lobby mezzanine of the Casino de Paris, 9ᵉ)
Pigall's (77 rue Pigalle, 9ᵉ)
Pile ou Face (59 rue Pigalle, 9ᵉ)
La Plantation (58 rue Notre-Dame de Lorette, 9ᵉ)
Le Princess (6 rue Fontaine, first floor, 9ᵉ)
Le Rat blanc (16 bis rue Fontaine, ground floor, 9ᵉ)
Le Rat mort (7 place Pigalle, 9ᵉ)
The Ritz Hotel (15 Place Vendôme, 1ᵉʳ)
The Ritz Hotel Bar (38 rue Cambon, 1ᵉʳ)
Romano's (14 rue Caumartin, in the Hôtel Grande Bretagne, 9ᵉ)
Le Samovar (16 bis rue Fontaine, mezzanine, 9ᵉ)

Le Sans-Gêne (17 rue Caumartin, 9ᵉ)

Le Sans Souci [prewar] (17 rue Caumartin, 9ᵉ)

Le Sans Souci [postwar] (17 rue Caumartin, 9ᵉ)

Savoy Dancing Club (25 rue Caumartin, 9ᵉ)

Shanley's (6 rue Fontaine, ground floor, 9ᵉ)

So Different [Le Grand Teddy] (24 rue Caumartin, 9ᵉ)

Le Tempo Club (16 bis rue Fontaine, mezzanine, 9ᵉ)

Théâtre Caumartin (25 rue Caumartin, 9ᵉ)

Théâtre des deux masques (6 rue Fontaine, ground floor, 9ᵉ)

Théâtre des Champs-Elysées (15 avenue Montaigne, 8ᵉ)

Théâtre Marigny (Avenue des Champs-Elysées and the avenue de Marigny, 8ᵉ)

La Troïka (26 rue Fontaine, 9ᵉ)

Le Ver luisant (61 rue Blanche, 9ᵉ)

Washington Palace (14 rue Magellan, 8ᵉ)

Le Yar (63 rue Pigalle, 9ᵉ)

Zelli's Club (17 rue Caumartin, 9ᵉ)

Zelli's Royal Box (16 bis rue Fontaine, ground floor, 9ᵉ)

NOTES

INTRODUCTION. "A JOYOUS TOWER OF BABEL"

The epigraph is from Gravigny, *Montmartre en 1925*, 46. Unless otherwise indicated all references are to the 1924 Editions Montaigne edition. All translations of foreign languages are my own.

1. On the cabarets of the Place Pigalle see Cazaux, *Les Boulevards de Clichy*. For the location of bars, cabarets, restaurants, and theaters cited in the text, see the appendix.
2. Woon, *Paris That's Not*, 247.
3. Ibid., 245. Florence's maiden name is given variously as "Emery," "Embry," or "Emory." Magloire states that her death certificate and passport application record it as Emery ("Florence's Place," 38n1). However, notices of early appearances almost always use "Emory" (see, for example, "Theatrical Jottings," *New York Age*, August 6, 1914, 6). In one exception, she appears as "Emery" on a program with singer Marjorie Sipp, but three months later, with the same Miss Sipp as cohostess, she is advertised at the Libya Café as "Emory" ("Happy Rhone and His Orchestra of Thirty," *New York Age*, April 17, 1920, 6; "Manhattan and the Bronx," *New York Age*, July 17, 1920, 8).
4. See H. C. Morris, "The Story of Corporal Mouvet, Yankee in the Foreign Legion," *Des Moines Sunday Register*, August 11, 1918, Feature Sec., n. pag. [3]. See also *New York Herald* (European ed.), June 1, 1919, 2. Unless otherwise indicated, citations refer to this continental edition.
5. French scholars are often equally ill-informed about the specifics of Montmartre. When Aragon writes of "Cruykshank . . . who was assassinated by his wife one evening in 1926," it is obvious that consciously or unconsciously he is misspelling the name of hapless Black pianist Leon Crutcher. Yet his French editor notes, "We have been unable to find any trace of this musician, or of his tragic end" (*Le Mauvais Plaisant*, 346 and note 2).
6. He writes that in 1919 Eugene Bullard "was hired to play in the band at the Chez Florence in the Théâtre Caumartin at 17 rue de Caumartin. Another source places Chez Florence in the rue Pigalle . . . founded as Mitchell's by Louis Mitchell in 1924 but renamed for the singer and hostess, Florence Embry Jones. . . . In time Chez Florence was sold to Joe Zelli who . . . owned and managed several other Parisian clubs, including the Royal Box at 16 rue Fontaine and the Tempo Club above Zelli's in the rue Caumartin" (Shack, *Harlem in Montmartre*, 30).

These few lines represent a compilation of errors. The Théâtre Caumartin was located at 25 rue Caumartin, not 17. Bullard was hired by Zelli to play at Cadet Rousselle, 17 rue Caumartin. After they departed in 1921, Florence sang there but by that time it had become the Sans Souci. Chez Florence in the rue Pigalle was not founded until 1924 and was named by Florence and her husband, Palmer. Joe Zelli had no connection to Chez Florence, and the Tempo Club was located on the mezzanine at 16 bis rue Fontaine. Citing the unreliable *New*

Grove Dictionary, Shack compounds these mistakes by stating that Chez Florence was in rue Pigalle until autumn 1926 (30n17). In fact, Florence left the rue Pigalle in October 1925. These misrepresentations are then perpetuated by subsequent scholars; Edwards, for example, cites Shack on some of these supposed facts (Edwards, *Practice of Diaspora*, 63n105), and Roueff repeats the mistaken belief that Zelli bought Chez Florence (Roueff, *Jazz, les échelles du plaisir*, 99).

7. Chevalier, *Montmartre du plaisir*.

8. Citing Shack in his brief chapter on "Wartime and the Années Folles" (145–69), Nicholas Hewitt claims that Bullard "celebrated the Armistice by founding L'Escadrille" (*Montmartre*, 161). He was not in Paris in 1918, and L'Escadrille was founded ca. 1932.

9. Colin Nettlebeck, *Dancing with de Beauvoir: Jazz and the French* (Melbourne: Melbourne University Press, 2004); Gendron, *Between Montmartre and the Mudd Club*.

10. Wambly Bald, *On the Left Bank, 1929–1933* (Athens: Ohio University Press, 1987); Sisley Huddleston, *Back to Montparnasse: Glimpses of Broadway in Bohemia* (Philadelphia: J. B. Lippincott, 1931).

11. On the role of the Black Press see Gillet, "Jazz and the Evolution."

12. Jackson, *Making Jazz French*, 67. His first three chapters deal superficially with the concrete life of Montmartre and, as we shall see, accumulate many errors (Louis Mitchell at the Casino de Paris in 1917, recruitment of the Jazz Kings at that time, etc., 18). Jackson cites names mentioned in Sem's *La Ronde de Nuit* ([Le Grand] Teddy, Maurice's Club, the So different), but lacking detailed knowledge of these clubs he comes to the false conclusion that they were named to draw Americans (68).

13. It is therefore unsurprising that much useful scholarship is found in the work of jazz historians. However, as Andy Fry points out, Ludovic Tournès' widely cited *New Orleans sur Seine*, while ostensibly covering the whole century, is rooted in the 1940s and 1950s, dealing only briefly with the twenties, and the major focus is French cultural identity (*Paris Blues*, 20). Gendron's *Between Montmartre and the Mudd Club* describes links between jazz and modernism, high and low culture, but says almost nothing about the material existence of Montmartre. Other more pertinent studies like Denis-Constant Martin and Olivier Roueff's *La France du jazz* or Roueff's *Jazz, les échelles du plaisir* are riddled with errors. More useful for my purposes were the works of jazz and dance scholars like Chris Goddard, Robert Pernet and Howard Rye, Mark Miller, Sophie Jacotot, Rainer E. Lotz, and Yannick Séité, which do not focus mainly on the interactions of jazz and French cultural institutions or the acculturation of jazz in France.

14. Roueff, *Jazz, les échelles du plaisir*, 99.

15. A parodic allusion to the "Great White Way," a nickname for New York's Broadway propagated in the twenties (Basil Woon, "Mirrors of Paris," *Courier Journal* [Louisville, Ky.], December 5, 1926, 23). The phrase was adopted by other journalists.

16. Bennett, "Wedding Day," 202. The story was loosely inspired by the life of Eugene Bullard.

17. Tyler Stovall, "Murder in Montmartre: Race, Sex and Crime in Jazz Age Paris," in *Minor Transnationalism*, ed. Françoise Lionnet and Shu-mei Shih (Durham, N.C.: Duke University Press, 2005), 137.

18. Boittin, *Colonial Metropolis*.

19. See the two invitations reproduced in Emile Derlin Zinsou and Luc Zouménou, *Kojo Tovalou Houénou, Précurseur, 1887–1936: Pannégrisme et Modernité* (Paris: Maisonneuve & Larose, 2004); Edwards, *Practice of Diaspora*, 100, and Sparrow Robertson, "Sporting Gossip," *New York Herald*, February 10, 1924, 6.

20. Miller, *Some Hustling This!* 11. Rachel Anne Gillett points out that prominent Black American performers ignored the existence of racially discriminatory practices vis-à-vis Black French from the colonies and were "not very involved in various anticolonial groups and activist associations" ("Jazz and the Evolution," 490 and note 80). Gillett's article and her dissertation ("Crossing the Pond") form the basis of her 2021 book *At Home in Our Sounds*), but in this work she is concerned with a broad range of diasporan life.

21. McAlmon, *Nightinghouls of Paris*, 49.

22. Fry, *Paris Blues*, 6.

23. Robert Sandler, ed., *Northrop Frye on Shakespeare* (New Haven: Yale University Press, 1986), 186. The reference is to Gonzalo's utopian evocation of a new golden age in *The Tempest* (II.1. 148–69) and to Sebastian and Antonio's banter on apples and islands (II.1. 91–94).

24. *Tender Is the Night* (Melarky and Kelly versions), 1:261.

CHAPTER 1. SHIMMY PARLORS AND DELUXE DIVES

The epigraph is from Sem, *La Ronde de Nuit*, 110.

1. For a typical program, see "15th Gives Show in France," *New York Age*, May 11, 1918, 6. Until March 1918 the 369th Infantry Regiment was known as the 15th New York National Guard Regiment.

2. Chevalier, *Ma route et mes chansons*, 281.

3. Jacotot, *Danser à Paris dans l'entre-deux-guerres*, 96.

4. On "surprise parties" see Leiris, *L'Age d'homme*, 157, and Sachs, *Au Temps du Bœuf*, 87.

5. Warnod, *Les Bals de Paris*, 295.

6. *Paris-Danse*, February 13–19, 1920, 1; "Paris Dance Halls Closed to Save Coal Consumption," *New York Times*, November 27, 1919, 17.

7. Wales, "Dance Halls of Paris," 1.

8. Warnod, *Les Bals de Paris*, 301–2.

9. "Cardinal Amette Protests American Dances in Paris," *Boston Daily Globe*, November 29, 1919, 5. See also Wales, "Dance Halls of Paris."

10. "Informations," *Dansons*, December 1926, 157.

11. Sem, *La Ronde de Nuit*, 11.

12. Warnod, *Les Bals de Paris*, 304.

13. "American Arrivals," *New York Herald*, June 8, 1917, 2.

14. Nevill, *Days and Nights*, 50.

15. Woon, *Paris That's Not*, 250–54.

16. Woon, "Parisians Ready."

17. Weber, *News of Paris*, 205.

18. "Soldiers Try to Make Money"; advertisement, *New York Herald*, April 23, 1919, 2.

19. "Day by Day in Paris."

20. Woon, *Paris That's Not*, 173.

21. Wales, "Chicago 'Scribe' Coins Dough."

22. Bertelli, "Ice Cream King"; "Soldiers Try to Make Money."
23. Wales, "Dance Halls of Paris."
24. "Paris Cops Find Hop in U.S. Jazz Hall; Put Lid On," *Chicago Tribune*, February 9, 1920, 5.
25. Inconsistently, in 1924 he situated Kiley's failure in early December (Woon, "Parisians Ready").
26. See Bertelli, "Ice Cream King."
27. Born Georges Goursat, "Sem" was art director of *Le Journal*, owned by the fabulously wealthy Henri Letellier. There, he published drawings and texts skewering the foibles of an upper-class public that he stalked in Montmartre's night haunts. According to O. O. McIntyre, Sem's acerbic caricatures suggested "the unlovely etchings of Hogarth—raw and searing with realism" ("New York Day by Day," *Carbondale Daily Free Press* (Carbondale, Ill.), February 19, 1931, 2).
28. Wales, "Dance Halls of Paris."
29. Paul Brach, "Dans le tunnel . . . La Nuit noire," *Comœdia*, November 12, 1925; Johnson: perhaps William A. Johnson, an ex-member of the Clef Club in New York (Miller, *Some Hustling This!* 42).
30. Sem, *La Ronde de Nuit*, 14, 17. The Aladdin's Lamp Club was located at 21 boulevard de la Seine, in Neuilly ("'*Comœdia* au Palais," *Comœdia*, March 30, 1920, 2). Sem situates his *dancing* on a "long suburban boulevard, veiled by the mists of the Seine" (*La Ronde de Nuit*, 31). And, compare Sem's text with Parke's description of Aladdin's Lamp: "a dignified old family mansion sitting far back in a park surrounded by a high wall and plenty of trees" (Newton C. Parke, "Dance Halls in Paris Being Run by Americans," *Evening News* [Harrisburg, Pa.], March 30, 1920).
31. Sem, *La Ronde de Nuit*, 19.
32. "The *dancing* . . . destroyed": Magloire, "Florence's Place," 34; "hookers . . .": Sem, *La Ronde de Nuit*, 27.
33. Sem, *La Ronde de Nuit*, 28.
34. *Revue de la Danse*, March 1921, 3.
35. "Paris Dancing Professors in War Against the Shimmy," *Topeka Daily Capital* (Topeka, Kans.), December 24, 1921, 2.
36. French performers: The most notable was Léo Vauchant (Noel Léon Marius Arnaud) who played in American and French bands. Vauchant later worked in Hollywood where he composed "Bugler's Dream," used as theme music for the Olympic Games. The White Lyres: The White Lyres appeared at the Washington Palace in April of 1920, followed by two months at Ciro's, a stint at Frolics, and another at the Clover.
37. Jody Blake rightly presents the drawing as an example of Black stereotypes, musicians "in a rhythmic frenzy . . . abandoning themselves to the mysterious forces the surrealists courted," but she seems unaware of the precise context (*Le Tumulte Noir*, 121).
38. Sem, *La Ronde de Nuit*, 27–28.
39. A small American handgun, popular in Montmartre.
40. Sem, *La Ronde de Nuit*, 30.
41. Ibid., 31.
42. Warnod, *Les Bals de Paris*, 296.

43. Advertisement, *Le Journal*, January 25, 1918, 4. The Seven Spades were essentially former members of the Ciro's Club Coon Orchestra, minus its leader, Dan Kildare, plus Seth Jones, and dancer Fernando (Sonny) Jones.
44. "Courrier des Théâtres," *Le Figaro*, March 17, 1918, 3.
45. Cooke, "Mitchell Loves His Baseball." In this, one of a series of articles based on interviews with Mitchell, it is not always clear who is speaking: Cooke, Mitchell, or Cooke paraphrasing Mitchell. Included are newspaper clippings, but dates are often lacking or incorrect.
46. "Next Wednesday Will Be Big Night at S. and S. Club," *New York Herald*, June 30, 1918, 4.
47. "Spectacles et concerts," *Le Figaro*, April 20, 1919, 6; June 3, 1919, 3.
48. "then a satirical cabaret": "Concerts et spectacles," *Le Journal*, October 11, 1915, 4.
49. "News of Paris Day by Day; Police Slice High..."
50. A rich source on Stavisky's early career is the series of articles by Stéphane Manier titled "La Vie prodigieuse et néfaste de l'escroc Stavisky," published shortly after the "Affaire" and the "suicide" of its protagonist. Written some twenty years after the facts, it contains useful if sometimes fictionalized detail.
51. Jankowski confuses her with Jeanne Bloch, a stout, five-foot-four actress popular before the war, and repeats the fat jokes of her self-deprecating routine (*Cette vilaine affaire Stavisky*, 27). The source of this error lies in contemporary magazines (see *Détective*, January 11, 1934, numéro spécial, 7).
52. Advertisement, *Le Journal*, May 25, 1919, 3; "Spectacles et concerts," *Le Figaro*, September 19, 1919, 4.
53. "Tribunaux. Le Zelli's Club," *La Presse*, November 17, 1920, 1. Except for an affair of falsified checks in 1923, Stavisky scholars do not mention Zelli, and those who write about the restaurateur never allude to Stavisky. Nor does Zelli himself. See Louis Sobol's interview, "Voice of Broadway," 6, the closest thing to an autobiography.
54. Lloyd, *Eugene Bullard*, 77–78. Despite excellent qualities, Lloyd's biography sometimes errs, particularly in chapter 5, "Man of Montmartre," which relies heavily on Bullard's self-serving memoirs.
55. See "Sports divers. La Mort du nègre," *La Presse*, May 30, 1919, 3, and "L'Affaire du nègre... continue!" *La Presse*, May 31, 1919, 3.
56. Lloyd, *Eugene Bullard*, 73–74. Based on Bullard's claims, this is an approximation. The Spades had disbanded before his arrival in Paris, and Mitchell was in New York recruiting a band for the Casino de Paris. He may have tutored Bullard between July and December.
57. Ibid., 70.
58. Quoted by Carisella and Ryan, *Black Swallow of Death*, 202.
59. Le Noctambule, "Une soirée au Zelli's Club." In Bullard's memoir, it is identified as the Zig-Zag Band, but a correspondent of *Paris-Danse* calls it "Jack, the incomparable Negro band" ("Zelli's Club," *Paris-Danse*). Bullard's middle name was James, in French Jacques. Another Anglo-Saxon equivalent is Jack.
60. Warnod, *Les Bals de Paris*, 304.
61. "Zelli's Club," *Paris-Danse*. Monzat is one of the "shadowy business partners" mentioned in my introduction, but until now his identity has remained a mystery.

62. Ibid.
63. Woon, *Paris That's Not*, 231; "News of Paris Day by Day; Police Slice High..."
64. Le Noctambule, "Une soirée au Zelli's Club"; "Papotages," *Paris-Danse*, June 11–17, 1920, 2.
65. "Nouvelles diverses," *Le Journal*, June 12, 1920, 3. Evidently the *Journal* had not integrated the Savoy's recent transformation into the Clover Club. The designation Cadet Rousselle perhaps reflects the fictive nature of "Zelli's Club."
66. Heilig, "Heilig Says Paris Is Mad Over Dancing"; "Everything Is Peaches down in Georgia" (music by Milton Ager and George W. Meyer, lyrics by Grant Clarke) vaunted folksy pleasures. Equally mawkish, "Just a Baby's Prayer at Twilight" (music by M. K. Jerome, lyrics by Sam M. Lewis and Joe Young) depicts a child praying for her soldier father "over there." Both were 1918 hits.
67. "News of Paris Day by Day; Police Slice High..."
68. Le Noctambule, "Les potins des dancings et... d'ailleurs," *Paris-Danse*, July 2–8, 1920, 3.
69. "A great sort of family": "Zelli's Club," *Paris-Danse*; "'the same *dancing*'": Claretie, "Gazette des Tribunaux."
70. Claretie, "Gazette des Tribunaux." The Clover was also raided but not closed. See "News of Paris Day by Day; Police Restrict Dancing Resorts," *New York Herald*, November 29, 1920, 1.
71. *Paris-Danse* states unequivocally that Zelli had been "accorded the management" ("Zelli's Club").
72. "Tribunaux. Procès de théâtre," *Le Journal*, October 21, 1920, 3.
73. Charlier and Montarron, *Stavisky*, 70.
74. "Volunteers Honor Fallen Comrades," *New York Herald*, August 2, 1920, 4.
75. Lloyd, *Eugene Bullard*, 78.
76. This information appears in a manuscript note on a Sûreté Générale report. See Jankowski, *Cette vilaine affaire Stavisky*, 44, and 414n38.
77. Ibid., 45.
78. Advertisement, *New York Herald*, January 19, 1921, 3.
79. "L'Escroc Stavisky continue à mener grande vie même en prison," *Le Journal*, August 4, 1926, 3.
80. "Les Enquêtes au Palais," *Le Journal*, May 7, 1921, 3.
81. "*Comœdia* au Palais," *Comœdia*, June 4, 1921, 2.
82. Advertisements, *Le Journal*, June 4, 1921, 3; June 9, 1921, 3. She was doubtless inspired by a revival of Victorien Sardou and Emile Moreau's historical comedy-drama *Madame Sans-Gêne*, starring music hall icon Mistinguett.
83. Manier, "La Vie prodigieuse."
84. "Spectacles et concerts," *Le Figaro*, September 23, 1921, 5.
85. *His Memories of Paris and Europe*, available at http://www.todotango.com.
86. Charlier and Montarron, *Stavisky*, 72.
87. "Deux aigrefins lavaient et transformaient des chèques," *Le Petit Parisien*, March 18, 1924, 3; "Le Roumain et le chèque maquillé," *Le Petit Parisien*, March 30, 1924, 2; "Truquage de chèques," *Le Petit Parisien*, April 25, 1924, 2.

88. "A la poursuite de Staviski [sic]," *Le Journal*, June 11, 1926, 3.
89. Sem, *La Ronde de Nuit*, 110.
90. Woon, *Paris That's Not*, 245.
91. Nevill, *Days and Nights*, 182.

CHAPTER 2. THE DANCER AND THE DRUMMER

The epigraph is from Warnod, *Les Bals de Paris*, 292.

1. Apropos of Mitchell's band, cited by Pernet and Rye, "Visiting Firemen 18," 231. This is the most extensive biography of Mitchell but in the Montmartre section the authors are too willing to credit the statements made in the Cooke interviews.
2. Woon, *Paris That's Not*, 181–82.
3. Martine Clément, *Music-Hall* (Paris: Du May, 2008), 122.
4. For pertinent remarks on this new format see Roueff, *Jazz, les échelles du plaisir*, 76–96.
5. Sirkis, *Les Années Deslys*, 163.
6. Ibid. Anonymous critic, quoted by Sirkis.
7. Cocteau, *Le Coq et l'Arlequin*, 21–22.
8. Interviewed in Goddard, *Jazz Away from Home*, 268.
9. Gustave Fréjaville, "Music-Halls et Cabarets. Harry Pilcer à l'Alhambra," *Comœdia*, October 10, 1922, 6.
10. Interviewed in Goddard, *Jazz Away from Home*, 276.
11. See, for example Goffin, *Jazz*, 69, or Lloyd, *Eugene Bullard*, 74. See also Pernet, "Quiproquo."
12. *Casino de Paris. Programme Officiel, Laisse-les tomber!* (Paris: n. p., n. d. [December 11, 1917–?]), n. pag.
13. "Corporal James Roney Writes from Paris; Longs to See More Santa Cruz Boys," *Santa Cruz Evening News*, March 18, 1918, 7.
14. Leiris, *L'Âge d'homme*, 159.
15. Sirkis, *Les Années Deslys*, 168. Tournès states that Mitchell and the Jazz Kings took Murray Pilcer's place in October (*New Orleans sur Seine*, 16), but all evidence points to Pilcer's departure in March, when his band was playing at the Folies-Bergère ("Spectacles et concerts," *Le Figaro*, March 9, 1918, 4).
16. "Pernet and Rye assume": Pernet and Rye, "Visiting Firemen 18," 233; "but the advertisements specify": advertisement, *Le Journal*, April 14, 1919, 4.
17. Quoted in Pernet and Rye, "Visiting Firemen 18," 233.
18. "Spectacles et concerts," *Le Figaro*, June 26, 1918, 4.
19. Advertisement, *Le Journal*, October 17, 1918, 3. Tournès claims that they were a rebaptized Murray Pilcer's Band, which is not the case (*New Orleans sur Seine*, 15).
20. Pénet, *Mistinguett*, 513; advertisement, *Le Journal*, October 26, 1918, 4.
21. Lester A. Walton, "French Now Want Colored Musicians from United States," *New York Age*, February 8, 1919, 6.
22. Advertisement, *Le Journal*, October 26, 1918, 4.
23. Mitchell's letter can be found among Eubie Blake's papers (Maryland Historical Society). Quotations are from the transcriptions of Miller, *Some Hustling This!* 49–50, and Pernet and Rye, "Visiting Firemen 18," 234.

24. Advertisement, *Le Petit Parisien*, August 11, 1918, 3.
25. Advertisement, *New York Herald*, September 1, 1918, 2. Denis-Constant Martin and Olivier Roueff confuse both the date of the engagement (1917) and the band, believing that it was the Seven Spades performing under the name of the Jazz Kings (*La France du jazz*, 30).
26. Interviewed in Goddard, *Jazz Away from Home*, 17–18.
27. "Spectacles et concerts," *Le Figaro*, July 13, 1918, 4.
28. Wales, "Chicago 'Scribe' Coins Dough."
29. In an example of misinformation that seriously distorts the historical record, Jackson states that "in 1917, Mitchell was drumming at Le Casino de Paris when the management sent him back to New York to recruit a jazz band" (*Making Jazz French*, 18). As we know, Mitchell did not play at the Casino until mid-1918.
30. "The first allusion": advertisement, *Le Petit Parisien*, July 4, 1919; "after one week": James M. Shaw, "Still Jazzing," *Chicago Defender*, March 10, 1920, 7. All references to the *Chicago Defender* are to the national edition; advertisement, *Le Journal*, July 12, 1919, 3.
31. Jean Cocteau, "Carte Blanche: Jazz Band," *Paris-Midi*, August 4, 1918, 3.
32. Cocteau, *Le Coq et l'Arlequin*, 29.
33. Goddard, *Jazz Away from Home*, 66.
34. Several Pathé recordings made between 1921 and 1923 are available on YouTube.
35. Quoted by Pernet and Rye, "Visiting Firemen 18," 239.
36. Goddard, *Jazz Away from Home*, 7, 16.
37. Advertisement, *New York Herald*, February 21, 1920, 2.
38. Interviewed by Goddard, *Jazz Away from Home*, 296–303. See Miller, *Some Hustling This!* 69n14.
39. Seth Weeks, "Weeks Writes from Paris," *Chicago Defender*, March 27, 1920, 5.
40. "Spectacles et concerts," *Le Figaro*, February 14, 1920, 3.
41. Cooper, "Musical Career of Opal Cooper." In March, they appeared as the "Melody Monarchs' Jazz Band" (Impartial, "D'un dancing à l'autre: Morgan's Dancing," *Paris-Danse*, March 19–25, 1920, 4), but the name change took place before June ("Items of Personal Intelligence," *New York Herald*, May 4, 1920, 2.
42. O. O. McIntyre, "New York Day by Day," *Pittsburgh Press*, January 13, 1920, 12.
43. Advertisement, *Le Journal*, November 27, 1919, 3.
44. See Yvonne Du Clos, "Suitor vs. Sister for the Gems of Gaby Deslys," *Palm Beach Post*, February 13, 1927, Magazine Sec., 2.
45. Woon, *Paris That's Not*, 220; Jean Prasteau, *La Merveilleuse aventure du Casino de Paris* (Paris: Denoël, 1975), 91.
46. Aragon, *Le Mauvais Plaisant*, 371–72.
47. See Georges Barbier's cover for *Les Modes*, April 1912.
48. See *Décor for Scheherazade* (Musée des Arts décoratifs, 1910).
49. "Even the Daring Mlle Dherlys."
50. Sabourin's photos are reproduced in "Distressing Predicament of the Famous and Frivolous Beauties of Paris," *Philadelphia Inquirer*, June 5, 1921, Feature Sec., 3, and "Even the Daring Mlle Dherlys."
51. "the slightly servile": Mathias Auclair and Sarah Barbedette, *Bakst: Des ballets russes à*

la Haute Couture (Paris: Albin Michel, 2016), 126; "was at odds with": Martha H. Patterson, ed., *The American New Woman Revisited: A Reader, 1894–1930* (New Brunswick, N.J.: Rutgers University Press, 2008).

52. "'L'Oasis' Is the Brilliant Gala Spot," 65, British edition of *Vogue*. Unless otherwise indicated all *Vogue* references are to the French edition.

53. Nancy Cunard's diary, quoted by Chisholm, *Nancy Cunard*, 53; "'L'Oasis' Is the Brilliant," 67.

54. "'L'Oasis' Is the Brilliant Gala Spot," 65.

55. "temple of Jazz": Parker, "Paris, Madly Jazzing"; "King of Jazz": "Dans les Dancings," *Le Gaulois*, May 31, 1921, 6.

56. "Jazzbandism," *Georgia Review* 60, no. 1 (2006): 73.

57. Kate Buss, "Paul Poiret, the Greatest Personality Artist," *Greenville News* (Greenville, S.C.), October 16, 1921, Comic and Magazine Sec., n. pag. [3].

58. Karl K. Kitchen, "If You Must Tour, Stop in Paris," *Arkansas Gazette* (Little Rock, Ark.), October 3, 1920, part 2, 13.

59. Reproduced in Hammond and O'Connor, *Josephine Baker*, 27.

60. Advertisement for ukuleles, *Daily Missourian* (Columbia, Mo.), February 7, 1917, 4.

61. Leiris, *L'Âge d'homme*, 163.

62. Music by Maurice Yvain, lyrics by Albert Willemetz and Georges Arnoux.

63. In fact, only William (Billy) Kanui was Hawaiian; Lula was Parisian, born Lucie Schmidt.

64. Advertisement, *Evening World* (New York), June 23, 1916, 7. On jazz and Hawaiian music see Okihiro, "Afterword," 322–24.

65. A review of *Paris qui Jazz* by Charles Méré, a reactionary critic quoted by Miller, *Some Hustling This!* 74.

66. Parker, "Paris, Madly Jazzing."

67. Advertisement, *Comœdia*, October 7, 1920, 4.

68. Referring to the shrine that Pilcer had erected to Gaby Deslys' memory, Woon makes a gratuitous remark: "Though the altar may have disappeared, it is still . . . enshrined in the little Jewish boy's heart" (*Paris That's Not*, 220). Doubtless, there was also a degree of antisemitism in the way he was viewed by the Casino audience.

69. Roger de Valerio (Roger Laviron, 1892–1970) was a painter and graphic artist who designed numerous covers for the music editor, Francis Salabert.

70. Badger, *Life in Ragtime*, 116.

71. Francis Salabert, 1920.

72. Gillett, "Crossing the Pond," 61–62.

73. Georges Bourden, "*Madame Sans-Gêne*," *Comœdia*, March 9, 1921, 1.

74. "Theater Monument to Memory of Gaby Deslys," *Akron Beacon Journal* (Akron, Ohio), March 2, 1921, 10.

75. "on the eve": Bastia, "La Soirée"; "and that summer": "Perroquet Magnet at Montmartre," *Pittsburgh Daily Post*, August 7, 1921, Sec. 1, 7.

76. "This was the Perroquet": One of Tournès' errors is situating the Perroquet's opening in 1923 (*New Orleans sur Seine*, 16); "known as the": Nevill, *Days and Nights*, 42.

77. Nevill, *Days and Nights*, 42.

78. See, for example, Charles Stern, *Les Jets d'eau et perroquets* (damask silk and cotton fabric, 1917), and Jean Dupas, *Les Perruches* (Xavier Roberts Coll., 1925).

79. See the photo taken by the Séeberger frères, FSK10-01, 1926. In 1923 the Séeberger brothers, Jules, Louis, and Henri, aided by Louis' sons Jean and Albert, were commissioned by a Hollywood agency, International Kinema Research, to provide photographs of Parisian *dancings* for the frequent studio recreations. Their work may be found online in the archives of the Médiathèque de l'Architecture et du Patrimoine, Paris.

80. See the photo taken by the Séeberger frères, FSK10-04, 1928.

81. Pernet and Rye, "Visiting Firemen 18," 238.

82. Ibid., 238; Blake, *Le Tumulte Noir*, 64.

83. On Blazer see Henry Wales, "Albert Marks Twenty Years at Maxim's Café?" *Chicago Sunday Tribune*, February 27, 1956, part 6, 7.

84. Woon, *Paris That's Not*, 243.

85. *Avec le sourire* (1921), *Dans un fauteuil* (1921), *Paris en l'air* (1921), *La Revue des étoiles* (1922).

86. Williams, "Americans in Paris."

CHAPTER 3. AMERICA'S SWEETHEART," THE "JAZZ BABY," AND THE SISTER OF THE "COLORED GENTLEMAN"

The epigraph is from "American Ballet in Paris Tonight."

1. Sem, *La Ronde de Nuit*, 121.

2. Ibid.

3. Woon, *Paris That's Not*, 2.

4. Ibid., 232.

5. "Again Shack": Shack, *Harlem in Montmartre*, 53; "but as usual": Without specifying dates, Woon proposes the following chronology (*Paris That's Not*, 231–35). I have added the actual opening dates in brackets: Zelli's Club, "when Kiley abandoned jazz to go into the ice cream business" (October 1919) [mid-April 1920]; the Clover Club, "after Zelli closed his Caumartin club to go into business on a legitimate scale" (mid-February 1921) [May 1920]; Harry Pilcer's Sans Souci (Chez Harry Pilcer) [March 1921]; Maurice's Club (in the Hotel Grande-Bretagne) [April 12, 1921]; Maurice Chevalier and Saint-Granier's Acacias [June 2, 1921]; Le Sans Souci [September 23, 1921]; Elsa Maxwell's Acacias ("the following summer") [May 24, 1922]; Maurice's Club (at the Théâtre Caumartin), "when it [Elsa's Acacias] closed down" (July 14, 1922) [April 21, 1922]; The So-Different, "later on" [December 15, 1921].

6. "Eté tardif," *Le Journal*, October 14, 1921, 1.

7. Mary Brush Williams, "The Last Word in Paris Fashions," *Chicago Tribune*, August 27, 1922, part 5, 1.

8. Warnod, *Les Bals de Paris*, 298–99.

9. Basil Woon, "Americans Play Big Part in Business Life of Paris," *Bridgeport Telegram*, June 7, 1922, 18.

10. "Gloves, of Course, with Carpentier," *New York Herald*, June 4, 1922, 2.

11. Sem, *La Ronde de Nuit*, 122.

12. "Vocal Jazz Enters Paris in Tommy Lyman's Songs," *New York Herald*, May 18, 1922, 2; Bricktop, *Bricktop*, 51.

13. Sem, *La Ronde de Nuit*, 124–25.

14. "American Ballet Pleases Gathering at Paris Theatre," *New York Herald*, October 26, 1923, 4.

15. For a photo of Gerald Murphy's back curtain, and costume sketches by his wife Sara, see *La Danse*, a revue created to promote Rolf de Maré's company (*"Within the Quota,"* October 1923, n. pag.)

16. Leiris, *L'Âge d'homme*, 188.

17. "American Ballet in Paris Tonight."

18. See James Abbé's photo of the Jazz Baby, the Immigrant, and the Sweetheart, reproduced in Mathias Auclair, Frank Claustrat, and Inès Piovesan, *Les Ballets Suedois: Une compagnie d'avant-garde, 1920–1925* (Paris: Opéra National de Paris, 2014), 125.

19. "Within the Quota," *La Danse*, October 1923.

20. "World-Famed Dancer Says He'd Pick Prettier Girl," 2.

21. Several variants exist but the most legible is the text given above by Milton A. Cohen (*Hemingway's Laboratory*, 25).

22. "World-Famed Dancer Says He'd Pick Prettier Girl," 2.

23. C. F. Bertelli, "Peggy Hopkins Gilded Butterfly, Admiration Is Food and Drink for Her," *Shreveport Times* (Shreveport, La.), June 9, 1921, 1.

24. "World-Famed Dancer Says He'd Pick Prettier Girl," 1.

25. "Evoking a turn": Henry Wales, "It Is a Terrible Blow for Maurice the Dancer," *Arkansas Gazette* (Little Rock), April 14, 1921, 12; "she confided": Peggy Hopkins Joyce, "My Life with My Millionaire Husbands, Chap. III," *St. Louis Star and Times*, March 12, 1922, Magazine Sec., n. pag. [6, 7].

26. Basil Woon, "'I Love 'Em All,' Says Jack, Denying Peggy Is Cause of Paris Visit," *Washington Times* (Washington, D.C.), May 4, 1922, 2.

27. Most details of the evening are drawn from the *New York Times* report ("Errázuriz, Blanca de Saulles' Brother, a Suicide in Paris over Peggy Joyce," May 2, 1922, 1).

28. "Peggy Joyce Seriously Ill from Overdose of an Opiate; Like Cleopatra She Declares," *Evening World* (New York), final ed., May 3, 1922, 1.

29. C. F. Bertelli, "Favorite Suitor of Peggy Joyce, Jealous, Ends His Life," *Washington Times* (Washington, D.C.), May 2, 1922, 3.

30. Woon, *Paris That's Not*, 183–84.

31. Sem, *La Ronde de Nuit*, 123.

32. Barbara Zabel, *Assembling Art: The Machine and the American Avant-Garde* (Jackson: University Press of Mississippi, 2004), 161.

33. [Mouvet], "Latest Dances."

34. Sem, *La Ronde de Nuit*, 46.

35. [Mouvet], "On with the Dance."

36. "While praising": [Mouvet], "Shall America Have a Distinctive Social Dance?"; "he added": [Mouvet], "Latest Dances," 24.

37. "Bending to fashion": Sem, *La Ronde de Nuit*, 124; "damning praise": O. O. McIntyre, "New York Day by Day," *Wilkes-Barre Times Leader* (Wilkes-Barre, Pa.), July 9, 1927, 16.

38. Marcel Rieu, "Le Bal Noir et Blanc," *Comœdia*, May 8, 1921, 1.
39. "Perroquet Magnet at Montmartre," *Pittsburgh Daily Post*, August 7, 1921, Sec. 1, 7.
40. Bertelli, "Britain Owes Gratitude."
41. Jacques Moreau, *Americanization of a Hotel-Restaurant "Grand Teddy," Rue Caumartin, Paris* (1918?), photographic print, Archives Larousse, Paris.
42. "Informations," *Le Figaro*, January 6, 1920, 3; Tise, "Francis Jourdain," 265.
43. "Informations," *Le Figaro*, December 15, 1921, 4.
44. Advertisement, *Le Figaro*, January 2, 1919, 3.
45. Fan by the Pierre Morgue, in the Hélène Alexander Collection, The Fan Museum, Greenwich, Great Britain.
46. Wiggins ["The Street Wolf of Paris"], "Paris Is My Beat."
47. Hughes, *Big Sea*, 160.
48. "Chez Florence," *Time Magazine*, 14.
49. Bricktop, *Bricktop*, 189.
50. Hughes, *Big Sea*, 172.
51. Woon, *Paris That's Not*, 235; Nevill, *Days and Nights*, 53.
52. Gramont, *Souvenirs du monde*, 338.
53. Advertisement, *Le Figaro*, December 15, 1921, 4.
54. Woon, *Paris That's Not*, 235.
55. Maxwell, *R. S. V. P.*, 170.
56. Advertisement, *Le Figaro*, October 6, 1922, 3.
57. [May Birkhead], "Parties in Paris Celebrate Gaily," *New York Herald*, November, 12, 1921, 6.
58. "Elsa Maxwell's Party Line," *Pittsburgh Post-Gazette*, August 30, 1945, 19. Elsa seems to have hedged her bets as she also engaged the White Lyres (advertisement, *New York Herald*, May 21, 1922, 3), but they are not mentioned in subsequent ads, and in August they sued Elsa for "violation of contract" ("California Girl in Paris Manages Most Popular Café," *San Francisco Examiner*, August 27, 1922, Society and Clubs, 2S).
59. Bricktop, *Bricktop*, 104.
60. Woon, *Paris That's Not*, 235.
61. Advertisement, *New York Herald*, January 13, 1923, 3. The last soirée was a gala with a promise to reopen. It never did.
62. Maxwell, *R. S. V. P.*, 171; "Famous Paris Dancer and Brother Manager at Outs," *St. Louis Star*, July 2, 1922, 8A.
63. Birkhead, "Americans Attend Gala Outdoor Events." Based in Paris, Ms. Birkhead was a society reporter for the New York and Paris *Heralds*.
64. "La Mode à Paris," *Comœdia*, June 4, 1922, 3.
65. "Les Dancings," *Vogue*, July 1, 1922, 11.
66. Maxwell, *R. S. V. P.*, 172.
67. Nash, "Best-Dressed," [6].
68. "Kills Himself When Peggy Ridicules Love," *Buffalo Morning Express* (Buffalo, N.Y.), May 2, 1922: 1, 3; Floyd Gibbons, "Paris Warms Up to Jack in Montmartre," *Chicago Tribune*, April 24, 1922, 21.
69. Hurston, "How It Feels to Be Colored Me," 117.

70. "*Within the Quota*," *La Danse*, October 1923, n.p.
71. Maxwell, *R. S. V. P.*, 173.
72. "Americans at Biarritz," *New York Herald*, August 16, 1922, 4.
73. May Birkhead, "War Talk Fails to Dampen Gayety of Paris Society," *New York Herald* (New York ed.), October 15, 1922, Sec. 6, 4.
74. See Basil Woon, "Dance Hall War Is on as Usual in Giddy Paris," *Oakland Tribune*, November 12, 1922, 10B. The So-Different closed on January 13, 1923 (advertisement, *New York Herald*, January 13, 1923, 3), and the International Five debuted at Le Jardin in February 1923—without Florence ("With the Entertainers," *New York Herald*, February 28, 1923, 2).

CHAPTER 4. A GALA IN MY SISTER'S GARDEN

The epigraph is from Woon, *Paris That's Not*, 243.

1. Birkhead, "Paris Is Deserted."
2. Maxwell, *R. S. V. P.*, 172.
3. Ibid., 174.
4. "U. S. Girl Retires from Partnership in Gay Paris Café," *Oakland Tribune*, December 24, 1922, 5A.
5. Nevill, *Days and Nights*, 52.
6. Loos, *A Girl Like I*, 251.
7. Birkhead, "Paris Is Deserted."
8. Image by Leslie Saalburg in "La Journée d'une Américaine à Paris," *Vogue*, July 1, 1923, 4.
9. C. F. Bertelli, "Chefs Aghast When Yank Cooks Invade Kitchens of France," *Indianapolis Star*, May 28, 1923, 10.
10. "La Journée d'une Américaine," 54.
11. Bertelli, "Fantasy Reigns in New Paris Café."
12. "'Chemise Envelope' as Sole 'Undie' for Women Makes Debut; Mystery of Paris' Missing Cats Revealed," *Buffalo Courier* (Buffalo, N.Y.), January 19, 1925, 1. On Sturges and Porter's friendship see Porter, *Letters of Cole Porter*, 51.
13. Newton C. Parke, "Plan May Day Terrors," *Hamilton Evening Journal* (Hamilton, Ohio), April 22, 1921, 6.
14. "Prince Leaves Paris for Home," *New York Herald*, January 14, 1924, 1.
15. Woon, "Presence of Wales." A minor writer, Gwynne was known as "the Playboy of Paris."
16. "Informations," *Dansons*, February 1924, 61.
17. Ibid.
18. Woon, "Presence of Wales."
19. "Many Playboys in Paris Who Have Big Bankrolls and Bigger Thirsts," *Berkeley Daily Gazette*, December 31, 1931, 7.
20. Sections of this paragraph in quotes refer to Woon, "Presence of Wales."
21. "The crowd of spenders": Louis Chevalier found the "Tout-Paris" insipid (*Montmartre du plaisir*, 320–29); "Americans and English": Woon, *Paris That's Not*, 138.
22. Fitzgerald, *Tender Is the Night*, ed. Goldman, 88.
23. Woon, "Presence of Wales." See "Mrs. Corey Insists Engagement Was Not Disclosed in Interview," *New York Herald*, February 23, 1924, 1.

24. Beer, *Playboy Princes*, 222.
25. "Autour du globe," *Dansons*, March 1, 1922, 2; Miller, *Some Hustling This!* 137.
26. "nicknamed the 'Modern Solomon'": C. F. Bertelli, "British Woman Dazzles Paris; Has $1,500,000 Jewels in Attire," *San Francisco Examiner*, June 20, 1921, 1; "one of his younger sons": Woon, *Paris That's Not*, 96.
27. Woon, *Paris That's Not*, 144.
28. May Birkhead, "Paris Season Gives Promise of More Than Usual Gayety," *New York Herald* (New York ed.), November 5, 1922, Sec. 6, 4.
29. Bricktop, *Bricktop*, 274.
30. Cunard, "Black Man and White Ladyship," 183.
31. Ibid., 189.
32. "Prince's Flying Visit to Paris Brings Record Crush to Gala Dance," *New York Herald*, April 15, 1924, 1.
33. Maxwell, *R. S. V. P.*, 23.
34. Ibid., 173–74.
35. Cunard, "Black Man and White Ladyship," 184.
36. Reproduced in Chisholm, *Nancy Cunard*, between pages 176 and 177.
37. Rogers, "Paris Notes."
38. Fitzgerald, *Tender Is the Night*, ed. Goldman, 279.
39. Rose, *Woman Before Wallis*, 116–17.
40. At an Embassy Club gala in February, she "attracted interested attention" ("Brilliant Party Welcomes Dancer," *New York Herald*, February 7, 1924, 2).
41. "Murdered Egyptian Is Described as 'Vile Sadist' in London Trial," *New York Herald*, September 12, 1923, 1.
42. *The Curzon Papers*, British Library, September 9, 1923 (cited in Rose, *Woman Before Wallis*, 193).
43. See "Fahmy Bey Widow Has Spotlight," *Los Angeles Daily Times*, April 11, 1924, 10, and Rose, *Woman Before Wallis*, 295–99.
44. Freddy Bate was a journalist attached to the American delegation to the Reparations Commission. Born Arkwright, his wife Vera was rumored to be the illegitimate daughter of the Duke of Westminster. A childhood companion of the Prince of Wales, she introduced him to Coco Chanel, for whom she handled public relations.
45. Bertelli, "Britain Owes Gratitude."
46. Woon, "Presence of Wales."
47. Bertelli, "Wales Is Some Stepper-Out."
48. "Having flabbergasted": Wales, "Prince of Wales Becomes Jazz Band Addict"; "causing Kiley to comment": Woon, "Presence of Wales."
49. Woon, *Paris That's Not*, 186, 184.
50. Interviewed by Goddard, *Jazz Away from Home*, 287.
51. Gravigny, *Montmartre en 1925*, 162. Gravigny may be confusing Shanley's and the preceding Kiley's. Shanley's opened on September 9, 1924, and the first edition of his book was published on December 29. For much of that time the prince was in America.
52. Bertelli, "Wales Is Some Stepper-Out."
53. Woon, "Presence of Wales." On Tuesday morning the prince was the guest of the

Baron de Rothschild at a deer hunt in Chantilly ("Paris Oscillates to Quivering Knee of Dancing Wales," *Daily News* (New York), April 17, 1924, 7.

54. Bertelli, "Wales Is Some Stepper-Out."
55. Ibid. According to the often-unreliable Marvel Cooke interviews, Mitchell had already met the prince in London ("Mitchell, Sensation of Europe," *New York Amsterdam News*, March 2, 1940, 15).
56. Bertelli, "Wales Is Some Stepper-Out."
57. Miller, *Some Hustling This!* 113.
58. Birkhead, "Paris Is Deserted."
59. "Maurice Mouvet May Never Dance Again," *Akron Beacon Journal*, August 18, 1922, 10.
60. J. M. Shaw, "Shaw Writes from Paris," *Chicago Defender*, July 21, 1923, 7.
61. "Americans Will Be Many at Embassy Club Opening," *New York Herald*, November 24, 1923, 2; "Thanksgiving Fare Indulged in Early," *New York Herald*, November 28, 1923, 2.
62. "Dish Fit for King—Griddle Cakes and Bacon," *New York Herald*, April 26, 1924, 2.
63. Advertisement, *New York Herald*, May 24, 1924, 6. Several days earlier, Maurice and Leonora had appeared before the royal couple, but this is not mentioned in the ads ("To Dance Before King," *New York Herald*, May 19, 1924, 5).
64. *New York Herald*, November 18, 1924, 5. Cf. the ad for Mitchell's: "Surprise Opening Tonight," *New York Herald*, November 27, 1924, 8.
65. "Prince in Paris Dines Privately," *New York Herald*, April 17, 1924, 1. On Charlie and Dorothy Munn see Woon, *Paris That's Not*, 66.
66. William Ivy, "William Ivy's Letter," *Port Huron Times-Herald* (Port Huron, Mich.), last ed., July 1, 1924.
67. Robert Destez, "Les Argentins de Paris," *Le Figaro*, August 22, 1925, 7.
68. Woon, "Presence of Wales."
69. "La fin d'une idylle," *Le Journal*, October 13, 1924, 3.
70. "Prince to Visit Canada. To Open Exhibition," *Singapore Free Press and Mercantile Advertiser*, March 5, 1931, 12.
71. C. De Vidal Hunt, "Little Miss Bennett and the Rich South American," *Ogden (Utah) Standard Examiner*, August 30, 1925, Comic Sec., n. pag. [4].
72. Advertisement, *New York Herald*, June 4, 1925, 8.
73. Advertisement, *New York Herald*, February 26, 1925, 8; Eugene J. Bullard, "Shooting at Us," *Chicago Defender*, April 4, 1925, 7. On the Princess di San Faustino see Bricktop, *Bricktop*, 111.
74. "Opening of Parisian Supper-Dances Gives Promise of Gay Winter Season," *New York Herald*, October 13, 1922, 6.
75. "Biarritz, Fille du Soleil, Fleur Nocturne, Ville des Contrastes," *Vogue*, November 1, 1925, 5.
76. Advertisement, *New York Herald*, October 7, 1925, 8.
77. [Woon], "'Fashionable' Americans in Paris."
78. Nash, "Best-Dressed," [6].
79. "Oscar to Open New Place," *New York Herald*, August 31, 1924, 2.
80. "'Smart, yet not too formal'": advertisement, *New York Herald*, September 13, 1924; "'a lively place'": Nash, "Best-Dressed," [6].

81. C. F. Bertelli, "Author Has Influence on Fashion," *Tampa Bay Times*, November 29, 1925, Sec. 5, 8.
82. Advertisement, *New York Herald*, October 22, 1925, 8.
83. Advertisement, *New York Herald*, October 9, 1925, 7.
84. "News of Americans in Europe," *New York Herald*, October 11, 1925, 4.
85. Jocelyn Augustus "Frisco" Bingham, prominent Jamaican entertainer and club owner. He had worked on freighters to the Far East, spoke eight or nine languages, and earned his nickname as a longshoreman in San Francisco.
86. Advertisement, *New York Herald*, December 31, 1925, 8.
87. Henry Périer, "De la Poudre des bals et des dancings," *Dansons*, February 1926, 187.
88. Woon, *Paris That's Not*, 182.
89. "The Truth," *New York Herald*, April 27, 1926, 4.
90. Advertisement, *New York Herald*, May 19, 1926, 8.
91. O. O. McIntyre, "New York Day by Day," *Wilkes-Barre Times Leader*, July 9, 1927, 16.
92. Nevill, *Days and Nights*, 53.
93. "Paris Amusements," *New York Herald*, March 16, 1926, 7.
94. Advertisement, *New York Herald*, October 27, 1927, 4.
95. C. F. Bertelli, "American Demand Stifles Changes in Paris Styles," *Bridgeport Telegram*, October 24, 1927, 5.
96. Vaughn, *Sleeping with the Enemy*, 38; Rose, *Woman Before Wallis*, 300.
97. "Why a Poor Girl Gave Up a Billion," *St. Louis Star*, September 25, 1921, Magazine Sec., n. pag. [3].
98. "'Where did Alfonso get so much virtue?'": "Too Outrageous"; "the latter being no stranger": Bertelli, "Shah of Persia's New Dance"; "American Girls Rush to Biarritz to Win King's Dance Decoration," *Minneapolis Morning Tribune*, October 21, 1922, 8.
99. "In a cellar cabaret in the rue des Tournelles near Bastille he spied two sailors and sent his henchman, Antonio Vasconcellos, to bring them to his table. Their conversation resulted in a frightful row, in which the two tars appeared to take the offensive. Don Luis and his Portuguese friend were saved from complete wreckage by the arrival of the police" ("Too Outrageous").
100. Bertelli, "Shah of Persia's New Dance."
101. "King and Shah Had to Beg the Dolly Sisters for Dance Favors Like Any Lowly Commoner," *Evening Public Ledger* (Philadelphia), October 14, 1922, 17.
102. "Le Shah de Perse rentrerait dans ses états," *Le Journal*, April 9, 1924, 1.
103. "Why the Young Shah Lingers in Paris," *Houston Post*, March 30, 1924, Magazine Sec., n. pag. [8].
104. "Prince of Wales Quits Paris Still Wearing Captivating Smile," *New York Herald*, April 19, 1924, 2.
105. Rose, *Woman Before Wallis*, 295.
106. Cited by Rose, ibid., 300.
107. Basil Woon, "Prince of Wales Refuses to Wed; Loves Woman Who Can't Be Queen," *Journal News* (Hamilton, Ohio), October 1, 1926, 2.
108. Basil Woon, "Presence of Wales."
109. Cooke, "Mitchell, American Boy."

CHAPTER 5. "SMOKE UPON THE WATERS"

The epigraph is from "Une descente dans un tripot," *Le Figaro*, May 1, 1922, 4.

1. Aragon, *Mauvais Plaisant*, 341–42.
2. Ibid., 340.
3. Ibid., 347. Lionel Follet, editor of *Le Mauvais Plaisant*, finds no trace of Omar Khayyâm (347n1), clearly visible in a photo taken by the Séeberger brothers (see gallery 1).
4. Séité, *Le Jazz à la lettre*, 60.
5. Dennie, "News from Abroad"; Séité, *Le Jazz à la lettre*, 58–66; Miller, *Some Hustling This!* 93–94.
6. "Chronique des Tribunaux. Les soirées du Tempo Club," *Le Journal*, October 22, 1922, 3.
7. Fourès, "Tribunaux: Jazz-band."
8. Interviewed by Goddard, *Jazz Away from Home*, 17.
9. Fitzgerald, *Tender Is the Night* (Melarky and Kelly versions), 256.
10. Cited by Pernet and Rye, "Visiting Firemen 18," 235.
11. Olin Downes, "Clef Club Players," *New York Age*, August 24, 1918, 6.
12. Soupault, *Terpsichore*, 11.
13. Quoted by Miller, *Some Hustling This!* 94.
14. "Mazie Mullen [sic] Dead," *New York Age*, November 5, 1921, 6.
15. Interviewed by Goddard, *Jazz Away from Home*, 267, 266.
16. Antoine Banès, "Les Premières. Théâtre des Champs-Elysées," *Le Figaro*, May 9, 1922, 3.
17. Montboron, "Synco-Synco Orchestra."
18. Carlish and Bestic, *King of Clubs*, 27.
19. Soupault, *Le Nègre*, 21–22.
20. Baron, *L'An I du Surréalisme*, 175.
21. On the Dadaists and jazz see Blake, *Le Tumulte Noir*. Blake's aesthetic evaluations are judicious but her comments on "Mily" remain vague. Moreover, she makes misleading factual errors, maintaining that the Tempo Club was established "before 1920 by Louis Mitchell" (113).
22. Soupault, *Mémoires de l'oubli*, 30–31.
23. *Librairie Six, Exposition Man Ray, 3–31 décembre 1921*, Yale University, Beinecke Rare Book and Manuscript Library. On the exhibition see Soupault, *Mémoires de l'oubli*, 163–65.
24. David Belasco (1853–1930), director and playwright, noted for his realistic sets.
25. Demuth, *Letters of Charles Demuth*, 25.
26. Ibid., 25n2.
27. To my knowledge, the only extant image of the Grand Duc is a drawing by Pierre Brissard (see gallery 2).
28. "Courrier des Théâtres," *Le Matin*, October 27, 1921, 5. Gillett cites only a November article to document their presence ("Crossing the Pond," 137n286).
29. See Jennifer Fronc, "The Horns of the Dilemma: Race Mixing and the Enforcement of Jim Crow in New York City," *Journal of Urban History* 33, no. 3 (2006): 3–25.
30. 1915, Demuth Museum (Lancaster, Pennsylvania).
31. *Marshall's*, 1915 (private collection); *The Jazz Singer*, 1916 (private collection); *Negro Jazz Band* [*Negro Girl Dancer*], 1916 (private collection).

32. Leonard Walton, "Hotel Marshall, Place of Unique Entertainment Closes," *New York Age*, October 9, 1913, 6.
33. Advertisement, *New York Age*, August 13, 1914, 5.
34. "Theatrical Jottings," *New York Age*, October 29, 1914, 6. Duchamp arrived in June 1915. Edward A. Berlin confirms that Florence was still at the Dunbar (*King of Ragtime: Scott Joplin and His Era*, 2nd ed. [New York: Oxford University Press, 2016], 14).
35. Haggerty, "Michel Leiris," 35.
36. Ibid., 36.
37. Blake, *Le Tumulte Noir*, 120.
38. Soupault, *Terpsichore*, 9–11.
39. Ibid., 9.
40. Dennie, "News from Abroad." For a time a Red Devil, after the Tempo Club's fall, Wilson joined the Jazz Kings (J. A. Jackson, "Grundy Tells Story of Success Abroad," *Afro-American*, October 13, 1922, 7), but he is best known as the singer-pianist in *Casablanca*.
41. Soupault, *Terpsichore*, 9.
42. Ibid.
43. Williams, "Americans in Paris."
44. French gangsters noted for their skill with long-bladed knives. See Nevill, *Days and Nights*, 203–7, and Chevalier, *Montmartre du plaisir*, 298–99.
45. Carlish and Bestic, *King of Clubs*, 111–12.
46. "Montmartre Scene of Dramatic Raid"; "Paris Court's Fine of Ex-Jazz King"; "Chronique des Tribunaux, les soirées du Tempo Club," *Le Journal*, October 22, 1922, 3; Fourès, "Tribunaux: Jazz-band."
47. "Une descente de police au 'Tempo-Club.'"
48. "African Golf": An implicitly racist phrase referring to craps. Hemingway shows his "literary flair" by inventing the term "Senegambian Polo" (see Hemingway, "Galloping Dominoes," 34); "the Paris temple": "Paris Court's Fine of Ex-Jazz King."
49. "Une descente de police au 'Tempo Club.'"
50. Vautel, "Mon Film."
51. Ibid.
52. "Montmartre Scene of Dramatic Raid."
53. "Paris Black and Tan Club Raided," *Los Angeles Times*, May 2, 1922, 2.
54. "Raid American's Paris Club."
55. Vautel, "Mon Film," 1.
56. "*The New York Times*": "Raid American's Paris Club"; "the *Herald*": "Paris Court's Fine of Ex-Jazz King."
57. Rose, *Woman Before Wallis*, 117.
58. From drafts in *The Sun Also Rises*, Hemingway Library ed. (New York: Scribner's, 1954), 226.
59. Demuth, *Letters of Charles Demuth*, 24n3.
60. "Une descente de police au 'Tempo Club'"; Fourès, "Tribunaux: Jazz-band." At the Capitole Boyd sang "Ida Sweet as Apple Cider" and " Rolly Bolly Eyes" (advertisement, *New York Herald*, April 8, 1920, 3).
61. "Joe Boyd," *Le Journal*, November 9, 1927, 4. In 1929 he toured with Wellmon and his

Darktown Follies ("Colored Americans in Paris Stage Big Christmas Party," *Philadelphia Tribune*, January 24, 1929, 7). On Boyd at Louigi's see "Doings in Gay Paree," *Chicago Defender*, January 15, 1927, 7.

62. *La Semaine à Paris*, June 13–20, 1924, 12; "Life in Paris," *New York Herald*, October 29, 1924, 2; advertisement, *New York Herald*, March 28, 1925, 5; "Fire Destroys Russian Cabaret," *New York Herald*, March 3, 1927, 1.

63. Soupault, *Le Nègre*, 125, 131.

CHAPTER 6. ZELLI'S ROYAL BOX

The epigraph is from Aragon, *Aurélien*, 121.

1. On New Year's Eve 1920, La Féria reopened at 16 bis rue Fontaine with Oscar Mouvet as artistic director ("Voir la Féria," *Comœdia*, December 31, 1920, 2). It was replaced by Le Rat Blanc, an ephemeral supper club (advertisements, *New York Herald*, February 25, 1921, 3; *Le Journal*, March 2, 1921, 3). On April 22, 1921, the first ad for "Au Zelli's" appeared in the *Herald*, p. 3.

2. Carlish and Bestic, *King of Clubs*, 119.

3. A stairway on the balcony to the left of the bandstand may have mounted to the Tempo Club (see the photo taken by the Séeberger frères, (FSK04–10, 1925).

4. Woon, *Paris That's Not*, 248.

5. "Jazzers in Row with Paris Club," *New York Herald*, November 13, 1923, 6; advertisement, *Comœdia*, October 18, 1923, 6.

6. Abbott, "My Trip Abroad."

7. In *Aurélien*, Zelli's masquerades as "Lulli's." For convenience's sake I will use Zelli's. Louis Chevalier relies on Aragon, but it is not clear if he is aware that Lulli is Joe Zelli, and he situates the club in the rue Frochot (*Montmartre du plaisir*, 332).

8. Aragon, *Aurélien*, 120.

9. Ibid., 109.

10. Aragon, *Mauvais Plaisant*, 361.

11. Impartial, "D'un dancing à l'autre: Cadet Roussel," *Paris-Danse*, February 13–19, 1920, 4.

12. Woon, "Mirrors of Paris," July 3, 1927.

13. Aragon, *Mauvais Plaisant*, 355.

14. Aragon, *Aurélien*, 447, 449, 451.

15. Ibid., 112.

16. Gravigny, *Montmartre en 1925*, 153, and see the photo taken by the Séeberger frères (FSK04–10, 1925).

17. Arthur Moss, "Cocktails Round Town," in McElhone and Holcomb, *Barflies and Cocktails*, 83.

18. See Nevers, "Tom Waltham."

19. Goddard, *Jazz Away from Home*, 75.

20. Interviewed by Goddard, *Jazz Away from Home*, 268.

21. Touzot, *Jean Cocteau*, 298.

22. Quoted in Goddard, *Jazz Away from Home*, 149.

23. Nevers, "Tom Waltham," 29.

24. Interviewed by Goddard, *Jazz Away from Home*, 269.

25. Such as trumpeter Arthur Briggs (Nevers, "Tom Waltham," 27).
26. Carlish and Bestic, *King of Clubs*, 27.
27. "to give patrons": Sobol, "Voice of Broadway," 6; "Variety's London": Jolo, "One Night in Paris."
28. Jolo, "One Night in Paris."
29. Baron, *L'An I du Surréalisme*, 177.
30. Aragon, *Aurélien*, 127.
31. Ibid., 127–30.
32. The photo was taken June 7, on the roof garden. See "Fourteen Nurses Graduated from American Hospital," *New York Herald*, June 8, 1928, 11. The image is reproduced by Goddard (*Jazz Away from Home*, 50–51) and elsewhere but usually misidentified and/or misdated.
33. Reproduced by Lloyd, *Eugene Bullard*, between pages 102 and 103. The carousel nearest the camera is often wrongly designated as Zelli.
34. Ibid., 78.
35. Lloyd, *Eugene Bullard*, 90; Florence Richardson, "Notes of Paris," *New York Amsterdam News*, July 3, 1929, 12.
36. Advertisement, *New York Herald*, May 15, 1930, 11; "Paris Gossip," *Philadelphia Tribune*, July 17, 1930, 6.
37. After leaving the Casino, Crickett and the ex–Jazz Kings (joined by saxophonist Sidney Bechet, star of *La Revue Nègre*) ventured to the fringes of Europe. Led by Frank Withers, in early 1926 they spent several months in Moscow and the Ukraine. See Miller, *Some Hustling This!* 142–44.
38. Rogers, "The Paris Pepper Pot," *Afro-American*, June 22, 1929, 11.
39. "Le Jazz tragique," *Le Matin*, October 16, 1926, 1.
40. "Léonie Boyard qui tua son mari le chef du jazz-band Crutcher comparait devant le jury," *Le Petit Parisien*, October 7, 1926, 2.
41. Nevill, *Days and Nights*, 182.
42. Aragon, *Mauvais Plaisant*, 354.
43. Aragon, *Aurélien*, 108.
44. Geo London, "La meurtrière du maestro noir son mari est acquittée par le jury de la Seine," *Le Journal*, October 8, 1926, 1.
45. Aragon, *Aurélien*, 134.
46. Ibid., 449.
47. Nevill, *Days and Nights*, 48.
48. The first version appeared in Leiris, *Journal*, 106; the second in *L'Age d'homme*, 51.
49. O. O. McIntyre, "New York Day by Day," *Wilmington Morning News* (Wilmington, Del.), June 11, 1926, 4.
50. J. A. Rogers, "The Paris Pepper-Pot," *Pittsburgh Courier*, June 29, 1929, Sec. 2, 1. See also "Glover Compton Returns After 4 Years in Paris," *Chicago Defender*, January 25, 1930, 7.
51. Aragon, *Mauvais Plaisant*, 358, 360.
52. Ursula Petrie, "How King Edward 'Put Out the Eye' of the Society Peeper," *El Paso Times*, October 4, 1936, Sunday Home Magazine, 10; Samuel Dashiell, "Montmartre to Get Long Rest," *Pittsburgh Press*, January 26, 1930, 9. Arsène's was owned by Anatole Désiré and Arsène Moreau, father and uncle of actress Jeanne Moreau. In early 1928 it was sold and

became La Cloche d'Or, featuring ragtime pianist Les Copeland (advertisement, *New York Herald*, April 23, 1928, 12).

53. J. A. Rogers, "Foreign Observations," *Birmingham Reporter*, June 15, 1929, 2. Illustrator Armand Vallée (1884–1960) often treated the subject. For example, in "Aujourd'hui, dans les dancings. C'est le triste frôlement des métèques," *Fantasio* (1921): 334

54. Advertisement, *Le Journal*, October 31, 1926, 4.

55. Cited by Hammond and O'Connor, *Josephine Baker*, 45.

56. Bricktop, *Bricktop*, 108–9. According to Josephine they met in a club in Montmartre; Abatino claimed it was at the Folies Bergère, perhaps to obscure his dubious past (J. A. Rogers, "Rogers Interviews Count and Countess Albertini [sic] in France," *Pittsburgh Courier*, extra, July 9, 1927, Sec. 1, 1).

57. Giuseppe (Pepito) Abatino, "Letters to Josephine Baker," September 24, 1926, MS, auctioned by Ader Nordmann, 3 rue Favart, November 26, 2016.

58. "De la Poudre des bals et des dancings," *Dansons*, July 1928, 66.

59. Baker and Chase, *Josephine Baker*, 142.

60. See his self-portrait in "Immortalized on the Walls of Paris's Pet Night-life Café," *Hamilton Evening Journal*, May 25, 1929, Editorial, Pictorial, and Magazine Sec., 8. Gomina was an Argentinean hair oil popular in Paris in the late twenties.

61. Cited by Hammond and O'Connor, *Josephine Baker*, 45.

62. Bricktop, *Bricktop*, 109.

63. Foster Dulles, "Princess Leads Paris Merry Chase," *Philadelphia Inquirer*, March 15, 1925, 1; Chevalier, *Montmartre du plaisir*, 345–46.

64. Abatino, "Letters to Josephine Baker," September 24, October 13, 1926, MS, auctioned by Ader Nordmann, 3 rue Favart, November 26, 2016.

65. His comment may reflect the Jones' summer hiatus in Biarritz prior to moving to the rue Blanche.

66. "How Marilyn Scared Away the Mashers," *Pittsburgh Press*, September 6, 1925, American Weekly Sec., n. pag. [3].

67. J. A. Rogers, "Foreign Observations," *Birmingham Reporter*, June 15, 1929, 2.

68. Nevill, *Days and Nights*, 44–45.

69. "Sermons on Paris Opium Addicts by an Artist," *Pittsburgh Press*, April 13, 1924, American Weekly Sec., n. pag. [15].

70. Woon, "Powerful World Drug Ring," 34, and see Chevalier, *Montmartre du plaisir*, 385–87.

71. Baron, *L'An I du Surréalisme*, 174.

72. Bedu, "Avant-propos," 675.

73. "What Olive Thomas Saw in the Early Morning Hours Before She Killed Herself," *Pittsburgh Press*, October 31, 1920, American Weekly Sec., 2, 3.

74. Avocat, "Defiant Confessions," [5].

75. "Paris Bartenders Growing Rich by Vending Cocaine," *Philadelphia Inquirer*, April 3, 1921, 1.

76. Woon, "Powerful World Drug Ring," 33–34.

77. Ibid., 33.

78. Bricktop, *Bricktop*, 152–53.

79. "Joe Zelli Himself Limns Vivid Picture of Nights in Paris," *Palm Beach Post* (West Palm Beach, Fla.), February 20, 1930, 11.

80. Aragon, *Mauvais Plaisant*, 355.

81. Jolo, "One Night in Paris," 2.

82. Aragon, *Mauvais Plaisant*, 354–56.

83. Gilbert Swan, "In New York," *Olean Evening Times* (Olean, N.Y.), February 5, 1930, 10.

84. Sobol, "Voice of Broadway," 6.

85. "$250,000 Oasis Drained as Drys Stab New Year," *Daily News* (New York), January 1, 1932, 3–4.

86. "Paris Producer Dropped Big Roll," *Standard-Sentinel* (Hazelton, Pa.), February 12, 1932, 3.

87. "French Capital Gay During Late Spring," *Cincinnati Enquirer*, May 15, 1932, Sec. 5, 4.

88. Advertisements, *New York Herald*, November 24, 1933, 8; *Paris-Soir*, February 15, 1934, 6.

89. "Noted Host Finds World at His Doorstep," *Chatham Courier* (Chatham, N.Y.), July 24, 1958, n. pag.

90. Paul Yawitz, "Walter Winchell on Broadway," *Waco News Tribune*," August 25, 1934, 4.

CHAPTER 7. "M'SOO KEE-LAY AND HIS SNOW-WHITE RUSSIAN WOLFHOUND"

The epigraph is from Woon, *Paris That's Not*, 248.

1. Jim Mitchell, "Jed Kiley, 'The Fatal Man' Home from the Wars, Parisian Boulevards," *Tennessean* (Nashville), October 14, 1929, 5.

2. Woon, *Paris That's Not*, 249.

3. "Tragic Death," [2].

4. Woon, *Paris That's Not*, 249–50.

5. Ben Hecht, "Charlie's First Days of Soldiering—and Col. Foreman," *Chicago Tribune*, July 16, 1957, part 2, 1.

6. "Quiz Young Man for Light on Ebba Johnson's Death," *Chicago Tribune*, January 1, 1915, 17.

7. "Tragic Death," [3].

8. Ibid., [2].

9. "Doughboy Millionaire Has Last Best Laugh," *Courier* (Harrisburg, Pa.), June 27, 1920, 7.

10. Floyd Gibbons, "The Author," *St. Louis Post-Dispatch*, April 4, 1937, part 6, 1H.

11. *Le Figaro* confirms the call ("Nouvelles diverses: La Mort de la princesse Rospigliosi," June 14, 1920, 2) but not the dialogue.

12. "Princess Rospigliosi Dies," *New York Times*, June 11, 1920, 13.

13. "A. E. F. Hero Making Fortune on Dances," *Wisconsin Rapids Daily Tribune*, May 3, 1921, 2; "News of Americans Day by Day," *New York Herald*, May 3, 1921, 2.

14. Albert Curtis, "Arrogant Americans Slugged in Paris Streets: French Hero, Georgia Born, Whips White Bully in Paris," *Chicago Defender*, January 6, 1923, 1.

15. Charles B. Driscoll, "New York Day by Day," *State Journal* (Lansing, Mich.), May 1, 1940, 8.

16. Wales, "Yankee Negroes in Paris"; and see Lloyd, *Eugene Bullard*, 81–85.
17. "'Jed' Kiley Purchases Theatre in Montmartre," *Bridgeport Telegram*, December 27, 1923, 10.
18. Woon, *Paris That's Not*, 254.
19. Maurice Bourgeois, "Paris et la littérature américaine," *Le Figaro*, March 7, 1924, 4.
20. "Paris Won't Have Volstead Café," *New York Herald*, February 7, 1924, 1.
21. "Paris to Honor Mister Volstead," *New York Herald*, January 7, 1924, 1.
22. "Volstead Café in Paris Now Renamed," *Los Angeles Daily Times*, February 7, 1924, part 1, 8.
23. "No Heat at the Volstead," *New York Herald*, January 14, 1924, 2.
24. See also the photo taken by the Séeberger frères (FSK04–09, 1925).
25. Reproduced in "Triumphant Revenge of the English Dancer," *Houston Post*, June 22, 1924, Magazine Sec., n. pag. [9].
26. Kiley, *Hemingway*, 34.
27. "Blink" was one of the picturesque figures who enliven the history of Montmartre. Although fighting under an Irish surname, he was a Philadelphian Jew named Lewis Silverman. His nickname was due to the glass eye he confided to his second before each fight.
28. "Kiley Renames Volstead Café," *New York Herald*, February 11, 1924, 2.
29. Advertisement, *La Presse*, February 10, 1924, 2.
30. Kiley claims the incident occurred two weeks after the opening (Kiley, "My Friend Edward"). Actually, it was the early morning of April 17. After the dinner at the Munns, where Florence and Palmer Jones entertained, the party adjourned to Kiley's.
31. Kiley, "Man Behind the Mask."
32. "Why the Prince of Wales Took Ham-and-Eggs," *Pittsburgh Press*, May 25, 1924, American Weekly Sec., n. pag. [3]; Kiley, "Man Behind the Mask."
33. O'Brien, "American Is King."
34. Wales, "Prince of Wales Becomes Jazz Band Addict."
35. McAlmon, *Being Geniuses Together*, 244.
36. Martin, "Wales Plays Around Paris."
37. Woon, *Paris That's Not*, 255.
38. "Kiley's Becomes French Café; Owner to Open New Rendezvous," *New York Herald*, August 9, 1924, 3.
39. "*Moulin Rouge Program. New York-Montmartre*" (Paris: [1925]). The likeness is striking when compared with a caricature of Paris-American newsmen by Pandl. Kiley appears on the far right of the first panel (reproduced in Weber, *News of Paris*, between 118–19).
40. Goddard, *Jazz Away from Home*, 70.
41. "Harry's New York Bar": Harry McElhone acquired the bar in February 1923 ("Bar Ownership Changes," *New York Herald*, February 21, 1923. 1); "charter members": 1. O. O. McIntyre; 2. Arthur Moss; 31. John O'Brien; 34. Sparrow Robertson; 41. Henry Wales; 42. Joe Zelli; 72. Sinclair Lewis; 76. Bill Henley; 90. Billy Arnold; etc. Non-charter members were Ernest Hemingway and F. Scott Fitzgerald (McElhone and Holcomb, *Barflies and Cocktails*, 95–101).
42. Moss, "Birth of the I.B.F.," 84.
43. Ibid.

44. Woon, "Mirrors of Paris," May 16, 1926.
45. Basil Woon, "'Bat' Siki Hopes American Promoter Will Bar Him," *Shreveport Times* (Shreveport, La.), November 19, 1922, 11. Louigi's owner was Gaspard Luigi Palma, an Italian American friend of Zelli's. Carlish confirms that Louigi's was one of the few clubs that barred "negroes" (Carlish and Bestic, *King of Clubs*, 113).
46. Music by Roy Henderson, lyrics by Buddy G. de Sylva and Lew Brown.
47. Woon, *Paris That's Not*, 173.
48. Woon, "Mirrors of Paris," August 8, 1926.
49. "Montmartre Welcomes New Music Hall," *New York Herald*, October 9, 1925, 5.
50. Avocat, "Defiant Confessions," [4].
51. Horatio, "Les Echos," *Comœdia*, October 10, 1926.
52. Arthur Moss, "Around the Town," *New York Herald*, July 5, 1926, 8.
53. Henry Wales, "The *Tribune* Covers the Lindbergh Story," *Chicago Sunday Tribune*, June 27, 1937, Graphic Sec., 3.
54. For an account of Henry Wales and the Lindbergh story see Weber, *News of Paris*, 87–88.
55. Kiley, *Hemingway*, 21.
56. Ibid., 48.
57. "In the Latin Quarter," *New York Herald*, February 20, 1929, 10.
58. Woon, *Paris That's Not*, 256.
59. Nevill, *Days and Nights*, 51.
60. Michael S. Reynolds, "The *Sun* in Its Time: Recovering the Historical Context," in *New Essays on The Sun Also Rises*, ed. Linda Wagner-Martin (Cambridge: Cambridge University Press, 1987), 59.
61. Built in 1898 as the Théâtre des Fantaisies-Parisiennes, it was renamed by director Léo Berryer and opened on December 24, 1924, with a nude revue.
62. Aragon, *Mauvais Plaisant*, 344.
63. Ibid., 343–46.
64. "indeed vast": Turner, "Summer in Paris"; Danny Wilson: Antoinette [Tony] Mitchell, "Afro-American Artists Latest Sensation in Europe," *Pittsburgh Courier*, December 20, 1924, part 2, 9. Wilson was married to blues singer Edith Wilson. He died from tuberculosis in 1928.
65. O. O. McIntyre, "New York Day by Day," *Evening News* (Harrisburg, Pa.), October 26, 1929, 8.
66. "Prince of Wales Sets New Deauville Styles," *St. Louis Post Dispatch*, August 20, 1924, 2; Kiley, "Man Behind the Mask"; Arthur Moss, "Around the Town," *New York Herald*, August 24, 1924, 4.
67. A genteel Irishwoman, despite her scandalous career: three daughters married English peers.
68. Carlish and Bestic, *King of Clubs*, 111.
69. Ibid., 114–15. She calls it "Meyrick's Gaity," but advertising spells it "Merrick's."
70. Meyrick, *Secrets of the 43*, 118–20.
71. Carlish and Bestic, *King of Clubs*, 115; "People Here and There," *New York Herald*, November 14, 1925, 2.

72. Meyrick, *Secrets of the 43*, 120–21.
73. Ibid., 120.
74. In October 1925 C. F. Bertelli speaks of a sale ("Gaming Table Kills Dancing," *Shreveport Times*, October 6, 1925, 16), but the *Pittsburgh Press* says she "leased" the club from Kiley ("Daughter of Most Notorious Woman in England Weds a Lord," May 16, 1926, American Weekly Sec., n. pag. [3]).
75. C. F. Bertelli, "Paris's New Gambling Fever Outstrips Klondyke Days," *Buffalo Courier*, October 27, 1924, 2.
76. "University of Alabama Orchestra Returns After Tour Across Seas," *Birmingham News*, September 13, 1925, Social Sec., 2.
77. Meyrick, *Secrets of the 43*, 120, 124.
78. Ibid., 124.
79. [C. F. Bertelli], "'Jed' Kiley of Paris to Marry American Girl," *El Paso Times*, February 2, 1925, 2.
80. "En douce," *Comœdia*, December 22, 1922, 3.
81. Quoted by Séité, *Le Jazz à la lettre*, 326.
82. Basil Woon, "Broadway Air at Paris Race," *Shreveport Times* (Shreveport, La.), June 22, 1925, 10.
83. "'Ketchup' King Has Girl Arrested on Blackmail Charge," *Arizona Republican* (Phoenix), November 15, 1924, 4; "Bay Heiress Tries Death in Romance," *Oakland Tribune*, November 12, 1926, 56; "U. S. Woman Tries to End Life with Poison in Paris," *Chicago Tribune*, November 12, 1926, 2; C. F. Bertelli, "Mrs. Caples Sues U. S. Grid Star in Paris," *San Francisco Examiner*, December 27, 1926, 1.
84. In a letter to Kiley, Hemingway declared, "you were never a friend of mine in Paris nor anywhere else" ("Beating the Drum About a Book Written 46 Years Ago," *New York Herald*, June 26, 1972). Critics agree that Kiley's narration is largely fictional, even if some details seem too precise to be totally invented.
85. Kiley, *Hemingway*, 40, 45.
86. Ibid., 42.
87. "Beauties of Paris Scoff at Budapest Legs and Ankles," *Pittsburgh Press*, June 12, 1921, Editorial and Automobile Sec., n. pag. [10]; "Tragic Death," [2].
88. "Tragic Death," [2].
89. Kiley, *Hemingway*, 119.
90. O. O. McIntyre, "New York Day by Day," *Evening News* (Harrisburg, Pa.), February 25, 1936, 6.
91. Walter Winchell, "Along Broadway," *Dayton Herald* (Dayton, Ohio), May 8, 1946, 15.
92. "New York Day by Day," *Evening News*, October 26, 1929, 8.
93. Woon, "Mirrors of Paris," May 23, 1926.
94. Basil Woon, "Paris Prepares to Receive Legion Invaders with Cash Registers," *Warren Tribune* (Warren, Pa.), April 19, 1927, 12.
95. Kiley, *Hemingway*, 25, 31.
96. See Weber, *News of Paris*, 204.
97. Gerald Kiley, "Three of a Kind," *Baltimore Sun*, April 12, 1936, Magazine Sec., 10.
98. James Leveque, "Hawaii," *Honolulu Star-Bulletin*, December 11, 1961, 34.

99. Henry Wales, "Letters from Geneva-Germany," *Chicago Sunday Tribune*, May 30, 1954, part 1, 9.

100. "the association of white girls with men of colour": Meyrick, *Secrets of the 43*, 127; "University of Alabama Capstone Orchestra": advertisement, *New York Herald*, October 10, 1925, 8. The orchestra was a college jazz band seeking a summer job and adventure—a far cry from the Crackerjacks! See Turner, "Summer in Paris"; and "Mrs. Merrick Opens the 'Gaity,'" *New York Herald*, July 20, 1925, 4.

CHAPTER 8. "AN OSTRICH FEDDAH SUIT O' CAT'S PAJAMAS"
The epigraph is from "Chez Florence," *Time Magazine*, 14.

1. Pernet and Rye, "Visiting Firemen 18," 241.
2. Cooke, "Mitchell, American Boy," 13.
3. McMullin, "Paris and London," 35.
4. Cooke, "Mitchell, American Boy," 13.
5. Dougherty, "About Things Theatrical."
6. Miller, *Some Hustling This!* 106; Lotz, *Black People*, 310.
7. See Shack, *Harlem in Montmartre*, 30.
8. "Le music-hall et les cirques" in *Oeuvres complètes*, vol. 1, ed. Maxime Morel (Eds du Sandre, 2014), 488.
9. Hemingway, "European Nightlife," 406; Magloire, "Florence's Place," 23.
10. Advertisement, *New York Herald*, December 22, 1923, 3.
11. Around March 11, 1924, Florence was still at the Grand Duc (Sam Jay Bush, "Paris Dope," *Chicago Defender*, June 21, 1924, 7). Thus, her move occurred between that date and April 14.
12. O. O. McIntyre, "New York Day by Day," *Pittsburgh Press*, January 13, 1920, 12.
13. O'Brien, "American Is King," 2.
14. Mitchell's passport application lists New York as his birthplace (Pernet and Rye, *Visiting Firemen 18*, 223), but bandleader Noble Sissle says he was born in New Jersey and brought to New York as a baby ("Show Business," *New York Age*, March 12, 1949); "his stock of 1911 Cordon Rouge": Jolo, "One Night in Paris," 2.
15. "Hon. Mrs. Norton Feather-Footed Chum of Prince," *Daily News* (New York, N.Y.), September 10, 1924, 4. "Plantation songs," popular airs sung by "Negro planters" ("slaves"), formed a large part of the repertoire of the popular Fisk Jubilee Singers (See "Les Concerts," *Comœdia*, May 4, 1925, 4).
16. Goffin, "*Jazz*," 77.
17. "Prince of Wales Tarries in Paris," *Hartford Courant*, April 18, 1924, 28.
18. Music by Walter Donaldson, lyrics by Joe Young, Sam M. Lewis, 1919.
19. Martin, "Wales Plays Around Paris," 1.
20. Nash, "Best-Dressed," [7].
21. Cooke, "Mitchell, American Boy," 13; "Wales Knee Lobs Where Races Mix and Night's Long," *Daily News* (New York), first ed., April 19, 1924, 10.
22. "Wales Sees Bit of Gayest Paree," *Binghamton Press* (Binghamton, N.Y.), April 18, 1924, 36.
23. "Flo Jones Dies."

24. "Aimée Sees Paris Montmartre as 'Brink of Hell,'" *El Paso Evening Post*, September 24, 1928, 7.
25. "Mlle Parisys and Her Fighting Argentine Admirers," *Pittsburgh Press*, October 18, 1925, American Weekly Sec., n. pag. [11].
26. Rogers, "Paris Notes."
27. "Informations diverses: Les étrangers en France," *Le Temps*, August 2, 1923, 3.
28. "Chronique des Tribunaux: Le Prince noir Tovalou molesté dans un établissement de nuit obtient réparation," *Le Journal*, October 19, 1923, 3.
29. "Americans Making Trouble in the Gay Paris Cafés," *Pittsburgh Press*, February 3, 1924, American Weekly Sec., n. pag. [8].
30. [Woon], "'Fashionable' Americans in Paris."
31. Woon, "Mirrors of Paris," May 16, 1926.
32. "Mirrors of Paris," *Albuquerque Journal*, January 9, 1927, Editorial Page, 6.
33. O. O. McIntyre, "In Paris with McIntyre," *Akron Beacon Journal*, March 26, 1925, 4.
34. Hughes, *Big Sea*, 161.
35. Music by Richard A. Whiting, lyrics by Dave Redford, 1916.
36. Aragon, *Mauvais Plaisant*, 352.
37. Raymond G. Carroll, "Paris Day by Day: Montmartre," *Los Angeles Daily Times*, May 24, 1924, part 1, 5.
38. "Lizzie Miles Forced to Vacate Gay Paree," *Pittsburgh Courier*, February 14, 1925, 10.
39. "Lizzie Prognosticates," *Chicago Defender*, March 21, 1925 [datelined March 2], 8.
40. Antoinette (Tony) Mitchell, "French Chorus Girls Protest High-Salaried Colored Dancers," *Pittsburgh Courier*, March 21, 1925, part 2, 11.
41. A tax fraud conviction led to bankruptcy ("Le fisc et la boîte de nuit," *Le Populaire*, May 16, 1933, 1).
42. Advertisement, *New York Herald*, April 17, 1924, 4.
43. "Lizzie Prognosticates," 8. "Skarjinsky" is the correct spelling.
44. "Miss Lizzie Miles Is Montmartre's Smart Entertainer," *New York Age*, March 21, 1925, 6; advertisement, *New York Herald*, February 1, 1925, 5.
45. Bullard, "Shooting at Us," 7. His memoirs are filled with questionable statements, such as being hired by Oscar Mauvais [sic] to organize a 1931 gala in honor of the exiled Spanish king—a year and a half after Mouvet's death (Lloyd, *Eugene Bullard*, 108–9)!
46. Advertisement, *New York Herald*, January 25, 1925, 5.
47. Advertisement, *New York Herald*, April 11, 1925, 5.
48. Classified Advertisement, *New York Herald*, July 29, 1925, 6.
49. Most persuasively, on December 28, 1925, Frisco is reported to be giving Charleston lessons at "Mitchell's" and at the same time teaching at "Chez Florence" (Henry Wales, "Rudy Wins Prize for Charleston in Montmartre," *Chicago Tribune*, December 29, 1925, 5; Stéphane Manier, "Les Américains chez nous. Le Triomphe du Nègre," *Paris-soir*, April 28, 1926, 1). And see Woon, "Mirrors of Paris," August 8, 1926.
50. Wiggins, "Paris Is My Beat."
51. Advertisement, *New York Herald*, September 12, 1925, 5.
52. *Morning Telegraph* (New York), January 24, 1926, cited in Cooke, "Mitchell, American Boy," 13.

53. See Bricktop, *Bricktop*, 153–54.

54. "Three Bejeweled Beauties Gleam in Paris Night Life," *Daily News* (New York), main ed., November 16, 1925, 2.

55. See "Leonora Hughes, Noted Dancer, Engaged Again," *Wilmington Morning News (Wilmington, Pa.)*, October 1, 1924, 8; "Pretty Leonora Won from Stage by Rich Youth," *Harrisburg Telegraph* (Harrisburg, Pa.), February 24, 1925, 1; "Unpleasant Consequences of Mrs. Nash's Newest Marriage," *Pittsburgh Press*, November 21, 1926, American Weekly Sec., n. pag. [3]; "Now Peggy Joyce Plans a Brand New Divorce Say the Paris Society Dames," *News-Press* (Fort Myers, Fla.), November 20, 1925, 1, 7; "Valentino and Party Visit Paris Night Resorts," *Sioux City Journal (Sioux City, Iowa)*, November 29, 1925, 1. Quoted by Cooke without a source ("Mitchell, American Boy," 13), the bottle throwing incident was first published in the *Pittsburgh Press* ("How Mrs. Jean Nash Rebuked Her," November 22, 1925, American Weekly Sec., n. pag. [3]).

56. Bart A. Lynch, "Comstock, Detroit Go-Getter, Loses Peggy Joyce," *Detroit Free Press*, August 8, 1926, Feature Sec., 1.

57. Cooke, "Mitchell, American Boy," 13.

58. Bullard is often credited with introducing pancakes (Lloyd, *Eugene Bullard*, 92) but Mitchell was serving them in June 1923, and Clarence Glover was already offering pancakes at the Aladdin's Lamp in 1919 (Wales, "Dance Halls of Paris," 1).

59. Nash, "Best-Dressed," [6].

60. Bricktop, *Bricktop*, 115.

61. Ibid., 116–17.

62. Ibid., 115.

63. Advertisement, *New York Herald*, October 7, 1926, 7.

64. Pernet and Rye, *Visiting Firemen 18*, 241.

65. Lotz, *Black People*, 61.

66. Barbara Lewis, "When Paris Adored Flo-Jo Jazz Goddesses," *New York Amsterdam News*, May 18, 1996, 24; Sharpley-Whiting, *Bricktop's Paris*, 59.

67. Gillett accords the text three sentences apropos of Florence's association with Black women entertainers ("Crossing the Pond," 138). The only substantive article on Florence is Magloire's recent "Florence's Place," but even she allots it only a long paragraph and ignores the crucial role of the Prince of Wales (34–35).

68. Nevill, *Days and Nights*, 43.

69. A. Montillot, "La Mort du Fox-Trot," *Dansons*, January 1927, 163.

70. "In its turn": Harry Pilcer popularized the dance in the revue *Palace aux Femmes* ("Au Palace. *Palace aux Femmes*," *Dansons*, October 1926, 119), but at the same moment Josephine Baker was black bottoming at the Impérial; "the dance à la mode": Although the *Time* story is dated June 20, 1927, the contest took place on June 7 ("Prince Is Winner of Cat's Pajamas," *Detroit Free Press*, June 8, 1927, 1).

71. "When Death Played for the Dance," *Philadelphia Inquirer*, June 19, 1927, Magazine Sec., 3.

72. "Chez Florence," *Time Magazine*, 14.

73. "Prince Henry Is Made Captain in the Hussars," *Indiana Evening News* (Indiana, Pa.), June 1, 1927, 12.

74. He may be referring to the "hostesses" who came in at 6 a.m. to eat breakfast and work on crossword puzzles ("Paris High Hat Golden Nights," *Daily News* (New York), May 10, 1925, 10).

75. "Chez Florence," *Time Magazine*, 14. Between April 1924 and June 7, 1927, the P.O.W. made four visits to Paris: September 11–15, 1926, when he listened to Tommy Lyman at Louigi's; October 28–November 1, 1926, when he met Bricktop; April 14–19 and May 6–11, 1927. The flashback likely occurred on one of the latter occasions.

76. Woon, "Mirrors of Paris," July 3, 1927.

77. Hughes, *Big Sea*, 160–61.

78. Kiley, "My Friend Edward."

79. Woon, *Paris That's Not*, 19.

80. Hemingway, "European Nightlife," 406.

81. Zora Neale Hurston recycled it in "How It Feels to Be Colored Me": "I am the only Negro in the United States whose grandfather on the mother's side was *not* an Indian chief" (114).

82. Bricktop, *Bricktop*, 98.

83. Magloire, "Florence's Place," 24.

84. "Chez Florence," *Time Magazine*, 14.

85. "People Here and There," *New York Herald*, October 10, 1927, 9.

86. On November 27, 1927, Harlem Renaissance patron Carl Van Vechten wrote in his *Daybooks*, "A. gets very drunk & goes out when I do, taking me to Florence Embry Jones's." He notes further visits on January 3 and February 9, 1928 (*Splendid Drunken Twenties*, 184, 191, 195).

87. Ibid., 196 (February 12, 1928).

88. Advertisement, *New York Herald*, April 19, 1928, 7.

89. Vincent Price, "My First Trip Abroad" (July–August 1928), entry for August 24, 1928, available at https:/vincentpricejournal.wordpress.com/tag/florence-emery/; "Just Bill": music by Jerome Kern, lyrics by P. G. Wodehouse and Oscar Hammerstein II, 1927.

90. Lois Bancroft Long ("Lipstick"), "Tables for Two," *New Yorker*, May 5, 19285; Tom Pettey, "Liquor Clubs Run Wide Open in New York," *Chicago Tribune*, May 14, 1928, 1.

91. "Orchestra Leader Dies Suddenly," *New York Herald*, September 1, 1928, 3.

92. Advertisement, *New York Herald*, February 23, 1929, 6; "Rumor Hubby of Florence Mills May Marry Soon," *Pittsburgh Courier*, January 26, 1929, 1.

93. Chappy Gardner, "Along the Rialto," *Pittsburgh Courier*, March 16, 1929, 2.

94. "Night Club Draws," *Afro-American*, November 23, 1929, 9.

95. Gerry, "New York," *Afro-American*, April 11, 1931, 7.

96. Snelson, "Once Toast of Europe's Gayest Resorts." Later critics like Magloire also exaggerate her impoverishment ("Florence's Place," 24). Her apartment at 148 West 142nd Street possessed a manned elevator, and at her death she left some $10,000 in jewels and expensive furs ("Meet Florence, a Nation's 'It' Lady," *Chicago Defender*, January 2, 1932, 5).

97. Snelson, "Once Toast of Europe's Gayest Resorts."

98. Bricktop, *Bricktop*, 89.

99. Hughes, *Big Sea*, 174, 172.

100. "Flo Jones Dies."

101. "Theatrical Celebrities Honored," *Afro-American*, October 4, 1930, 7.

CHAPTER 9. BRICKTOP AND BUDDIE AT THE GRAND DUC

The chapter title is from Langston Hughes, *Big Sea*, 162; the epigraph is from Baron, *L'An I du Surréalisme*, 179.

1. Aragon, *Mauvais Plaisant*, 384. Curiously, his poetic fantasy was concretized by Harlem, opened on the site of the Harem (advertisement, *New York Herald*, November 15, 1926, 7).
2. Leiris, "Paris-Minuit," 61.
3. Lloyd, *Eugene Bullard*, 93, 97.
4. In his letter to the *Chicago Defender*, Bullard stated that he left the Grand Duc on August 2, 1924. Apparently, his defense of Lizzie Miles hides his chief concern: "Bricktop remained with my previous partner as a singer and entertainer.... But she has not the direction of the Grand Duke" ("Shooting at Us," 7). Nevertheless, she was undeniably the director (Evans, "Letter from Paris"; advertisement, *New York Herald*, October 1, 1924, 5, and Sparrow Robertson, "Sporting Gossip," *New York Herald*, October 20, 1924, 6). Bricktop suggests that he later returned as her manager, but that time frame is unclear (118).
5. Advertisements, *New York Herald*, October 1, 1924, 5; October 3, 1924, 5.
6. Gravigny, *Montmartre en 1925*, 172.
7. Fitzgerald, *Crack-up*, 114; "Buddie would come in": McAlmon, *Being Geniuses Together*, 115.
8. Socrates: Plato, *Symposium*, trans. Alexander Nehamas and Paul Woodruff (Indianapolis: Hackett, 1989), 214A; "Bricktop 'drank'": Leiris, "Paris-Minuit," 61.
9. "He used to do": Interviewed in Goddard, *Jazz Away from Home*, 289; Kiley's, etc.: His appearances at the Grand Duc were "with approval of Ritz" (advertisement, *New York Herald*, October 3, 1924, 5. And see Woon, *Paris That's Not*, 159).
10. See "Leeds Gets Drum, Gives House, Lot," *New York Herald*, December 17, 1925, 4.
11. "young Maharajah of Indore": Yeshwant Rao Holkar II (1908–1961). The screen is in *verre églomisé*, a technique involving painting between layers of mirror and glass (Piramal Museum of Art, Mumbai, India, ca. 1930). For a photo see exh. cat. *Moderne Maharajah: Un mécène des années 1930* (Musée des Arts Décoratifs, 2019), 130; "for the music room": See Géraldine Lenain, *Le Dernier Maharaja d'Indore* (Paris: Seuil, 2022), 133.
12. *New York Herald*, October 1, 1924, 5.
13. Reproduced in Bastia, "La Soirée."
14. Old Chum, "Paris Dope," *Chicago Defender*, December 13, 1924, 8.
15. Bricktop offers the only evidence (*Bricktop*, 98). In a radio interview with journalist Studs Terkel she gave a more neutral version. Fitzgerald says, "I knew Brick before Cole Porter did" ("Brick Top discusses her career, her colleagues, and the jazz scene," Studs Terkel Radio Archive, May 6, 1975).
16. The text dates the hero's dissipations from 1927, and his return to Paris in fall 1930. Bricktop's was then at 59 bis-61 rue Pigalle, on the site of the Floresco (*New York Herald*, April 25, 1930, 14), but for narrative reasons, Fitzgerald blurs the distinction. A rapid look at Bricktop's poorly documented peregrinations may be useful. After the Music Box's demise in January 1927, Georges Jamerson welcomed her back. In 1928 she moved "across the street" (Bricktop, *Bricktop*, 119). This has been taken to mean she had only one club between then and Bricktop's Monico (November 1931). In fact, there was the former Floresco and two others: "Bricktop's Impérial" at #59 rue Pigalle (*New York Herald*, March 14, 1928, 12), and

a club at #53, home of the Harem (advertisement, *New York Herald*, June 20, 1928, 2). By Christmas she was back at the Grand Duc (J. A. Rogers, "Ada Smith, Chicagoan, Runs Her Own Cabaret," *Afro-American*, January 26, 1929, 6).

17. Scott and Zelda: Fitzgerald, *Ledger*, 180; Cole Porter: In her memoirs Bricktop specifies "late fall or early winter of 1925 (*Bricktop*, 100). Her comment to Studs Terkel stating that she knew Fitzgerald in 1925, the year before meeting Porter, is more accurate ("Brick Top discusses her career"). In October 1925, Porter was still frequenting Le Jardin ("News of Americans in Europe," *New York Herald*, October 11, 1925, 4), and on November 4 he sailed for New York (Porter, *Letters of Cole Porter*, 66).

18. Woon, "Mirrors of Paris," May 23, 1926.

19. Bricktop, *Bricktop*, 100–101.

20. Quoted in Gill, *Cole*, 70.

21. Bricktop, *Bricktop*, 101.

22. Basil Woon, "Mirrors of Paris," *Wisconsin State Journal* (Madison, Wis.), December 5, 1926, 23. He is evidently referring to the Music Box, which was not across from the Impérial.

23. Basil Woon, "Mirrors of Paris," *Wisconsin State Journal* (Madison, Wis.), June 14, 1926, 2. In preparation, Elsa had taken a private lesson from Bricktop (*Diary, 1926* [Holograph MS], May 7, 1926, Ada "Bricktop" Smith Papers, 1926–1983, box 1, folder 1, Schomburg Center for Research in Black Culture, New York Public Library). Her energetic performance of the Black Bottom was commemorated in Sem's satirical album *White Bottoms* (Succès, 1927). Sisley Hiddleston accused the artist's "*bottomiers*" of imitating "the least admirable qualities of the basest Negroes" (*Back to Montparnasse: Glimpses of Broadway in Bohemia* [Philadelphia: J. B. Lippincott, 1931], 35).

24. Bricktop, *Bricktop*, 105.

25. Ibid., 89.

26. Ibid., 90–92.

27. Ibid., 94.

28. "Fanny Ward Visits Beach," *Miami Daily News*, home ed., February 26, 1925, 26; "Liner Fleet Brings 3000 More to Crowded Paris," *New York Herald*, June 20, 1925, 1.

29. [Basil Woon], "'Fashionable' Americans in Paris," 1.

30. In her interview with Goddard, a vague "months and months and months" after her arrival is specified, the dialogue is not identical, and Fanny and her husband are said to have deserted when "they had to come back home . . . and then the Left Bank started coming in" (*Jazz Away from Home*, 193).

31. Bricktop, *Bricktop*, 91.

32. Ibid., 105.

33. Stovall, *Paris Noir*, 80.

34. Fitzgerald, *Crack-up*, 84.

35. Fitzgerald, *Tender Is the Night*, ed. Goldman, 88.

36. Fitzgerald, *Tender Is the Night* (Melarky and Kelly versions), 250. My comments concern the third and fourth drafts of the "Melarky Narrator Version."

37. Other than the page on Le Grand Duc, the most direct reference to Black Montmartre concerns Louis Mitchell. During the summer of 1929 Fitzgerald's wallet was stolen in a Montmartre club by a Black client. Having accused the wrong man, and caused Mitchell to

be arrested, he spent the night at the police station trying to straighten out the imbroglio. The incident is the subject of a cryptic *Ledger* entry: "Nigger affair—Buck, Michell [sic] in prison. Dane" (Fitzgerald, *Ledger*, 183). The manuscript contains a more detailed version (Fitzgerald, *Tender Is the Night* [Melarky and Kelly versions], 256). With Mitchell's name changed to Freeman, the story is expanded into a major episode in *Tender Is the Night* where Fitzgerald examines the racial issues underlying the confrontation (108–21).

38. Fitzgerald invents a pseudonym for the Grand Duc, the "Georgia Cabin." The former is crossed out, but I restore it in my transcription. *Tender Is the Night* (Melarky and Kelly versions), 251–52.

39. "Nos Echos," *L'Intransigeant*, November 1, 1926, 2.

40. Nevill, *Days and Nights*, 59–60. The most notable Russian aristocrat at that time was the Grand Duke Boris Vladimirovich who, despite straightened circumstances, kept an expensive suite in the chic Bois de Boulogne.

41. "Echoes of the Jazz Age," *Scribner's Magazine* 90, no. 5 (1931): 464.

42. Fitzgerald, *Ledger*, 180 (October 1925).

43. Alan Patrick Herbert, *She-Shanties* (London: T. Fisher Unwin, 1926). Nevill cites it as "*Sea-Shanties* by H. P. Herbert" (*Days and Nights*, 12).

44. "heir to a Scandinavian throne": Fitzgerald, *Tender Is the Night*, ed. Goldman, 88; "the most famous young Englishman in the world": Fitzgerald, *Tender Is the Night* (Melarky and Kelly versions), 249.

45. Baron, *L'An I du Surréalisme*, 180.

46. Rye, "Southern Syncopated Orchestra," 38.

47. Hughes, *Big Sea*, 180.

48. Leiris, "Paris-Minuit," 61.

49. "Montmartre Just a Glorified Broadway," *Daily News* (New York), home ed., November 16, 1924, 20.

50. Magloire, "Florence's Place," 31.

51. Bricktop, *Bricktop*, 145–46. Henley's racist attitudes were perhaps more structural than personal.

52. Reproduced in Lloyd, *Eugene Bullard*, between pages 102 and 103. The presence of "Blink" McCloskey dates it to early 1924.

53. Evans, "Letter from Paris."

54. "Singers Obliged to Leave France," *Afro-American*, February, 1925, 4; Henry Wales, "France Banishing American Negro Players of Jazz," *Chicago Tribune*, May 31, 1924, 3.

55. See, for example, Fry, *Paris Blues*, 7.

56. Stovall, *Paris Noir*, 72.

57. "More's Utopia": Fry, *Paris Blues*, 9; "T.O.B.A.": Bricktop, *Bricktop*, 30.

58. Music and lyrics: Cliff Richards and Gilbert Wells (1924).

59. Stovall, *Paris Noir*, 78.

60. Ibid., 79.

61. Bricktop, *Bricktop*, 97.

62. Ibid., 106.

63. "Echos," *Comœdia*, March 18, 1922, 1.

64. Stovall, *Paris Noir*, 78.

65. Bricktop, *Bricktop*, 112.
66. "Italian and British Nobility and U. S. Heiress Perform for Charity," *New York Herald*, August 29, 1926, 7.
67. Bricktop, *Bricktop*, 111.
68. Marquise Nina de Polignac, "Mme de Polignac to Ada 'Bricktop' Smith" [Holograph MS], July 1, 1926, Ada "Bricktop" Smith Collection, Personal Correspondence: 1920–29, box 1, folder 2, Delilah Jackson Papers, Emory University, Atlanta, Ga.
69. Bricktop, *Bricktop*, 116.
70. Ibid., 204–6.
71. Ibid., 174, 130.
72. See Matthew McMahan, "'Let Me See You Dance': Ada Bricktop Smith, the Charleston, and Racial Commodification in Interwar France," *Journal of Dramatic Theory and Criticism*, 29, no. 2 (2015): 54
73. McAlmon, *Nightinghouls of Paris*, 48.
74. Bricktop, *Bricktop*, 129. Interpreting "I'm in Love Again" in early 1926, she was probably thinking of Black Crackerjack Bobby Jones, and when she married, it was with a Black saxophonist, Peter Ducongé.
75. Ibid., 128–29.
76. Ibid., 131, 130.
77. Stovall, *Paris Noir*, 88.
78. Ibid., 46.
79. Jameson, "Of Islands and Trenches," 97.
80. Glassco, *Memoirs of Montparnasse*, 57, 58.
81. Gill, *Cole*, 70.
82. Baron, *L'An I du Surréalisme*, 179.
83. Leiris, "Paris Minuit," 60–61.
84. Ibid., 61.
85. Aragon, *Mauvais Plaisant*, 344. La Perle was a club that preceded the Floresco and catered to lesbians.
86. F. Scott Fitzgerald, "The Offshore Pirate," in *The Short Stories of F. Scott Fitzgerald*, ed. Matthew J. Bruccoli (New York: Scribner's, 1989), 91.
87. Langston Hughes, *Big Sea*, 162.

CHAPTER 10. "STILL LONGING FOR DE OLD PLANTATION"

1. "Paris Night Clubs Get Merger Idea but Shun Standardized Whoopee," *Brooklyn Daily Eagle*, January 16, 1929, 5.
2. "Echoes et Nouvelles," *Comœdia*, October 10, 1929, 2.
3. Schmitt, "Un animateur."
4. Advertisement, *Comœdia*, October 5, 1928, 4.
5. "Nouvelles diverses," *Le Journal*, October 28, 1920, 3; Dashiell and Cope, "Mysterious Baron." Hewitt's comments on Montmartre as "a centre of crime" neglect this enigmatic figure (*Montmartre*, 154). For example, Louis Chevalier, on whom Hewitt relies, mentions Stavisky several times but never links him to the baron (*Montmartre du plaisir*, 399n2, 400, 432).
6. Courrière, *Joseph Kessel*, 435. Geo London adds that de Lussats claimed he broke with

Stavisky around 1928 over mistreatment of a friend ("Le Baron de Lussats nous révèle les étonnantes relations de Bonny avec Stavisky," *Le Journal*, March 18, 1935, 2).

7. "La Mort tragique du conseiller Prince," *Le Matin*, March 30, 1934, 1, 5.

8. "Louis Mitchell," *Afro-American*, January 25, 1930, A11.

9. Aldington, *An Autobiography in Letters*, 87.

10. Egan, *Florence Mills*, 87; "'Plantation Revue,' New Negro Show..."

11. Sampson, *Blacks in Blackface*, 815.

12. Birkhead, "Americans Attend Gala Outdoor Events."

13. Advertisement, *New York Herald*, October 5, 1928, 7.

14. Advertisement, *New York Herald*, October 18, 1928, 9.

15. "a nigger songstress": Undoubtedly Lydia Bourke, wife of the Alabamians' drummer—"an extremely beautiful colored girl" whose looks caused a sensation in Venice (Crowder with Speck, *As Wonderful as All That?* 68); see Aldington, *Autobiography in Letters*, 87–88.

16. Advertisement, *Le Journal*, November 10, 1928, 4.

17. Lotz, *Black People*, 340; Florence Richardson, "Notes of Paris," *New York Amsterdam News*, February 20, 1929, 8. Warner danced with the "Black Follies Bronz Girls," directed by Sidney Bechet (Adriano Mazzoletti, *Il jazz in Italia: Dalle origini alle grandi orchestre* [Turin: EDT, 2004], 208–9).

18. Crowder with Speck, *As Wonderful as All That?* 52; and see Lois Bancroft Long ("Lipstick"), "Tables for Two," *New Yorker*, May 5, 1928, 85.

19. Crowder with Speck, *As Wonderful as All That?* 55.

20. Ibid., 57–58.

21. *Chicago Defender*, December 12, 1931, quoted in Mazzoletti, *Il jazz in Italia*, 234.

22. "Elsa-Valse," sixth poem of the "Cantique à Elsa," *Les Yeux d'Elsa* (1942), *Œuvres complètes*, vol. 1., ed. Olivier Barbarant (Paris: Gallimard [Pléiade 503], 2007), 802.

23. Forest, *Aragon*, 301.

24. Crowder with Speck, *As Wonderful as All That?* 61.

25. Cunard, *These Were the Hours*, 26.

26. Bob Slater, "Theatrical Jottings," *New York Age*, October 20, 1928, 6.

27. Aldington, *Autobiography in Letters*, 92.

28. Crowder with Speck, *As Wonderful as All That?* 70.

29. Aldington, *Autobiography in Letters*, 88. Nancy's libertinism extended to women; she had a fondness for La Perle. See Chisholm, *Nancy Cunard*, 66, and Crowder with Speck, *As Wonderful as All That?* 77, 106–7. Dolly Wilde was the witty niece of Oscar Wilde.

30. Crowder with Speck, *As Wonderful as All That?* 98.

31. See Gordon, *Nancy Cunard*, 176, and Crowder with Speck, *As Wonderful as All That?* 104–7, 98–99.

32. Crowder with Speck, *As Wonderful as All That?* 104.

33. Ibid., 68.

34. Cunard, *These Were the Hours*, 26, 29.

35. James J. Wilhelm, *Ezra Pound in London and Paris* (University Park: Pennsylvania State University Press, 1990), 293; "Venice Witnesses Historic Umbrian Candle Game," *New York Herald*, September 19, 1928, 7; Crowder with Speck, *As Wonderful as All That?* 71.

36. Robert L. Allen, "Epilogue," in Crowder with Speck, *As Wonderful as All That?* 195.
37. Cunard, *These Were the Hours*, 53.
38. Aldington, *An Autobiography in Letters*, 88.
39. Crowder with Speck, *As Wonderful as All That?* 78–79.
40. "Inexplicably, they always drifted back": Wiggins, "Paris Street Scene"; "rejoining what Aragon described": Aragon, *Mauvais Plaisant*, 343.
41. "Le Costa-Bar, rue Fontaine à Pigalle" (1930), Paris, Galérie au Bonheur du Jour.
42. "Combat de nègres à Montmartre," *Comœdia*, January 3, 1929, 4.
43. "Rue Fontaine à Paris: des musiciens nègres échangent 16 balles de revolver et blessent trois passants," *Le Petit Journal*, December 23, 1928, 8.
44. Bechet, *Treat It Gentle*, 151.
45. Crowder with Speck, *As Wonderful as All That?* 80.
46. Olivier Weber, *Dictionnaire amoureux de Joseph Kessel* (Paris: Plon, 2019), 1003; Courrière, *Joseph Kessel*, 316.
47. Courrière, *Joseph Kessel*, 311–13.
48. Ibid., 317, 391.
49. Crowder with Speck, *As Wonderful as All That?* 80.
50. Lloyd, *Eugene Bullard*, 103. Unaware that Hubert was Bechet's lawyer, Lloyd speculates that Bullard sought assistance from his friend Robert Henri (104).
51. "Baron de Lussats": Dining with Torrès at Chez Nine, Rosenthal noted that "at the next table the Baron de Lussats downed his clear, fruit brandy. The night before, at the Capitole, he had lodged a bullet in the wrist of a rich American" (Rosenthal, *Avocat de Trotsky*, 65). Police had not identified the gunman, but Nine regulars would have been better informed. For the sources of this story see "Le Capitole ensanglanté," *Paris-Soir*, February 8, 1928, 1; "Montmartre la nuit," *L'Humanité*, February 8, 1928, 2; "Des Bagarres dans un restaurant de nuit," *Le Journal*, February 8, 1928, 3; "White Southerners Cause Paris Riot," *Afro-American*, March 3, 1928, 2.
52. She refers to him only as "the Baron" (Bricktop, *Bricktop*, 166–70). Courrière (*Joseph Kessel*, 314) and Patrice Bollon (*Pigalle: Le Roman noir de Paris* [Paris: Hoëbeke, 2004], 120) claim, without evidence, that after the Capitole, de Lussats managed the Grand Duc.
53. Fitzgerald, *Tender Is the Night*, ed. Goldman, 245.
54. Bricktop, *Bricktop*, 167.
55. Chevalier, *Montmartre du plaisir*, 395.
56. Aragon, *Les Beaux Quartiers*, 208.
57. Bullard's resistance to intolerance earned him the title of "tamer of wild crackers" (Abbott, "My Trip Abroad," 1).
58. Bechet, *Treat It Gentle*, 156.
59. "U. S. Musicians Duel in Paris," *Detroit Free Press*, December 24, 1928, 8.
60. Bechet, *Treat It Gentle*, 153.
61. "Musicians in Gun Battle Over Girl in Paris Café," *Chicago Defender*, December 29, 1928, 1.
62. Glover Compton, "Chicago Musician Brands Tale in American Papers," *Chicago Defender*, February 9, 1929, 2.

63. London, "Une bataille de nègres."
64. Bechet, *Treat It Gentle*, 152.
65. London, "Une bataille de nègres."
66. Crowder with Speck, *As Wonderful as All That?* 81.
67. Advertisement, *New York Herald*, June 21, 1929, 11.
68. *Comœdia* thought the latter played "with taste" but lacked "force and emotion" ("Les Attractions de la Quinzaine," November 21, 1928, 4).
69. Louis Fourès, "Tribunaux: Joséphine Baker's Impérial," *Comœdia*, January 26, 1926, 2.
70. Advertisements, *New York Herald*, October 19, 1928, 9; February 9, 1929, 2.
71. Classified advertisement, and advertisement, *New York Herald*, January 5, 1929, 10; June 11, 1929, 15.
72. Advertisement, *New York Herald*, March 12, 1929, 6; Florence Richardson, "Notes of Paris," *New York Amsterdam News*, June 5, 1929, 12.
73. Florence Richardson, "Notes of Paris," *New York Amsterdam News*, August 21, 1929, 9; September 25, 1929, 8; Cooke, "Mitchell Closes Paris Nightclub."
74. Cooke, "Mitchell Closes Paris Nightclub."
75. Advertisement, *Comœdia*, December 11, 1929, 2.
76. "a young 'buck'": A racial slur, referring to a violent, African American male, a danger to white women.
77. "Ethel Waters to Open at Parisian Nite Club," *Chicago Defender*, January 4, 1930, 6; J. A. Rogers, "Foreign Observations," *Birmingham Reporter*, December 14, 1929, 4; Bricktop, "Letter to Carl Van Vechten" (October 5, 1929), quoted in Sharpley-Whiting, *Bricktop's Paris*, 61.
78. "Ethel Waters in 'Londontown,' Makes Big Hit," *Pittsburgh Courier*, December 21, 1929, 11.
79. Advertisement, *New York Herald*, December 13, 1929, 9.
80. Lotz, "Black Diamonds Are Forever."
81. Alain Romans, interviewed by Goddard, *Jazz Away from Home*, 278.
82. Miller, *Some Hustling This*, 173.
83. Ibid.
84. "Powerful Paris Newspaper Presented Negro Stars to Aid Flood Sufferers," *New York Amsterdam News*, April 16, 1930. 11.
85. "Entertain War Mothers," *Afro-American*, August 9, 1930, 9.
86. J. A. Rogers, "Foreign Observations," *Birmingham Reporter*, June 14, 1930, 4.
87. Cooke, "Mitchell Closes Paris Nightclub."
88. "Six-Day Bicycle Races Stir Parisians," *Brooklyn Eagle*, April 27, 1930, Sec. B, 7.
89. Advertisements, *Comœdia*, February 5, 1931, 5; February 19, 1931, 5; March 1, 1931, 3. Like Napoleon, Santo lived his "one hundred days." Leaving behind his Riviera Elba in 1932, he set out to reconquer Paris, launching the Atlantide. In his case, it lasted three years.
90. See Deyle, *Carry Me Back*, 243–44. The term derives from Black composer James A. Bland's "Carry Me Back to Old Virginny" (ca. 1878).
91. Fréjaville, "Paris sans voiles."
92. Ibid.

93. Raymond G. Carroll, "Nine Super Cabarets Are Operating Within Small Area in New York City; Patrons of Jazz Night Life Happy," *El Paso Herald*, extra, February 21, 1922, 4.

94. Maxwell, *R. S. V. P.*, 173. Tropical gardenias thrived during scorching southern summers.

95. Moore, *You're Only Human Once*, 70–71.

96. See "'Pickaninny' Ban Urged by Negroes," *New York Herald*, March 17, 1930, 1.

97. "journalist queried": Quoted in Hammond and O'Connor, *Josephine Baker*, 97; "jeeringly linking": "Joséphine Baker n'est comtesse qu'au cinéma," *Paris-Soir*, June 24, 1927, 1. Surprisingly, scholars still maintain that Josephine and Pepito were married (see, for example, Jayna Brown, *Babylon Girls: Black Women Performers and the Shaping of the Modern* (Durham, N.C.: Duke University Press, 2008), 256, or Gillett, "Crossing the Pond," 176. Questioned on the subject Pepito observed: "To divorce, one must first have been married" ("Joséphine Baker ne divorcera pas," *Le Journal*, January, 1936, 2).

98. Jules-Rosette, *Josephine Baker in Art*, 55.

99. On the Nardals see Edwards, *Practice of Diaspora*, 147–68.

100. Boittin, *Colonial Metropolis*, 125.

101. Edwards, *Practice of Diaspora*, 168.

102. Jane Nardal, "Pantins exotiques," 2.

103. Boittin, *Colonial Metropolis*, 21.

104. In *Paris Noir* Stovall analyzes *Bâton Rouge*, the story featuring Congo (71), and see Magloire, "Florence's Place," (31). On Morand and Nardal see Edwards, *Practice of Diaspora*, 169–71.

105. Jules-Rosette, *Josephine Baker in Art*, 43.

106. Lyrics and music: Tony Town, 1927. A segment of the Plantation tableau can be seen in *La Sirène des tropiques* (Siren of the tropics), Henri Etiévant and Mario Nalpas (1927).

107. See the photos in Hammond and O'Connor, *Josephine Baker*, 24–25.

108. Ashton Stevens, quoted in Robert Kimball and William Bolcom, *Reminiscing with Sissle and Blake* (New York: Viking Press, 1973), 180.

109. Cited by Boittin, *Colonial Metropolis*, 124.

110. McMullin, "Une Nuit à Paris," 12.

111. Schiller, "On Naïve and Sentimental Poetry," 232. In Greek mythology Elysium is the site of a future felicity.

112. Samuel Dashiell, "Paris Letter," *Vidette Messenger* (Valparaiso, Ind.), April 4, 1930, 4.

113. "'Plantation Revue,' New Negro Show..."

114. The number was sung by a Black jockey, Boule de Neige (act 1, scene 5).

115. Marin, *Utopics*, 199.

116. Jameson, "Of Islands and Trenches," 81.

EPILOGUE. "NO DOUBT ONE MUST BID THEM ADIEU"

The epigraph is from Sachs, *Au Temps du Bœuf*, 123.

1. Bricktop, *Bricktop*, 171.

2. "Oscar Mouvet, Noted Paris Night Club Owner Dies," *Chicago Tribune*, January 23, 1930, 14.

3. Minott Saunders, "France Thinks Stock Crash Will Check U.S. Spenders," *Appleton Post-Crescent* (Appleton, Wis.), November 29, 1929, 20.

4. Goffin, *Jazz*, 75.

5. Maxwell, *R. S. V. P.*, 210–11.

6. Vauchant, interviewed by Goddard, *Jazz Away from Home*, 268.

7. "Harry Pilcer Dies: Gaby Deslys Partner," *New York Herald*, January 18, 1961, 2.

8. Miller, *Some Hustling This!* 175; Bricktop, *Bricktop*, 205.

9. "Seeing the Sights of Paris," *Owensboro Messenger* (Owensboro, Ky.), August 14, 1940, 3. The article includes a chilling photograph.

BIBLIOGRAPHY

Abbott, Robert S. "My Trip Abroad." *Chicago Defender*, November 23, 1929, 1.
Aldington, Richard. *An Autobiography in Letters*. Edited by Norman T. Gates. University Park: Penn State University Press, 2010.
Allen, Robert L. "Epilogue." In Crowder and Speck, *As Wonderful as All That?*
"American Ballet in Paris Tonight." *New York Herald*, October 25, 1923, 6.
Aragon, Louis. *Aurélien*. Paris: Gallimard (Coll. Folio), 1972.
Aragon, Louis. *Le Mauvais Plaisant. La Défense de l'infini*. Edited by Lionel Follet. Paris: Gallimard, 1997.
Avocat, M. L'. "Defiant Confessions of an American Divorce Shark in Paris. Chap. VI." *Shreveport Times* (Shreveport, La.), May 29, 1927, Magazine Sect., n. pag.
Badger, Reid. *A Life in Ragtime: A Biography of James Reese Europe*. Oxford: Oxford University Press, 1995.
Baker, Jean-Claude, and Chris Chase. *Josephine Baker: The Hungry Heart*. New York: Cooper Square Press, 2001.
Baron, Jacques. *L'An I du Surréalisme*. Paris: De Noel, 1969.
Bastia, Jean. "La Soirée." *Comœdia*, May 10, 1921, 1.
Bechet, Sidney. *Treat It Gentle*. New York: Hill and Wang, 1960.
Bedu, Jean-Jacques. "Avant-propos." In Francis Carco, *Rue Pigalle*. Edited by Jean-Jacques Bedu. Paris: Laffont, 2004.
Beer, Peter J. *The Playboy Princes: The Apprentice Years of Edward VII and Edward VIII*. London: Peter Owen, 2014.
Bennett, Gwendolyn. "Wedding Day." In *Ebony Rising: Short Fiction of the Greater Harlem Renaissance Era*, edited by Craig Gable. Bloomington: Indiana University Press, 2004.
Bertelli, C. [Charles] F. "Britain Owes Gratitude to U. S. Dancer." *Shreveport Times* (Shreveport, La.), home ed., June 12, 1921, 15.
Bertelli, C. [Charles] F. "Fantasy Reigns in New Paris Café." *Washington Herald* (Washington, D.C.), December 1, 1922, 1.
Bertelli, C. [Charles] F. "Ice Cream King Hoists Stars and Stripes After Victory on Paris Front." *Buffalo Courier*, August 23, 1920, 2.
Bertelli, C. [Charles] F. "Shah of Persia's New Dance, 'Harem Hug,' Good Example of How World Advances." *Akron Beacon Journal* (Akron, Ohio), September 18, 1922, 1.
Bertelli, C. [Charles] F. "Wales Is Some Stepper-Out Like Granddad." *Davenport Democrat and Leader* (Davenport, Ia.), July 25, 1924, 19.
Birkhead, May. "Americans Attend Gala Outdoor Events in Paris." *New York Herald*, New York ed., June 11, 1922, Sec. 3, 9.
Birkhead, May. "Paris Is Deserted by Many for Riviera and St. Moritz." *New York Herald*, New York ed., December 24, 1922, Sec. 6, 5.

Blake, Jody. *Le Tumulte Noir: Modernist Art and Popular Entertainment in Jazz Age Paris, 1900–1930*. University Park: Pennsylvania State University Press, 1999.

Boittin, Jennifer Anne. *Colonial Metropolis: The Urban Grounds of Anti-Imperialism and Feminism*. Lincoln: University of Nebraska Press, 2015.

Bricktop [Ada Louise Smith], with James Haskins. *Bricktop*. New York: Atheneum, 1983.

Bricktop [Ada Louise Smith]. *Diary* [Holograph Manuscript]. Ada "Bricktop" Smith Papers, 1926–1983, Schomburg Center for Research in Black Culture, New York Public Library.

Bullard, Eugene J. "Shooting at Us." *Chicago Defender*, April 4, 1925, 7.

Carisella, P. J., and James W. Ryan. *The Black Swallow of Death*. Boston: Marlborough House, 1972.

Carlish, Richard, and Alan Bestic. *King of Clubs*. London: Elek Books, 1962.

Cazaux, Thierry. *Les Boulevards de Clichy et de Rochechouart*. Paris: Editions des Musées de la Ville de Paris, 2004.

Charlier, Jean-Michel, and Marcel Montarron. *Stavisky: Les secrets du scandale*. Paris: Laffont, 1974.

Chevalier, Louis. *Montmartre du plaisir et du crime*. Paris: Laffont, 1980.

Chevalier, Maurice. *Ma route et mes chansons*. Paris: Flammarion, 1998.

"Chez Florence." *Time Magazine* 9, no. 25 (1927): 14.

Chisholm, Anne. *Nancy Cunard*. New York: Knopf, 1979.

Claretie, Georges. "Gazette des Tribunaux. Night Club." *Le Figaro*, November 19, 1920, 2.

Cocteau, Jean. *Le Coq et l'Arlequin*. Paris: Editions de la Sirène, 1918.

Cohen, Milton A. *Hemingway's Laboratory: The Paris in Our Time*. Tuscaloosa: University of Alabama Press, 2012.

Cooke, Marvel. "Mitchell, American Boy Host to Prince." *New York Amsterdam News*, March 16, 1940, 13.

Cooke, Marvel. "Mitchell Closes Paris Nightclub; Returns." *New York Amsterdam News*, March 23, 1940, 4.

Cooke, Marvel. "Mitchell Loves His Baseball." *New York Amsterdam News*, March 9, 1940, 15.

Cooke, Marvel. "Mitchell, Sensation of Europe." *New York Amsterdam News*, March 2, 1940, 15.

Cooke, Marvel. "Step Up Mr. Louis Mitchell." *New York Amsterdam News*, February 24, 1940, 15.

Cooper, Opal. "Musical Career of Opal Cooper" [As told to Bertrand Demeusy]. *Record Research* 90 (1968): 3.

Courrière, Yves. *Joseph Kessel ou Sur la piste du lion*. Paris: Plon, 1985.

Crowder, Henry, with Hugo Speck. *As Wonderful as All That?* Navarro, Calif.: Wild Trees Press, 1987.

Cunard, Nancy. "Black Man and White Ladyship: An Anniversary." In *Essays on Race and Empire*, edited by Maureen Moynagh: Peterborough, Canada: Broadview Press, 2002.

Cunard, Nancy. *These Were the Hours. Memories of My Hours Press, Réanville and Paris: 1928–1931*. Edited by Hugh Ford. Carbondale: Southern Illinois University Press, 1969.

Dashiell, Samuel, and Thomas Cope. "Mysterious Baron a Central Figure in Stavisky Case." *Evening Times* (Sayre, Pa.), April 25, 1934, 3.

"Day by Day in Paris and Other Cities in France." *New York Herald*, August 10, 1919, 4.

Demuth, Charles. *Letters of Charles Demuth, American Artist, 1883–1935*. Edited by Bruce Kellner. Philadelphia: Temple University Press, 2000.

Dennie, Frank A. "News from Abroad." *Chicago Defender*, October 22, 1921, 6.
Deyle, Steven. *Carry Me Back. The Domestic Slave Trade in American Life*. New York: Oxford University Press, 2005.
Dougherty, Romeo L. "About Things Theatrical." *New York Amsterdam News*, February 7, 1923, 5.
Driggs, Frank, and Harris Lewine. *Black Beauty, White Heat: A Pictorial History of Classic Jazz, 1920–1950*. New York: William Morrow, 1982.
Edwards, Brent Hayes. *The Practice of Diaspora: Literature, Translation, and the Rise of Black Internationalism*. Cambridge: Harvard University Press, 2003.
Egan, Bill. *Florence Mills: Harlem Jazz Queen*. Lanham, Md.: Scarecrow Press, 2004.
Evans, George H. "Letter from Paris." *Chicago Defender*, July 18, 1925, 6.
"Even the Daring Mlle Dherlys Was Ashamed." *Pittsburgh Press*, April 17, 1921, American Weekly Sec., n. pag. [9].
Fitzgerald, F. Scott. *The Crack-up*. Edited by Edmund Wilson. New York: New Directions Paperbacks, 1956.
Fitzgerald, F. Scott. *Ledger, 1919–1938* [Holograph Manuscript]. University of South Carolina. Irwin Dept. of Rare Books and Special Collections.
Fitzgerald, F. Scott. *Tender Is the Night*. Edited by Arnold Goldman. London: Penguin Classics, 2000.
Fitzgerald, F. Scott. *Tender Is the Night: The Melarky and Kelly Versions. Part 2*. Edited by Matthew J. Bruccoli. New York: Garland, 1990.
"Flo Jones Dies; Heart Failure." *Inter-State Tattler* (New York), January 7, 1932, 2.
Forest, Philippe. *Aragon*. Paris: Gallimard, 2015.
Fourès, Louis. "Tribunaux: Jazz-band et Passe anglaise." *Comœdia*, October 23, 1922, 7.
Fréjaville, Gustave. "Paris sans voiles." *Comœdia*, May 30, 1923, 1.
Fry, Andy. *Paris Blues*. Chicago: University of Chicago Press, 2014.
Gendron, Bernard. *Between Montmartre and the Mudd Club: Popular Music and the Avant-Garde*. Chicago: University of Chicago Press, 2002.
Gill, Brendan. *Cole: A Biographical Essay*. Edited by Robert Kimball. New York: Holt, Rinehart & Winston, 1971.
Gillett, Rachel Anne. *At Home in Our Sounds: Music, Race, and Cultural Politics in Interwar Paris*. New York: Oxford University Press, 2021.
Gillett, Rachel Anne. "Crossing the Pond: Jazz, Race and Gender in Interwar Paris." PhD diss., Northeastern University, 2010.
Gillett, Rachel Anne. "Jazz and the Evolution of Black American Cosmopolitanism in Interwar Paris." *Journal of World History* 2, no. 3 (2010): 471–95.
Glassco, John. *Memoirs of Montparnasse*. Toronto: Oxford University Press, 1970.
Goddard, Chris. *Jazz Away from Home*. New York: Paddington Press, 1979.
Goffin, Robert. *Jazz: From the Congo to the Metropolitan*. Translated by Walter Schaap and Leonard G. Feather. New York: Doubleday, Doran, 1944.
Gordon, Lois. *Nancy Cunard: Heiress, Muse, Political Idealist*. New York: Columbia University Press, 2007.
Gramont, Elisabeth de (duchesse de Clermont-Tonnerre). *Souvenirs du monde*. Grasset, 1966.
Gravigny, Jean. *Montmartre en 1925*. Paris: Editions Montaigne, 1924.

Haggerty, Michael. "Michel Leiris: L'Autre qui apparaît chez vous [Interview with Michel Leiris]." *Jazz Magazine* 325 (1984): 34–36.

Hammond, Bryan, and Patrick O'Connor. *Josephine Baker*. Boston: Little Brown, 1988.

Heilig, Sterling. "Heilig Says Paris Is Mad Over Dancing." *Sunday Star* (Washington, D.C.), December 28, 1919, part 2, 3.

Hemingway, Ernest. *Dateline Toronto: The Complete "Toronto Star" Dispatches, 1920–1924*. Edited by William White. New York: Scribner's, 1985.

Hemingway, Ernest. "European Nightlife: A Disease." In *Dateline Toronto*.

Hemingway, Ernest. "Galloping Dominoes." In *Dateline Toronto*.

Hewitt, Nicholas. *Montmartre: A Cultural Study*. Liverpool: Liverpool University Press, 2017.

Hughes, Langston. *The Big Sea: An Autobiography*. London: Pluto Press, 1986.

Hurston, Zora Neale. "How It Feels to Be Colored Me." In *The Best American Essays of the Century*, edited by Joyce Carol Oates and Robert Atwan. Boston: Houghton Mifflin, 2000.

Jackson, Jeffrey H. *Making Jazz French: Music and Modern Life in Interwar Paris*. Durham, N.C.: Duke University Press, 2003.

Jacotot, Sophie. *Danser à Paris dans l'entre-deux-guerres: lieux, pratiques et imaginaires des danses de société des Amériques (1919–1939)*. Paris: Nouveau Monde, 2013.

Jameson, Fredric. "Of Islands and Trenches: Neutralization and the Production of Utopian Discourse." In *The Ideologies of Theory: Essays 1971–1986*. Vol. 2, *The Syntax of History*. Minneapolis: University of Minnesota Press, 1988.

Jankowski, Paul F. *Cette vilaine affaire Stavisky: Histoire d'un scandale politique*. Translated by Patrick Hersant. Paris: Fayard, 2000.

Jolo. "One Night in Paris." *Variety*, October 22, 1924, 2.

Jules-Rosette, Bennetta. *Josephine Baker in Art and Life: The Icon and the Image*. Urbana: University of Illinois Press, 2007.

Kiley, John Gerald (Jed). *Hemingway: An Old Friend Remembers*. New York: Hawthorn Books, 1965.

Kiley, John Gerald (Jed). "The Man Behind the Mask." *St. Louis Post-Dispatch*, May 9, 1937, part 8, 6.

Kiley, John Gerald (Jed). "My Friend Edward." *St. Louis Post-Dispatch*, April 4, 1937, part 6, 4.

Leiris, Michel. *L'Âge d'homme*. Paris: Gallimard (Coll. Folio), 1939.

Leiris, Michel. *Journal. 1922–1989*. Edited by Jean Jamin. Paris: Gallimard, 1992.

Leiris, Michel. "Paris-Minuit." *Magazine Littéraire: Michel Leiris*, no. 302 (September 1992): 60–61.

"'L'Oasis' Is the Brilliant Gala Spot for Paris Fêtes." *Vogue*, British edition, December 1919, 65.

Lloyd, Craig. *Eugene Bullard: Black Expatriate in Jazz Age Paris*: Athens: University of Georgia Press, 2000.

London, Géo [Samuel Georges London]. "Le Baron de Lussats nous révèle les étonnantes relations de Bonny avec Stavisky." *Le Journal*, March 18, 1935, 2.

London, Géo [Samuel Georges London]. "Une bataille de nègres a son épilogue en correctionnelle." *Le Journal*, March 1, 1929, 1.

London, Géo [Samuel Georges London]. "La meurtrière du maestro noir son mari est acquittée par le jury de la Seine." *Le Journal*, October 8, 1926, 1.

Loos, Anita. *A Girl Like I*. New York: Viking Press, 1966.

Lotz, Rainer E. "Black Diamonds Are Forever: A Glimpse of the Prehistory of Jazz in Europe." *Black Perspective in Music* 12, no. 2 (1984): 214–36.
Lotz, Rainer E. *Black People: Entertainers of African Descent in Europe and Germany*. Bonn: Birgit Lotz, 1997.
Magloire, Magali. "Florence's Place: Host(ess)ing Revolution in Interwar Black Paris." *Palimpsest: A Journal on Women, Gender, and the Black International* 10, no. 1 (2021): 23–42.
Manier, Stéphane. "La Vie prodigieuse et néfaste de l'escroc Stavisky: Des amours mouvementées." *Paris-Soir*, April 15, 1934, 3.
Marin, Louis. *Utopics: Spatial Play*. Translated by Robert A. Vollrath. Atlantic Highlands, N.Y.: Humanities Press, 1984.
Martin, Denis-Constant, and Olivier Roueff. *La France du Jazz: Musique, modernité et identité dans la première moitié du XXe siècle*. Marseilles: Parenthèses, 2002.
[Martin, Lawrence]. "Wales Knee Lobs Where Races Mix and Night's Long." *Daily News* (New York), first ed., April 19, 1924, 10.
Martin, Lawrence. "Wales Plays Around Paris." *Mount Carmel Item* (Mount Carmel, Pa.), April 1, 1924, 1.
Maxwell, Elsa. *R. S. V. P.: Elsa Maxwell's Own Story*. Boston: Little, Brown, 1954.
Mazzoletti, Adriano. *Il jazz in Italia: Dale origini alle grandi orchestra*. Turin: EDT, 2004.
McAlmon, Robert. *Being Geniuses Together*. London: Secker & Warburg, 1938.
McAlmon, Robert. *The Nightinghouls of Paris*. Edited by Sanford J. Smoller. Urbana: University of Illinois Press, 2007.
McElhone, Harry, and Wynn Holcomb. *Barflies and Cocktails: 300 Recipes*. Paris: Lecram, 1927.
McMullin, John. "Une Nuit à Paris." *Vogue*, June 1, 1927, 12, 33.
McMullin, John.. "Paris and London When Night-Life Is in Flower." *Vogue*, New York ed., June 15, 1923, 35.
Meyrick [Merrick], Kate. *Secrets of the 43*. London: John Long, 1933.
Miller, Mark. *Some Hustling This! Taking Jazz to the World: 1914–1929*. Toronto: Mercury Press, 2005.
Montboron. "The Synco-Synco Orchestra." *Comœdia*, February 16, 1922, 2.
Montmartre: Album descriptif de Montmartre en 1927. Paris: Editions artistiques de Paris, 1927.
"Montmartre Scene of Dramatic Raid on Gambling Club." *New York Herald*, May 1, 1922, 6.
Moore, Grace. *You're Only Human Once*. New York: Doubleday, 1944.
Moss, Arthur. "The Birth of the I.B.F." In McElhone and Holcomb, *Barflies and Cocktails*.
[Mouvet], Maurice. "The Latest Dances and How to Dance Them." *El Paso Herald*, weekend ed., April 6, 1912, 24.
[Mouvet], Maurice. "On with the Dance. Maurice Protests Against the Tendency to Artistic Bolshevism in Ballroom." *Ogden Standard Examiner* (Ogden, Utah), July 26, 1920, 5.
[Mouvet], Maurice. "Shall America Have a Distinctive Social Dance?" *Sun Telegram* (Clarksburg, W.Va.), October 3, 1915, 28.
Nardal, Jeanne, "Pantins exotiques." *La Dépêche africaine*, October 1928, 2.
Nash, Jean. "The Best-Dressed and Most Extravagant Woman in the World." *Pittsburgh Press*, March 22, 1925, American Weekly Sec., n. pag. [6– 7].
Nettlebeck, Colin. *Dancing with de Beauvoir: Jazz and the French*. Melbourne: Melbourne University Press, 2004.

Nevers, Daniel. "Tom Waltham: Un Anglais à Paris." *Sonorités* 12 (1985): 27–32.
Nevill, Ralph. *Days and Nights in Montmartre and the Latin Quarter*. New York: George H. Doran, 1927.
"News of Paris Day by Day; Police Slice High Cost of Drinking." *New York Herald*, June 12, 1920, 6.
Noctambule, Le. "Une soirée au Zelli's Club." *Paris-Danse*, June 11–17, 1920, 5.
O'Brien, John. "American Is King in Paris Cabarets and Dollar Shouts." *Pittsburgh Daily Post*, May 26, 1924, 2.
Okihiro, Gary Y. "Afterword: Toward a Black Pacific." In *AfroAsian Encounters: Culture, History, Politics*. Edited by Heike Raphael Hernandez and Shannon Steen. New York: New York University Press, 2006.
"Paris Court's Fine of Ex-Jazz King Reveals Tragi-Comedy of Montmartre." *New York Herald*, October 22, 1922, 1.
Parker, R. A. "Paris, Madly Jazzing, Sees Jazz as the Music of the Future." *New York Tribune*, March 20, 1921, part 7, 3.
Pénet, Martin. *Mistinguett: La Reine du music-hall*. Paris: Editions Du Rocher, 1995.
Pernet, Robert. "*Quiproquo*—Louis Mitchell or Murray Pilcer? Robert Goffin vs. Jean Cocteau." *Record Memory Club Magazine* 50 (March 2000): n. pag.
Pernet, Robert, and Howard Rye. "Visiting Firemen 18: Louis Mitchell." In *Storyville 2000–2001*, edited by Laurie Wright. Chigwell, Essex: L. Wright, 2001.
"'Plantation Revue,' New Negro Show Is Like Minstrels." *New York Herald*, July 18, 1922, 8.
Porter, Cole. *The Letters of Cole Porter*. Edited by Cliff Eisen and Dominic McHugh. New Haven: Yale University Press, 2019.
"Raid American's Paris Club," *New York Times*, May 1, 1922, 7.
Rogers, J. A. "Paris Notes." *Pittsburgh Courier*, November 3, 1928, Sec. 1, 5.
Rose, Andrew. *The Woman Before Wallis: Prince Edward, the Parisian Courtesan, and the Perfect Murder*. New York: Picador, 2013.
Rosenthal, Gérard. *Avocat de Trotsky*. Paris: Laffont, 1975.
Roueff, Olivier. *Jazz, les échelles du plaisir*. Paris: La Dispute, 2013.
Rye, Howard. "Southern Syncopated Orchestra: The Roster." *Black Music Research Journal* 30, no. 1 (2010): 19–70.
Sachs, Maurice. *Au Temps du Bœuf sur le toit*. Paris: Grasset, 1987.
Sampson, Henry T. *Blacks in Blackface: A Sourcebook on Early Black Musical Shows*. 2nd ed. Lanham, Md.: Scarecrow Press, 2014.
Schiller, Friedrich. "On Naïve and Sentimental Poetry." In *Essays*, edited by Walter Hinderer and Daniel O. Dahlstrom. New York: Continuum, 1933.
Schmitt, Georges. "Un animateur." *Comœdia*, December 4, 1929, 2.
Séité, Yannick. *Le Jazz à la lettre: La littérature et le jazz*. Paris : Presses Universitaires de France, 2010.
Sem [Georges Goursat]. *La Ronde de Nuit*. Paris: Arthème Fayard, 1923.
Sem [Georges Goursat]. *White Bottoms*. Paris: Succès, 1927.
Shack, William A. *Harlem in Montmartre: A Paris Jazz Story Between the Great Wars*. Berkeley: University of California Press, 2001.
Sharpley-Whiting, T. Denean. *Bricktop's Paris: African American Women in Paris Between the Two World Wars*. Albany: State of New York University Press, 2015.

Sirkis, Jean-Jacques. *Les Années Deslys*. Paris: Jean Lafitte, 1990.
Snelson, Floyd G. "Once Toast of Europe's Gayest Resorts, America's Brown Beauty Passes Away Minus Funds, Friends." *Pittsburgh Courier*, January 30, 1932, Sec. 2, 6.
Sobol, Louis. "The Voice of Broadway [Interview with Joe Zelli]." *Minneapolis Tribune*, December 24, 1931, 6.
"Soldiers Try to Make Money in France." *Chanute Daily Tribune* (Chanute, Kans.), November 18, 1919, 1.
Soupault, Philippe. *Mémoires de l'oubli, 1914–1923*. Paris: Lachenal & Ritter, 1997.
Soupault, Philippe. *Mémoires de l'oubli, 1927–1933*. Paris: Lachenal & Ritter, 1997.
Soupault, Philippe. *Le Nègre*. Paris: Gallimard, 1997.
Soupault, Philippe. *Terpsichore*. Paris: Hazan, 1986.
Stovall, Tyler. *Paris Noir: African Americans in the City of Light*. Boston: Houghton Mifflin, 1996.
Tise, Suzanne. "Francis Jourdain." In *Jourdain. Frantz 1847–1935, Francis 1876–1958, Frantz-Philippe 1906*, translated by Philippe Bonnet. Paris: Editions du Regard, 1988.
"Too Outrageous to Be Allowed to Live Even in Gay Paris," *Pittsburgh Press*, April 18, 1926.
Tournès, Ludovic. *New Orleans sur Seine: Histoire du Jazz en France*. Paris: Fayard, 1999.
Touzot, Jean. *Jean Cocteau*. Lyon: La Manufacture, 1989.
"Tragic Death Overtakes Every Woman He Loves." *Pittsburgh Press*, November 2, 1924, American Weekly Sec., n. pag. [2–3].
Turner, Jack. "A Summer in Paris: Memories of College Jazz Band out on the Town." *Chicago Tribune*, October 28, 1984, Sec. 12, 3.
"Une descente de police au 'Tempo-Club' de la rue Fontaine." *Le Petit Parisien*, May 1, 1922, 2.
Van Vechten, Carl. *The Splendid Drunken Twenties: Selections from the Daybooks, 1922–1930*. Urbana: University of Illinois Press, 2003.
Vaughn, Hal. *Sleeping with the Enemy: Coco Chanel, Nazi Agent*. London: Chatto and Windus, 2011.
Vautel, Clément. "Mon Film." *Le Journal*, May 2, 1922, 1.
Wales, Henry. "Chicago 'Scribe' Coins Dough in Paris Jazz-House." *Pittsburgh Daily Post*, August 10, 1919, Sec. 5, 2.
Wales, Henry. "Dance Halls of Paris Are Closed." *Spokesman-Review* (Spokane, Wash.), November 28, 1919, 1.
Wales, Henry. "Prince of Wales Becomes Jazz Band Addict." *Chicago Tribune*, April 17, 1924, 3.
Wales, Henry. "Yankee Negroes in Paris Beat Up Man with Bride." *Chicago Tribune*, January 2, 1923, 17.
Warnod, André. *Les Bals de Paris*. Paris: Grès, 1922.
Weber, Ronald. *News of Paris: American Journalists in the City of Light Between the Wars*. Chicago: Ivan R. Dee, 2006.
Wiggins, Edgar A. "Paris Is My Beat." *Philadelphia Tribune*, October 26, 1971, 11.
Wiggins, Edgar A. "Paris Street Scene." *Chicago Defender*, June 3, 1933, 11.
Williams, A. Wilberforce. "Americans in Paris; What They Are Doing." *Chicago Defender*, November 19, 1921, 3.
[Woon, Basil]. "'Fashionable' Americans in Paris Find Thrills in Tiny 'Dive' as Guests of Negress." *Buffalo Courier* (Buffalo, N.Y.), July 13, 1925, 1.
Woon, Basil. "Mirrors of Paris." *Albuquerque Journal*, July 3, 1927, 16.

Woon, Basil. "Mirrors of Paris." *Courier Journal* (Louisville, Ky.), August 8, 1926, Sec. 2, 11.
Woon, Basil. "Mirrors of Paris." *Courier Journal* (Louisville, Ky.), May 16, 1926, Sec. 4, 6.
Woon, Basil. "Mirrors of Paris," *Courier-Journal* (Louisville, Ky.), May 23, 1926, Sec. 2, 12.
Woon, Basil. *The Paris That's Not in the Guide Books*. New York: Robert M. McBride, 1931.
[Woon, Basil]. "Parisians Ready for Influx of Good American Dollars During 1924 Olympic Games." *Shreveport Times* (Shreveport, La.), March 30, 1924 B2.
[Woon, Basil] "Powerful World Drug Ring Stirs European Police." *Indianapolis Sunday Star*, April 22, 1922, 33–34.
[Woon, Basil]. "Presence of Wales 'Makes' Monday Night for Parisian Cafés; Otherwise It's Dull Time; Prince Displays Keen Delight for Dancing." *Cincinnati Enquirer*, May 11, 1924, News Sec., 36.
"World-Famed Dancer Says He'd Pick Prettier Girl than 'Peggy' Hopkins." *Pittsburgh Press*, April 13, 1921, 1–2.
"Zelli's Club." *Paris-Danse*, April 16–4 June 1920, 5.

INDEX

Abatino, Giuseppe ("Count" Pepito "Pepy"), 103–5, 153
Abbaye de Thélème, L', 1, 29, 74–75, 100
Abbott, Berenice, 148–49
Acacias, Les (Maxwell), 62, 164, 176–77
Acacias, Les (Maxwell and O. Mouvet), 57–60, 62
Ad-Libs, 96–99
Aflalo, Albert (Gros Albert), 170
Ahmad Shah Qajar, Shah of Persia, 65, 66, 68, 76–77, 104, 115
Alabama, evocation of, 71, 130–31, 134, 164, 165, 178, 181
Alabamians (band), 165–73, 176
Aladdin's Lamp Club, 17, 18, 21, 123, 194n30
Aldington, Richard, 163–64, 167–68
Alfonso XIII, king of Spain, 76–77, 115
Alhambra Theater, 13, 95
Allen, Ferdie, 100
Ambrose, Eleanora, 74, 75
American Federation of Musicians, 36
American Foxtrot Club, 16–17, 35, 113
American Soldiers and Sailors' Club, 21
America's Sweetheart. *See* Hughes, Leonora
Amette, Léon-Adolphe, 15
Ansaldi, Jules, 47
Apollo Theater, 29, 43; Harry Pilcer's *Dancing*, 15, 35–38, 131
Aragon, Louis: as actor-witness in Montmartre, 5; and N. Cunard, 166–73; on exoticism, 38, 41; on gangsters, 171; on Harlem compared to Montmartre, 146; at Kiley's Gaity, 119–21, 125; on Russians, 135; at Tempo Club, 85–86; Zelli's Royal Box, novelization of, 95–96, 98, 101–3, 107–8
Argentineans, 14, 73
aristocracy and royalty, 57, 65–68, 76–78, 115, 140, 142–44, 148, 153–54. *See also*

Ahmad Shah Qajar, Shah of Persia; Edward David, Prince of Wales
Armistice, 57
Arnold, Billy, 116, 155
Arsène's, 103, 170
"Aunt Jemima," 134, 174, 175
Author's Club, 17–18

Baby Doll (Mme Zelli), 95, 108
Baker, Josephine: and Abatino, relationship, 103–5; banana skirt, 103; and Black Bottom, 218n70; in blackface, 177; Charleston Jazz Band, 75; and Chez Joséphine, 105; and exoticism, 178–79; and Grand Duc, 153; and Grand Duc (Bricktop), 103–4; and L'Impérial, 103, 104–5, 153, 173; and plantation-themes setting, 164; and racism, 177; *La Revue nègre*, 16, 75
ban on modern dances, in England, 54–55, 69
Baron, Jacques, 106, 154
Baron, the (Gaëtan Lherbon de Lussats), 163, 170, 171, 225n51
Barreto, Marino, 174
Barton, Roy, 48
Basualdo, Carlos Ortiz, 73
Bate, Freddy, 65, 204n44
Bate, Vera, 65, 77, 115, 204n44
Bayes, Nora, 142–43
Bechet, Sidney, 162, 168–73
Bennett, Barbara, 73–74
Bennett, Gwendolyn, 7, 146
Berryer, Léo, 121, 214n61
Berschad, Bobby, 33
Bey, Ali Kamel Fahmy, 68–69
Bey, Princess Marguerite (Maggie) Marie Laurent Meller Fahmy, 68–69, 141
Biarritz Acacias, 60, 74, 77

237

Bingham, Jocelyn A. "Frisco," 75, 139, 164, 206n85, 217n49
Birth of a Nation, 117
Black Bottom, 15, 54, 138–40, 142–43, 150, 218n70, 221n23
blackface, 40, 49, 57–58, 84, 135, 141–44, 176–77
Black Gold Star mothers, 175
Black-owned clubs: Morgan's *Dancing*, 37; need for, 129–30; Tempo Club first Black owned and managed in Pigalle, 81–82; white patrons, reliance on, 149–61. *See also* Tempo Club
Black performers: audience demands for, 35; erasure of, 117–18; Le Jardin de ma Soeur, 75; and racism, 5, 67, 94–96, 111, 125–26. *See also* Bricktop; Bullard, Eugene; Jones, Florence; Jones, Palmer; Mitchell, Louis
Blazer, Albert (Glazer), 44
Bloch, Fanny (aka Jeanne "Lulu" Darcy), 21–22, 25, 26–27, 47
Boll, Mabel, 137–38
Boucot, Louis, 29–30, 41–42
Bouquin, Regina "Bouglor," 136, 145
Boyard, Marie-Louise (Madame Crutcher), 100, 170
Boyd, Joe, 82, 89, 175
Bricktop: and birthday party in Venice, 157; and Black Gold Star mothers, 175; on cocaine use of patrons, 107; on decline of Montmartre, 183; departure from Paris, 185; description of, 147–48, 160–61; and Edward, Prince of Wales, 67, 138; and Fitzgerald, 149, 151–54, 157; and Le Floresco, 176; on gangster violence, 171; and Gilmore, 147–50; and Grand Duc, 146–47, 220–21n16; and Harem, 220–21n16; on Hemingway, 142; and Impérial, 173, 220–21n16; and F. Jones, 56, 151; and Maxwell, 150; miscegenation, views on, 159; Mitchell partnership with, 138; and Le Monico, 220–21n16; at Music Box, 138, 220–21n16; and de Polignac, 158; and Porter, 49, 149–50, 157, 160; on race, 132, 157–59; and Ward, 151–52; and white patrons, 149–61; on Zito and Abatino, 103–4
Briggs, Arthur, 70
British King of Jazz (Jack Hylton), 97

"Broadway in miniature," 46
Brodmann-Alfaro, 172–73
Brooks, Antoinette, 137
"buck," 174
Bullard, Eugene: arrival in Paris, 23; and Bechet and McKendrick, 170–71; and Cadet Rousselle, 22–24; and charity concert for flood victims, 175; and Comedy Club, 100; and L'Escadrille, 100, 185; espionage work, 185; and Grand Duc, 99, 130; life before Paris, 3, 171; on Mitchell, 136; photograph with crowd, 155; race-based attacks on, 23, 113–14, 133, 171; scholarship on, inaccuracies, 191n6; United States, return to and death in, 185; Zelli relationship with, 99–100. *See also* Grand Duc (Bullard)
Burke, Jerome (Romie), 166
Burke, Lydia, 224n15
Burleigh, Bertram, 121

Cadet Rousselle, 21–28, 135; scholarship on, inaccuracies, 191n6
Capitole, Le, 29, 162–63; under Jules Volterra, 171
Caples, Muriel Buell, 122
Carlish, Dick, 84, 89, 94, 98, 120
Caron, commissioner of the Sureté Générale, 106, 107
Carpentier, Georges, 117, 142–43
"carry-me-backs," 176–79
Casino de Paris, 29–45, 122; scholarship on, inaccuracies, 192n12
Catholic church, 15
Caulk, Joe, 8, 115, 158
Chanel, Coco, 75, 76, 204n44
charity concert for flood victims, 175
Charleston (dance), 49, 75, 139, 150, 164, 218n70
Charleston Jazz Band, 75
Château et Caveau caucasiens, 135
Chevalier, Louis, 4
Chevalier, Maurice, 32
Chez Florence (36 rue Pigalle), 72–73, 105; and racism, 134–35; scholarship on, inaccuracies, 191n6
Chez Florence (61 rue Blanche), 74, 139–44; after Florence's death, 145; and Mitchell's, same address, 136; and

Palmer's death, 168–69; and racism, 134–35
Chez Florence (New York City), 144
Chez Harry Pilcer: at Cadet Rousselle former location, 42–43; inaccuracies in scholarship, 46–47; and Kiley, 123; in Poiret's garden, 38; and Red Devils, 85
Chez Henri, 76
Chez Joséphine, 105
Chez Nine, 170
Chez Vous (Venice), 139, 157
Chief Mogul of Montmartre. *See* Zelli, Giuseppe Salvatore "Joe"
Chimot, Edouard, 106
Cid of the Charleston (Leon Crutcher), 100, 191n5
Clarke, Charlie, 174
Clef Club, 36
Clover Club, 21, 24, 25, 40
Club Daunou, 94–95
Club des Lapins, 109, 184
coal, shortages of, 14–15, 17–18
cocaine, 77, 106–8
Cocteau, Jean, 30–31, 35–36, 97
College Inn, 118, 125
Colored Don Juan (Leon Crutcher), 100, 191n5
"Colored Gentleman." *See* Mitchell, Louis
Colored Nightingale of Montmartre. *See* Jones, Florence
Colored Queen of Montmartre. *See* Jones, Florence
Comedy Club, 100
Compton, J. Glover, 100, 168–73
Cook, Will Marion, 83, 84
Cooper, Opal, 36, 144
Cossitt, James "Jimmy," 125
Costa Bar, 169–70
"Countess" Abatino. *See* Baker, Josephine
"Countess" Arabella von Frankenstein, 120, 125
Crackerjacks, 70, 114, 115, 116, 170
Crewe-Milne, Robert, 69, 77
Crowder, Henry, 67, 162, 165–73, 175
Crutcher, Leon, 75, 100, 158, 191n5
Cunard, Edward, 166
Cunard, Maud, 65, 66, 67–68, 77
Cunard, Nancy, 67, 68, 162, 165–73
Cunard, Victor, 166, 170

Curzon, George, 54, 69
Curzon, Grace, 54, 65, 69

Dadaists, 85–86, 87–88, 119, 160
Dance Hall King. *See* Kiley, John Gerald "Jed"
dancings: ban, lifted, 14, 34–35, 55; legalization of, 20; operating hours and curfews, 14–16, 18–19, 24–25, 43, 46; pretensions of, 17–18; as term, use of, 2, 14
Darcy, Jeanne (Jane). *See* Bloch, Fanny
Davis, Deering, 74
Day, June, 165
Dean, Jack, 151
Deauville Casino, 51, 120
demographics of Montmartre, 65–66, 102–3, 135, 136, 152–54
Dempsey, Jack, 60
Demuth, Charles, 86–87, 91–92
Désiré, Anatole, 210n52
Deslys, Gaby, 37–38; memorial to, envisioned, 43; and Pilcer, 29–32
Dherlys, la belle (Simone d'Herlys), 38–39
Diamond, Jack "Legs," 171
"Diamond Queens," 137–38
Dietrich, Marlene, 117
Dimitri, Grand Duke, 57, 65, 66
Dixie Club, 16
Dixie Ice Cream Company, 17–18
Dolly, Jenny, 58, 60, 71–72, 74, 77, 150, 176–77, 185
Dolly, Rosie, 60, 72, 74, 77, 150, 176–77, 185
Don Luis-Ferdinand of Bourbon-Orleans, 76–77
Dora (German ice skater), 113, 123
Drian, Etienne, 148–49
Driscoll, Charles B., 124–25
drugs, 18, 22, 77, 106–8
Duchamp, Marcel, 85–86
Duke of Westminster, 76
Dunbar Hotel (New York City), 87
Dynamo from Keokuk. *See* Maxwell, Elsa

Earl of Chester. *See* Edward David, Prince of Wales
Edward David, Prince of Wales: and Arsène's, 103; and Bricktop, 138, 158; and Crackerjacks, 115; Good Friday regrets, 77–78; at Le Jardin de ma Soeur, 64–71;

Edward David, Prince of Wales (*continued*) and F. Jones, 72–73, 76, 130–32, 140, 142–44; and Kiley, 69–70, 115, 120, 123; and Mitchell's (36 rue Pigalle), 130–32; at Music Box, 138; Paris, list of trips to, 219n75; and prostitutes, 140, 141

Edward VIII, king of England. *See* Edward David, Prince of Wales

El Garrón, 29, 133, 173

Emanuel, Victor, 175, 184

Embassy Club. *See* Jardin de ma Soeur, Le

Embassy gala. *See* Jardin de ma Soeur, Le

Emergency Quota Act (1921), 49

Errázuriz, Guillermo (Billy), 51–52, 60, 102

Escadrille, L', 100, 185

Esperanto, L', 175

Europe, James Reese, 13, 82, 96, 117

Evans, George, 155

Ex-Mogul of Montmartre. *See* Kiley, John Gerald "Jed"

exoticism, 81, 86, 162–64, 177–81

Fatal Man. *See* Kiley, John Gerald "Jed"

Faurens, Clara, 20–21

Fitch, Harold, 16, 17

Fitzgerald, F. Scott, 8–9; on American violence, 171; on Black musicians, 161; and Bricktop, 149, 151–54, 157; on Mitchell, 82

Flirting Club, 17, 18

Floresco, Le, 176, 220–21n16

Florida (club), 163

Folies Bergère, 103, 178–79

Folies Marigny, 34

Forde, Marion, 45, 121–22

43 Club, 120

foxtrot, 24, 38–39, 47–50, 51, 104, 113, 135, 160; in England, 54–55

Fox Trot King. *See* Kiley, John Gerald "Jed"

France as colonial power, 7, 133, 177–79

Francesca Rospigliosi, 112–13

gambling, 22, 82, 89–92, 137

gangsters, 89, 129, 163, 170

Garvey, Marcus, 132–33, 177

Gautier, Suzanne, 121

Gay Brummel Band, 172–73

gigolos, 102–6

Gilmore, Buddie: on Black musicians, status of, 157; celebrity of, 114–15, 147–50; at Clover Club, 40; at Tempo Club, 84–85; United States, return to, 184; and white patrons, 149–50; at Zelli's Royal Box, 98–99

Gilmore, Martha (Mattie) "Lady," 84, 148

Glover, Clarence M., 18, 21, 113

Gold Club, 17–18

Goudie, Frank "Big Boy," 100

Gould, Edith Kelly, 95

Grand Duc, 86; and Crutcher, 100; and Hemingway, 141–42; and F. Jones, 141–42

Grand Duc (Bricktop): and Baker, 103–4, 153; and Bricktop, 220–21n16; and Jardin de ma Soeur, 155; management of, 147; and Tempo Club legacy, 154–55, 159

Grand Duc (Bullard), 8, 130, 134–35, 145, 146–47

Grand Duc (Mitchell), 45, 78, 129–30

Grand Hotel Luna (Venice), 166

Grand Teddy, 55, 56

"Great Black Way," use of term, 7, 133–34

Gri-Gri d'Amour, The (*Paris qui Jazz* at the Casino), 38, 41–42

Guinan, Texas, 144

Guinan, Tommy, 144

Guitton, Maxime, 22, 25, 27

Gustaf V, king of Sweden, 153–54

Gwynne, Erskine, 64, 67, 118

Hall, Joseph, 88, 154

Harem, 220–21n16

Harem, The (*Paris qui Jazz* at the Casino), 38–40

Harlem Hellfighters, 13

"Harlem in Montmartre," 7, 129, 134, 146, 180

Harot and Léonard, 173

Harry Pilcer's *Dancing* at the Apollo Theater, 15, 35–38; Jazz Kings and racist white Americans, 131

Harry's Pilcer's *Dancing* at the Oasis, 40

hashish, 106

Havemeyer, Mrs. Freddie, 115

Hawaiians, 38, 41–42, 175

Hemingway, Ernest, 50–51, 91–92, 122–23, 130, 141–42

Henley, Bill, 16, 113, 116, 155
Henri, Robert, 22
Henry, prince of Britain, 140, 142–44
Hitler, Adolf, 183
homosexuality, 77, 158
Hubert, Raymond, 170, 225n50
Hughes, Langston, 56, 134–35, 140–41, 161
Hughes, Leonora, 47–48, 50, 53–54, 63–64, 73, 76
Hutchinson, Leslie, 158
Hylton, Jack, 97

I.B.F. (International Bar Flies), 116–18
I.B.F. Band, 116
Ice Cream King. *See* Kiley, John Gerald "Jed"
Impérial: and Baker, 103, 105, 153, 173; and Bricktop, 173, 220–21n16
International Five: and Biarritz Acacias, 74, 77; and Cooper, 144; France, expulsion from, 155; and Le Jardin de ma Soeur, 60, 71–73; and F. Jones, 203n74; at Mitchell's (36 rue Pigalle), 72; and M. Mouvet, 74; and racism, 94–95; at So-Different, 55. *See also* Jones, Palmer

Jack's Negro Band. *See* Bullard, Eugene
Jamerson, Georges, 129
Jardin de ma Soeur, Le: Black performers, 60, 71–73, 75; decline of, 71–72, 73–75; description of, 63, 67–68; directors and business partnerships, 60, 62–64, 71–72; and high society, 63–71; and Porter, 149, 221n17
jazz: Black performers, synonymous with, 19–20, 23; early jazz in Paris on rue de Clichy, 29–45; French performers as rare, 19; French views on, 35–36; improvisation, 84, 88, 97; musical critics on, 116; "soft jazz" versus "hot jazz," 97
jazz ballet, 48–50
Jazz Band du Majestic Hotel de New York, 36
Jazz Kings, 35, 43–45, 82–83, 122, 131, 173
Joe Puni's island ensemble, 43
Johnson, Ebba, 112
Johnson, William A., 18
Jolson, Al, 135, 141

Jones, Bobby (Bobbie), 88, 92, 115, 174
Jones, Fernando (Sonny), 113, 155
Jones, Florence: and Les Acacias, 60; arrival in Paris, 47–48; arrogance, charges of, 140–44, 151; and Bricktop, 151; and the Charleston, 139; and Edward, Prince of Wales, 71, 72–73, 130–32, 140, 142–44; fame of, 138–39; health decline and death of, 144, 184; and International Five, 203n74; legacy for Black musicians, 146–47; and Mitchell, 136–38, 145; at Mitchell's (36 rue Pigalle), 71; at Mitchell's Grand Duc, 78, 130, 141–42; and M. Mouvet, 71–73; and Palmer, 144–45; and racism, 130–36, 140–44; rue Pigalle, move to, 60–61; and Le Sans Souci, 57, 87; scholarship on, inaccuracies, 191n6; at So-Different, 53, 55; and Tempo Club, 86–87, 130; United States, visit to, 144; wealth of, 219n96; women, protection of, 145. *See also* Chez Florence (36 rue Pigalle); Chez Florence (61 rue Blanche)
Jones, Palmer: and Les Acacias, 60; death of, 144, 168–69; and Edward, Prince of Wales, 72–73; extramarital affairs, 145; fame of, 138–39; as Fisk graduate, 142; and Florence, 47, 144–45; at Le Jardin de ma Soeur, 71–73; and M. Mouvet, 71–73; and Le Sans Souci, 87; scholarship on, inaccuracies, 191n6. *See also* International Five
Joyce, Peggy Hopkins, 50–52, 59–60, 137–38, 157, 168
Joyce, Stanley, 51

Kanui and Lula, 41
Keech, Alvin, 41
Keech, Kelvin, 41
Kelly's Jazz Band, 22
Kiley, John Gerald "Jed": American Foxtrot Club, 16–17, 35, 113; arrival in Paris, 15–16; Author's Club, 17–18; as college athlete, 125; College Inn, 118, 125; curfews, 35; departure from Paris, 184; and Edward, Prince of Wales, 70, 123; as "fatal man," 111–13, 122, 125; Florida, move to, 124; and Hemingway, 122–23; with I.B.F., 116–18, 119;

Kiley, John Gerald "Jed" (*continued*)
and ice cream, 16, 17–18, 112–13; insolvency, 121, 122; Kiley's, 69–70, 71, 114–16; Kiley's Gaity, 119–20, 136; literary aspirations, 118–19, 123–26; Meyrick relationship with, 121; Mr. Will Stay-Up-Late Club, 18; racial views of, 70, 71, 111, 113–15, 116–18, 119, 125–26, 133; and romance, 111–13, 115, 121–23
Kiley's, 69–70, 71, 114–16
Kiley's Gaity, 119–20, 136
King of Cabaret Keepers. *See* Zelli, Giuseppe Salvatore "Joe"
King of Jazz. *See* Gilmore, Buddie
King of Negro Singers (Joe Boyd), 82, 89, 175
King of the Banjo (William A. Johnson), 18
Ku Klux Klan, 117, 143, 156

la Belle Dherlys (Simone Dherlys), 38–39
La Belle Leonora and Signor Valentino, 13
Lady Gilmore (Martha Gilmore), 84, 148
Lattimore, George William, 83, 84
le beau Sacha. *See* Stavisky, Serge Alexandre
Le Croque-mort (Gaëtan Lherbon de Lussats), 163, 170, 171, 225n51
Legare, Oliver (Ollie), 135–36
Leiris, Michel, 32, 41, 49, 87–88, 147, 160
Leslie, Lew. *See* Leslie's Plantation Room
Leslie's Plantation Room (New York City), 164, 175, 176–77
Letellier, Henri, 51–52
Livingston, "Ketchup King" Jefferson, 122
Louigi's, 78, 92
Love, Bessie, 74–75
"Lulu." *See* Bloch, Fanny
Lussats, Gaëtan Lherbon de, 163, 170, 171, 225n51
Lyman, Tommy, 48, 52, 219n75

MacArthur, Charles, 112
Madden, Owney "Killer," 25, 108
Maharajah of Indore, 66, 148, 220n11
Maharajah of Kapurthala, 65, 67, 68, 76
Manassa Mauler (Jack Dempsey), 60
Man Ray, 85–86, 148
Maré, Rolf de, 49
Marie, Grand Duchess, 65, 66

Marquis di Medici, 137
Marshall's (New York City), 86–87
Mary, queen of England, 54–55, 69
Maurice. *See* Mouvet, Maurice
Maurice and Eleanora's Club, 75
Maurice's Club at the Hotel Grande Bretagne, 47–48, 51, 54
Maurice's Club at the Théâtre Caumartin, 48, 51, 52, 92–93
Maxwell, Elsa: and Les Acacias, 57–61, 62; and Bricktop, 150; at Bullard's Grand Duc, 147; and M. Cunard, 67–68; departure from Paris, 184; and Grand Duc, 150; as I.B.F. member, 117; and Le Jardin de ma Soeur, 60, 62–63, 75; and O. Mouvet, 62–63, 72; and Porter, 150; racial views of, 57–58, 150, 177; and So-Different, 56–60, 62; in Venice, 157; and Ward, 151–52; and White Lyres, 202n58
May, Jack, 109
McClelland, Harry, 113
McCloskey, "Blink," 114, 155, 213n27
McElhone, Harry, 116
McIntyre, O. O., 116, 123–25, 131, 134
McKendrick, Mike, 162, 166–67, 168–73, 185
Mendl, Lady (Elsie de Wolfe), 158
Merrick's Gaity, 120–21, 125
Metten, Captain, 24–25, 90
Meyrick, Kate, 120–21, 125–26
Miles, Lizzie, 135–36, 155
Mills, Florence, 164
"Mily," 82–84, 88–89. *See also* Tempo Club
miscegenation: interracial interactions, 130–36, 152–54; interracial romance, 158–59, 162, 165–73; violence linked to, 172; white Americans' fear of, 8, 20, 42, 105, 125–26; and white-Indian relationships, 68–69. *See also* Crowder, Henry
Mistinguett, 32, 38–42, 130
Mitchell, Louis: and Black Gold Star mothers, 175; and Bricktop, 138; at Casino de Paris, 21, 32–34, 44–45; and charity concert for flood victims, 175; as "Colored Gentleman," 52, 53; family life, 137–38; Fitzgerald's fictional account of, 221–22n37; on French musicians, 33–34; gambling and finances of, 137, 138, 173,

175, 184; and Grand Duc, 129–30; jazz, role in establishment in Montmartre, 82–83; and F. Jones, 136–38, 145; legacy for Black musicians, 146–47; and Miles, 135–36; Pilcer collaboration begins, 34–35; and La Plantation, 173, 175; on race relations in France, 129; rue Pigalle, move to, 60–61; scholarship on, inaccuracies, 191n6, 192n12; and Seven Spades, 13, 20–21, 23; and Tempo Club, 82, 129–30; United States, return to, 145, 184. *See also* Casino de Paris; Jazz Kings

Mitchell's (36 rue Pigalle): and Black performers, 71, 72; and Chez Florence, 72–73; and Edward, Prince of Wales, 71, 130–32; integrated audiences, 131–32; scholarship on, inaccuracies, 191n6

Mitchell's (61 rue Blanche), 73, 120, 126, 135–38

Mitchell's Midnight Frolic Jazz Band, 34

Mitchell's Quick Lunch, 138, 173

Molyneux, Edward, 58–60, 62–63

Monico, Le, 171, 220–21n16

Monzat, Pierre, 24–25

Morand, Paul, 178

More, Thomas, 2, 156, 159

Moreau, Arsène, 210n52

Morgan's *Dancing*, 37

Mörner, Gösta, Countess. *See* Joyce, Peggy Hopkins

morphine, 106

Moss, Arthur, 116, 118

Moulin-Rouge, 81

Mouvet, Maurice: and Ambrose, 74; and Bennett, 73–74; exclusivity, use of, 59; health and death of, 71–72, 75–76, 139; and Hughes, 54, 73; at Le Jardin de ma Soeur, 63–64; and Joneses, 71–73; Maurice and Eleanora's Club, 75; Maurice's Club at the Hotel Grande Bretagne, 47, 51, 54; Maurice's Club at the Théâtre Caumartin, 48, 51, 52, 92–93; and Oscar, rift, 58; at Le Perroquet, 54; on race and jazz, 53, 71–73, 74

Mouvet, Oscar: and L'Abbaye de Thélème, 74–75; and Les Acacias, 57–60, 62; and Black performers, 73; death of, 184; and International Five, 60, 72, 74; and Le Jardin, 60, 62–63; and Maurice, rift, 58; Maurice's Club at the Hotel Grande Bretagne, 47; Maurice's Club at the Théâtre Caumartin, 48; on Maurice's health, 72; and Maxwell, 62–63, 72

Mr. Will Stay-Up-Late Club, 18

M'soo Kee-lay. *See* Kiley, John Gerald "Jed"

Mullins, Mazie, 82–84, 88–89. *See also* Tempo Club

Munn, Charlie, 73, 115

Munn, Dorothy, 73, 115

Murat, Violette, 140, 148, 168

Murphy, Gerald, 48–50

music, income for, 90–91

Music Box 1 (41 rue Pigalle), 83, 138, 173, 220–21n16

Music Box 2 (53 rue Pigalle): Bullard manager of, 100; Mitchell manager of, 173

Napoleon of the Night Clubs. *See* Santo, Paul

Nardal, Jane, 177–79

Nardal, Paulette, 177–79

Nash, Jean, 137–38

Nazis, 158, 185

negritude movement, 177

New Woman, 39, 41, 52, 167–68

New York Bar, 113, 116, 117

Normandy (club), 135

Old King Kiley. *See* Kiley, John Gerald "Jed"

Olympia Theater, 5, 41

Omar Khayyâm's, 81, 86, 92

opium, 106–7

Pagès, J.-B., 173

Palermo, Le, 118, 163

Palmer, Bee, 165

Paradise, Le, 110

Paris qui Jazz (at Casino de Paris), 38–42

Parrish, Dan, 167

Pensacola Kid (Paul Wyer), 130

Perrene, Ivia, 172–73

Perroquet, Le (Léon Volterra), 43–44, 83

Perroquet, Le (Santo), 163, 176

Phal, Louis "Battlin' Siki," 117, 143

"pickaninny," 174, 177

Pickford, Jack, 105
Pickford, Mary, 50
Pilcer, Harry: and Cadet Rousselle, 26–27; and Carpentier, 143; and Casino de Paris, 38–42, 45; and the Charleston, 218n70; collaboration with Mitchell begins, 34–35; and June Day, 165; death of, 185; and Deslys, 29–32, 37–38, 43; Harry's Pilcer's *Dancing* at the Oasis, 40; *Paris qui Jazz*, 38–42; United States, return to, 184–85. *See also* Casino de Paris; Chez Harry Pilcer; Harry Pilcer's *Dancing* at the Apollo Theater; Sans Souci, Le
Pilcer, Murray, 31–32, 36, 165
Pile ou Face, 173
Pizarro, Manuel, 27, 47
Plantation, La (Mitchell), 162, 173–75, 180
Plantation, La (Santo), 162–64, 167–73; in Monte Carlo, 175–76
plantation life, nostalgia for, 8, 176–81
Playboy of Paris (Erskine Gwynne), 64, 67, 118
Poincaré, Raymond (president of France), 117, 133
Poiret, Paul, 38, 39–40, 43–44
Polignac, Nina de, 65–66, 69, 76, 78, 158
Popovici (student), 27
Porter, Cole: and Les Acacias, 149; and Bricktop, 149–50, 157, 160; dance lessons, 49; Harlem and Montmartre, comparison, 180; and Hutchinson, 158; and Le Jardin de ma Soeur, 63, 149, 221n17; and Maxwell, 150; and Royal Box, 108; and society *dancings*, 149; *Within the Quota*, 48, 50
Pound, Ezra, 166, 168
P.O.W., the. *See* Edward David, Prince of Wales
Price, Vincent, 144
Prince of Persia. *See* Ahmad Shah Qajar, Shah of Persia
private club licenses, 24–25
professional dancers, 101–3, 105–6. *See also* prostitution
prohibition in United States, 108, 114, 144
prostitution, 101–3, 106, 140, 141; and professional dancers, 101–3, 105–6

Queen of Montmartre. *See* Bricktop
Queen of New York night clubs (Texas Guinan), 144
Queen of the Shimmy. *See* Joyce, Peggy Hopkins

race relations, American, 15, 87, 116–18, 129–36, 152–53, 155–61, 171, 179–81
race relations, French, 34, 38–42, 105, 117, 129, 131, 133–34, 138, 155–61, 166, 179; France as colonial power, 133, 177–79; racial categories, 84
ragtime, 29–31, 33–34
Raux, Fernand, 14
Real Jazz Kings, 45, 64, 100
Red Devils, 37, 42–43, 57, 85
Red Summer of 1919, 131
Reed, Mr. (partner at Tempo Club), 89
Rentschler, Joan Sawyer, 18, 123
Richardson, Sammy, 36, 144, 146–47
Romans, Alain, 174
Rosenthal, Gérard, 170, 171, 225n51
Royal Box Orchestra, 99–100
Russians, 65–66, 135, 136, 153

Sacha. *See* Stavisky, Serge Alexandre
Saint-Martin district, 16, 20, 27, 163
Samovar, 92
Sanford, Stephen "Laddie," 141
Sans Souci, Le, 27, 46–47, 57, 87, 191n6
Santo, Paul (aka Paul Santolini), 118, 162–73, 175–76
Savoy Dancing Club, 20–21, 24
Sawyer, Joan (Rentschler), 18, 123
Scanlon, Bob, 167, 175
Séeberger brothers, 200n79
Sem (Georges Goursat), 15, 18–20, 22–28, 46, 48, 52–53, 140, 158, 189n27
Serge. *See* Stavisky, Serge Alexandre
Seven Spades, 13, 20–21, 23, 43
Shakespeare, William: *Othello* reversal and interracial relationships, 167–68; *The Tempest*, 8
Shanley's, 70, 115–16, 118, 204n51
Sherbo American Band, 31, 32, 36
shimmy, 19–20, 24, 28, 50–51, 66; in England, 54–55

Simpson, Wallis, 77–78, 123
"Sister" of the Colored Gentleman. *See* Jones, Florence
Smith, Ada. *See* Bricktop
Smith, Crickett, 45, 100, 173, 175
Smith, Norris, 174
society *dancings*: dance clubs, early, 20–28; jazz, introduction of, 13–15; operating hours, unrestricted, 46; versus rue Pigalle, 76, 77–78; society *dancings*, emergence of, 46. *See also* Casino de Paris; Clover Club; Jardin de ma Soeur, Le; Maurice's Club at the Hotel Grande Bretagne; Maurice's Club at the Théâtre Caumartin; Sans Souci, Le
So-Different, 48, 53, 55–58; closing of, 203n74
Soupault, Philippe, 85, 88, 93, 160
South, Eddie, 165–66
Southern Syncopated Orchestra, 39, 43, 54, 82, 83, 84, 88, 148–49
Stavisky, Serge Alexandre, 21–22, 25, 26–28, 47, 136, 163, 223n5
Straumann, Marcelle, 99
Sturges, Howard, 63
suburbs of Paris, 17–19
"surprise parties," 14
Surrealists, 85–86, 87–88, 119, 160
Synco-Synco Orchestra, 84

tango, 14–15, 24, 40, 44, 47, 55–56, 98, 163; Black origins of, 53–54; at El Garrón, 29, 133, 173
Tempo Club: as Black cultural center, 82, 87, 92; and Black musicians, 85; Black-owned and managed, 81–82; and Dadaists and Surrealists, 85–86; and gambling, 82, 86, 89–92, 94; and Joneses, 86–87, 130; legacy of, 92–93, 129–30, 154–55, 159, 180–81; Mitchell inspired by, 129–30; New York, similar club to, 86–87; police raid on, 89–92; scholarship on, inaccuracies, 191n6; and white patrons, 82, 85–89; and Zelli, 94
Tempo Club (New York City), 82
Théâtre Caumartin, 20–21, 191n6
Théâtre des Champs Elysées, 16, 48–49

Théâtre des Deux Masques, 114
Thomas, Olive, 106
Thomson Jazz Band, 178
Torrès, Henry, 170
Tovalou Houénou, prince of Dahomey, 7–8, 133
Trittle, Billy, 116
Troïka, Le, 135
Tuck, Anthony, 174

"Uncle Tom," 174
Undertaker, the (Gaëtan Lherbon de Lussats), 163, 170, 171, 225n51
U.S. immigration policy, 49
Utopia, 7, 29, 82, 88, 92, 99, 129, 140, 145, 162; versus American prejudice, 5, 8, 135; More's image of, 2; as unrealized, 154–56, 159, 161, 176, 179–81, 183, 185

Valentino, Rudolph, 49, 137
Valerio, Roger de, 42, 199n69
Vauchant, Léo, 34, 82, 83–84, 185
Vautel, Clément, 91
Venice, Italy, 139, 157, 166–67
Ver luisant, Le, 136
Versatile Four, 174
Villa, Pancho, 112, 115
violence, 23, 113–14, 133, 168–73. *See also* gangsters
Volterra, Albert, 29
Volterra, Elie, 29
Volterra, Joseph, 29
Volterra, Jules, 29, 92, 162–63
Volterra, Léon, 29, 35. *See also* Apollo Theater
Vuillard, Edouard, 55

Walker, A'lelia, 144
Wall Street crash of 1929, 100, 118–19, 174, 183
Waltham, Tom, 96–99
Walton, Florence, 142–43
Ward, Fanny, 46, 65, 66, 78, 129, 147, 151–52, 155
Warner, Louise, 164–65
Warnod, André, 14, 15, 20, 30, 47
Waters, Ethel, 174

Watts, Usher, 72
Webb, Clifton, 58, 177
Weeks, Seth, 36
Wellmon, Harry "General," 84, 92, 98, 120
White, Harvey, 175
White Lyres, 41, 113, 202n58
Whiteman, Paul, 97
Wilkins and Riley, 164–65
Wilson, Arthur (Dooley), 88
Wilson, Danny, 135–36; at Kiley's Gaity, 120; at Mitchell's (52 rue Blanche), 120, 126
Wilson, Edith, 144, 164
Wilson Welcome Ball, 16
Windsor, Duchess of (Wallis Simpson), 77, 123
Windsor, Duke of. *See* Edward David, Prince of Wales
Withers, Frank, 82–84, 88–89, 185
Within the Quota (Porter), 48–50
Wolfe, Elsie de (Lady Mendl), 158
Woon, Basil, 4–5, 16, 18, 28, 52, 64–68, 134, 140, 150, 199n68
World War I, 13–14, 15
World War II, 183, 185
Wyer, Paul, 130

Yar, Le (club), 135
Yvain, Maurice, 38–39, 41

"Zazz," 47
Zelli, Giuseppe Salvatore "Joe": arrival in Paris, 23; and Black musicians, 23, 94–96, 99–100, 109; bouncer, role of, 107–8; and Bullard, 99–100; and Cadet Rousselle, 22–24; fictionalization of, 25; as master of ceremonies, 98; personality of, 111, 121; Pigalle, move to, 26; prestige, decline of, 108–10; scholarship on, inaccuracies, 191n6; and Wall Street crash, 184. *See also* Zelli's Royal Box
Zelli, Mme, 95, 108
Zelli's Chez les Nudistes, 109, 110
Zelli's Club, 25–26
Zelli's Royal Box: and Baker, 103; and Black musicians, 98; closing of, 184; closing of, temporary, 99–100; description of, 81, 96, 99, 101–2; fictionalization of, 95–96; jazz, description of, 97–98; opening of, 26, 43, 94; and professional dancers, 101–3; racism of patrons, 95; respectability, mask of, 100–101, 107–8; Royal Box Orchestra, 99–100; and Stavisky, 27; successors, 108–10; white musicians, early, 97
Zelli's Royal Box (New York), 108
Zig-Zag Band, 195n59
Zito, Vincenzo Maria, 103–5, 109, 116

www.ingramcontent.com/pod-product-compliance
Lightning Source LLC
Chambersburg PA
CBHW030506291225
37390CB00004B/17